World

Volume I: The British Isles

Also available from Bloomsbury:

Corpus Linguistics and World Englishes, by Vivian de Klerk

World Englishes: A Critical Analysis, by Mario Saraceni

World Englishes Volume II: North America, edited by Tometro Hopkins

World Englishes Volume III: Central America, edited by Tometro Hopkins and Ken Decker

World Englishes

Volume I: The British Isles

Edited by
Tometro Hopkins and John McKenny

Bloomsbury Academic
An imprint of Bloomsbury Publishing Plc

B L O O M S B U R Y
LONDON • OXFORD • NEW YORK • NEW DELHI • SYDNEY

Bloomsbury Academic
An imprint of Bloomsbury Publishing Plc

50 Bedford Square
London
WC1B 3DP
UK

1385 Broadway
New York
NY 10018
USA

www.bloomsbury.com

BLOOMSBURY and the Diana logo are trademarks of Bloomsbury Publishing Plc

First published 2013

First published in paperback 2017

British Library Cataloguing-in-Publication Data
A catalogue record for this book is available from the British Library.

ISBN: PB: 978-1-4742-9846-9

Library of Congress Cataloging-in-Publication Data
A catalog record for this book is available from the Library of Congress.

Typeset by Deanta Global Publishing Services, Chennai, India
Printed and bound in Great Britain

Contents

Acknowledgements

The *World Englishes* series could not have gone forth without the help of many who tirelessly contributed in various ways. First, I am indebted to Loreto Todd for imparting this project to me and for giving me advice, support and encouragement along the way. In the early stages of the project, I consulted with Braj Kachru, who provided invaluable guidance for the development of the series.

The editors are grateful to all those who have identified contributors and provided advice or research materials for various chapters. For Volume I, John McKenny and I express our gratitude to Dave Britain, Graeme Davis, Christina Lee, Richard Marsden, Esther Asprey, Gerald Kelly, Kim Willcocks, Bill Griffiths, Lifang Wang, William Lancaster, Peter Sercombe, Gus John, Peter Craumer, Lynn Berk, Marian Demos, Joan Baker, Heather Blatt; for Volume II, I am grateful to Michael Montgomery, Barbara Burnaby and William Kretzschmar; and I am grateful to John Holm for his comments on Volume III.

I am especially thankful for the encouragement and support of my colleagues in the Linguistics Program and the English Department at Florida International University: Ellen Thompson, Mehmet Yavas, Feryal Yavas, Virginia Mueller Gathercole, Asher Milbauer, Kemp Williams, Meri-Jane Rochelson, Kathleen Mccormack and Donna Weir-Soley. During the course of the project, the students in my World Englishes seminars always kept me upbeat and motivated.

Both John McKenny and I are thankful to the University of Nottingham Ningbo China and Florida International University respectively for the faculty development grants we received for the production of the maps.

Also, I would like to acknowledge the staff at Bloomsbury: Jennifer Lovel, formerly of Continuum, made helpful suggestions in the early design of the series; and Colleen Coalter and Gurdeep Mattu provided unwavering support, guidance and patience throughout this publication. The editors owe an enormous debt to Subitha Nair for her painstaking work in the final editing and typesetting of the volumes.

These acknowledgements would be incomplete without an expression of gratitude to my friend, Robert Kohn; he is always a source of advice and inspiration.

As one would expect in a project of this size, there were many others who contributed in multiple ways. I have benefitted from them all and to them I give my heartfelt thanks. Any omission of their names is unintentional.

Text

Permission has been granted to Ramish, H. 2008. Channel Island English: Phonology. in B. Kortmann and C. Upton (eds), Varieties of English. *The British Isles.* Vol. 1. Berlin: Mouton de Gruyter. 223–236.

We are pleased to grant permission for the non-exclusive use of your article.

Decker, K. 'Belize Kriol', in Vol. III: *Central America,* "Portions of this chapter were published previously in Decker, Ken. 2005. The Song of Kriol: A Grammar of the Kriol Language of Belize. Belize Kriol Project: Belize City".

Permission has been granted by the Belize Kriol Project for this chapter to be published as an abridgement of a book previously published as: Decker, Ken. 2005. The Song of Kriol: A Grammar of the Kriol Language of Belize. Belize Kriol Project: Belize City.

Maps/Illustrations

Regional maps, Vol. I–III, prepared by Himadri Biswas, GIS-RS Center, Florida International University.

Map of South east Englishes produced by the author.

Map language data adapted from 2009 *Ethnologue: Languages of the World, Sixteenth Edition,* (C) SIL International, Inc. Used by permission.

"Indigenous Peoples and Languages of Alaska, compiled by Michael E. Krauss. Copyright 2011 Alaska Native Language Center and Institute of Social and Economic Research. Used with permission."

"Canada population centres" compiled by J.K. Chambers. Copyright 1999. Used with permission.

"Route of the African Seminoles," compiled by Ian Hancock.

Simon, Beth Lee, "Midwest American English," Vol. II, ***North America.***

All map figures were generated by Erica Wyss to whom I am grateful.

Figure 1. Murrray, T. E., Frazer, T. C., and Simon, B. (1996), 'Need + Past Participle in American English'. *American Speech,* 71, 259.

Figure 2. Lavov, W., Ash S., and Boberg, C. (2003), Atlas of North American English, www.ling.upenn.edu/phono_atlas/.

Figures 3, 14. Ash, S. (2006), 'The North American Midland as a dialect area', in Murray, T. and Simon, B., *Language Variation and Change in the Midland; a new look at 'Heartland' English,* pp. 41, 47.

Figure 4, 5, 6, 10, 11, 12, 13. Responses to *Dictionary of American Regional English (DARE) Questionnaire* prompts and material from DARE files compiled from data provided by Joan Hall and Luanne von Schneidermesser.

Figure 7. Murray, T. E., Frazer, T. C., and Simon, B. (1996), 'Need + Past Participle in American English', *American Speech,* 71, 159.

Figure 8. Murray, T. E. and Simon, B. (1999), 'Want + Past Participle in American English', *American Speech,* 74.

Figure 9. Benson, E. J., (2009), 'Everyone Wants In: Want + Prepositional Adverb in the Midland and Beyond', *Journal of English Linguistics.* 37, 33.

Every effort has been made to trace copyright holders and to obtain their permission for the use of copyright material. The publisher apologizes for any errors or omissions in the above list and would be grateful if notified of any corrections that should be incorporated in future reprints or editions of this book.

Contributors

Paul Cavill
University of Nottingham
School of English Studies
University Park
Nottingham NG72 RD
United Kingdom
Email: Paul.Cavill@nottingham.ac.uk

John Corbett
The Department of English
Faculty of Social Sciences and Humanities
University of Macau
Av. Padre Tomás Pereira, Macau
Email: jcorbett@mac.mo

The late Bill Griffiths
Formerly at Centre for North East England History
Balbee Hall
Newcastle upon Tyne, NE1 SE
United Kingdom

Andrew Hamer
School of English
University of Liverpool
Modern Language Building
Chatham Street
Liverpool L69 7ZR
United Kingdom
Email: hamer@liverpool.ac.uk

Sharon Millar
Institute of Language and Communication
University of Southern Denmark
Campusvej 55, DK-5230
Odense M, Denmark
Email: smi@language.sdu.dk

Heli Paulasto
English language and Culture School of Humanities
University of Eastern Finland
P.O. Box 111
80101 Joensuu, Finland
Email: heli.paulasto@vef.fi

Heinrich Ramisch
Otto-Friedrich-Universität Bamberg
Englische Sprachwissenschaft
An der Universität 9, R. 103
96045 Bamberg
Germany
Email: heinrich.ramisch@uni-bamberg.de

John Mckenny
Division of English
University of Nottingham
Ningbo, China
199 Taikang East Road
Ningbo 315100, China
Email: john.mckenny@nottingham.edu.cn

Klaske van Leyden

Tometro Hopkins
Linguistics Program
Department of English
Florida International University
MMC
11200 SW. 8th Street
Miami, Florida 33199, USA
Email: hopkinst@fiu.edu

Barry J. H. Rawling
Stillington
North Yorkshire
United Kingdom
Email: barry@yorkshiredialect.com

Joanna Ryfa
Department of Language and Linguistics
University of Essex
Wivenhoe Park
Colchester
Essex CO4 3SQ
United Kingdom
Email: joanna.ryfa@googlemail.com

Jane Stuart-Smith
University of Glasgow
Department of English Language
12 University Gardens
Glasgow G12 8QQ
United Kingdom
Email: jane.stuart-smith@glascow.ac.uk

Steve Thorne
15 Fairfield Road
Kings Health,
Birmingham B14 7QY
England

Phillip Tipton
School of Languages
University of Salford
Salford M5 4WT
United Kingdom
Email: ptipton@salford.ac.uk

Susanne Wagner
English Language and Linguistics
Chemnitz University of Technology
D-09107 Chemnitz Reichenhainer StraBe
39, zi 221
Email: susanne.wagner@phil.tu-chemnitz.de

John Wilson
School of Communication
University of Ulster
Jordanstown campus
Shore Road
Newtownabbey
Co. Antrim
BT37 0QB
Email: j.wilson@ulster.ac.uk

List of Maps

List of Tables

List of Abbreviations

COLT	Bergen Corpus of London Teenager Language
CP	Communist Party
CSc	Mid or Central Scots
DAR	definite article reduction
Du	Dutch
EDD	English Dialect Dictionary
EDS	English Dialect Society
ER	East Riding
EModE	early Modern English
EngE	English English
FC	Football club
FRED corpus	The Freiburg English Dialect Corpus
Ger.	German
Gmc	Common Germanic
GONW	Government Office of the North West
IM	Imperfective marker
IPA	International Phonetic Alphabet
IRA	Irish Republican Army
ISc	Insular Scots
MC	Middle class
MDu	Middle Dutch
ME	Middle English
MHG	Midddle High
Mod.Du.	Modern Dutch
NE	North East
NELP	North East Language Project
NER	North and East Ridings
NHS	National Health Service
NORMs	non-mobile older rural males
NR	North Riding
NSc	Northern Scots
OE	Old English
OED	Oxford English Dictionary

OFr	Old French
ON	Old Norse
ONS	Office for National Statistics
PDE	Present-Day English
PIE	Proto-Indo-European
PRES	Present tense
RP	Received Pronunciation
SAWD	Survey of Anglo-Welsh Dialects
SCCC	Scottish Consultative Council on the Curriculum
SED	Survey of English Dialects
SG	Singular
SND	*Scottish National Dictionary*
SSc	Southern or Border Scots
SSE	Scottish Standard English
StE	Standard English
St.F.	Standard French
TL	target language
VN	Verbal noun
WC	Working class
WE	Welsh English
WR	West Riding

Series Preface

World Englishes surveys the huge richness and varieties of the English language and its diffusion worldwide, looking beyond the documented popular English varieties to include lesser known varieties and emerging English varieties, especially in geographical regions where English has not been previously documented.

Given that we are surrounded by the global presence of English written and spoken – from its proliferation in the mass media, the translation of works from other languages into English to the internet, online communication and its use as the main language in medical, diplomatic, scientific and international discourses – it would not be practical in a series of this kind to focus only on the structural features of an English variety. The globalization of English is a topical issue in geography, international relations, anthropology, sociology, political science and other related fields. Consequently, chapters have been structured in such a way to give liberty to those contributors with expertise in various disciplines, or who could co-author with contributors who have, to include chapter sections that would reflect the needs of the other social sciences.

While the primary aim of *World Englishes* is to appeal to linguists and English language specialists, the series focuses more on the geographical region and the variety of English spoken there than on the type of English variety involved. For instance, English as a first language, a second language, a third language, an International language and English pidgin and creole varieties.

Each chapter follows a general template that reflects the linguistic, social and historical needs of the English variety. The chapters consist of a linguistic description, as applicable to that particular English variety, of the components of the grammar: phonetics/phonology, morphology, syntax and semantics. Chapters also include demographic data, a brief description of the historical and sociocultural background of the English variety, the present and (if possible) future social, political and economic implications of English language use within the region, its use in literary works and in the social media, and wherever the use of English is applicable and of its importance in the region.

In Volumes I, II and III, the contributors are considered to be well informed of the particular English variety in the region, The chapters are illustrated with maps outlining the region or location of the particular English variety. Each volume will describe several varieties of English within the specified territory.

Some descriptions will be more detailed than others, depending on the variety described and its use of English.

World Englishes serves to function as a reference book, an educational tool and a work of history, geography and anthropology. The series aims not only to appeal to linguistic and English language scholars and students but also to scholars and students in other of the social sciences: geographers, anthropologists, sociologists and economists. The volumes are accessible to undergraduates, as well as graduate and postdoctoral students: any student or scholar who is interested in a comprehensive guide that encompasses all aspect of a particular English variety as a new line of research or expanding existing knowledge of a particular English variety.

The *World Englishes* series is intended to be the first series of volumes to offer comparable, accurate descriptions of English varieties within a given territory and to provide a systematic model for linguistic description and comparison. We hope that as the volumes become available, our efforts will complement previous works on world Englishes, contribute to the growing knowledge of English as a global language and support the development of research in this area.

Bibliography

Crystal, D. (2003), *English as a Global Language*, 2nd edn, Cambridge: Cambridge University Press.

Kachru, B. B., Kachru, Y. and Nelson, C. L. (eds) (2006), *The Handbook of World Englishes*, Malden, MA: Blackwell Publishing.

Kachru, Y. and Smith, L. E. (2008), *Cultures, Contexts, and World Englishes*, New York and London: Routledge.

Kortman, B. and Schneider, E. W. (eds) (2006), *A Handbook of Varieties of English: A Multimedia Research Tool*, Berlin: Mouton de Gruyter. (Edited together with Kate Burridge, Rajend Mesthrie, and Clive Upton.)

McArthur, T. (ed.) (2002), *The Oxford Guide to World Englishes*, Oxford: Oxford University Press.

Svartvik, J. and Leech, G. (2006), *English: One Tongue, Many Voices*, London: Palgrave MacMillan.

Introduction

John McKenny

This first volume, *The British Isles,* is in many ways a key to the entire series to follow, namely *World Englishes.* This volume is a compilation of close studies of the regional varieties of English spoken in Britain and Ireland. It tells the story of the varieties of English which developed as Old English spread, starting from the fifth century (CE), from the eastern seaboard of Britain and came into contact with various Celtic languages to the West on the mainland and on the many islands which make up the archipelago called The British Isles. The centrality of this volume in a series of books with the overall title *World Englishes* is clear. The forebears of all the Englishes in the world can be traced back to the linguistic events during this period in this group of islands, the birthplace of English.

The English varieties which began to develop are important for the history of World Englishes not only because of their chronological primacy but also because users of these varieties would go to distant shores through the centuries and bring their own particular dialects with them. Examples of this propagation would be the influence of Scottish and Irish migrants in shaping varieties of North American English or the influence of Londoners on emergent Australian English. Another tremendously fortuitous aspect of the spread and development of English is that the so-called standard dialects lost certain lexis, grammatical structures and pronunciations, which are well preserved in different parts of these islands down to the present day. * colonial lag? Often it was rivers, mountains or the sea in the case of the many islands that allowed the language to be, as it were, 'frozen in time'.

The first challenge that presented itself to the editors of this first volume was how it should be titled. The geographical and political term *The British Isles* was no longer acceptable to many of the inhabitants of Ireland. The designation *The Isles of the North Atlantic,* which yields the attractive acronym IONA, fails to exclude Iceland and Greenland among others. Another leading candidate, *The Western Isles of Europe* does not pick out all and only those islands whose varieties of English we wish to study. In the end, rather than gamble on which term will emerge historically as the favoured place name, a decision was taken to choose the term currently used to denote the area under investigation. This at least would connect our work with that of other researchers working in this area of scholarship.

In the arrangement of the chapters in *The Englishes of the British Isles* our sequential path through the regions tries to emulate the historical course of English from the southeast and Midlands westward to the southwest of England and to

Wales and eventually to Ireland and northward to northwest England, Scotland and the Scottish Isles. In establishing this chronological sequence, the time references of the various authors were used. This attempt to follow the progress of early English through the islands can always be called into question due to simultaneous language-shaping events and processes taking place at geographically separated places. Thus various synchronicities occur along the timeline.

Contributors to this volume were given a matrix to guide them in the elaboration of their chapter, which provided them with a set of broad headings to work with. This was not meant to be in any way a straitjacket but rather a broad set of parameters within which they could develop their own unique account, drawing on their own blend of methodologies, including philology, dialectology, sociolinguistics, contact linguistics, diachronic linguistics and historical linguistics. While the contributors are aware of the debates within each of these subdisciplines, their chapter contains their own position as to the major issues facing scholars of their particular region.

This volume opens with Paul Cavill's overview of the history of the English language in the millennium and a half since its inception. As well as deftly underpinning the whole of this volume, this chapter also has resonances for the rest of the series: readers will be able to come back to it for orientation about how English emerged as a world language.

In Chapter 2, Joanna Ryfa set herself the daunting task of examining the constellation of south-east Englishes. This meant she had to grapple with the question of Standard English as well as the new controversial dialect, Estuary English, which some people in Britain see as the new language of power, given that it is widely used among Members of Parliament at Westminster and by prominent figures in the mass media. Joanna examines the arguments for and against viewing Estuary English as a variety of English on the same level as the other varieties discussed in the volume.

Barry Rawling, himself a Yorkshireman, writes lovingly in Chapter 3 of the varieties of English to be found in Yorkshire today and we see how the hills and dales there have preserved distinctive ways of talking down through the centuries.

Bill Griffiths in Chapter 4 shows how a 'blow-in' can make himself more of a Geordie than the Geordies themselves. Bill, a southerner, established himself as one of the leading authorities on NE English. He was also an important poet, essayist and raconteur and his death during the making of this volume was a sad blow not only to the team working on this volume but to the whole NE community. This chapter is one of the last pieces of writing he completed before his untimely death. A notable aspect of this work is his illustration of the huge influence of Dutch on the lexis of NE English.

Steve Thorne's Chapter 5 captures the vitality and dynamism of the huge crossroads which is the West Midlands, which locals like to refer to as 'the heart of England'. Steve's work includes a critique of 'dialectalism' and is a plea for its avoidance. In the past there has sometimes been a tendency for comedians to make fun of the rising intonation of 'Brummies' or folk who hail from Birmingham.

Susanne Wagner in Chapter 6 shows how English gradually prevailed over the Cornish language in the South-west of England. The variety she describes here is important for World Englishes because, like Irish English and Scottish English, Southwest English is a rhotic variety and therefore has contributed to the rhoticity found in various parts of the English-speaking world.

Chapter 7 is in many ways monumental, dealing as it does with one of the most influential of all the varieties of English, particularly of the last four centuries. John Corbett and Jane Stuart-Smith marshal their sources well and give us a view of the sweep of the Scots tongue down to the noughties. They are dealing with a number of languages and varieties which have been in continual contact (English, Gaelic, French and Norn).

In Chapter 8, Phillip Tipton sets himself the task of describing the varieties of English found in the Northwest. This region contains two cities, Manchester and Liverpool, which have been incredibly influential since the industrial revolution, and their importance in modern pop culture and music from the 1960s until today. The rivalry between these two cities is recounted and in the discussion Phillip has included an excellent comparison of the two methodologies used in such an analysis, the ethnographic and the sociolinguistic. He transcends his region when he asks whether there is a wider Northern identity and not just a North-western identity.

Chapter 9, *English in Wales* is the work of Heli Paulasto. Wales is an interesting region where a Celtic language is still alive and well and where a delicate ecology of Welsh and English coexists. One of the main questions Heli sets herself is whether a case can be made for a regional standard Welsh English and she takes the reader through the intricate discussion surrounding this question.

Chapter 10 by John Wilson and Sharon Millar discusses the varieties comprising *English in Ireland.* Like Scotland, Ireland has had massive emigration. Scottish and Irish varieties of English have influenced many varieties of world Englishes. This chapter was written at a time of great political change when political peace finally seemed attainable between the two communities in warring Northern Ireland: those who wished to be part of Ireland and those who wanted to maintain the link with the United Kingdom. Both communities in Northern Ireland were struggling hard to revive their distinctive language or dialect: Irish Gaelic for the nationalists and Ullans or Ulster Scots for the loyalists to the British crown.

Andrew Hamer tells us the story of English in the Isle of Man in Chapter 11. Although there were several invasions and attempted invasions in its history (the Irish came in the fourth century CE; the Norse ruled from the ninth century CE until 1266) this sheltered island has managed to hold on to more political independence from London than any of the other islands in the archipelago with the exception of the Republic of Ireland and the Channel Islands. Given its shelteredness it is not surprising how much influence of Manx Gaelic can still be found in present day Manx English. Manx Gaelic died in the twentieth century but its spirit lives on in Manx English. This is one of the most interesting features of Volume 1: how the various islands of the peninsula act as laboratories or hothouses where language varieties can lag centuries behind the varieties they once belonged to. Indeed this will be a feature of World Englishes. Strains of English will be found in colonies or outposts but meanwhile the originals of these will have continued to develop at home. The conservatism is sometimes found in the implanted variety but is not inevitable and instead rapid innovation can take place.

In Chapter 12 Klaske van Leyden gives us a history of the languages spoken in the Orkney and Shetland Isles from the days when the islanders spoke Pictish. The introduction of Norn by Scandinavian colonizers and the development of this language and the bilingualism which became increasingly widespread are described. The death of Norn is discussed but it seems that this is not such a final death as that suffered by the Brythonic language spoken in England before the arrival of the Anglo-Saxons in the fifth century as described in Chapter 1. Van Leyden shows how Norn pervades Insular Scots to this day at the phonological, lexical and syntactic level and so lives on.

In Chapter 13 Heinrich Ramisch details the evolution of the English language in the Channel Islands. This chapter comes so late in the volume because the English language began gradually to replace Norman French dialect only in the late eighteenth century. In the following century the arrival of a large garrison of English soldiers accelerated the process of Anglicization so that by the end of the following century only 15 per cent of the islands' population could speak any of the Norman French dialects. The author describes what he calls transference phenomena, the influence of Norman French on the English spoken in the Channel Islands. Certain phonological and syntactic features resulting from this language contact are shown. Several of these features, for example, H-dropping, could have several explanations besides crosslinguistic influence (e.g. they could be due to contact with various UK dialects). It could be said that there is a surprising lack of influence of French.

Scholars of World Englishes will find it useful to have access in this volume to the exhaustive analyses of the phonology, lexis and syntax of the varieties of English which spread from Britain and Ireland to several parts of the world. In colonial situations many speakers of many different varieties came face to face and in the short term the result was a period of diversity with each accommodating to the others. Eventually a mixed dialect or new variety would emerge, perhaps dominated by the variety spoken by the majority of immigrants in a particular place. The varieties analysed in this book provide the ingredients for many of the Englishes found throughout the world.

I am privileged to have mediated among so many brilliant scholars and helped the Chief Editor, Tometro Hopkins, to bring this dazzling collection of chapters to the reading public.

Bibliography

Marckwardt, A. H. (1958), American English. New York: Oxford University Press.

Regional British Isles

Chapter 1

Historical Perspectives on the Development of English

Paul Cavill

Introduction

Painting the background with the broadest possible strokes, the history of English reflects a change from a predominantly synthetic to a predominantly analytic language. A majority of modern users of English, even those familiar with the German or Scandinavian languages most resembling it in the modern world, are unable to read the earliest written form of English, Anglo-Saxon. The difficulties are both immediate and visual – unfamiliar letters (þ, ð, æ and others) and lack of modern punctuation or formatting in the original texts (verse is written in continuous lines, capital letters are rare); and more profound, in the sense that the inflectional morphology, the syntax and the lexis have changed beyond recognition.

The development of the language is traditionally divided into periods. The beginnings of English lie in Common Germanic (Gmc) which developed as a dialect of Proto-Indo-European (PIE); West Germanic, the immediate ancestor of Old English (OE) derived from the Common Germanic stock, influenced on the Continent by the Latin of the Roman empire. Following the invasion of Britain in particularly the fifth and following centuries CE, and the introduction of manuscript writing by Latin Christianity, OE in several different dialects came to be written down, and in due course was influenced by the North Germanic dialect of the Vikings. With the establishment of a Norman French aristocracy after the Conquest of 1066, the predominant languages of administration and social hierarchy were French and Latin, and Middle English (ME) developed pronounced regional dialect features, significantly influenced by lexical borrowing from the superstrate languages. In the early Modern period, the rise of Latin and Greek in religion, education and learned discourse coincided with the commercial exploitation of printing with movable type, discoveries in geography and science, and a fairly general desire for a standard vernacular language and led to the suppression and disparagement of regional dialect.

In terms of geography, the earliest OE is closely related to Frisian and dialects of the North Sea coasts. Following the Anglo-Saxon invasion of Britain, the language spread with Anglo-Saxon political power, and within perhaps 300 years was the main language spoken in territories from Lowland Scotland south and east to Kent. Though it was largely understood in the west of (modern) England and the Marches, Cornwall, Wales and Cumbria retained their Brittonic dialects in this early period, and further north and west, Gaelic dialects were spoken. Later in history, there was at least a theoretical possibility that English would die out under the political and military dominance of the Scandinavians and Normans, much as early Celtic in England and later Cornish were expunged under English dominance. But for reasons that are still debated, English conquered the conquerors.

With English colonial and imperial expansion in the Modern period, the growth in political and commercial power of North America, and the development of international media, computing and telecommunications technology, Present-Day English (PDE) is now the most important language in the world, with more than 400 million native speakers and many times that figure using it as a second or other language (Crystal 2006: 424–425). But such a summary could give the impression that 'English' is a monolithic entity, a universal currency with a consistent value throughout the world. That impression would be entirely false: though scholars speak of a 'standard core', particularly in relation to the written forms of the language, the recent development of Englishes is one of protean dialects, pidgins and creoles, each with its own grammar and morphology, pronunciation and lexis, and indeed each with its own social and political significance within the speech community.

The History of English in the Earliest Period

OE is descended from PIE via Common Germanic and latterly West Germanic. It shares the Gmc phonological changes categorized in Grimm's Law (or First Consonant Shift) and Verner's Law. Grimm demonstrated that the voiceless stops /p, t, k, k^w/ in PIE correspond to the voiceless fricatives /f, θ, x, x^w/ in Germanic (Latin *piscis, tres, caput, quis* = PDE *fish, three, head, who*); the voiced stops /b, d, g/ in PIE correspond to the voiceless stops /p, t, k/ (Latin *cannabis, pedis, genus* = PDE *hemp, foot, kin*); and the voiced aspirated stops /b^h, d^h and g^h/ correspond to the voiced stops /b, d, g/ in Gmc (slightly more difficult to illustrate, but, e.g. PIE **bhráter*, Latin *frater*, PDE *brother*). Thus, though a new word for 'god' was introduced in early Gmc, and the Gmc pantheon was given a new leader, Woden/Óðinn, Gmc mythology preserves the name *Tiw* (< Gmc **Tiwaz*; Icelandic *Týr*, PDE Tuesday), cognate with Latin *deus* 'god', Sanskrit *dyaus-pitar*.

Verner showed that in certain contexts the voiceless fricative consonants were voiced, namely in medial positions in the word, following an unstressed syllable and between voiced sounds. The PIE **pətér* 'father' (appearing as, e.g. Latin *pater*) regularly has PIE *p* > Gmc *f*, but instead of the unvoiced /θ/, has the voiced /ð/ in PDE. In PIE the stress fell on the second syllable, and thus the consonant originally followed an unstressed syllable and was subject to voicing. This illustrates in passing the Gmc stress-shift whereby the variable stress of PIE was firmly located on the root syllable of the word in Gmc: it was thus *after* the sound-changes of Grimm's Law had taken place in the word now appearing as *father*, but before OE was written down, that the stress-shifting occurred.

PIE was morphologically complex. It had eight cases for nouns and adjectives; three of these, the vocative, ablative and locative were lost by the time OE was written, and the instrumental appears in only a few fossilized forms. However, names like Altrincham (Cheshire), and the dialect pronunciation of Birmingham, namely *Brummagem*, are argued by Dodgson (1967) to preserve the locative case of an earlier stage of Gmc: the element *-ing*(-) is palatalized and assibilated, implying the front-vowel inflection of the locative (**-ingi-*) here. The mutated plurals of *man, foot, mouse* and others also preserve the relics of PIE inflection. The nominative and accusative plural inflections of these nouns in early Gmc contained a high front vowel (e.g. **fōtiz*) which mutated the back vowel of the stem by drawing it forward in the mouth, giving *men, feet, mice*; this is known variously as i-mutation, i-umlaut or front mutation.

Gmc inherited PIE words for relationships, numerals, parts of the body and in many other lexical fields. But it also developed distinct lexis of its own and borrowed words, particularly from the Romans. Lexis borrowed from the Romans in this period tends to be broadly technological: to do with trade (*mint, cheap*), building (*pitch, wall, tile, street*) and culinary matters (*cheese, butter, cup, dish, kitchen*); some appears only in place-names (*chester/cester/caster* 'city, fortification' and *wich/wick* 'dairy farm, depot'). The words *north, south, east* and *west, sea, ship, cliff, sail, steer* are Gmc words with no known PIE source, and suggest that the technology of sailing underwent a development in the Gmc period. Similarly, *ale, beer* and *drink* are Gmc; the name Woden, chief of the Gmc gods from about the second century CE, possibly earlier (Turville-Petre 1964: 73), is related to OE *wōd* 'mad' and the idea of intoxication and inspiration. Together these words provide a partial but suggestive sociological background to the great Gmc migrations of the first centuries CE, one of which was the invasion of Britain.

Language Contact: Old English and Celtic

Though the Celtic languages spoken in Britain when the Anglo-Saxons arrived and the Gmc language spoken by the invaders were both descended from PIE, there was virtually no overlap between them. Indeed, even if some inkling of common ancestry between the languages might have been sensed, semantic change would have made some connections obscure. The PIE word **kait-* developed into Celtic and Gaulish **cēto-*, whence Welsh *coed* 'wood'; and also into Old English *hǣð* 'heath, open land, land without trees'. The modern reflexes are common place-name elements in Welsh (Bettws-y-coed) and English (Hampstead Heath), but with quite different, not to say contradictory, meanings.

A debate currently rages about the precise nature of the fifth-century Anglo-Saxon conquest of parts of Britain and the subsequent establishment of the English language in England and southern Scotland (Higham). Why, when major features of the landscape retained their Celtic names (Rivers Trent and Derwent, areas Kent and Craven, hills Cheviots and Mendips, woods Charnwood and Savernake), did so few Celtic words become lexicalized in English after the Anglo-Saxon settlement? Richard Coates discusses the handful that made the transition to English (Coates 2007: 177–181). Elements that continued in use in Celtic areas were not understood by the English: Celtic **penno-* 'a head(land)' in Pendle (Lancashire) has the explanatory and tautological addition of Old English *hyll* 'a hill'; Celtic **cēto-* 'a wood' in Chetwoode (Berkshire) has Old English *wudu* 'a wood' added.

Hildegard Tristram proposes that Celtic influence on the morphosyntax of Old English did not appear in the record until after the Norman Conquest because of the control exercised by the Anglo-Saxon elite. She particularly believes that periphrastic aspect (PDE *-ing* forms) and periphrastic *do* might represent morphosyntactic influence from Celtic (Tristram 2007: 208–213). But the linguistic control of the Anglo-Saxon elite did not prevent substantial influence from Scandinavian speakers on OE, and these particular features of late ME or early Modern English (EModE) cannot be securely related to the reconstructed Old Welsh forms on which the theory is based, but can be explained by other developments closer in time to the actual changes. Explanations vary, but the lack of linguistic impact from Celtic at this stage of English suggests the significant marginalization or removal of Celtic speakers.

Old English

OE inherited from PIE ablaut changes in the vowels of past tenses of strong verbs, as in PDE *swim – swam – swum*, or *sing – sang – sung*. There were seven classes of strong verbs in OE, each with its characteristic series of vowel gradations. The (West Saxon) verb *crēopan* 'to creep' had the first and third person singular past tense (*ic, hē*) *crēap*, the plural (*wē, gē, hīe*) *crupon* and the past participle *cropen* (Mitchell and Robinson 2007: 93). This particular verb is one of the numerous examples of OE strong verbs that became weak, PDE *creep, crept*, thus joining the large class of OE and later verbs, and the default weak paradigm of PDE verbs, in adding a dental suffix to indicate the past tense. However, the *Magnificat* in the *Book of Common Prayer* preserves the form *he … hath holpen* (PDE 'helped') as late as 1662, and this is still used in some liturgical circles.

The main dialects of OE were Anglian (predominantly north and east), Mercian (midlands and west) and West Saxon (the south-west). The early political dominance of the Anglian and Mercian kings gave way in the later OE period to the West Saxon, and most of written OE is in the West Saxon dialect. But not all: *Cædmon's Hymn*, one of the relatively few OE poems preserved in more than one manuscript, may serve briefly to illustrate dialectal and other differences in OE. Cædmon (*fl.* before 680) is reputedly the first English Christian poet in the vernacular; his nine-line poem in characteristic OE alliterative metre praises the deity for his creation. The poem is preserved in 21 manuscripts, including two which were written in Cædmon's early Northumbrian dialect of the eighth century, and others in the West Saxon dialect of the tenth century and later; line 7 reads as follows (Robinson and Stanley 1991: 2.3 and 2.8):

Northumbrian:	tha middingard moncynnæs uard
West Saxon:	þa middangeard moncynnes weard
PDE (literal):	then [the] middle-enclosure [the] guardian of humankind [adorned]

The West Saxon version shows the adoption of runic letters *þ* (thorn) and *w* (properly the wynn-rune, a letter shaped like *þ* but without the pointed ascender). Both of these letters survive into late ME, and the former is still used not infrequently in the forms *y*[e], *y*[t] (the, that) in the eighteenth century. Unstressed vowels are represented differently (early and Northumbrian inflectional *-æ-* or *-ae-* is regularly represented in West Saxon as *-e-*). But the West Saxon line also shows the 'breaking' or diphthongization of OE front vowels (*æ* long or short, *e* short and *i* long or short) before velarized consonants (*ll* or *l* + *C*, *rr* or *r* + *C*, *h* or *h* + *C*). In this case Gmc **a* fronted to early OE *æ* shows retraction to *a* in Northumbrian but breaking to *ea* in West Saxon before *r* + consonant: thus Gmc **ʒardaz*, Northumbrian *gard*, West Saxon *geard*; Gmc **warðo*, Northumbrian *uard*, West Saxon *weard*.

Breaking has often happened in Northumbrian by late OE, but the *Durham Ritual* and the glosses to the Lindisfarne Gospels of *c.*960 (*Dictionary of OE Corpus*), still have dialect forms such as *biðon* for the present plural of *bēon* 'to be', West Saxon *bēoð*. Some place-names preserve spellings like *Cerlintone* 1086, *Cherlenton* 1297 (Charlton, Northamptonshire: Watts 2004: 126) which indicate a weak genitive plural *ceorlena* (West Saxon *ceorla*) for some strong nouns (here *ceorl* 'a peasant'), spellings later restricted to northern texts (Campbell 1959: 572–573).

The Old English language was highly inflected, with singular and plural, three genders and four main cases for nouns, articles and adjectives. In addition to the cases nominative, accusative, genitive and dative, there is an instrumental, for example, in the *Anglo-Saxon Chronicle* entries beginning *þȳ gēare* 'in this year'. There were, furthermore, strong (or definite) and weak (or indefinite) versions of the adjectives, representing a broad distinction between predicative and attributive adjectives, as in *se ceorl is eald* ('the peasant is old', where *eald* is masculine, singular, nominative and strong/definite/predicative) and *se ealda ceorl* ('the old peasant', where *ealda* is weak/indefinite/attributive).

Personal pronouns included first and second person dual forms *wit* 'we two' and *git* 'you two' and their inflectional forms. The second person pronouns also discriminated between singular *þū* and plural *gē*, later a status distinction in EModE. The third person pronoun-noun gender distinctions were at least theoretically preserved in narrative syntax, so that the feminine pronoun *hēo* would normally refer to an antecedent feminine noun; but by the end of the OE period natural gender is appearing in this kind of context, and *hēo* could refer to a female whatever the grammatical gender of the antecedent noun (e.g. OE *wīf* neuter, *wīfmon* masculine 'woman').

Verbs had two tenses, past and present, and two principal moods, indicative and subjunctive. The verb 'to be' had two forms, *bēon* which had no past tense and was the preferred form for future time reference; and *wesan*, for present and past. Normally the present tense can extend into the future, not unlike some common forms of the present tense in PDE: *ic gā tō þǣm cyninge* 'I go/am going/will go to the king'. The subjunctive is often used for hypothetical conditions:

Onsend Higelāce, gif mec hild nime,
beaduscruda betst (*Beowulf* 452–3a)

[Send (imperative sing.) to Higelac, if battle should take (pres. subjunctive sing.) me, the best of war-garments]

There are some periphrastic verb forms, such as *hīe feohtende wǣran* 'they were fighting', but it is arguable that this has a more limited semantic focus than immediately appears, as in 'they *kept on* fighting'. By the end of the OE period, verbs such as **sculan* 'to be obliged to' and *willan* 'to wish to' are beginning to reflect the development of modality as in PDE *shall* and *will.*

In syntax, whether prose or verse, OE prefers parataxis to hypotaxis and generally word-order is more flexible than in PDE. The order SVO predominates in main clauses, but SOV in subordinate clauses. An exception to this is in correlative clauses, common in OE with identical adverb-conjunction pairs such as *þā – þā* (when – then), *þonne – þonne* (when – then), *þǣr – þǣr* (where – there) where VS marks the principal clause and SV the subordinate: 'Þā (conjunction) se cyning ūt ēode, þā (adverb) slōh hē þone dracan' [When the king went out, (then) he killed the dragon].

Verse technique involves the deployment of variation, iteration of nominal groups of minimally variant semantic content around relatively few verb-phrases. Thus in the West Saxon *Cædmon's Hymn*, the last three lines read:

þā middangeard moncynnes weard
ēce drihten æfter tēode
fīrum foldan frēa ælmihtig

[then the earth (var1) the guardian of humankind (var2), the eternal Lord (var2), afterwards created for the children of earth [*or* the earth (var1) for men], the Lord almighty (var2)]

The subject, varied three times, is placed after the object, which may here be varied later. In the whole of the poem, there are only four verb phrases as against eighteen or nineteen (pro)nominal groups. The time-sequencing is simple: *Nū* – *ærest* – *þā* – *æfter* (Now – first – then – afterwards).

In prose, more complex time-sequencing is difficult: in the annal for 992 in the E version of the *Anglo-Saxon Chronicle* (Plummer 1952: vol. I, 127), there is the phrase '[ond] þa on þere nihte ðe hi on ðone dæi togædere cumon sceoldon …' [and then in the night that they in the day must come together …] where the writer is expressing the notion 'the night before the day when they would fight'. The writer of the F version struggles similarly (Plummer 1952: vol. I, 126: '[ond] on ðare nihte ða hi scolde an morgen togædere cuman …' [and then in the night that they in the day must come together …]). As frequently in subordinate clauses, the verb is placed at the end in both.

The lexis of OE is overwhelmingly Gmc, with the Continental Latin borrowings and a few Celtic words mentioned above adopted in the early stages. The poetic style noted above interacts with lexical inventiveness. Since both the stress pattern of the alliterative metre and the technique of variation tend to privilege nouns and adjectives over verbs, poets use and make compounds. One of the more common methods is to modify a noun or adjective with another signifying 'battle' such as *beadu, gūð, here* or *hilde*. So the *Dictionary of Old English* lists 24 compounds premodified by *beadu* 'battle'. Both the simplex and the compounds are poetic and do not occur in prose. Of the 24 compounds, an astonishing 17 occur only once in the corpus. Most are clear enough (*beadu-mēce* 'battle-sword', *beadu-wang* 'battlefield'), and one or two are imagistic. *Beadulēoma* (*Beowulf* 1522) 'battle-light' is a sword, a conceit used by the same poet again at 1143 with a different modifier but the same meaning (*hildelēoma*); but in 2583 of the poem the compound *hildelēoma* means 'battle-flame' that is, 'destructive fire'.

A wide range of affixes modify verbs, nouns and other parts of speech. A verb like *beran* 'to carry' has relatively few related affixed forms: *forberan* 'to abstain', *onberan* 'to plunder, carry off' and *underberan* 'to support, endure', among them. But the verbal, adjectival, adverbial and nominal affixed and compounded derivatives in OE from a core verb like *niman* 'to take' run into hundreds. Though most noun-, adjective- and adverb-forming suffixes from OE still appear in PDE, not all of them are still productive. Noun-forming suffixes include *-nes, -scipe, -hād* and *-dōm* (sharpness, friendship, brotherhood and kingdom); adjective-forming suffixes include *-isc*, *-lēas*, *-full*, *-en* (English, heartless, fearful, wooden); adverb-forming suffixes include *-e* and *-līce* (the former often lost, but compare OE *fæst* 'firm', *fæste* 'firmly' and *fæstlīce* 'steadfastly').

The largest influx of lexis was from the Latin of Christianity. Christian missions began in earnest at the end of the sixth century CE and within little over a century, much of England was nominally Christian. Christianity introduced the technology of discursive writing and brought with it a Latinized religious vocabulary which OE borrowed: *abbod* 'abbot', *munuc* 'monk', *nōn* 'the monastic service at the ninth hour' > PDE 'noon', *mynster* 'monastery' > PDE 'minster'. OE also augmented its wordstock with translation compounds like *þrīnes* 'trinity' (lit. 'three-ness') and *leornung-cniht* 'disciple' (lit. 'learning-youth').

The outline above gives a general synopsis of the OE language as it appears in the records. Much of the known range of vocabulary has been lost: since the replacement of OE *niman* with the Scandinavian *take*, nearly all of the derived lexis from *niman* has been lost. The precarious survival of OE manuscripts (the fire of 1731 which ravaged Sir Robert Cotton's library destroyed several and damaged many) suggests that there were others of which we know nothing. But much of the vocabulary cannot have been recorded: by far the most *hapax legomena* are poetic, and poetry was predominantly an oral form. And non-literary language has a slimmer chance of surviving.

Language Contact: The Vikings

'Vikings' is a convenient term for the predominantly Danish and Norwegian Scandinavian attackers and settlers who came to Britain and Ireland in numbers in the last years of the eighth century CE and onwards through the OE period. In England, the effects of the early raids were felt principally by coastal monasteries and trading centres. Later Viking settlement in the north and east after the disbanding of the 'Great Army' which had successfully campaigned throughout the country in the third quarter of the ninth century, and the division of England into the Danelaw and Wessex along the course of the River Thames and Watling Street from London to Chester, gave rise to linguistic change. This was very likely reinforced by the reign of the Scandinavian king Cnut 1017–35. The effects of Scandinavian influence on English were most apparent in the ME period.

Sharing roots in Gmc, OE and Scandinavian might have been mutually intelligible (Baugh and Cable 2002: 96). But characteristic sound differences, many surviving in PDE, distinguish the languages. Palatalization of OE *sc*, and of *g* and *c* before front vowels (OE *scip* 'ship', *gēar* 'year' and *cild* 'child') did not occur in the languages of the Vikings, and this differentiation in sound yields etymologically identical but semantically distinct words such as *shirt* and *skirt*, *church* and *kirk*. The Gmc vowel /ai/ becomes that found in OE *stān* 'stone' and *hāl* 'whole', and in Old Norse *steinn*, *heill*. The latter yields the doublet *whole/hale* (Kastovsky 1992: 332), the former is found in place-names originally containing OE *stān* but now spelt and pronounced Stainburn, Stainley and so on (Smith 1956: vol. II, 143).

The Scandinavian language added many new words to English, including those most famously mentioned by Jespersen, 'An Englishman cannot *thrive* or be *ill* without Scandinavian words; they are to the language what *bread* and *eggs* are to the daily fare' (Jespersen 1938: 74). Before the Norman Conquest and the compilation of Domesday Book, hundreds of Scandinavian place-names appeared, often containing the elements *by* 'farm', *thorp* 'outlying farm', *thwaite* 'cleared land'. In northern counties fairly generally, some Scandinavian-derived toponymy replaced English: *beck*, *carr* and *gate* replaced *brook*, *marsh* and *way*. Legal language is also early borrowed: *lagu* 'law' and *grið* 'peace' are OE words adopted from ON; and OE *eorl* 'nobleman, warrior' adopts the ON sense 'underking' (Pons-Sanz).

But Scandinavian also changed the grammar and morphology of the language, most obviously the third person plural pronouns and the present plural of the verb 'to be', but also possibly the third person singular present tense inflection *-s* and even the third person feminine pronoun. The Scandinavian *they*, *their* and *them* forms of the third person pronouns gradually replace the ambiguous *hī*(*e*), *hira* and *him* forms of OE during the ME period, as does the present plural *are*(*n*) for OE *bēoð* (or, as noted earlier, Northumbrian *biðon*). The *-s* third person present tense inflection is similarly found first in the north and slowly infiltrates southern dialects, and the feminine singular pronoun *she* may be a Scandinavian pronunciation of OE *hēo* or a transferred use of the definite article *sēo*.

Middle English

The Norman Conquest of 1066 did not immediately change the English language, but it established a new aristocracy, and in succeeding years most positions of authority in church and state came to be occupied by French speakers. French influence at the court of Edward the Confessor (1042–66) had been a bone of contention and French nobles had small armies and castles of some kind in England even before the Norman Conquest (*Anglo-Saxon Chronicle* E 1052, Plummer 1952: vol. I, 181, *castel*). Although there was significant communication between the new masters and their English serfs, it was probably not until the loss of Normandy to the English crown in 1204 that French-speaking landowners in England seriously took to learning English and this process was given additional impetus by the Hundred Years War with France from 1337. The patterns of language development that emerge include changes that broadly continue what had already been happening before the Conquest, namely the loss of inflections and associated loss of grammatical gender; French influence that can be traced through documentation, before large-scale borrowing of French lexis; and the growth and subsequent waning of dialectal differences in English.

The loss of distinct quality in vowels of unstressed syllables is observable in OE and goes back ultimately to the Gmc root-initial stress-shifting which meant that grammatical endings would be unstressed. This was compounded in OE by contact with the Scandinavians where languages similar in etymology had different inflectional morphology and where communicative efficacy might have been achieved through inflectional compromise. A late OE inscription on a stone sundial from Aldbrough (East Yorkshire) has a peculiar mix of Scandinavian and OE: 'Ulf het aræran cyrice for hanum [and] for Gunwara saula' [Ulf commanded the church to be built for himself and for Gunnvor's soul(s)] (Binns 1966: 20–1). The names are Scandinavian, as is the third person dative masculine pronoun *hanum*. But the nouns *cyrice* and *saula* are essentially ME in form, with indistinct vowel endings where standard OE would have *cyrican* (acc. sg. fem. weak) and *saule* (dat. sg. fem. strong) or *saulum* (dat. pl. fem.). An alternative possibility is that these forms represent pidginization, as the spellings could be nominative singular *cyrice* and nominative plural *saula* in place of the oblique cases.

The loss of inflections characteristic of ME reduced the oblique cases of weak nouns and adjectives (OE *-an*), the dative plural of nouns (OE *-um*), the infinitive (OE *-an*) and past plural indicative (OE *-on*) and subjunctive (OE *-en*) of verbs to a sound represented most frequently by *-en*. The nasal was lost and in due course the weakened schwa vowel was lost too. The *-s* plural and genitive from the strong noun paradigm was applied to nouns with a very few exceptions (*oxen, shoon*). The articles of OE, declined for gender (masc. *se*, fem. *sēo*, neut. *þæt*) and number (plural all genders *þā*) were reduced to two, singular *the* and (sometimes) plural *tho*. The indefinite article *a*(*n*) has also emerged as a distinct grammatical category from the cardinal numeral *ān* of OE. By the end of the ME period noun and adjective morphology was essentially that of PDE and grammatical gender had disappeared except in third person singular pronouns.

Other simplifications and changes are observable. An eleventh-century OE version of the Lord's Prayer, Matt. 6.12, has 'forgyf us ūre gyltas swā swā we forgyfað ūrum gyltendum' [lit. forgive us our sins just as we forgive our sinners] as against a Wycliffite version, *c.*1389, 'forȝeue to vs oure dettis as we forȝeue to oure dettours' (Bosworth and Waring 1888: 24–5). In these phrases, the OE singular imperative is preserved in *forȝeue* and the sounds are broadly similar – with, for example, the OE *ū* being represented by *ou*. But the OE nominative and dative plurals *gyltas* and *gyltendum* have been replaced by *-s* plurals of nouns of French origin (*dettis, dettours*); the distinctive OE present plural in *forgyfað* has been lost, replaced by the *-e(n)* of Midlands dialects and falling together with the infinitive; the accusative/dative case in *us* and the dative plural in *gyltendum* are represented by *to* ~; the comparative conjunction *swā swā* is reduced to *as*; and OE *f* (/f/ before a back vowel, /v/ in the vicinity of a front vowel) is spelt *u* medially and *v* initially, and represents both vowel and consonant /v/ sounds.

Major changes in morphology tend to reflect dialectal developments in ME, and are therefore treated in the section on dialects below. Syntax was naturally affected by trends in morphology, as prepositions and word order replaced OE endings in indicating the function of words and the meaning of sentences. A wide range of prepositions replaced the OE dative, and semantic overlap between *of* and *from* in OE, both usually meaning 'from', made the refashioning of *of* as a marker of possession possible. By the end of the ME period, syntax is very similar to that of PDE; the predominant word-order is SVO and variations from that are usually either poetic or in marked syntactic structures.

Language Contact: French

The earliest general French influence can be illustrated from official documents. Nottingham 'the settlement of Snot's people' is first recorded as *Snotengaham* in the ninth century; in Domesday Book 1086 it is *Snotingeham* illustrating the weakening of the inflectional vowel to schwa; and by the early twelfth century it appears as *Not(t)ingham*, with the vowel having been lost (Gover et al. 1940: 13). The simultaneous loss of the initial consonant shows the influence of French, where initial *sn-* does not occur. This may be sociolectal: the same phenomenon may appear in Trafford Park Manchester (Old English *strǣt* 'Roman road' with *ford*), an estate occupied by Norman French aristocracy (Watts 2004: 625).

At no point in the ME period was there a majority of the population who spoke French, and the early impact of French spelling and pronunciation on these English names is the impact of an aristocracy keeping records for administrative purposes. Not unnaturally, their own vocabulary for legal and religious administration entered the language. *Court, crime, judge* and *sentence*; *clergy, disciple, religion* and *virtue* are among the many words borrowed (see further Burnley, Serjeantson, Sheard). Words for arts, leisure and cooking are prominent in the borrowed lexicon, particularly the last of these when compared with the English lexicon: *boil, fry, grill, roast,* as well as *beef, mutton, pork* and *veal.* Alongside the words, of course, came the leisured practices: for example, though there is a revival of alliterative verse in the fourteenth century, verse rhymed after the French pattern predominates. In the General Prologue to *The Canterbury Tales,* Chaucer begins by rhyming predominantly English with English (*soote-roote, breeth-heeth* etc.), French with French words (*licour-flour, corages-pilgrimages* etc.), but in the lines relating to the Parson (477–528), he rhymes English and French-origin words freely (*religioun-toun, werk-clerk, preche-teche* etc.) (Chaucer 23–36).

Latin words were also introduced in semantic fields related to the exercise of power, in religion and in the arts: *arbitrator* and *conviction*; *requiem* and *psalm*; *simile* and *allegory* all enter the language from Latin (Burnley 1992: 428–434). It is often unclear whether these loans were mediated through French or in some sense direct from Latin. Latin and French were also the source of a wide range of affixes: *de-, dis-, im-/in-/em-/en-, re-* and *-al, -ate/-ation, -ence, -ity, -ize, -ment* and others. The decades either side of the end of the thirteenth century saw a peak in the number of French words being borrowed, but the process is continuing. Studies suggest that even though there was a particular literary taste for borrowed, learned words towards the end of the ME period (so-called 'aureate' diction) and into the EModE period ('ink-horn' terms), the proportion of such words is rarely more than about one-fifth in surviving ME texts (Burnley 1992: 432).

Medieval English Dialects

In most features of the developing pronoun system and verb morphology the northern and midland dialects were more radical than the southern, which tended to be conservative. The administrative and commercial power in London and the cultural and educational importance of the south-west midlands preserved the older forms and inflections for longer, but resistance to innovation gave way eventually to the demands of clarity.

In Chaucer's London dialect at the end of the fourteenth century, the Scandinavian-derived third person plural pronoun *they* was used for nominative and accusative cases, but the older *hire* and *hem* were used for the genitive and dative cases. In his *Reeve's Tale*, Chaucer makes fun of the northerners John and Aleyn and their dialect: their talk of how the grain hopper 'wagges til and fra', with the northern third person present singular *-es* and the Scandinavian-derived *til and fra* is offered for the amusement of the cultured (southern) reader (4039, Chaucer 80). At the very end of the ME period, Caxton the printer tells an anecdote in his *Eneydos* which illustrates his perplexity at dialectal variation. A sailor called Sheffelde (and so probably from the northern English city of Sheffield) asks a woman on the banks of the River Thames for *eggys* and she replies that she does not speak French; but another man 'translates' by saying that he is asking for *eyren* (Caxton *Eneydos* Preface). The Scandinavian-derived *egg* with the northern plural ending, which becomes standard, has not yet (in about 1490) supplanted the OE-derived *ey* in an anomalous southern plural form.

The following table gives a synopsis of the main dialectal differences (there is a good deal of variation in some of the vowels and letter forms which cannot easily be represented here):

14th-cent. form	North	Midlands	South
Fem. sg. nom. pronoun	scho	heo, sche	heo, hu
3rd person plural pronouns	thay, thayr, thaym	they, (t)her, (t)hem	hi, hire, hem
3rd person sing. pres. tense	he loves	he loves, he loveth	he loveth
3rd person plural present tense	thay are thay loves	they aren, hi ben they loves, hi loven	hi beth hi loveth
Present participle	lovand	lovend, loving	lovind, loving

In these main areas, the standard dialect of the south-west midlands and later London was essentially adopting the most distinctive forms. The northern pronouns and third person singular present tense, and the northern third person plural of ‘be’, are distinct and therefore maximally functional. The northern third person plural present tense is the same in most cases as the singular and thus the midland form (*-en* > *-e*) was adopted. Caxton’s southern farmer’s wife notwithstanding, most of these changes had entered the standard written language by the end of the ME period.

Early Modern English

A notional cut-off date for this period is 1800, and the period itself fairly neatly divides into an earlier part to 1660, characterized by political, colonial, cultural and linguistic expansion; and a later part characterized by stability and standardization. Into the first part fall global exploration and discovery bringing new trade and new words; the Renaissance and Reformation bringing new art, culture, literary styles and a revived interest in theology; and printing, with its potential to spread ideas and encourage literacy; but also the major upheavals of international and civil wars and the English republic under Cromwell. Into the second part fall the restoration of the monarchy, the (re-)establishment of the Church of England, the associated quests for taxonomy, order and regularity in science and language.

A number of texts show a concern about the pronunciation of English. Sir Thomas Elyot writes in 1531 that it is appropriate for well-born boys to have nurses who only speak English that is ‘cleane, polite, perfectly and articulately pronounced, omitting no lettre or sillable’ (Elyot Book I, Chapter V folio 18v); George Puttenham in 1589 recommends that poets use the language of ‘educated, not common people ... the vsuall speach of the Court, and that of London and the shires lying about London within lx myles, and not much aboue' (Puttenham Book III, Chapter IIII). Swift's famous letter to the *Tatler* of 1710, despite its written form, is essentially a castigation of the elisions and cant terms of spoken English: 'I *cou'dn't* get the things you sent for all *about Town.* — I *thôt* to *ha'* come down myself, and then *I'd ha' brout'um*; but I *han't don't*, and I believe *I can't do't*, that's *pozz*' (italics Swift's). There is a direct line of descent between this kind of concern and that expressed by John Reith in 1924, that the BBC's announcers should be 'men who ... can be relied upon to employ the correct pronunciation of the English tongue' (McArthur 1992: 110), and indeed more recent views.

In the EModE period the principal phonological change was the raising and diphthongizing of long vowels known as the Great Vowel Shift. This was a systemic change in that it affected all the long vowels in chains, but there is still debate as to which vowels were affected first (McMahon 1994: 31 'the vowel to start the whole process may have been /ɔ:/ (and similarly front /ɛ:/)'; Barber 1976: 290 'The process began with the close vowels'), and not all regional varieties were equally affected. The close (high) front /i:/ and back vowels /u:/ were diphthongized to /aɪ/ and /aʊ/ respectively, so OE *wīd* /wi:d/ became PDE *wide*, and OE *hūs*/hʊs/ became PDE *house.* The back vowels were raised, /ɔ:/ to /o:/ and /o:/ to /u:/: so, OE *cōl* /co:l/ became PDE *cool.* The front vowels similarly were raised, /a:/ to /ɛ:/, the half open /ɛ:/ to half close /e:/, and /e:/ to close /i:/: so, OE *grēne* /gre:n/ became PDE *green.*

It was in this period, too, that the standard dialect of English lost postvocalic *r.* In ME the *r* in words like *bird, corn, moor* and *flower* was almost invariably sounded, and in some standard Scottish, Irish and American English dialects still is. But in ME short vowels, the effect of loss of postvocalic *r* was generally to lengthen the vowel sound, and in both long and some short vowels, the vowel quality was changed. So the short vowels in ME *bird* /bird/ and *corn* /korn/ became PDE /bə:d/ and /kɔ:n/, and the long vowels in ME *moor* /mo:r/ and *flower* /flu:r/ became PDE /mɔ:/ and /flaʊə/. Another sound change which adds to the unrepresentative character of English spelling is the loss of earlier /x/ in such words as *night, brought* and *laugh.* Once again, this change tends to lengthen and/or change the quality of the vowel.

The syntax of English by the end of EModE is little different from that of PDE. It is in this period that the *do*-periphrasis is formed and becomes standard: the *do*-periphrasis barely exists before 1400, and its use is established practically as in PDE by 1700, in negative direct questions ('Didn't you say that?'), in affirmative direct questions ('Do you say that?'), in negative declarative sentences ('You don't say that') and in negative imperative sentences ('Don't say that'). The other main type, affirmative declarative sentences ('They do say'), common enough in EModE, is now reserved for emphasis. Interestingly, the King James

Bible (1611) uses this latter type of *do*-periphrasis ('ye know not [negative declarative without *do*] what hour your Lord doth come' [affirmative declarative with *do*], Matt. 24.42) almost to the exclusion of the others.

The subjunctive mood remains important, though modal verbs and greater emphasis on conjunctions with modal content (*if, though* etc.) replace many of the functions of the subjunctive in due course. Subjunctives are now mainly used in fossilized phrases such as 'if I were you' or 'if need be', but were a much more significant feature of EModE syntax. Also common is the use of the auxiliary *be* with verbs of motion: Jane Austen's 1813 novel *Pride and Prejudice* has Mrs Bennett exclaiming, 'He is come — Mr. Bingley is come. — He is, indeed' (Chapter 55). Progressive tenses were less commonly used than in PDE and passive progressives were not yet employed: in the same author's *Sense and Sensibility,* Mrs Palmer 'could soon tell at what coachmaker's the new carriage was building, by what painter Mr. Willoughby's portrait was drawn' (Chapter 32: PDE *was being built, was being drawn*).

Grammar and morphology are substantially similar to PDE by 1800. In particularly formal or religious contexts, the third person singular verbs *hath* and *doth* remain in standard English. The second person pronouns undergo development, possibly after the pattern of French. In OE and much of ME, the *þū/gē* (*thou/you*) denotes the distinction between singular and plural, a point made repeatedly in a pamphlet by George Fox in 1660, entitled 'A Battle-Door for Teachers and Professors to Learn Plural and Singular: *You* to *Many,* and *Thou* to *One*; Singular *one, Thou*; Plural *many, You*' (Fox Title page). Fox's point, of course, is a political and religious one about equality which he sees echoed in diverse languages. But it highlights the fact that the English language has changed and that *thou* was used for familiarity and sometimes contempt, *you* for respect, at the time; by the end of the period, however, the distinction is rare in standard English.

Other pronouns are also developing. The King James Bible retains the older forms of *his* for the possessive of the neuter (*h*)*it* where PDE has *its*; and the relative pronouns *that, which* relating to animate antecedents where PDE has *who.* So Matt. 5.13 has 'If the salt have lost *his* savour ...' and 6. 9 'Our Father *which* art in heaven' (italics mine); in both of these the verb forms are also conservative, *have* subjunctive, *art* second person singular present, familiar *thou* form.

The advent of printing soon brought some elements of standardization to the representation of language in writing. Early printed books retain elements of the manuscript tradition such as *&* (*and*) and the macron or tilde over a vowel to represent *m* or *n* (*whā* when), as well as variant forms of the letters *u* and *v*, *i* and *j*, and of *s*. Capital letters are used not only to begin sentences, but also for the initials of nouns, occasionally verbs and sometimes for emphasis; and different printing fonts, italic and bold, are used not very consistently for the same kinds of purpose. Punctuation such as colons and period stops is present, but other forms of punctuation such as the oblique slash/or virgule sometimes perform the same kinds of function. The comma and semicolon were introduced in EModE, as were the question and exclamation marks and various kinds of brackets. The apostrophe was first used to indicate what was thought of as suspension: Milton wrote in *Areopagitica*, 1644, 'We should be wary … how we spill that season'd life of man preserv'd and stor'd up in Books' (Milton 1644: 4). The possessive apostrophe may in part derive from the same notion of suspension or omission, as it was thought that the *-s* genitive was the suspension of *his*, as in 'the Kinge his fool' (Lass 1992: 146).

Studies of the vocabulary of EModE indicate that the period 1500–1700 saw a massive increase in borrowing and adaptation of words, particularly in the decades around the middle of that period (Nevalainen 1999: 336). The source of most loans and affixes, in the aftermath of the Renaissance and the Reformation is Latin: Latin is the language of learning and formal communication, of science and theology. Milton (a linguistically conservative author: note his affirmative declarative *do*) writes in his *Areopagitica*, mentioned above,

> For Books are not absolutely dead things, but doe contain a potencie of life in them to be as active as that soule was whose progeny they are; nay they do preserve as in a violl the purest efficacie and extraction of that living intellect that bred them (Milton 1644: 4).

The image is taken from the realm of science, a burgeoning pursuit at this time, and though many of the words are from Latin or French and borrowed in later ME (*active, progeny, violl* [phial], *preserve, intellect*), several are newly borrowed in the EModE period: *absolutely, potency, efficacy, extraction.* Shakespeare is more adventurous than Milton. The First Folio *King Lear*, 1623, has this speech:

> Blow windes, & crack your cheeks; Rage, blow
> You Cataracts, and Hyrricano's spout,
> Till you have drench'd our Steeples, drown the Cockes.
> You Sulph'rous and Thought-executing Fires,
> Vaunt-curriors of Oake-cleauing Thunder-bolts,
> Sindge my white head. (3. 2. 1–6)

Several of the words are relatively recent: *cataract* and *thunderbolt* are first recorded in ME, but not in any great numbers of instances. *Hurricane* is a recent borrowing from Spanish, and may represent the international expansion of trade and war at the time; *sulphurous* is borrowed from Latin, and is from the lexical field of natural science; *vaunt-courier* is borrowed from French *avant-courier* 'advance guard' and the military domain (though the simplex *courier* had been available in ME, the compound is first used in EModE; the first element is semantically changed by merging with *vaunt* 'boast'); and Shakespeare's is the first recorded use of the compound *thought-executing*. The richness of Shakespeare's lexical resources is demonstrated here.

By far the greatest number of lexical novelties were created by affixation. Some affixes that were borrowed from Latin (sometimes from Greek, and often through French) were *a-*, *ab-*, *ad-*, *anti-*, *con-/com-/co-*, *contra-*, *ex-*, *inter-/enter-*, *post-*, *pre-*, *sub-*, *super-*; and *-an*, *-able/-ible* and *-ist*. English-originating affixes were applied to borrowed words (*-like*, *-wise*, *-ish*, etc.), and foreign-originating affixes were applied to English words. Some linguistic purists disapproved of this tendency.

Mention has been made of some of the factors that made for the standardization of language in this period, printing, commerce and education among them. But there was also a great deal of theorizing about language, the writing of grammars and dictionaries, and plans for an Academy for the language after the model of the Académie française. Swift satirized what he saw as plebeian and careless use of language; Dryden famously had to translate his thoughts into Latin to put them into logical order. Samuel Johnson, as he tells his readers in the Preface to his *Dictionary*, 1755, embarked on the work with a view to fixing the language:

> Those who have been persuaded to think well of my design, require that it should fix our language, and put a stop to those alterations which time and chance have hitherto been suffered to make in it without opposition. With this consequence I will confess that I flattered myself for a while; but now begin to fear that I have indulged expectation which neither reason nor experience can justify … the lexicographer [may] be derided, who being able to produce no example of a nation that has preserved their words and phrases from mutability, shall imagine that his dictionary can embalm his language, and secure it from corruption and decay, that it is in his power to change sublunary nature, or clear the world at once from folly, vanity, and affectation.

While Johnson still sees change in language as 'corruption and decay' due to 'folly, vanity and affectation', he nevertheless did more than any to establish lexicology as a modern scientific, descriptive and taxonomic enterprise. But a predecessor of Johnson's, Robert Cawdry (or Cawdrey as he signs himself in the book), published *A Table Alphabeticall* in 1604,

> conteyning and teaching the true writing, and understanding of hard vsuall English words, borrowed from the Hebrew, Greeke, Latine or French & c. With the interpretation thereof by plaine English wordes, gathered for the benefit & helpe of Ladies, Gentlewomen or any other vnskilfull persons.

> Whereby they may the more easily and better vnderstand many hard English wordes, vvhich they shall heare or read in Scriptures, Sermons, or elsewhere ... (Cawdr(e)y Title)

This, almost in passing, reveals two important factors in both the expansion and standardization of the language: the wider education of women, and the influence of religious discourse, Bible and Prayer Book, in education more generally. While the influence of the former is only now being properly assessed, the latter have given the language hundreds of proverbial phrases and clichés, 'going the second mile', the concept of the *scapegoat* (from Tyndale), 'the apple of my eye' and more. The entry of these phrases into the language suggests that exposure to the Bible and Prayer Book (for most of the EModE period it was a legal requirement in England to attend church) was a significant standardizing influence on language.

The Beginnings of World Englishes

Little attention has been paid in this essay to the varieties of English spoken and written within the different kingdoms and provinces artificially united by the political power of the English crown. In the medieval and EModE periods, Scots was a distinct dialect, with its own flourishing literary culture; it was influenced by the developing southern varieties of English, and in due course by the union of the English and Scottish kingdoms in 1603. Scots in turn influenced the English used in Ireland. The English language was a relatively late arrival in Ireland and Wales, which not only had their own Celtic languages, but also, particularly in Ireland, French, as contenders for the status of *lingua franca.* Scottish and Irish English retain to the present day an eclectic mix of Celtic and Germanic vocabulary, distinct syntactic forms (e.g. uses of the *do*-periphrasis) and phonological features (e.g. postvocalic *r*).

Crucially, it is in this time of linguistic fluidity that the earlier English colonies were planted. The North American colony at Jamestown, Virginia, was planted in 1607; settlements were made in the Caribbean in the early seventeenth century; and the East India Company exercised political and commercial influence over much of South Asia from 1600. Towards the end of the period ending notionally in 1800, British settlement and political dominance became significant in Australia, New Zealand and South Africa. A substantial number of the early settlers in New England were from East Anglia, those in Virginia from the English West Country, and those in Australia from London, and some features of the present-day Englishes in these places may be traced to the seventeenth- or eighteenth-century dialects of the areas of origin of the settlers. But the sheer variety of dialectal, cultural, political, commercial and language-contact situations make generalizations hazardous here. In the 1776 Declaration, North America asserted not only its political, but also its linguistic, independence of Britain: Noah Webster, among others, made that independence linguistically tangible and effective.

Conclusion

Any survey such as this leaves out a great deal more than it includes, but it may serve to trace some of the main changes that occurred in English before it became, and as it was on the cusp of becoming, a world language: the change from a synthetic to an analytic language, and parallel processes of grammatical simplification and lexical expansion and diversification. Many regional and social dialect forms within the United Kingdom have their origins in the periods covered here, and other essays in this volume discuss these in detail. The world Englishes that grew from the trade and colonial expansion of the EModE period and developed independently will be treated in other volumes.

Bibliography

Austen, J. (1813), *Pride and Prejudice*, London: Thomas Egerton.

—. (1811), *Sense and Sensibility*, London: Thomas Egerton.

Barber, C. (1976), *Early Modern English*, London: Deutsch.

Baugh, A. C. and T. Cable (2002), *A History of the English Language*, 5th ed, Upper Saddle River, NJ: Prentice Hall.

Binns, A. L. (1966), *East Yorkshire in the Sagas*, York: East Yorkshire Local History Society.

Blake, N. (ed.) (1992), *The Cambridge History of the English Language*, Vol. II, pp. 1066–1476, Cambridge: Cambridge UP.

The Book of Common Prayer (1662), London.

Bosworth, J. and G. Waring (eds) (1888), *The Gothic and Anglo-Saxon Gospels … with the Versions of Wycliffe and Tyndale*, 3rd ed, London: Reeves and Turner.

Burnley, D. (1992), 'Lexis and Semantics', in N. Blake (ed.), pp. 409–499.

Cameron, A. et al. (eds) (2003), *Dictionary of Old English in Electronic Form, A–F*, Toronto: Dictionary of Old English, *Dictionary of Old English Corpus*, <http://quod.lib.umich.edu/o/oec/>.

Campbell, A. (1959), *Old English Grammar*, Oxford: Oxford UP.

Cawdrey, R. (1604), *A Table Alphabeticall*, London: Edmund Weaver, < http://gateway.proquest.com/openurl?ctx_ver = Z39.88-2003&res_id = xri:eebo&rft_id = xri:eebo:image:19240.>.

Caxton, W. (1490), *Eneydos*, London. Durable url for images of this edition: < http://gateway.proquest.com/openurl?ctx_ver = Z39.88-2003&res_id = xri:eebo&rft_id = xri:eebo:image:10136:2>.

Chaucer, G. (1988), in Benson, L. D. (ed.), *The Riverside Chaucer*, 3rd ed, Oxford: Oxford UP.

Coates, R. (2007), 'Invisible Britons: The View from Linguistics', in N. J. Higham (ed.), pp. 172–191.

Crystal, D. (2006), 'English Worldwide', in R. Hogg and D. Denison (eds), pp. 420–439.

Dodgson, J. McN. (1967), 'The *-ing-* in English place-names like Birmingham and Altrincham', *Beiträge zur Namenforschung* NF 2, pp. 221–245.

Elyot, Sir T. (1531),*The Boke Named the Gouernour*, London, Durable url for images of this edition: <http://gateway.proquest.com/openurl?ctx_ver = Z39.88-2003-&res_id = xri:eebo&rft_id = xri:eebo:image:23526>.

Fox, G. 'A Battle-Door for Teachers and Professors to Learn Plural and Singular', Durable url for images of this edition: <http://gateway.proquest.com/openurl?ctx_ver = Z39.88-2003&res_id = xri:eebo&rft_id = xri:eebo:image:61737>.

Freeborn, D. (1998), *From Old English to Standard English: A Coursebook in Language Variation Across Time*, 2nd ed, Basingstoke: Palgrave.

Görlach, M. (1991), *Introduction to Early Modern English*, Cambridge: Cambridge UP.

Gover, J. E. B., A. Mawer and F. M. Stenton. (1940), *The Place-Names of Nottinghamshire*, English Place-Name Society, Vol. XVII, Cambridge: Cambridge UP.

Higham, N. (ed.) (2007), *Britons in Anglo-Saxon England*, Publications of the Manchester Centre for Anglo-Saxon Studies, Vol. 7, Woodbridge: Boydell.

Hogg, R. (ed.) (1992), *The Cambridge History of the English Language*, Vol. I, The Beginnings to 1066, Cambridge: Cambridge UP.

Hogg, R. and D. Denison (eds) (2006), *A History of the English Language*, Cambridge: Cambridge UP.

Jespersen, O. (1938), *Growth and Structure of the English Language*, 9th ed, Oxford: Blackwell.

Johnson, S. (1755), *A Dictionary of the English Language*, 2 vols, London.

Kastovsky, D. (1992), 'Semantics and Vocabulary', in R. Hogg (ed.), pp. 290–408.

The King James Bible, (1611), London.

Klaeber, F. (ed.) (1950), *Beowulf and the Fight at Finnsburg*, 3rd ed, Boston, MA: Heath.

Lass, R. (ed.) (1992), *The Cambridge History of the English Language*, Vol. III, pp. 1476–1776, Cambridge: Cambridge UP.

—. 'Phonology and Morphology', in N. Blake (ed.), pp. 56–186.

McArthur, T. (ed.) (1992), *The Oxford Companion to the English Language*, Oxford: Oxford UP.

McMahon, A. (1994), *Understanding Language Change*, Cambridge: Cambridge UP.

Milton, J. (1644), *Areopagitica; A Speech of Mr. John Milton*, London, Durable url for images of this edition: http://gateway.proquest.com/openurl?ctx_ver = Z39.88-2003&res_id = xri:eebo&rft_id = xri:eebo:image:121215:4.

Mitchell, B. and F. C. Robinson (2007), *A Guide to Old English*, 7th ed, Oxford: Blackwell.

Nevalainen, T. (1999), 'Lexis and Semantics', in R. Lass (ed.), pp. 332–458.

Onions, C. T. (ed.) (1966), *The Oxford Dictionary of English Etymology*, Oxford: Oxford UP.

The Oxford English Dictionary, http://oed.co.uk.

Plummer C. (ed.) (1952), *Anglo-Saxon Chronicle. Two of the Saxon Chronicles Parallel*, 2 vols, Reissued with Bibliographical note by Dorothy Whitelock, Oxford: Clarendon.

Pons-Sanz, S. (2007), *Norse-Derived Vocabulary in Late Old English Texts: Wulfstan's Works, A Case Study*, North-Western European Language Evolution Supplement, Vol. 22, Odense: UP of Southern Denmark.

Puttenham, G. (1589), *The Arte of English Poesie*, London, Durable url for images of this edition: http://gateway.proquest.com/openurl?ctx_ver = Z39.88-2003 &res_id = xri:eebo&rft_id = xri:eebo:image:11025.

Robinson, F. C. and E. G. Stanley (eds) (1991), *Old English Verse Texts from Many Sources: A Comprehensive Collection*, Early English Manuscripts in Facsimile, Vol. XXIII, Copenhagen: Rosenkilde and Bagger.

Serjeantson, M. S. (1935), *A History of Foreign Words in English*, London: Kegan Paul.

Shakespeare, W. (1955), *Mr. William Shakespeares Comedies, Histories, & Tragedies* in H. Kökeritz (ed.), Facsimile of the First Folio, London: Oxford UP.

Sheard, J. A. (1954), *The Words We Use*, London: Deutsch.

Smith, A. H. (1956), *English Place-Name Elements*, 2 vols, English Place-Name Society, Vols XXV–XXVI, Cambridge: Cambridge UP.

Tristram, H. (2007), 'Why Don't the English Speak Welsh?', in N. J. Higham (ed.), pp. 192–214.

Turville-Petre, E. O. G. (1964), *Myth and Religion of the North: The Religion of Ancient Scandinavia*, London: Weidenfeld and Nicolson.

Watts, V. (2004), *The Cambridge Dictionary of English Place-Names*, Cambridge: Cambridge UP.

The Home Counties Modern Dialect Area

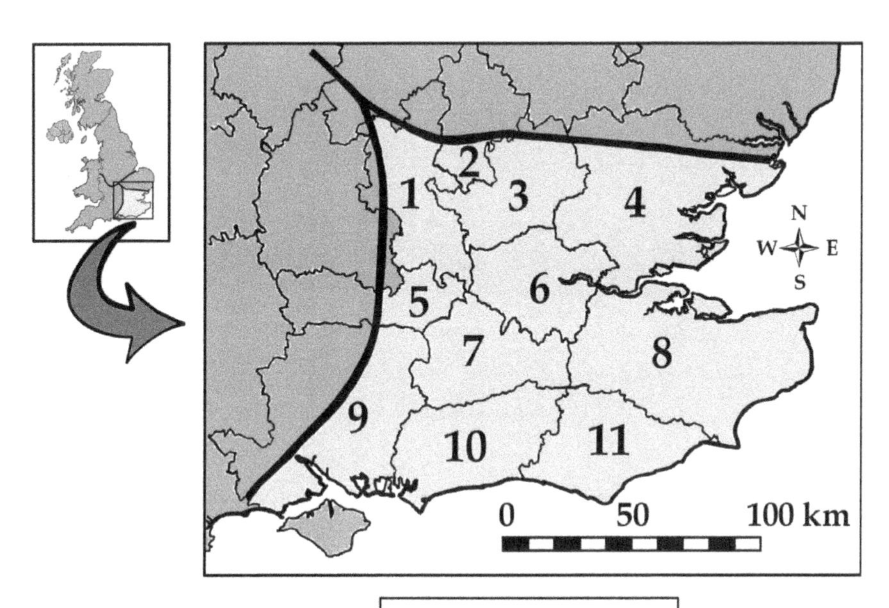

1. Buckinghamshire
2. Bedfordshire
3. Hertfordshire
4. Essex
5. Berkshire
6. Greater London
7. Surrey
8. Kent
9. Hampshire
10. West Sussex
11. East Sussex

Chapter 2

Englishes of London and the Southeast of England

Joanna Ryfa

London and the Southeast of England

The political and geographical definitions of the 'South East of England' do not correspond directly to what is, or rather used to be, considered the Southeast in dialectology. Officially, the region encompasses nineteen county and unitary authorities and fifty-five districts, which stretch around London, from Milton Keynes and Aylesbury Vale in the north-west to the New Forest in the south-west and to Thanet in the south-east (i.e. Buckinghamshire, Oxfordshire, Berkshire, Hampshire, Surrey, West Sussex, East Sussex, Kent and the Isle of White). With 8,634,800 (according to the 2011 Census) inhabitants, it is considered to be the most populous region of England. Historically, the Southeast included also the counties of Essex, Hertfordshire, Bedfordshire and Greater London. In dialectology, what used to be called the 'Southeast', and what roughly corresponds to the older 'official version' of the Southeast is now called the 'Home Counties Modern Dialect Area' (see MAP 1), which 'centres on the counties immediately around London, but includes also parts of Hampshire, Berkshire and Buckinghamshire' (Trudgill 1990: 75). When the term 'Southeast' appears in this chapter, it should be equated with the Home Counties Modern Dialect Area rather than with the current political division of the same name. The reason behind this is to look for a fairly uniform construct where, to a greater or lesser extent, certain linguistic features would be shared by its substrata. Allegedly, the Southeast has developed a set of characteristic features, which are often perceived as an outcome of two processes, namely regional dialect levelling and the diffusion of linguistic features from London, the capital and biggest cultural centre in Britain, and, as some authorities claim, the biggest source of linguistic innovations in the region and beyond. Regional dialect levelling, or supralocalization, is a result of increased dialect contact triggered by high degrees of mobility and migration in the region, whereby very local forms, especially those perceived as 'old-fashioned' or particularly stigmatized on account of sounding 'provincial', lose in a competition with the more neutral, regionally acceptable, but not necessarily standard, forms. The reality, however, is much more complex than the dialectological and sociolinguistic literature tells us, and the regional dialect levelling, or supralocalization, forces do not operate with the same pace and strength in all towns, villages or neighbourhoods, leaving the surviving forms to coexist alongside the 'new' features.

Non-specialists associate London English itself with a specific linguistic, especially phonetic, make-up, popularized by lay, often satirical, literature and the media. The variety in question is popularly called 'Cockney' and was, in fact, confined to English spoken by white working-class East-End London residents (traditionally, those born within the sound of Bow-bells, where 'Bow' represents the historic church of St Mary-le-Bow). The perception that 'Cockney' is a London-wide variety, however, is mistaken and such a perception of London English obscures the fact that London is a multi-ethnic home to 8,173,900 people (according to the 2011 Census). The traditional home of Cockney, the East End, has changed dramatically in terms of its demography over recent years and is now, like many other areas of London, a multi-ethnic community. Indeed, 'Cockney', at least as it is traditionally characterized, is no longer representative even of the white working-class population of the East End.

It is impossible to define very precisely what London English or Southeastern English is, also because the Southeast is a fuzzy concept, a product of a whole set of fairly recent political, economic and social changes. Nonetheless, certain linguistic phenomena can be observed at the level of the region, and some generalizations based on both clear-sighted observation and empirical research can be attempted. This chapter aims at presenting general tendencies found in the Englishes, rather than English, of London and the Southeast, as well as providing detailed descriptions of actual realizations of a set of linguistic variables constituting the core of those varieties. It has to be remembered, though, that using particular features in isolation does not make someone's speech sound London or Southeastern.

Linguistic Characteristics

Before any description of the Englishes of the Southeast of England (or any other region) is made, the reader needs to understand that language is a variable construct and that that variability is fairly complex and dependent on many social and linguistic factors. The extent to which particular linguistic features 'typical' of the region are adopted by individual speakers is affected by their age, gender, social class, ethnicity, length of stay in and attitudes towards the region and its speakers, the amount of contact with other speakers of the same or other language varieties and many more. The subtle interplay between all those factors influences the degree to which particular features or groups of features are incorporated into the speech of an individual. One has to bear in mind that for economic and political reasons London and the Southeast are particularly good places to observe extensive dialect contact, resulting from high rates of mobility and migration from other regions of Great Britain and different parts of the world. Only recently have the scholars practising the disciplines of dialectology and sociolinguistics begun to acknowledge the scale of inter-ethnic influences on the outcomes of dialect contact. It also needs to be mentioned that particular linguistic processes may not necessarily be unique to the Southeast of England. Therefore, it is their co-occurrence in the region which makes its speech distinguishable from the speech heard in other regions within England. A warning needs to be made – the Southeast is relatively big; therefore, despite extensive regional dialect levelling, the distribution of specific features is uneven throughout the region, which manifests itself in both qualitative and quantitative differences from county to county, or even from town to town within a single county. Nevertheless, to a certain degree, generalizations can be made, and this chapter is an attempt to put together the various pieces of knowledge and research results related to varieties of English spoken in London and the rest of the Southeast of England.

Another warning must be made at this point. Empirical speech research findings are not comparable in a straightforward way. It should be taken into consideration that each research takes place under a set of unique circumstances and is driven by different motivations, which again makes straightforward comparisons impossible. This does not mean that they should be disbelieved. In fact, all findings complement rather than discredit each other.

Phonological Features

Vowels

In order to facilitate the recognition of which vocalic features are being discussed, I will be using the concept of lexical sets (Wells 1982: 127–165; Tipton, this volume). The phonetic symbols used to represent vowel qualities and consonantal realizations are based on the International Phonetic Alphabet, the IPA – vowels are described in relation to the closest cardinal vowels, along three dimensions: closeness/openness, fronting/backing and, when necessary, lip rounding.

Short monophthongs

KIT

In the Southeast of England, including London, the vowel of KIT, /ɪ/, such as in *kit, thin, big,* is relatively uncontroversial – as in the case of other short front vowels, that is, DRESS and TRAP, it is evidenced to have had closer realizations in the past than it does now. For instance, in nineteenth-century English it may have been in the region of [i] (Trudgill 2004: 47). At present, in Southeastern accents its quality is closer than in Received Pronunciation [RP] (Cruttenden 2001: 87). Nevertheless, this change towards a more open vowel quality has been progressing at such a slow pace and to such a small extent that some linguists remark on its 'considerable stability since Old English' (Gimson 1962: 98). A more contemporary sociolinguistic study in London conducted by Tollfree demonstrates that this vowel has undergone the process of laxing, and for some speakers centralization; she finds that KIT is realized as [ɪ] ~ [ɪ̈] by both middle- and working-class speakers who participated in her study. That coincides with Wells's description that the vowel 'may be somewhat more central at times' (1982: 305). However, a project called ***Linguistic innovators: the English of adolescents in London*** (Kerswill et al. 2007) demonstrates that the KIT vowel is undergoing fronting in inner-London Hackney, but raising in outer-London Havering (Torgersen et al. 2006), albeit in Hackney statistically not significantly (Kerswill at al. 2007: 5, Cheshire et al. 2008).

To the best of my knowledge, the only published data from empirical studies regarding the KIT vowel in the Southeast come from Williams and Kerwill's study in the New Town of Milton Keynes, Buckinghamshire, and an earlier established town of Reading, Berkshire, as well as Torgersen and Kerswill's study in Ashford, Kent. The standard variant [ɪ] constitutes the most frequent realization of the vowel in both Milton Keynes and Reading, but slightly lower variants also occur. In Reading they range from [ɪ] > [ɪ̞]~[e̞]. Interestingly, in Milton Keynes, higher variants than the standard also appear, giving a range between [ɪ̞] ~ [i̞] (Williams and Kerwill 1999). In Ashford the vowel is reported to be undergoing the process of fronting (Torgersen and Kerswill 2004, Torgersen et al. 2006).

DRESS

Like the vowels of KIT and TRAP, the vowel of DRESS, /ɛ/, such as in *dress, fetch, set,* in London and the Southeast is said to have had closer qualities than nowadays (Wells 1982: 128, Trudgill 2004: 47), and in contemporary London varieties probably closer than in mainstream RP (Cruttenden 2001: 87), although there is evidence that this distance may be disappearing at least in the less basilectal varieties of English spoken in London. In London's East End Bethnal Green Sivertsen observes that the vowel is 'an unrounded, front, between half-close and half-open vocoid' (1960: 53). In 1962 Gimson writes that popular London realizes the DRESS vowel in the region of Cardinal [e], but almost forty years later in her South East London Regional Standard [SELRS] sample, Tollfree finds realizations ranging between [ɛ] and [ɛ̞]. Similar qualities were found in her South East London English (a basilectal, working-class variety) data. A recent project conducted in London demonstrates that the DRESS vowel in inner-London (Hackney) and outer-London (Havering) is undergoing a process of centralization (Torgersen et al. 2006). However, the change is not yet statistically significant (Cheshire et al. 2008); therefore, at this stage we cannot talk of a generational change for this vowel in the aforementioned boroughs of London (Kerswill et al. 2007). The centring of the DRESS vowel as a result of backing and lowering in the upper-middle class speech of London is also reported by Kamata (2006). Therefore, there is evidence that the two extremes on the social scale, that is, the lower-working and upper-middle class residents of London are undergoing the same change. It remains to be seen which group in London is leading this change.

In the Southeast of England, the contemporary DRESS vowel is rather poorly documented. Again we must rely on Williams and Kerswill's Milton Keynes and Reading data. In the New Town the variants tend to be slightly closer, [ɛ̝] > [e̞], than in Reading, [ɛ̝] > [e̞], where the vowel is relatively stable. Stability is also documented for the DRESS vowel in Ashford (Torgersen and Kerswill 2004, Torgersen et al. 2006).

TRAP

On the basis of historical evidence it is assumed that the vowel of TRAP, /æ/, as in *trap, cat, van,* used to have a much closer quality than it does at present and closer than in RP of the period in question (like the vowels of KIT and DRESS). Ellis (1889: 226) interpreted various accounts of the quality of TRAP as equivalent to the IPA [ɛ] (in his transcription system, E; see Eustace 1969 for an interpretation of Ellis's transcription system). Similarly, later accounts of Englishes of London oscillate around the same vowel quality, around Cardinal Vowel 3, [ɛ] – in Cockney 'it is an unrounded, front, half-open vocoid' (Sivertsen 1960: 59) and in popular London /æ/ is raised to 'approximately C [ɛ]' (Gimson 1962: 101; for linguistic constraints on the allophonic variation, including diphthongization, and vowel length for TRAP; see Sivertsen 1960: 59–63). Later descriptions of London vowels by Wells (1982: 129, 305) and Cruttenden (2001) point to the same vowel quality. However, empirical research reveals that the lowering of the TRAP vowel to lower qualities, at least in some London residents' speech, must have started at least as early as the 1960s, if not earlier – Labov's Hackney female speaker, recorded in 1968, for instance, realizes /æ/ as an open, quite front vowel, with high F2 (acoustic measurements for this speaker can be seen in Labov 1994: 169). Thirty years later Tollfree's South East middle- and working-class speakers demonstrate more open qualities, around [æ] as well. The lowering of TRAP has been a rather slow process and unevenly distributed across different boroughs of London and individual speakers; presumably with East London speakers acquiring more open qualities quite late and to a lesser extent, for instance Przedlacka's Bethnal Green speakers use variants ranging between [æ] and [ɛ], yet never reaching Cardinal [ɛ] (2002: 53). A recent sociolinguistic project in London reveals yet another important dimension in the change of this vowel's quality, namely its movement on the horizontal axis. While older speakers in inner-London Hackney have fully front [æ]-type qualities, acoustic measurements demonstrate a great degree of backness (in addition to lowering the quality of the vowel) among young speakers. The same kind of change is taking place in outer-London Havering, even though TRAP in the speech of elderly Havering speakers is already much less front than it is in the speech of people of the same age residing in Hackney (Kerswill et al. 2006, 2007, 2008, Torgersen et al. 2006 and Cheshire et al. 2008). Also Kamata's (2006) acoustic measurements demonstrate the process of backing for TRAP in the speech of working- and upper middle-class speakers (in the former accompanied by lowering, but in the latter slight raising).

In the Southeast, outside London, TRAP is also said to have been closer in the past than it is now. Trudgill (2004: 45) goes back to as early as the middle of the nineteenth century and claims that at that period regional accents in the whole area around London had much closer TRAP, in some cases even closer than [ɛ]. The lowering of the quality of TRAP could have taken place in the second half of the nineteenth century as Wright's (1905: 22) descriptions of Kent, Middlesex (now part of Greater London), south-western Essex, southern Hertfordshire and southern Buckinghamshire may suggest – his TRAP representation, 'e', can be interpreted, in compliance with his descriptions, as a vowel with a quality intermediate between [ɛ] and [æ]. Wright's descriptions are further supported by evidence from elderly speakers, some born as early as at the end of the nineteenth century, included in the Survey of English Dialects, SED (1950s). Further lowering evidence comes from Przedlacka's (2002: 57) research in the Home Counties, where she finds all but one of the localities to currently have more open qualities than in the past (i.e. in comparison with the SED data): in Little Badow, Essex, TRAP lowered from [ɛ] ~ [ɛᵊ] (SED) to [æ] ~ [ɛ̞], and in Farningham, Kent, and Walton-on-the-Hill, Surrey, from [æ] ~ [æ̝] and [æ], respectively, to [a] (Cardinal 4) ~ [æ]. On the other hand, her speech data from Aylesbury, Buckinghamshire, show significant raising from [a] ~ [a̝] (SED) to [a] ~ [æ] ~ [ɛ̞]. Williams and Kerswill's studies demonstrate the use of extremely open qualities, ranging from Cardinal 4, [a], to slightly raised [a̝] in Milton Keynes, Buckinghamshire, and Cardinal 4, [a], to retracted [a̠] in Reading, Berkshire (1999: 142 and 145). Acoustic measurements indicate that in Ashford the vowel has moved backwards (Torgersen and Kerswill 2004).

All in all, the empirical evidence supports the claims that the quality of the TRAP vowel is more open now both in London and the rest of the Southeast, and might suggest a further direction of change towards a backer realization, though we would need more evidence to be able to state which other areas of London and the Southeast have been involved in that change.

STRUT

In the Englishes of London and parts of the rest of the Southeast, the vowel of STRUT, /ʌ/, such as in *strut, cup, mud,* has undergone significant fronting: Wells claims that its quality can range from a fronted [ɐ̟] to Cardinal 4, [a]; similarly Cruttenden states the short vowel /ʌ/ 'moves forward to almost C [a]'

(2001: 87), Hughes et al. (2005: 73) say that in traditional Cockney, /ʌ/ is realized as [a̝], Tollfree's (1999: 166) middle-class London speakers' qualities of /ʌ/ range from [ʌ̟] to [ɐ], and her working-class speakers have even fronter variants, [ɐ] ~ [a]. Przedlacka's (2002: 53) teenagers from Bethnal Green also extensively front their STRUT vowel up to open front slightly raised with reference to Cardinal 4 [a̝] ~ [a] ~ [ɐ̟], but she finds less open and more back variants [ə] ~ [ʌ̟] as well. However, the most recent results of acoustic studies for inner-London (Hackney) and outer-London (Havering) seem to suggest that (at least for Hackney under the influence of dialect contact with residents of Creole/Jamaican English descent), the STRUT vowel is now in the dramatic process of backing and raising, and is realized as a back half-close vowel by non-Anglo, as well as white Anglo teenagers (Torgersen et al. 2006, Kerswill et al. 2007, 2008 and Cheshire et al. 2008). Similarly, Kamata (2006) reports backing and 'being more close' but only in the speech of upper-middle class speakers in the sample; working-class speakers in the study display a tendency to front STRUT.

Nevertheless, the process of fronting seems to be progressing in certain places in the Southeast, although we still find intra-regional variation. Milton Keynes and Reading still have some backer variants along with central variants, [ʌ] > [ʌ̟] ~ [ɐ] and [ə] (elderly speakers) and [ʌ] > [ʌ̟] ~ [ɐ] and [ə̟ː] (elderly and some younger speakers), respectively. Compared to the 1950s Survey of English Dialects (SED), Przedlacka's data (2001, 2002: 61–62, 65) also demonstrated fronting in progress: in the four localities she studied, the SED speakers exhibited no fronting, whereas in her speakers' speech fronting was already on the way, in Little Baddow, Essex, Farningham, Kent and Walton-on-the-Hill, Surrey, the [ʌ̟] variant was the most frequent, whereas in Aylesbury, Buckinghamshire, fronting was even more advanced, and the most widely used variants were [ɐ̟] – [ɐ]. In Colchester the STRUT vowel has reached the quality of [ɐ] (Britain and Johnson 2004/5). In Ashford, however, STRUT seems to be undergoing the process of backing and raising, as in London's Hackney and Havering (Torgersen and Kerswill 2004, Torgersen et al. 2006).

LOT

Early descriptions of the quality of the LOT vowel, /ɒ/, as in *lot, pot, flock,* in London revolve around two dimensions, that is, its openness and the degree of lip rounding. Sivertsen describes the 'simple syllable peak /o/ as in *pot*' as a 'slightly closer, rounded, back, half open vocoid' (1960: 71), and adds that its allophonic variants are conditioned by the adjacent consonants; namely, after the onset /w/ (as in *what*) 'both lip rounding and tongue position are closer', before /l + vowel/ and /r/ after velar consonants the articulation is significantly backer, and in unstressed positions it is closer and more centralized. Wells claims that the London LOT vowel is 'somewhat less open' [ɔ] (1982: 305). Both middle-class and working-class informants in Tollfree's study produce a fully back, rounded [ɒ] vowel, and as she notices, a slightly centralized variant [ɒ̈] in 'less formal styles', which adds the third dimension to the LOT vowel description, namely frontness/backness (1999: 166). No recent changes in the quality of the vowel of LOT have been detected in inner-London (Hackney) or outer-London (Havering) (Torgersen et al. 2006, Kerswill et al. 2007 and Cheshire et al. 2008).

Kurath and Lowman's descriptions (1970: 22), based on 1930 research, led to the conclusion that most counties in the South of England had an unrounded LOT vowel, around [ɑ], and those within the Southeast with the rounded variants were Essex, Hertfordshire and Middlesex (now part of Greater London). Later descriptions by Wells show the direction of change in the realization of this vowel towards the back and rounded variants [ɒ, ɔ] – yet he claims that the 'recessive' (1982: 130) unrounded LOT variant [ɑ] can still be found in parts of the South of England. That claim is supported by Williams and Kerswill's findings in the well established town of Reading, where old people still use the unrounded variant [ɑ], but younger people use the rounded variant [ɒ̞]. In the New Town of Milton Keynes, only the rounded variant [ɒ̞] is found, giving further evidence of the change in the quality of this vowel from unrounded to rounded in the Southeast of England. In Ashford, though, the vowel has been undergoing raising (Torgersen et al. 2006). It also needs to be mentioned that the LOT lexical set is realized in the same way as the CLOTH lexical set.

FOOT

More and more evidence suggests that the vowel of FOOT, /ʊ/, as in *foot, book, full*, has been in the process of fronting 'from a back to a central or front realisation' (Torgersen 2002: 26). A fronter quality of this vowel in London was commented on several decades ago by Sivertsen, who wrote that /ʊ/ 'differs slightly from RP in being a little more fronted'; she described /ʊ/ as 'a rounded, between central and back, between close and half-close vocoid' (1960: 79). According to this author, the exact quality of the vowel depended on its phonological environment – it was 'slightly more back after labials ..., also more back after velars', but 'after the consonant /j/, and to some extent after the strongly palatalized /ʃʒ/, /ʊ/ is centralized'. Wells considered fronted variants, characteristic of 'innovative or urban speech' (1982: 133). Nevertheless, Labov's interviews recorded in London's East End in 1968 do not contain any tokens with fronted /ʊ/ (Labov 1994). However, the phenomenon of FOOT fronting is also reported in more recent works. Tollfree (1999: 166) finds an unrounded centralized variant [ʊ̜̈] in the speech of her younger SELRS (middle-class) speakers, but her older SELRS speakers and SELE (working-class) informants use a rounded close back variant [ʊ]. Fronter variants, of the [ü ~ ɵ] type, are found in London by Altendorf (2003). In inner-London Hackney, Torgersen et al. (2006; also Kerswill et al. 2006) find rather low amounts of FOOT fronting, and considerable inter-ethnic variation, with White British-heritage speakers fronting more than non-Anglos, regardless of their ethnic origins. Also rather limited FOOT fronting is reported for outer-London Havering, yet more extensive than for Hackney. In both boroughs the pronunciation of FOOT is more central/more front among younger speakers than it is among the elderly (Kerswill et al. 2007, Cheshire et al. 2008, 2011). All those research findings suggest that the fronting of /ʊ/ is not well advanced in London.

In many other varieties of English in the Southeast, though, /ʊ/ is observed to have been undergoing a process of more extreme fronting than is taking place in London. Britain (2005: 1007) talks of more than one dimension of change in the quality of the FOOT vowel, that is, 'fronting, unrounding and lowering of /ʊ/'. Britain and Johnson (2004/5) explain the interdependency of the three dimensions in the following way:

> Where the original [ʊ] has unrounded, it has also had the tendency to move forward. The further back in the mouth that sound is articulated, the greater the tendency of the lips to become rounded and the further forward the less the tendency towards rounding.

They point to a tendency for low vowels to be unrounded, therefore 'if the sound starts to become unrounded it will either lower or front' (Britain and Johnson 2004/5). Let us now review some of the empirical research findings for the FOOT vowel in the Southeast. In 1995 Laver conducted a rapid and anonymous survey in private and state schools in Hampshire (and East Anglian Suffolk), asking students a question which triggered the word 'book' in response. The findings were revealing – the tendency for /ʊ/ fronting to an unrounded, centralized variant, [ɨ], was greater among young females than males, and middle-class rather than working-class speakers (the latter tallies with Tollfree's South East London findings). Centralized and front variants, [ɵ > ʊ̟ ~ ø̠ ~ ʏ], were also found, especially among middle-class speakers in Milton Keynes and Reading (Kerswill and Williams 1994, Williams and Kerswill 1999); working-class informants used mainly a conservative short weakly rounded centralized back close-mid monophthong [ʊ̟], but to some degree also fronted realizations [ø] and [ʏ]. The most detailed acoustic analysis of the FOOT vowel in the speech of young and middle-aged residents of the Southeast thus far, by Torgersen (2002), also demonstrates that it is young middle-class women (like in Laver 1995) who are leading the change. The variants he finds in the speech of younger informants are [ɵ], short weakly rounded central close-mid monophthong, and [ʏ], short rounded front centralized close-mid monophthong, both are fronted; on the other hand, his older speakers use a short weakly rounded centralized back close-mid monophthong [ʊ̟] almost categorically. His analysis also shows that fronting was most favoured in the context of a following /k/ and prevented by the following /l/; the hierarchy for specific consonants in that study was as follows: following /k/ > following /t/ > following /d/ > following /l/ (for a further discussion of linguistic constraints as well as lexical incidence of FOOT fronting, see Torgersen 2002: 33–37). Fronted variants have been found in several other Southeastern towns as well. Altendorf (2003) finds centralized and close-mid central rounded variants ranging between [ü] and [ɵ] in Colchester, Essex, and Canterbury, Kent, whereas Carfoot (2004) reports considerable amounts of fronted variants for Romford in the London Borough of Havering. Carfoot analyses the linguistic constraints on FOOT fronting and finds that it is more likely to occur before a coronal consonant, but less likely to occur after a labial consonant or before 'dark' L, that is, velarized /l/, [ɫ] (Carfoot 2004: 35). Moreover, Carfoot (2004: 40) suggests that FOOT fronting may lead to restructuring of the phoneme inventory in the dialects with a high degree of fronting. She suggests that if a great proportion of the words in the FOOT lexical set move to fronter positions resulting in realizations such as [ɨ] or [ʉ], the place for [ʊ] in the vowel space will remain open for another phoneme to move into. Some words in the FOOT lexical set, especially those where the vowel is preceded by a labial consonant or followed by 'dark L' (e.g. 'wool' or 'bull'), are unlikely to be fronted; therefore, 'a possible outcome would be a three-way split between a "FOOT" set, a "WOOL" set and the "STRUT" set' (Carfoot 2004: 40).

To sum up, the existing evidence suggests that the fronting of the FOOT vowel has been less extensive in London than in the rest of the Southeast, and that the fronting of /ʊ/ can be seen as a levelled regional (supralocal) feature of the English Southeast. In addition, FOOT fronting may be accompanied by unrounding and lowering.

bettER/commA

The unstressed bettER/commA vowel, /ə/, such as in the final syllable of the words *better, comma, suffer*, has received extremely little attention from commentators describing Englishes of the Southeast of England. In London, the exact quality of this vowel varies. Sivertsen, for instance, reported that 'it may vary in tongue position within the central vocoid area from half-close to half-open ... it is always short, and the lip position is neutral' (1960: 84). Twenty years later, Wells (1982: 305) talks of very open realizations of /ə/ by broad Cockney speakers, in the region of [ɐ], and forty years later, Tollfree also reports very open quality, [ɐ], alongside central realizations [ə] ~ [ə̞] in her South East London English (working-class) sample; the latter variants also appear in her South East London Regional Standard (middle-class) informants' speech.

Even less is known about the phonetic qualities of the /ə/ vowel in the Englishes of the Southeast outside London. In Milton Keynes it can range from a slightly lowered central vowel, [ə̞], to an advanced back open unrounded vowel, [ɑ̟], with middle-class and older speakers using the former variant. The quality of the /ə/ vowel in Reading ranges from a slightly lowered central vowel, [ə̞], as in Milton Keynes, to an open central vowel [ɐ], as in broad Cockney described by Wells. Middle-class and older speakers most frequently use a central variant [ə]. Data from both places come from research conducted by Williams and Kerswill (1999: 143–145).

happʏ

The happʏ vowel, /i/, is the last segment in words such as *happy, city, lucky* or *coffee.* In London and the rest of the Southeast of England, two trends have been observed. One of them is the so-called 'happʏ-tensing'. The term has been coined by Wells (1982: 257–258), and is meant to indicate that the quality of the vowel is tense [i(ː)] rather than lax as in the case of traditional RP realization [ɪ], that is, more like in FLEECE than KIT. A similar observation has been made by Hughes et al. (2005: 74). The other trend is the diphthongization of this vowel – the diphthong would be a closing one with a starting point lower than [i], that is a range of variants between [i̞i] and [ɪi] can be found, the latter prevailing. Altendorf and Watt (2004: 187) state that diphthongs with more central starting points can be heard in the speech of working-class Londoners, and the more basilectal the speech, the more central the starting point of the diphthong, which can reach the quality of [əɪ]. That tallies with the findings for the FLEECE vowel (discussed further in this chapter), with which the final vowel of *happy* is equated in the Southeast. However, diphthongization is not present in the speech of all people living in the Southeast; Tollfree (1999: 165, 169) finds only tense monophthongal variants [i] and [iː] in London, both in her middle-class and working-class samples. In Milton Keynes and Reading, no diphthongal realizations were observed either; the happʏ vowel has the quality of [i̞] (Williams and Kerswill 1999: 143). On the other hand, Altendorf (2003) reports realizations ranging from [i(i)] to [ᵊi] both in London, and in Colchester and Canterbury (where [ᵊi] denotes a diphthong with a less central starting point than in the case of [əɪ]).

Long monophthongs

NURSE

We know extremely little about the vowel of NURSE, /ɜː/, as in *nurse, bird, church,* in London and the Southeast of England. Sivertsen describes the Cockney NURSE as differing from RP in that 'the tongue position is more open and front, the opening between the jaws is greater, and the lips are slightly rounded, or rather protruded', she then defines it as a long 'fronted central, almost half-open, slightly labialized vocoid'. She also claims that it may be followed by a short central off-glide (1962: 87). A similar description is given by Wells: 'the monophthong /ɜː/ in NURSE is on occasions somewhat fronted and/or lightly rounded'; he denotes Cockney variants as [ɜ̟ː] and [œ̈ː] (1982: 305). However, in Tollfree's South East London sample, there are no signs of lip rounding either in the middle-class or the working-class speech. She finds long central monophthongs ranging from [ɜː] to [əː], the former used predominantly by older speakers and the latter by younger speakers (1999: 166). Milton Keynes and Reading data demonstrate the use of a slightly lowered mid central long monophthong, [ə̞ː], again without lip rounding (Williams and Kerswill 1999: 143). These findings might suggest a change towards slight raising and complete unrounding of the vowel of NURSE, but we would need to consider much more data from various places in London and the Southeast to make such a claim.

BATH-PALM-START

The back quality of the BATH-PALM-START vowel sets, /ɑː/, as in *bath, palm, start, path, father,* is characteristic of some 'southern accents', not only in the Southeast of England, and it is a 'relatively new addition to the phoneme inventory of English' (Trudgill 2004: 60). These sets of vowels must be discussed in relation to the TRAP vowel as historical evidence shows that prior to what is termed the 'TRAP-BATH Split', the BATH, PALM and START sets used the same vowel as in TRAP. Why do we distinguish between BATH-PALM-START and TRAP now? Two processes are said to be responsible for the emergence of the two different phonemes, /æ/ and /ɑː/, that is, Pre-R Lengthening and Pre-Fricative Lengthening (Wells 1982: 201 and 203, respectively). Pre-R Lengthening resulted in an emergence of a lengthened version of the seventeenth-century TRAP vowel to what can be transcribed as [aː]; subsequent Pre-Fricative Lengthening produced a lengthened version of the eighteenth-century TRAP vowel, that is [æː]. After that process START and PALM became [aː] and BATH became [æː]. However, the BATH set merged with the START and PALM set and started being pronounced as [aː] (for the complications found within the BATH set see Wells 1982: 133–137 or Trudgill 2004: 61). Another change that happened to the START lexical set was its backing. START Backing is claimed to have taken place in the eighteenth century (Wells 1982: 234) but became socially acceptable probably by the late nineteenth century (MacMahon 1994: 456). MacMahon argues that the process started among the least socially privileged sections of the society. The 1950/1960s SED does not give accurate data related to its social distribution, but is indicative of its occurrence in the region surrounding London (and Birmingham). In contemporary London, the occurrence of the TRAP versus BATH-PALM-START distinction has recently been documented by Tollfree (1999: 166), who describes the vowel of TRAP as slightly lower than the vowel variant described by Hughes et al. (2005: 74) for Cockney: [ɛ̞], that is [æ] and [æː] for all her speakers. She also finds diphthongal realizations of TRAP, [ɛi]. In the START lexical set both middle-class and working-class speakers in Tollfree's sample use a fully open, fully back, [ɑː], as well as slightly advanced, [ɑ̟ː], variants; in addition, her working-class informants use back/slightly fronted variants with lip rounding, [ɒ̟ː]. Earlier descriptions of BATH-PALM-START, by

Beaken (1971) and Wells (1982), indicate the use of the full back unrounded vowel, 'qualitatively equivalent to cardinal 5' (Wells 1982: 305). A recent analysis of data recorded in inner-London Hackney does not reveal any significant changes in the START lexical set (Kerswill et al. 2007, 2008 and Cheshire et al. 2008). It is worth mentioning that the distribution of /a/ and /ɑː/ in London English coincides with the distribution of those vowels in RP. At present, the BATH-PALM-START sets in the Southeast of England are relatively uncontroversial, and have attracted very little attention on the part of researchers in the past decade; even if commented on, they are not well described in terms of the accurate vowel quality. What we have at our disposal once more is Williams and Kerwill's 1999 Milton Keynes and Reading study, where the former fully back fully open [ɑː] variants are used, alongside more advanced [ɑ̟ː] variants (frequently used by middle-class young speakers) and elderly working-class speakers use a fronter [a̠ː] variant. In Reading, that fronter variant is used by some working-class adolescents; elderly informants tend to use [ɑ̟ː].

THOUGHT-NORTH-FORCE

The THOUGHT-NORTH-FORCE vowel sets, /ɔː/, as in *thought, north, force, lord,* are yet another little-explored phonological feature in the Southeast of England, although some interesting patterns of variation have been commented on in popular, rather than specialized, literature. Trudgill (2004: 64) points to the recent history of /ɔː/ in English: 'The /ɔː/ vowel is also a relative newcomer to English phonology, and its occurrence and distribution vary widely from variety to variety.' Mainstream RP has an /ɔː/ vowel in all three sets (though elderly U-RP speakers may still be found to display variation between them). In London and the Southeast of England we can encounter, with various intensity and frequency in different localities and across individual speakers, a phenomenon called the THOUGHT Split (Wells 1982: 310–311), which consists in either using the standard variant [ɔː], as in RP, or a closer monophthongal variant [oː], around Cardinal Vowel 7 (Wells 1982: 310, Hughes et al. 2005: 74), on the one hand, or a diphthongal variant [ɔə] on the other, depending on the position of the vowel in the utterance. When /ɔː/ is 'non-final', the monophthong is used, whereas when /ɔː/ is in utterance-final position, or 'within the utterance ... where the syllable in question is otherwise prominent' the diphthong tends to be used (Wells 1982: 306). The close monophthongal variant [oː] and the diphthongal variant [ɔə] are associated with broad Cockney, and so are triphthongal realizations, such as [ɔːʊ̆ə] (Beaken 1971) or [ɔwə] (Cruttenden 2001: 87). Intermediate London accents may still have a close monophthong [oː], but on the other hand, [ɔ̝ː] in unchecked syllable, or a diphthong [ɔə]. Degree of lip rounding may also vary. For a description of factors complicating the monophthong versus diphthong choice, such as L vocalization and morpheme boundaries, see Wells (1982: 311). We know rather little about those linguistic constraints from empirical studies, which nevertheless provide valuable information on the exact phonetic qualities of the THOUGHT-NORTH-FORCE vowel sets. Tollfree (1999: 167) reports /ɔː/ to be realized in South East London as monophthongs of the [ɔː] ~ [o̞ː] range by her SELRS (middle-class) speakers, and either monophthongs [ɔː] ~ [o̞ː] ~ [o̞ː] or a diphthong [o̞ʊ] by her SELE (working-class) speakers. In Przedlacka's (2002: 53) Cockney sample, teenage speakers born and bred in Bethnal Green, in the East End of London, use monophthongal realizations in the [o] ~ [ʊ] range in open syllables, and diphthongal realizations of the [oʊ] type in closed syllables. She also notices that her female informants used more open variants, [o̞] ~ [o̞ʊ] and [ʊ] than her male informants.

In the Home Counties, in the 1950s data recorded for the Survey of English Dialects, both monophthongal and diphthongal realizations were present, for instance, in all four localities restudied by Przedlacka in the late 1990s (or in a close proximity to the ones she researched, i.e. Aylesbury, Buckinghamshire, Little Baddow, Essex, Farningham, Kent and Walton-on-the-Hill, Surrey). Her own data demonstrate a drop in the use of diphthongal variants to the extent that her Essex and Surrey data do not contain any diphthongs for the THOUGHT-NORTH-FORCE vowel sets (Przedlacka 2001, 2002: 62). My own (Ryfa 2005) corpus of recordings of teenage males from Colchester, Essex, however, does contain a number of instances of the [ɔə] diphthong (in fact, with an even more open end-point) uttered by an 18-year-old working-class man. On several occasions I have also heard working-class women in their late 50s from Colchester and nearby Wivenhoe using the same pronunciation in the word *more*. A rapid anonymous survey conducted in Colchester by Jenny Hall and Richard Meade in 2001 found that [ou] was the preferred variant among speakers under the age of 35, whereas [ɔː] was most common among older speakers (Britain, David p.c.). Also, Williams and Kerswill (1999: 143) report the use of a diphthong with a close-mid back rounded onset [oʊ], alongside a slightly lower than close-mid back rounded monophthongal variant [o̞ː] in the Southeastern towns of Milton Keynes and Reading.

GOOSE

The realization of the GOOSE vowel, /uː/, as in *goose, boot, loom,* is one of the most distinguished features in the phonetic make-up of the Englishes of the Southeast. In London it can be realized either as a monophthong or as a diphthong. Sivertsen's characterization of this vowel in Cockney indicates its strong diphthongization and considerable fronting; she states that 'the tongue glides upwards, but the starting-point may vary: it may be half-close to half-open, or it may be half-close'; she then goes on: 'it is central rather than back, and the lips, which may be neutral at the beginning, are fairly closely rounded at the end: [ə̆ü] or [ʊ̆ü]' (1960: 81). Almost twenty years later, the most common diphthongal realizations reported by Hudson and Holloway (1977) were [ʊü], but working-class boys and some working-class girls used an [ɤu] diphthong. Comments by Wells, that the starting point for the diphthong ranges from [ʊ] to [ə], 'the latter being the most Cockney-flavoured' (1982: 306), tally well with Sivertsen's observations. According to Wells, the end-point is centralized [ü], like in Sivertsen's notation, or central [ʉ]. The entire diphthongs then can be represented as [ə̆ʉ] and [əü]. Sivertsen remarks that 'the end of the glide is at least as prominent as the beginning' (1960: 81), similarly Wells talks of the 'crescendo' nature of the Cockney GOOSE diphthongs (1982: 306). Non-Cockney varieties of London English, which Wells terms as 'popular London', have qualities such as [ɨü], [ə̹ü] and [ʊ̹ü] (all end-points are centralized). In a more recent study conducted in London's East End, Przedlacka finds both monophthongs and diphthongs, the latter with a 'lowered and slightly fronted' onset, while the second element is 'a back vocalic segment' (2002: 53), and denotes them as ranging between [ɵʊ] and [ɘʊ̹]. Apart from diphthongs, London GOOSE can be realized as a monophthong: Hudson and Holloway (1977) reported that the most commonly used monophthong in working-class informants' speech was [ʊː], and middle-class speakers' [ü], whereas Wells talked of central monophthongs, either with lip rounding, [ʉː] or with 'little lip rounding', [ɨː] (1982: 306). Altendorf (2003) also finds advanced fronting, leading to alternation between [ɨː] and [ɪː]. Most recent data from inner-London Hackney demonstrates most extreme fronting of GOOSE among Non-Anglo teenage boys, then extensive fronting among Anglo teenagers who mix with Non-Anglo friends and slightly less fronting among Anglo teenagers who have Anglo friends; the degree of fronting in all those groups is higher than in the case of Anglo elderly informants. The innovation within that borough of London is led by Non-Anglo speakers (Torgersen 2006, Kerswill et al. 2006, 2007 and Cheshire et al. 2008, 2011). To sum up, within at least the last three decades, the monophthongal variants of the London English GOOSE vowel have undergone extensive fronting, and now range from central [ʉː] to lax front vowels with varying lip rounding, that is, [ɨː] and possibly [ʏː].

In the discussion of the GOOSE vowel there appear a set of linguistic constraints limiting the use of particular variants in London English. Sivertsen regards monophthongs as typical only of unstressed non-final syllables, and comments that 'diphthongization is not equally strong with all speakers, but it seems to be characteristic of unguarded style of speech' (1960: 81). Bowyer (1973) finds no monophthongs at all for particular lexical items, such as *boo* and *boot*. Hudson and Holloway (1977) claimed that the environment of a following nasal clearly favoured monophthongal realizations, whereas before a lenis consonant or at the word boundary before a following word starting with a consonant, diphthongal realizations were favoured. Diphthongal variants were very strongly favoured at the word boundary before another word starting with a vowel. Another factor which makes a difference in the realization of GOOSE is the occurrence of the following /l/ – Wells (1982: 315) claims that fronting does not occur before /l/, similarly Trudgill (2004: 58) remarks that central variants do not occur before /l/, Cruttenden (2001: 87) talks of monophthongization of /uː/ before vocalized /l/, and Altendorf and Watt (2004: 190) state that monophthongal variants are disfavoured by the following velarized, or 'dark', /l/, [ɫ] (they also point out that preceding /j/ favours monophthongal variants). From this evidence we can conclude that the following vocalized /l/ has an opposite effect to the following velarized /l/, [ɫ].

In the Southeast of England the process of GOOSE Fronting is not entirely new. Kurath and Lowman (1970: 13) report central vowel qualities among others for Kent and Surrey when discussing the traditional dialect of the 1930s. In the 1950s/1960s SED data, central variants [ʉ] are found, for instance, for Buckinghamshire. Gimson (1984: 192) regarded diphthongal variants such as [ʊu] and a front monophthong [y] as a characteristic feature of Southeastern English generally. More recently, various degrees of fronting of the GOOSE vowel have been found in Milton Keynes and Reading (Williams and Kerswill 1999: 145): [ʉː] ~ [ʉ̟ː] ~ [ʏː] ~ [yː] > [ᵊʉ̟ː], with young females leading in the use of most fronted [yː] variants and elderly speakers producing variants with slight onglides. Przedlacka (2001, 2002: 52, 62–63, 65) demonstrates the progress of fronting of the GOOSE vowel in the four localities she studied by comparing her data with the SED data from the same (or nearby) places. She shows more advanced fronting, [ʉ] – [ʏ], in Aylesbury, Buckinghamshire, now than it was reported in the SED, [ʉ] – [u], and finds fronted variants where they were not observed in the SED: [u̟] – [ʉ] in Little Baddow, Essex, [ʉ] – [ʏ] in Farningham, Kent, and [ʉ] in Walton-on-the-Hill, Surrey (the corresponding SED variants were [ʊu] – [u], [u] and [u], respectively). In Colchester, Essex, and Canterbury, Kent, new variants are found – both fronted and unrounded, [ɨː] ~ [ɪː], although the most frequently occurring ones still retain lip rounding, [ʉː] ~ [ʏː] (Altendorf 2003). Apparently, diphthongal variants are not reported in any of these studies.

Long vowels: closing diphthongs

FLEECE

The vowel of FLEECE, /iː/, as in *fleece, mean, cheat,* in RP is a long monophthong. However, in the Southeast of England, it is most commonly realized as a closing diphthong (the starting point is more open than the end-point, and the second element is a close vowel, [i]). Therefore, FLEECE is discussed here among the other closing diphthongs, especially as it is reported as taking part in the so-called 'Diphthong Shift', in which front closing diphthongs move counter-clockwise – in the case of FLEECE the onset becomes more open than [ɪ], as in *fleece* [fləɪs] (Trudgill 2004:49) and backer (for a detailed discussion of the idea of diphthong shifting, see Wells 1982: 308–310). Britain (2002: 35) and Trudgill (2004: 50) suggest that the shifting of this vowel started rather late in relation to the shifting of some other closing diphthongs. The change probably started in London and parts of the Southeast, as well as East Anglia – this claim is supported by Lowman's 1930 reports (in Trudgill 2004: 59) of slightly diphthongal [ɪi] realizations as opposed to [iː], in this area of England. In London's Cockney the FLEECE vowel is described as strongly diphthongized, 'the tongue glides upwards and forwards, but the starting point may vary: it may be central and half-close to half-open, or it may be more frontish and half-close: [ə̆i] or [ɪ̆i]' (Sivertsen 1960: 48). As Sivertsen observed, the starting point of the FLEECE diphthong may vary in quality along two dimensions: the onset height and frontness/backness; therefore, we get realizations ranging from [i̞i] (Przedlacka 2002) to [ɪi] in less basilectal varieties of London English, or with a central onset, [əi], strongly associated with traditional East End Cockney speakers (Sivertsen 1960, Bowyer 1973, Wells 1982, Tollfree 1999, Cruttenden 2001, Przedlacka 2002, Altendorf 2003). In fact, Wells (1982: 306) talks of onsets as low and back as [ɐ], in addition to [ə], in the Cockney FLEECE diphthong. Along with diphthongal variants, long monophthongs are also found. Tollfree (1999: 166) reports the use of monophthongs [iː] and centralized [ïː] among her older, and [iː] among her younger South East London Regional Standard speakers, whereas her South East London English speakers, regardless of age, use a whole range of variants, [iː] ~ [ï(ː)] ~ [ᵊiː] ~ [iːᵊ]. Altendorf (2003) also finds a range of realizations, and the most frequent ones are [iː] ~ [ɪi], then [ᵊi], followed by [əi]. Przedlacka (2002: 52), on the other hand, does not find any monophthongs in her Bethnal Green sample, where FLEECE is realized as a range of diphthongs [əi] ~ [i̞i].

We do not have many empirical studies dealing with the FLEECE vowel in the rest of the Southeast, yet those that exist demonstrate the same tendency as in London, that is, the prevailing use of diphthongal variants but also the presence of monophthongs. And so, Williams and Kerswill (1999: 143) find [ɪi] > [ᵊi] in Milton Keynes, and [iː] ~ [ᶦi] > [ᵊi] in Reading. Przedlacka (2001, 2002: 60) finds [ɪi] ~ [i] in all the localities she studied, that is, Aylesbury, Buckinghamshire, Farninghton, Kent, Little Baddow, Essex, and Walton-on-the-Hill, Surrey. Interestingly, the SED1950s data for the locality in Essex reveal the use of the Cockney-type realizations, [əi], which her present data do not contain. Ryfa's (2005: 46–47) detailed quantitative analysis of the speech of two groups of Colchester teenage males roughly corresponding to middle-class ('MC') and working-class ('WC') demonstrates monophthongal [i] realizations to be used only 20.49 per cent of the time by the 'MC' informants, and 18.71 per cent of the time by 'WC' speakers. 'MC' speakers also used diphthongs with fairly close starting point, [i̞i] and [ɪ̞i], 47.58 per cent and 31.94 per cent respectively. 'WC' speakers' range of diphthongs was twice as broad; they used [ɪ̞i] – 32.58 per cent, [i̞i] – 21.64 per cent, [əi] – 15.20 per cent and [ɪ̞i] – 12.87 per cent of the time.

To sum up, the typical FLEECE vowel realizations in London and the Southeast are diphthongal. There is enough empirical evidence to confirm the idea of diphthong shifting for this vowel in the region; however, unshifted forms co-exist. It also seems reasonable to claim that the lower the socio-economic status of the speakers of a variety, the more open and centralized the starting point of the diphthong.

FACE

There is historical evidence that the vowel of FACE, /eɪ/, as in *face, blade* and *shame*, used to be widely realized as a monophthong, as it still often is in northern varieties of English. The process which led to its diphthongization is called 'Long Mid Diphthonging' (for details, see Wells 1982: 210), and for this vowel it started over a century ago. Ellis (1889: 226), for instance, regarded diphthongal realizations of FACE as innovative forms characteristic of the regional speech of north and east London, as well as Essex and Hertfordshire. After the Long Mid Diphthonging, further changes have appeared in London and the Southeast of England, which involved lowering of the diphthong onset as part of the process called the Diphthong Shift (Wells 1982: 308–310). The 1950s/1960s SED data indicate the lowering of the starting point from open-mid front unrounded Cardinal Vowel 3, [ɛ], to near-open front unrounded vowel, [æ], resulting in forms such as [æɪ]. General London realizations are also presented as [æɪ] (Hughes et al. 2005: 74). Descriptions of London Cockney vowels indicate even further lowering of the FACE diphthong onset: Sivertsen (1960: 56) defines it as 'an unrounded front vocoid glide, where the starting-point is between half-open and open, and the end is half-close', similarly Cruttenden (2001: 87) points to a front open vowel [a]; thus [aɪ]. Backing and lowering to [ʌ] (Matthews 1938 [1972]: 79, Wells 1982: 307) are also possible; therefore: [ʌɪ]. But even within contemporary Cockney, relatively close variants are still found – Przedlacka's recordings of Bethnal Green teenagers do not contain any FACE diphthongs with lower onsets; she finds [e̝ɪ] and [ɛ̝ɪ] (2002: 53). In other varieties of English spoken in London, there is considerable allophonic variation in the actual realizations of FACE. Wells (1982: 307) observes centralized open-mid rounded [ɛ̹̈ɪ]-type variants and unrounded near-open central variants [ɐɪ] for Popular London. Socio-economic class, age and area of London seem to make a difference. Pointner's (1996) transcriptions of Romford speakers, in the London Borough of Havering, also point to very open [ʌɪ] realizations. Tollfree's (1999: 166) older South East London Regional English (middle-class) speakers use diphthongs with rather close onsets, [eɪ]/[eˑ] or [e̝ɪ], and younger speakers in this sample use diphthongal variants with more open and centralized starting points, [ë̞ɪ]. Her South East London (working-class) speakers demonstrate even further lowering to [a̝ɪ] or [aɪ], and some use a slightly rounded variant, [a̹ɪ]. For the East End's Tower Hamlets district, Fox (2003, 2007; also, Fox et al. 2011) reports the use of 'older' diphthongal forms with front unrounded near-open and open onsets, [æɪ] and [aɪ], as well as more frequent 'newer' variants with half-close to half-open onsets, [e̝ɪ], [eɪ] and [ɛɪ], by adolescent boys, especially those of Bangladeshi descent. The older generation of Tower Hamlets use only traditional variants with more open onsets, that is, [æɪ], [aɪ] and [ʌɪ]. Such a distribution of particular variants across ages points to the shift away from traditional Cockney forms towards those used by Bangladeshi teenage boys, 'leading to [ɛɪ] being the most favoured form among all ethnic groups' (Fox 2007; also, Fox et al. 2011). Similarly, young white British-heritage speakers in inner-London Hackney, and outer-London Havering (Cheshire et al. 2005, 2008, 2011 and Kerswill et al. 2005, 2006, 2007, 2008), demonstrate considerable diphthong onset raising (to half-open) in relation to older speakers. In addition, innovative monophthongal realizations and diphthongs with high-front onsets are found in Hackney, especially among non-white boys. Older speakers in those areas of London use diphthongs with open starting points. Cheshire et al. (2005) and Kerswill et al. (2005, 2006) refer to the spread of realizations with raised onset diphthongs within Hackney as 'reversing the "drift"' or 'reversal of diphthong shift' to front closing diphthongs (for a thorough discussion of this phenomenon, see Kerswill et al. 2008; also see Cheshire et al. 2008 and Fox et al. 2011 in relation to the 'diphthong shift reversal' in new varieties of English called 'Multicultural [London] English' emerging in [London and other] multi-ethnic urban centres in England).

The FACE vowel in the rest of Southeast of England is a diphthong typically perceived and commented as one with a low onset: 'Home Counties English is distinguished by having very wide diphthongs in *made*' (Trudgill 1990: 75). Yet, considerable allophonic variation in the actual realizations of FACE can be observed by examining findings of empirical research. Again the variability concerns the degree of openness of the diphthong onset, but also the phonetic quality of the endpoint. Williams and Kerswill (1999) report a whole range of realizations: [ɛi] ~ [æi] ~ [ɐɪ] ~ [ȩɪ] in Milton Keynes, and [ɛi] > [æi] ~ [ȩɪ] in Reading. Przedlacka's (2001, 2002: 63, 65) Home Counties speech data from teenage informants contain mainly diphthongal variants with onsets in the mid-open region, [ɛi] for Buckinghamshire, Kent and Surrey, and slightly closer, between [ɛi] and [ȩi] for Little Baddow, Essex. On the other hand, in Colchester, also Essex, in the speech of teenage males, the realization of the FACE vowel depends mainly on their socio-economic status and adherence to different teenage subcultures (Ryfa 2005: 48–50). The prevailing variant is the standard diphthong with an unrounded open, mid-front onset [ɛɪ], used 79.81 per cent of the time by a group of teenage boys whose socio-economic status can roughly be estimated as middle-class ('MC'), and 53.24 per cent of the time by boys from working-class background ('WC'). A slightly lower onset [ɛ̞ɪ] is found 15.75 per cent of the time in the speech of 'MC' boys and 19.04 per cent of 'WC' boys. Both 'MC' and 'WC' boys also use monophthongs [ȩː] ~ [ɛː], though very rarely – only 4.45 per cent and 2.27 per cent of the time, respectively. Single instances of [æ] and [æ̝] were found in the speech of one 'WC' boy. In addition, 'WC' boys frequently use diphthongs with more open onsets, that is, [æ̝ɪ] and [æɪ] – 13.56 per cent and 11.71 per cent of the time, respectively.

All in all, the majority of realizations of the FACE vowel in London and the Southeast are diphthongal. There is considerable variation in the onset of the diphthongs, ranging from unrounded close-mid front to unrounded fully open front vowel. Backer realizations are also found. Evidence supports the theory of diphthong shifting for this vowel, yet the distribution of shifted variants is complex. Monophthongal realizations are rare, but seem to be on the increase in inner London, especially in the speech of non-white boys.

PRICE

The vowel of PRICE, /aɪ/, as in *price, die, side,* is another vowel which is considered to be undergoing the process of Diphthong Shift (Wells 1982: 308–310). In RP it is predominantly realized as a closing diphthong with an unrounded front open onset /aɪ/, whereas it is said to be shifted backwards, resulting in closing diphthongs, but with an unrounded back open onset /ɑɪ/ in Popular London and rounded back open onset /ɒɪ/ in Cockney. However, such statements obscure the underlying variation within those varieties of English, which has been observed over the past century and longer. It does not tell us much about the geographical distribution of those features within London itself or the Southeast either. Let us now examine what has been known about the PRICE vowel from empirical research or popular literature. Ellis (1889) claimed that at the time of his writing, diphthong-shifted forms of PRICE were typical only of London, which implies that the Southeast did not have such forms. Matthews' (1938 [1972]: 79) account of Cockney for this vowel contradicts the concept of the anti-clockwise direction of the Diphthong Shift for front closing diphthong; he claims that /aɪ/ is replaced by a diphthong of the same type, but 'slightly raised and rounded'. He also observes monophthongal forms, which are mentioned in later descriptions of Cockney. Sivertsen (1960: 64) reports a completely different version of the PRICE diphthong, with 'a more truly back initial element' in relation to RP, which supports the idea of PRICE backing, where *price* is realized as [pɹɑɪs], that is, as a diphthong with an unrounded back fully open onset. It is quite intriguing, though, that in her Cockney informants' speech, Sivertsen does not mention diphthongs with rounded onsets: 'the initial element is generally unrounded ... an unrounded vocoid glide, from back open towards front half-close' (Sivertsen 1960: 64), since the 1950s/1960s SED indicates the spread of the use of diphthongs with Cardinal Vowel 5, that is, an unrounded back open vowel, [ɑ], and Cardinal Vowel 6, that is, rounded back open-mid vowel, [ɒ], as the diphthong onsets, outwards from London. The backing of PRICE in London and the Southeast is also commented on by Wells (1982: 3008), Cruttenden (2001: 87), Britain (2005: 1008) and Hughes et al. (2005: 75). Like Matthews, on the other hand, Sivertsen observes the occurrence of monophthongal variants, which she defines as 'more truly back ... and ... possibly also slightly closer' than in RP, so *price* is realized as [pɹɑːs] (cf. Wells, 1982: 3008, and Britain, 2005: 1008). More recent research results also confirm the occurrence of PRICE monophthongs in various areas in London, though their quality markedly varies. In South East London, Tollfree (1999) finds back monophthongs – [ɑ̹] and [ɑ̹ː] (with more lip rounding) in her working-class sample. In London's East End Bethnal Green, Przedlacka (2002: 54), for instance, records rare instances of a variant [æ̞ˑ] in her male informant's speech, and Fox (2006b, 2007; also, Fox et al. 2011) presents a case for an emergence of new monophthongal realizations of the [æ]-type, which appear approximately 5 per cent of the time in her Tower Hamlets adolescents speech data, with Bangladeshi teenage boys initiating this change (over 10 per cent of their PRICE realizations are [æ] monophthongs). In the same data, the traditional broadest local back monophthongal realization [ɑː] occurs only 1 per cent of the time. Acoustic measurements of inner-London Hackney and outer-London Havering speech reveal significant amounts of the 'new' monophthongs as well, yet inner-London is in the lead of this change (Cheshire et al. 2005, Kerswill et al. 2005, 2006). Again, ethnicity makes a great difference: non-Anglo boys pronounce PRICE as an 'innovative' monophthong more often than white British-heritage boys; and among white teenagers, it is males who win over females, especially those who have non-Anglo networks. However, monophthongal PRICE realizations are a fairly recent phenomenon, and have not spread widely into the periphery. In all those places, apart from the monophthongs, of course, diphthongs are found too, and, in fact, constitute the majority of all realizations. Przedlacka (2002: 54) finds [a̠ɪ] and [ɑ̹ɪ] in Bethnal Green, and Tollfree (1999) in South East London reports the use of [aɪ] ~ [a̠ɪ] ~ [äɪ] in the speech of her middle-class informants, and a diphthong with a backer onset and slight lip rounding, [ɑ̹ɪ], in her working-class sample. Fox (2006b, 2007) provides details of different phonetic qualities of the PRICE diphthong in Tower Hamlets' speech, where on average the most common is still a shifted (Popular London rather than broad Cockney) variant [ɑɪ] (used 30 per cent of the time); another older variant [ɑ̹ɪ] is used 12 per cent of the time. Newer diphthongal variants [ɐɪ] and [aɪ] occur frequently – 27 per cent and 25 per cent of the time respectively – especially in the speech of the younger generation. In the Tower Hamlets data there is no evidence of diphthongal variants with a rounded onset. Fox's findings may be indicative of a change in progress led by young Bangladeshi boys who use variants previously not found in Tower Hamlets, that is, [æ], [aɪ] and [ɐɪ] much more frequently than the well-established ones, that is, [ɑ̹ɪ], [ɑɪ] and [ɑː]. The use of the 'newer variants' is also on the increase among white and mixed-race boys and white girls[1], who nevertheless still prefer to use the older variants[2]. It is impossible to ascertain, at this stage, whether this variation in Tower Hamlets is indicative of language change or age grading. Similarly, Cheshire et al. (2005, 2008, 2011) and Kerswill et al. (2005, 2006, 2008) provide diachronic and synchronic evidence of a reversal of the Diphthong Shift for the PRICE vowel among young white British-heritage speakers in both inner-London Hackney and outer-London Havering. However, that reversal is more advanced in inner London than in the periphery, which

Cheshire et al. (2005, 2011), Kerswill et al. (2005, 2006, 2007, 2008) and Fox et al. (2011) also justify by means of a dialect contact model – young 'non-Anglos' are demonstrated to have the greatest long-term impact on the way the young population speak. The reversal of the Diphthong Shift for PRICE consists in raising and fronting of the onset of the diphthong – the process is found to operate in Hackney, especially among non-white boys. Older speakers in those areas of London use diphthongs with open starting points.

Interestingly, some fractions of the population in the Southeast of England seem to have adopted, in their phonetic repertoire for the vowel of PRICE, diphthongs with more rounded, back, and possibly also raised onsets than has been found in contemporary London, even among Cockney speakers. Trudgill (1990: 75) writes that the Home Counties English is 'distinguished by a pronunciation of long "i" as in *by* which is rather like "oi"...'. Such variants have been found in Milton Keynes, Buckinghamshire, and Reading, Berkshire (Williams and Kerswill 1999: 143) and Colchester, Essex (Ryfa 2005: 50–52). In some places, such pronunciations are recessive and other variants prevail, even if they used to be present in the past. The social distribution of particular variants also needs to be taken into account. For instance, for three out of the four localities studied by Przedlacka (2001, 2002: 52), that is, in Little Baddow, Essex, Farningham, Kent and Walton-on-the-Hill, Surrey, diphthongs of this type, [ɔ̈ɪ], [ɔɪ] and [ɔɪ] respectively, were present in the SED data from the 1950s. In addition, diphthongs with a back unrounded onset, [ɑɪ], were also found in the SED data for Kent and Surrey. For the fourth locality, that is, Aylesbury, only unrounded centralized diphthong onsets, [ɑ̈ɪ], were reported. Przedlacka's analysis does not demonstrate the use of diphthongal realizations with rounded onsets; instead, she finds [a̠ɪ] ~ [ɑ̟ɪ] in Essex, Kent and Surrey, and [ɑɪ] in Buckinghamshire (Przedlacka 2002: 63, 65). However, we need to bear in mind that Przedlacka did not interview speakers of all socio-economic classes and ages. The specificity of her research required targeting 'middle-class'-type teenagers rather than broad local speakers of the localities in question. In Milton Keynes New Town (Williams and Kerswill 1999: 143–144), [ɔɪ] pronunciations exist, but are relatively infrequent – giving way to closing diphthongs with unrounded back (or advanced) open onsets, [ɑɪ] and [ɑ̟ɪ], or a near-monophthong in fast speech, [ɑ]; older speakers show a tendency to use diphthongs with an unrounded raised centralized onset, [ʌ̟ɪ]. In old towns, though, diphthongal realizations with back rounded raised onsets around [ɔɪ] are thriving even though quantitative analyses show that they are not in the majority. There seem to be two tendencies going on in such towns – either the [ɔɪ] variant emerges (or re-emerges) in the speech of younger people, or the once well-established local [ɔɪ]-type pronunciations of the PRICE vowel are 'surviving' the process of dialect levelling observed in the whole of the Southeast. A case where the former appears to be taking place is Reading (Williams and Kerswill 1999: 143, 145), where older informants predominantly use diphthongs with an unrounded raised centralized onset, [ʌ̟ɪ], and other generations use a closing diphthong with an unrounded back open onset, [ɑɪ], or in fast speech a near-monophthong, [ɑ]. A good example of the latter is the speech of Colchester male teenagers of working-class backgrounds. Ryfa (2005: 50–52) demonstrates that the 'oi' forms of PRICE, which are very frequent among older working-class native Colchester residents, also frequently appear in the speech of very young working-class males – in her data, a diphthong with an onset which is fronter, lower and with less lip rounding than the Cardinal Vowel 6, for convenience denoted here as [ɔ̞̜̈ɪ], appears as frequently as 44.11 per cent of the time, and a diphthong with a rounded fully back raised onset, [ɔ̝ɪ], reaches 21.89 per cent. The same boys use a diphthong with an unrounded front open onset, [aɪ], 23.82 per cent of the time (monophthongal realizations [aː] and [a̝ː] ~ [ɑ̝ː] in this sample are extremely infrequent, and constitute below 1 per cent of all variants, and so do diphthongs [a̝ɪ] ~ [ɑ̝ɪ]). On the other hand, boys with middle-class backgrounds do not use diphthongs with rounded back open or open-mid onsets or unrounded fully back open onsets. They use the standard variant, [aɪ], 82.21 per cent, [a̝ɪ] ~ [ɑ̝ɪ] 7.61 per cent and monophthongs [a̝ː] ~ [ɑ̝ː] 6.49 per cent of the time, other variants are very rare.

To summarize, variation in the realizations of the PRICE vowel concerns the rounding, backing and possibly raising of the diphthong onset; however, monophthongal realizations are also found. In London innovative forms are found, which do not appear in the rest of the Southeast, where there is still enough evidence of diphthong shifting, yet levelled forms also appear with different speed and degree of adoption.

CHOICE

The vowel of CHOICE, /ɔɪ/, as in *choice, toy, boil,* is greatly underrepresented in this paper on account of very little information available on its actual phonetic realizations in the literature concerning London and the Southeast of England. The scarce comments that we find are that in London, the diphthong of CHOICE is characteristically closer than it is in RP, that is, its qualities range between [ɔ̝ɪ] and [oɪ], where the [ɔ̝ɪ] variant is used in Popular London, and a closer variant [oɪ] in broad Cockney (Wells 1982: 308). On the basis of evidence from one 39-year-old female speaker of Cockney, Labov (1994: 170) claims that the nuclei of the CHOICE and PRICE vowels are rising. More recent findings in South East London show that the distinction between the realization of the CHOICE vowel by different socio-economic classes is not so clear any more, as both working-class and middle-class informants exhibited the presence of variants ranging between [ɔɪ] and [oɪ], and in addition, younger middle-class speakers use a diphthong with an advanced or centralized first element, [öɪ] (Tollfree 1999: 168). In Milton Keynes and Reading, the most common realizations were between [ɔ̝ɪ] and [ɔɪ], the latter being most frequently used by middle-class speakers (Williams and Kerswill 1999: 143, 144).

MOUTH

The vowel of MOUTH, /aʊ/, as in *mouth, now, about,* belongs to the series of vowels which have allegedly undergone the process of Diphthong Shift (Wells 1982: 308–310), and Britain (2002: 35) and Trudgill (2004: 50) present historical evidence for their argument that it must have shifted before the other closing diphthongs. Wells (1982: 310) presents the process of shifting MOUTH in the following way: RP has a diphthong with an unrounded open back starting point /ɑʊ/, which in Popular London is shifted to a front and more close position, resulting in a diphthong of the /æʊ/-type, whereas in broad Cockney the offset is dropped and there is compensatory lengthening of the remaining vowel, which then produces a long front monophthong /æː/ between open and open-mid. The MOUTH vowel has been considered crucial in distinguishing between a 'true Cockney' and a Popular London speaker – the former uses monophthongal and the latter diphthongal realizations of MOUTH. However, Wells (1982: 309) warns that there is no sharp boundary between Cockney and other forms of Popular London. When referring to 'Cockney', we should bear in mind that stereotypically, the term denotes a working-class resident of London's East End (at this point that definition should be sufficient). Let us now examine some evidence, to either support or somewhat dilute this Cockney – non-Cockney MOUTH distinction, by looking at who (and where) in London has been using monophthongs and who diphthongs.

Before World War II, Matthews wrote that a monophthong was employed by the 'coarsest speakers', 'in the broadest end of the [Cockney] dialect' (1938 [1972]: 78), and it was a vowel 'between standard *ah* and short *u*' (i.e. between /ɑː/ and /ʌ/), and it was 'long and slightly nasalised'. About twenty years later, a more precise description of the Cockney MOUTH monophthong was provided by Sivertsen (1960: 66), who also claimed that such realizations were employed by 'men and boys of less polished type': 'a long fully open, front unrounded monophthong', [aː]. Fast forward twenty years and monophthongs appear again in London English descriptions: Hudson and Holloway (1977) mention [æː] and [aː], where the former is restricted to working-class boys, and the latter to all other groups (the distinction may, however, be more geographical than social as the boys in the study came from different parts of London). A few years later, Wells (1982: 306) writes that in 'true Cockney' MOUTH is a monophthong of the [æː] type. Cruttenden (2001: 87), on the other hand, states that in Cockney, /aʊ/ is monophthongized to [aː], which corresponds with earlier Sivertsen's estimation of the vowel quality. So far, we have two slightly different candidates for a 'true Cockney monophthong': [æː] and [aː]. It is not surprising then that Przedlacka (2002: 54) finds monophthongs similar to both of them, that is, [æː] and [a̩ː] (her female informant produces a slight offglide [æᶦː]) in her Bethnal Green sample, but interestingly only in the word *mouth*! All the other realizations are diphthongal. It would be unfair to overlook Tollfree's (1999: 169) findings for South East London, where apparently the 'typical Cockney' monophthong [æː],

appears in her data too, but only in the SELE (working-class) sample (just to remind, 'Cockney' was to be confined to London's East End). Cheshire et al. (2005, 2008, 2011) and Kerswill et al. (2008) point to the preservation and modification of the shifted variants in inner-London Hackney. Acoustic measurements of MOUTH tokens demonstrate stability of the diphthong-shifted variant (low front near-monophthong) across ethnicities and over time; they report that the levelled southeastern [aʊ] variant is very infrequent. This again casts a shadow on the exclusiveness of 'Cockney' in having monophthongal variants. On the other hand, they observe a 'reversal' of the Diphthong Shift for MOUTH in the periphery, among others in outer-London Havering.

Let us now move on to see who (and where) in London employs diphthongal realizations and what the quality of the MOUTH diphthong is. Matthews (1938 [1972]: 78) states that 'other Cockneys [less broad] employ a diphthong, with [ə] as the second element'. Sivertsen (1960: 67) claims that most common is 'one-directional glide', [ɛ̞ə̯̆] or [ɛ̞ʊ̆]. Hudson and Holloway (1977) find that diphthongs are used with greater frequency than monophthongs in all studied social groups, and the quality of the diphthong is usually [æɤ], but middle-class boys use [ɑ̝ʊ]. Wells states that /æʊ/ of MOUTH in Popular London can be a closing-backing diphthong of the [æʊ] or [æɤ] type (the latter without lip rounding), or a diphthong with a particularly back starting point, [ɑʊ], in middle-class Londoners' speech (1982: 309); in broad Cockney it can be a centring diphthong (1982: 305). Hughes et al. (2005: 74) also suggest that /aʊ/ may be [æə]. Przedlacka's (2002: 54) Bethnal Green speakers use diphthongs [æʊ] ~ [a̝ʊ] ~ [æɤ] (in the last one, the first element is open-front, raised; the second element is unrounded close-mid back), in lexical items other than the word *mouth* (where they used monophthongs). Variants of the same type, [aʊ] ~ [æʊ], are found by Altendorf (2003). South East London SELRS (middle-class) speakers in Tollfree's study (1999: 169) pronounced MOUTH as [aʊ] and [aɤ]; apart from monophthongs, her SELE (working-class) speakers generally used [æː⁽ᵘ⁾], but her younger, less broad informants used [aʊ] and [aɤ], and younger, broader speakers had closer diphthong onsets, [æ̝ʊ] or [ɛʊ], or a closer and retracted onset [ɜʊ]. Cheshire et al. (2005) and Kerswill et al. (2007, 2008) demonstrate the 'reversal' of the Diphthong Shift for MOUTH in outer-London Havering, where levelled southeastern forms, [aʊ], are found.

Other possible realizations of MOUTH, not further commented on in the literature concerning London, are monosyllabic two-directional vocoid glides [ɛɑ̆ə̯̆] or [ɛɑ̆ʊ̆] mentioned by Sivertsen (1960: 67) and a triphthong [æjə] (perceived as very strongly Cockney) observed by Beaken (1971).

Within the Southeast, diphthong-shifted variants of the MOUTH vowel were recorded well over a century ago. Ellis (1889) regarded diphthong-shifted MOUTH as typical of his eastern 'dialect area', including the present Southeastern counties of Bedfordshire, Buckinghamshire, Essex and Middlesex (now part of Greater London). In the 1950s SED the prevalent variant in most Southeastern accents used to be a 'provincial' [ɛʊ] type diphthong with a closer onset than nowadays. At present such pronunciation is rare or non-existent in most southeastern towns. For instance, two of the localities studied by Przedlacka (2001, 2002: 63, 65) which in the SED had [ɛʊ], that is, Little Baddow, Essex, and [ɛʊ] ~ [ɛʏ], that is, Aylesbury, Buckinghamshire, now have [æʊ] – [æʏ] and [aʊ] – [aʏ], and [aʏ], respectively. The other two localities, Farningham, Kent, and Walton-on-the-Hill, Surrey, had [æʊ] in the SED, but now have [æʊ] – [æʏ] and [aʊ] – [aʏ], like Essex. Williams and Kerswill (1999: 143–146) report some of those variants, that is, the preferred levelled variant [aʊ] and [æʊ], also for Milton Keynes, where monophthongs [aː] ~ [ɛː] are also found. In their Reading data the standard variant [aʊ] is prevalent too, but [aː] ~ [ɛɪ] ~ [ɛʊ̹] are found as well. Altendorf (2003) reports [æʊ] rather than [ɛʊ] in Canterbury, Kent, and Colchester, Essex. My own analysis (Ryfa 2005: 52–53) of the speech of teenage males in Colchester can confirm that [æʊ] rather than [ɛʊ] is found in my informants' speech, yet the prevalent realizations in both groups, that is, from middle-class ('MC') and working-class ('WC') backgrounds are not [æʊ], but levelled forms [aʊ] – [a̹ʊ], used 50.94 per cent and 31.25 per cent of the time, respectively. Interestingly, the next most popular realization was a long unrounded, front, fully open monophthong, [aː], which 'MC' boys used 30.85 per cent and 'WC' 25.27 per cent of the time. We have to wait until the next most popular realization to find [æʊ], and it was preferred by 'WC' boys who used it 23.67 per cent of the time; 'MC' boys pronounced it 13.03 per cent of the time. Another realization was [æːᵊ] used 8.00 per cent of the time by 'MC' boys and 19.32 per cent of the time by 'WC' boys. In addition, 'middle-class'-type Colchester boys used [a̹ː] ~ [ɑ̹] 4.35 per cent, [ɑː] 4.00 per cent and [a̹ː] 4.35 per cent of the time. It should be remembered that the Southeast is characterized by high mobility rates, and the fact that many 'East End Londoners' have been moving out of London into the surrounding areas since World War II, could have triggered the spread of 'London variants' into the speech of those areas. A good example is provided by Fox (2000) who finds 'Cockney' monophthongal and diphthongal variants of MOUTH, [ɑː] and [æə], in the speech of teenagers of the London overspill town of Basildon.

In view of the evidence presented above, we can no longer clearly distinguish between 'true Cockneys' and other Londoners, or Londoners from residents of the rest of the Southeast, by examining the MOUTH vowel in isolation. The popular assumption that a 'genuine Cockney' uses a monophthong and a non-Cockney Londoner uses a diphthong lost its currency long ago (and perhaps has always been based on somewhat exaggerated, often comic, and incomplete popular literature accounts). We have seen that there is considerable variation within London's East End and other London areas, and we have seen, likewise, that the rest of the Southeast has a whole range of MOUTH variants, including ones found in Cockney's East End and other parts of London.

GOAT

On the basis of historical evidence it is assumed that the vowel of GOAT, /ɘʊ/, such as in *goat, moan, soap*, used to be realized as a monophthong before the process of Long Mid Diphthonging (Wells 1982: 210–211) occurred, which turned this vowel into a diphthong. Trudgill (2004: 55) suggests that diphthonging appeared to a greater extent in 'urban speech and at higher social class levels'. Ellis considered rising diphthongs, such as in GOAT, as typical of London. What is then the quality of that diphthong, if indeed diphthongal realizations are typical of London? There seems to be an agreement in the relevant literature that the first element of the diphthong can be lower than in RP. For instance, Wells (1982: 312) claims that the London GOAT vowel is typically a wide closing diphthong, and implies that the more open the quality of the starting point of the diphthong, the lower the social status of the speakers using it. He denotes the starting point of the GOAT vowel in Cockney speech as [æ̈ – ɐ], and equates this quality with the vowel of STRUT. Then he goes on to say that the broadest Cockney variant approaches [aʊ], with a front open onset. Cruttenden (2001: 87) talks of [æ] and Hughes et al. (2005: 74) of [ʌ], again meaning a lower onset. The end point varies from a near-close near-back rounded vowel, [ʊ], to a centralized close-mid back one, [ɤ̈], which may be more open and/or lacking lip rounding. Several contemporary researchers simply denote it as [ɤ]. Beaken (1971) reports that girls use a diphthong ending with a front rounded vowel [ø] ([ʌø] or [œ̈ø]). Tollfree's study (1999: 167) in South East London demonstrated the use of a whole range of GOAT variants, not necessarily wide diphthongs. Her middle-class speakers use [ʌʊ$^{(w)}$] ~ [ɤʊ] ~ [ɤə] ~ [ə̹ʊ] and working-class speakers [ʌʊ] ~ [ʌə] ~ [ɐɤ] ~ [aː]. This supports Wells's suggestion concerning the social distribution of diphthongs with a varied openness of the starting point well, even almost twenty years after it was made. Altendorf's data (2003) are compatible with earlier ones: she finds [əʊ] ~ [ɐʉ] > [ɐʊ] (there can be open starting point and fronter end-points of the diphthong). However, in Przedlacka's Cockney sample (teenage informants born and bred in Bethnal Green, the 'cradle' of Cockney) there are only realizations ranging from a standard variant [əʊ] to a variant with an open-mid central unrounded starting point, [ɜʊ], and three tokens with [ə̹ʊ] (2002: 54). Her young speakers have quite close onsets and no fronted and/or unrounded end-points. The most recent data from inner-London Hackney support earlier findings that diphthongal realizations in London, especially used by non-Anglo boys, most typically do not have fronted offglides, even though they are found in girls' speech; in addition, the data reveal some unexpected use of an 'endogenous innovation' (Kerswill et al. 2006), monophthongs. This change (GOAT monophthongization) is assumed to have been initiated by a high degree of contact between Anglo and non-Anglo teenage males, with the latter boys using monophthongal variants most frequently. Data from outer-London Havering, on the other hand, contain diphthongs with fronted offsets across ethnicity among younger speakers, again with girls being in the lead (Cheshire et al. 2005, Kerswill et al. 2005, 2006). Kerswill et al. (2005, 2008) propose that monophthongization of GOAT is correlated with four interacting scales:

Non-Anglo > Anglo

Non-Anglo network > Anglo network

Male > Female

Inner London > Outer London > London Periphery

Indeed, in the rest of the Southeast, the GOAT diphthongs with fronted offsets are on the increase, and Cheshire et al. (2005), Kerswill et al. (2005, 2006) propose that GOAT fronting is a result of supralocalization/dialect levelling in the whole region of the Southeast, excluding Inner London. There is enough evidence to support this claim. Przedlacka's research in the Home Counties (2001, 2002: 63) demonstrates that fronting and unrounding of the second element of the diphthong are present in all the four localities that she was studying. She found the [əʏ] variant in Aylesbury, Buckinghamshire, Farninghton, Kent, Little Baddow, Essex, and Walton-on-the-Hill, Surrey. Standard variant, [əʊ], was also noted for the latter two localities. Williams and Kerswill (1999) similarly report fronting and unrounding of the end-point in the GOAT set of words for Milton Keynes, [əʏ ~ ɐʏ ~ əɪ ~ ɐɪ], and Reading, [əʏ ~ əɪ ~ ə̟ʏ ~ əʊ̟]. It should be noted that the open first element is present only in the Milton Keynes data. Britain (2005: 1007) refers to the recent trend involving using fronter elements as 'the fronting of /ʌʊ/' and gives examples of words pronounced in this way: *know* [nɐ̟ɨ] and *show* [ʃɐ̟ɨ], with a near-open slightly fronter than central onset and a close central unrounded end-point. Similar realizations, but with varying degrees of lip rounding in the diphthong end-point, [ɐɨ] and [ɐʉ], were reported for Colchester and Canterbury (Altendorf 2003). It should be mentioned that the GOAT diphthong was already present in the late-nineteenth-century Ellis's dialect survey, but it seems to have been less advanced than in the case of the FACE vowel.

Now that we are aware of the possible variations in the GOAT lexical set, we should perhaps mention a certain complication, which Wells calls 'the GOAT Split' (1982: 312). He remarks on allophonic variation (i.e. different sound is used, but the meaning is not changed by the use of that different sound) in the GOAT vowel depending on its phonological environment. If the GOAT vowel is followed by velarized ('dark') /l/, then the vowel is realized as [ɒʊ], in the environment of _lC and _l#, where C represents a consonant and # a pause; in other environments, it is realized as [ʌʊ]. Cruttenden (2001: 88) writes of 'special allophones' [ɒʊ] before '"dark" /l/'. The rule itself is simple, but there appear to be further complications, that is, L Vocalization (discussed further in this chapter) and morphological regularization (for a discussion see Wells 1982: 312–313, Harris 1990: 97–98), resulting in forms such as [rɒʊlɪn] rather than [rʌʊlɪn] for *rolling*, and pairs such as *bowl* [bɒʊl] versus *Bow* [bʌʊ]. According to Wells, the exact phonetic quality of London /ɒʊ/ ranges from [ɒʊ ~ ɔo] to broad Cockney [aɤ] or modified regional [əo] type. To the best of my knowledge, this phenomenon has not been explored by researchers in detail either in London or the Southeast of England, so no empirical evidence can be cited here.

Long vowels: centring diphthongs

NEAR

In the absence of elaborate studies, very little can be said about the phonetic qualities of the vowel in the NEAR lexical set, as in *near, beard, clear.* However, it has been observed that the centring diphthong /ɪə/ has a closer starting point in popular London speech than in RP, that is, [iə]. Tollfree, on the other hand, with her more recent data, reports 'much variation in the nucleus used for NEAR, from [ɪː] to [ɪːᵊ]' (1999: 169), which may suggest the lowering of the starting point over the two decades, although realizations with a close starting point (but much more open front end-point than Wells describes), [iːa], also occur in the speech of her working-class informants. NEAR can also be realized as a monophthong [ɪː] (Wells 1982: 305–306). Tollfree's data may again suggest some lowering in the realization of the vowel, as she talks of the occurrence of a monophthongal realization which 'can be quite open: [ɪ̞ː]', or even as open as [eː] (1999: 169). Very broad Cockney has been observed to have a triphthongal variant, [ɪjɐ] restricted to sentence-final position (Beaken 1971), though more recent literature does not mention its occurrence. Much more open qualities are found in Milton Keynes and Reading, [e̞ː] ~ [eə] (Williams and Kerswill 1999: 169).

SQUARE

The vowel of SQUARE, /eə/, as in *square, fair, Claire,* like the other centring diphthongs, NEAR and CURE, is little explored in the Southeast. Nevertheless, we know that it can be realized either as a diphthong [eə] in utterance-final position or where the syllable containing it is prominent, or a long front open-mid monophthong [ɛː] within the utterance (Wells 1982: 305–306), or even a triphthong [ɛjə] but only in sentence-final position (Beaken 1971). The accurate phonetic realizations found by Tollfree (1999: 169) in South East London were monophthongal. In the speech of older middle-class informants those were [e̞] or [ɛ̞ː], some with schwa-type off-glide [ɛ̞ːᵊ] and [ɛ̞ᵊ], whereas younger middle-class speakers have [ɛ̞ᵊ] and [ɛᵊ]. In the more basilectal variety, the variants found were closer, [eː], [eᵊ] and [eːᵊ]. Outside London, the only recent published study that considers the SQUARE vowel, to the best of my knowledge, was done in Milton Keynes and Reading (Williams and Kerswill 1999: 144, 146); in both places the variants used were similar to those in Tollfree's middle-class sample, that is, [ɛː] ~ [ɛ̞ə].

CURE

The vowel of CURE, /ʊə/, as in *cure* and *pure*, is yet another feature which attracted relatively little attention in dialectological literature concerning the Southeast. Sivertsen described the vowel as it was spoken in Bethnal Green, East London, as 'a vocoid glide where the starting point is rounded, back central, between close and half-close, and the end is unrounded, central between half-close and half-open' (1960: 80). However, over the last few decades, in various varieties of English, the diphthongal realization of this vowel is known to have become recessive. The centring diphthong /ʊə/ has increasingly merged with /oː ~ ɔə/, and undergone smoothing, that is, has acquired a monophthongal variant, of the [ʊː] type (Wells 1982: 305–306). Nevertheless, the diphthong perseveres in utterance-final position or where the syllable containing it is prominent; the monophthongal realization is most common utterance-medially. Tollfree's (1999: 169) South East London study reveals a dichotomy in terms of lexical incidence: if the nucleus of the item in question is preceded by [j], as in *pure* then the vowel is realized as a diphthong of the [ʉ̞ə]/[ʊ̞ə] type, in broader speech, that may be smoothed to monophthongs [ʉ̞ː] or [ʊ̞ː], respectively; other items merge with the THOUGHT/NORTH vowel (as it is realized in open syllables), and have [ɔ̈] or [ɔ̈ː]. The age of the speaker, rather than the socio-economic class, is a better predictor of the variation in the use of particular realizations, with younger speakers pronouncing [ɔ̈] and [ɔ̈ː] more frequently than older speakers.

Consonants

Below is a description of several developments found in the consonantal system of the Englishes of London and the rest of the Southeast, which have received widespread attention from linguists and journalists.

TH

The realization of the voiceless TH consonant, /θ/, as the first sound in *through*, or its voiced counterpart, /ð/, as in the word *mother*, has received a significant amount of attention from linguists and journalists. The reason for this is the rapid spread of a process called TH Fronting, that is, the replacement of traditional, 'standard' variants, a voiceless dental fricative /θ/ (in all positions in a word) and a non-initial voiced dental fricative /ð/, with labiodental fricatives /f/ and /v/, respectively, as in *fan* and *van*. The process 'collapses the distinction between labiodental and dental fricatives' (Trudgill 2004: 74), hence pairs such as *thought* and *fought* and *lather* and *lava* become homophonous. It is worth mentioning that initial voiced TH can be replaced by /d/ or entirely omitted rather than fronted (Matthews 1938 [1972]: 80, Wells 1982: 328, Hughes et al. 2005: 74), although very rare instances of fronted initial voiced TH in the words *this* and *the* have also been reported (Matthews 1938 [1972]: 80, Tollfree 1999: 172).

The merger of /θ/ with /f/ and /ð/ with /v/ is observed to have spread outwards from London into the surrounding areas but we have evidence of its occurrence in many urban centres outside the Southeast (see Foulkes and Docherty (eds) 1999). In London itself, TH Fronting is said to have been present for at least a hundred and fifty years, and it is strongly associated with stereotypical Cockney speech, although 'this habit is not consistent' (Matthews 1938 [1972]: 80). Variability in the realization of /th/ is also attested by Sivertsen (1960: 123), Wells (1982: 328), Trudgill (1986: 54), Cruttenden (2001: 88, 203), Przedlacka (2002: 55–56) and Altendorf (2003). The presence of TH Fronting in various areas of London and its geographical spread within the Southeast is not in doubt (Trudgill 1986: 54, Schmid 1999, Tollfree 1999, Williams and Kerswill 1999, Altendorf 1999b, 2003, Fox 2000, Przedlacka 2001, 2002, Kerswill 2003, Ryfa 2005, Torgersen 2006, Kerswill et al. 2006, 2007). Yet, we need more research on the social stratification of the spread of this 'innovation'. Until recently TH Fronting was believed to be confined to the speech of working classes; however, more recent research demonstrates that labio-dental fricative variants, [f] and [v], of /θ/ and /ð/ are more and more frequent in the speech of young middle-class speakers in Milton Keynes (Williams and Kerswill 1999: 160) and in Colchester (Ryfa 2005), occasional fronted variants were also found in Greater London (Altendorf 1999b), which may suggest its further spread, beyond those from working-class backgrounds, where it is claimed to have developed. The aforementioned replacement of initial voiced TH by /d/, called DH-stopping, was thought to be a recessive feature of traditional Cockney. Currently, it relatively frequently appears in the speech of young people in the London boroughs of Hackney and Havering (and possibly elsewhere in London). Kerswill et al. (2007) and Cheshire et al. (2008) speculate it to have been reallocated to function as an ethnicity marker, which, at least in Havering, has gained salience. In Hackney DH-stopping has 'presumably [been] reinforced by high frequencies amongst Afro-Caribbeans' (ibidem).

L

In the Englishes of London and the rest of the Southeast, /l/ has three possible allophonic realizations: a voiced lateral approximant called 'clear' L, [l], its velarized equivalent called 'dark' L, [ɫ], and vocalized /l/. L Vocalization is the replacement of a non-onset, that is, coda, clustered and syllabic /l/, with a back vowel. The phenomenon appears only in those varieties of English which have the clear-dark /l/ dichotomy, and in British English the vowel can only be found in those contexts in which /l/ can otherwise be velarized; in word-initial and word-internal intervocalic contexts L Vocalization is blocked. The quality of the vowel varies from a back rounded [ʊ] or [o], to slightly rounded [ö], to [ɤ] with weakly spread or neutral lips. Although it is typically associated with London English and its variable occurrence has been recorded in London by numerous authors (Matthews 1938 [1972], Sivertsen 1960, Beaken 1971, Bowyer 1973,

Hudson and Holloway 1977, Wells 1982, Trudgill 1990, Tollfree 1999, Przedlacka 2002, Altendorf 1999a, b, 2003), there is no proof that it originated there; in fact, the earliest written records of L Vocalization are found in Pewsey, Wiltshire (Kjederqvist 1903). Despite having been regarded as a speech defect or infantilism, it has managed to spread across the whole of the Southeast very rapidly indeed; in the 1950s/1960s SED, L Vocalization was recorded in northwestern Kent, Sussex, Surrey, Middlesex (now part of Greater London), southeastern Essex and southern Hertfordshire, while now it is found with varying frequency in the whole of the Home Counties in the speech of the working and middle classes, with the former still in the lead (Spero 1996, Williams and Kerswill 1999, Schmid 1999, Przedlacka 2002, Meuter 2002, Altendorf 2003, Ryfa 2005, Baker 2007), and that suggests that it is no longer highly stigmatized and confined to the broadest accent speakers (on the possible causes of spread, as well as the effects of phonological environment on the realization of /l/, see Johnson and Britain 2003, 2007, Meuter 2002). It has to be reiterated, though, that L Vocalization is variable, and not all residents of London or the rest of the Southeast pronounce a vowel in the place where a velarized, or 'dark', /l/ is possible; on the other hand, for some speakers L Vocalization can be categorical.

R

Typically, accents of London and the Southeast belong to the class of non-rhotic accents, that is, those in which /r/ 'is excluded from preconsonantal and absolute-final environments' (Wells 1982: 76) even though *r* is indicated by spelling, for example, *dark* [dɑːk] and *car* [kɑː]. Where <r> is pronounced, its quality is most typically defined as an apical post-alveolar approximant, [ɹ]. However, over the last few decades, a 'new' allophonic variant of /r/, the labio-dental approximant, [ʋ], has been noticed and widely commented on in the popular media, as well as more and more often also explored in linguistic literature. Once considered a speech defect, infantilism or affectation among upper classes, at present it is so widely spread in the southeast, especially among young people, that it is now perceived as a linguistic innovation, or a new accent feature (Trudgill 1999: 133), rather than a sign of immature speech. In London, the labio-dental approximant pronunciations for word-initial /r/ are reported to be found in the speech of young people in Hackney, with significant effects for the ethnicity of speakers' friendship groups (for details, see Kerswill et al. 2007). It is also a well-known characteristic of Cockney speech, commonly used by comedians mocking it, yet from the existing literature related to that variety of English, it can be deduced that it began entering the Cockney phonetic make-up no longer than about fifty years ago (some indications of its infrequent use are found in Sivertsen 1960: 139–140, Beaken 1971: 344, Wright 1981: 135, Tollfree 1999: 174), and then spread further into the Southeast. It has been reported for Milton Keynes and Reading (Williams and Kerswill 1999: 147), Colchester (Meuter 2002) and various other localities (Torgersen 1997), especially among younger speakers. But how did it get its way into Cockney in the first place? Why would this 'immature' or 'affectatious' way of speaking be adopted by the working-class, stereotypically 'rough', men? Foulkes and Docherty (2000) propose that [ʋ] has become established as an accent feature in East London as a result of intensive long-term contact between native inhabitants of London's East End and Eastern European Jews, who immigrated to Stepney in large numbers between 1880 and 1900. The migrants would originally speak Yiddish and have a uvular [ʁ], but in a failed attempt to modify their /r/-s towards the English alveolar approximant [ɹ], they would end up with a labiodental approximant [ʋ]. It would then no longer be perceived as 'childish pronunciation' as it would be heard pronounced by Jewish adults. There is sufficient evidence to support the claim that Hebrew and Yiddish influenced English at least at a lexical level, and the assumption is that they could have done so also at the level of phonology. The theory seems very feasible when we recall that the 'innovative' form [ʋ] had not been reported before the beginning of the twentieth century, and when we read descriptions of English spoken in London by a Jewish community in the twentieth century (Wells 1982: 303).

Another phenomena frequently occurring in the Southeast are the linking and intrusive /r/. The linking /r/ is inserted by speakers of non-rhotic accents word-finally after a vowel when the following word also begins with a vowel, for example, *car of mine* [ˈkʰɑːɹ əv ˈmɑɪn]; in a similar context, as well as intervocalically word-medially, where it is not indicated by spelling, some speakers insert an intrusive /r/, for example, *pizza on the plate* [ˈpʰɪitsəɹ ɒn ðə ˈplæɪʔ] or *drawing* [ˈdrɔːɹɪŋ]. Neither the linking nor intrusive /r/ are unique to the Southeast, yet they are very common. Interestingly, Britain and Fox (2006, 2008, 2009) show that in Tower Hamlets, linking and intrusive /r/s are being replaced by a glottal stop, [ʔ]. The same hiatus avoidance strategy is used in Bedford Italian English (Guzzo et al. 2007).

STR

A relatively recent development observed in the Southeast, and beyond, which has received some attention, especially in literature concerning the so-called 'Estuary English' (discussed later in this chapter), is an assimilation of an alveolar fricative [s] to the following [tr] in an STR cluster in words such as *strong, street, history*. In the process called 'palatalization', [s] becomes a post-alveolar fricative [ʃ], resulting in [ʃtr] (Cruttenden 2001: 187); sometimes /t/ gets retracted before /r/ and the STR cluster can sound like [ʃʧr]. In STR onsets, palatalization may be accompanied by lip-rounding. In the 1950s SED, only one instance of [ʃ] in STR was reported for the Home Counties, and that was in Goudhurst, Kent. Nowadays such pronunciations are popular, especially among young people, possibly more among men than women – Przedlacka (2002: 55, 64–65) reports 75 per cent usage of [ʃtr] by her young male Cockney informant, but complete absence of it in the speech of her young female Cockney speaker; in her Home Counties sample, she finds /s/ realized as [ʃ] in STR 42 per cent of the time by young males and 25 per cent of the time by young females. She does not find any geographical or social patterning of this pronunciation feature, and therefore claims that it is idiosyncratic, and generalizations are not possible. Altendorf proposes that the palatalization of /st/ in STR 'reflects and conveys an attitude of informality and nonchalance' (2003: 154), which may be true given that it is mostly young people who are inclined to do it.

YOD

Englishes of London and the rest of the Southeast, as well as other varieties of English, are traditionally characterized by variable Yod Dropping, that is, when /j/ is not pronounced when it follows an alveolar stop, /t, d, n/ or, much less frequently, /m, h, s, l, b/. Hence, *tune* is [tuːn], *duke* is [duːk], *new* is [nuː], rather than [tjuːn], [djuːk] and [njuː], respectively. That kind of pronunciation in London has been commented on since the eighteenth century (Wells 1982: 330), and is considered part of stereotypical Cockney's phonetic make-up (Matthews 1938 [1972]: 172, Sivertsen 1960: 143–144, Cruttenden 2001: 88, Przedlacka 2002: 56). For the Home Counties, Yod Dropping is reported in the majority of dialect surveys. However, more recent studies seem to suggest possible recession of this feature, for example, Przedlacka (2002: 65) demonstrates that while in her Kent data Yod Dropping is still categorical, in her Surrey and Essex recordings all tokens contain /j/ and in Buckinghamshire /j/ is most frequently retained. My own corpus of recordings of Colchester young males contains rather rare (unquantified) tokens with dropped /j/, but only in the speech of teenage males from working-class backgrounds. The recession of Yod Dropping is also apparent in Amos and Green's data (Amos 2006) from nearby Mersea Island, Essex. On average, the younger generation islanders pronounce /u/ rather than /ju/ 9 per cent of the time, which contrasts significantly with the older generation speakers, who drop their yods 61 per cent of the time (the percentages exclude those occurrences of Yod Dropping where the preceding consonants were /t/ and /d/). Amos (2006) shows that there are no preceding environments where the older informants demonstrate categorical use of either /ju/ or /u/. On the other hand, the younger speakers exhibit 100 per cent yod-retention following /f, v, k, g, h, l/ but not before /p, b, s, m, n/.

Another development in the realization of /j/ is Yod Coalescence, or palatalization, that is, the type of assimilation whereby /tj/ becomes /ʧ/ and /dj/ becomes /ʤ/, so that *tune* is [ʧuːn], *duke* is [ʤuːk], etc. Such pronunciations have recently provoked some critical remarks in the media, but have been treated more seriously in professional literature for much longer, and it seems that coalescent forms have co-existed with Yod Dropping, though to a much lesser extent (Sivertsen 1960, Hurford 1967, Beaken 1971, Bowyer 1973). At present, Yod Coalescence seems to be replacing Yod Dropping, especially in the speech of the young. Wells talks of 'a switch in Popular London speech towards Yod Coalescence' (1982: 330), Cruttenden (2001: 88) discusses it when describing features of London Regional RP (Popular London and London Regional RP can be equated these days with 'Estuary English'), and Altendorf speculates that people who use coalescent forms 'affiliate themselves with the "young" and the "cool" and distance themselves from the "formal" and the "stuffy"' (2003: 154).

H

In standard accents of English, /h/ in word-initial position is pronounced as a voiceless glottal fricative [h] (or rather a range of approximants the qualities of which vary depending on the following vowel). Omitting the [h] in word-initial position of stressed syllables is called H Dropping, and is perceived as 'uneducated' and 'vulgar', and acts as a symbol representing 'lower social classes' – Wells (1982: 254) calls it 'the most powerful pronunciation shibboleth in England' (for a detailed discussion on the symbolism of H Dropping see Mugglestone 2003: 95–134). Not all instances of not pronouncing initial /h/ can be classified as H Dropping, though. Function words such as *he, his, him, her, have, has, had* are normally pronounced without the initial <h>; therefore, they are not candidates for social marking. Lack of /h/ in loan words borrowed from French, for example, *honest* or *honour*, with spelling indicating the presence of <h> is not considered H Dropping. Nor is the lack of /h/ word-medially in words such as *vehicle* or *exhibition*, where every native speaker of English lacks an /h/. H Dropping has for many years been very strongly associated with broad London accents (Matthews 1938 [1972]: 80, Sivertsen 1960: 141, Wells 1982: 321, Cruttenden 2001: 88, Hughes et al. 2005: 74), and frequently incorporated in the speech of comedians mocking Cockney speech. As is the case of some other consonants, the pronunciation of /h/ is variable within London too, depending on factors such as socio-economic class, age and ethnicity. For instance, middle-class speakers in South East London (Bowyer 1973, Tollfree 1999) tend to avoid non-standard H Dropping, and Tollfree finds that within that socio-economic group, younger speakers avoid the stigmatized realization even more than older speakers. In inner-London Hackney the amount of H Dropping has dramatically dropped in comparison with the past, and now reaches only 9 per cent, with young white British-heritage speakers approaching 16 per cent, and non-Anglos only 4 per cent. H Dropping among young residents of outer-London (predominantly white) Havering totals 32 per cent, with Anglos reaching 40 per cent and non-Anglos 9 per cent (Kerswill et al. 2006, 2007 and Cheshire et al. 2008).

In the rest of the Southeast, H Dropping has been common in the speech of the working classes for a long time, except in a substantial area of Kent (Ellis 1889). At present, in Southeastern towns, the amount of H Dropping seems to be decreasing, for example, Kerswill et al. (2006) report /h/ loss of 92 per cent among older speakers in both Milton Keynes and Reading, but only 14 per cent in Milton Keynes and 35 per cent in Reading among 14-year olds (based on data recorded in 1995). H Dropping is generally avoided by middle-class speakers – in Colchester, Ryfa (2005) finds it absent in the speech of a group of teenage males from middle-class backgrounds, and only 14.16 per cent from working-class backgrounds. The only recent study which demonstrates high amounts of H Dropping among young people in the Southeast is that in the London overspill town of Basildon – in interview style, Fox (2000) reports 85–90 per cent for most of her young working-class informants (on the basis of this, as well as findings for the other features examined, Fox concludes that Basildon speech is 'Cockney transplanted East'; hence this iconic Cockney pattern for /h/). The general tendency in the Southeast is for accents to undergo levelling, where highly stigmatized realizations are avoided; hence the employment of more standard pronunciation, especially by young people.

T, P, K

Depending on the social factors and phonetic environment, in London English the voiceless plosives /p, t, k/ can be glottalled, pre-glottalized, aspirated, affricated or voiced; Wells (1982: 322) points out that a combination of these processes is also possible.

A well-known feature of Cockney is the heavy aspiration of initial /p, t, k/, [p^h, t^h, k^h] (Pointner 1996: 66, Hughes et al. 2005: 76), which Wells (1982: 322) considers the phonemic norm. Non-final /t/ can sometimes be affricated – 'the tongue tip/blade leave the alveolar ridge slowly, so that [s] is produced before the vowel begins' (Hughes et al. 2005: 76), and the resulting realization of /t/ is [ts], thus *tea* is [tsəi/tsɪi]. In non-initial positions, /p, t, k/ can be pre-glottalized, that is, preceded by a glottal stop, [ʔ], or completely replaced by it (a glottal stop is a sound <or in fact its lack> which is produced by closing the epiglottis by holding the vocal folds tightly together). Pre-glottalization passes unnoticed and is rarely commented on, whereas glottalling, the realization of the plosive /p, t, k/ as a mere glottal stop, has been considered a feature typical of Cockney, observed in London (and simultaneously in Scotland) since 1860 (Bailey 1996: 76 in Trudgill 2004: 81) and examined for many years (Matthews 1938 [1972]: 80, Sivertsen 1960: 114, Beaken 1971, Hudson and Holloway 1977, Wells 1982: 322, Cruttenden 2001: 88, Przedlacka 2002: 55, Altendorf 1999a, b, 2003). Research has demonstrated an increase in T glottalling over the recent few decades and its extension to previously socially 'sensitive' contexts – there seems to be a greater tolerance to this previously frowned upon phenomenon. Glottalling of /t/, the most affected voiceless plosive, can occur after vowels, laterals and nasals, between vowels and before a pause; /p/ and /k/ can be replaced by a glottal stop before a following consonant (Cruttenden 2001: 88, Hughes et al. 2005: 74; for a detailed description, see Wells 1982: 322–327, Pointner 1996: 51–65, Altendorf and Watt 2004: 192–195). When used intervocalically (between vowels) word-medially or word-finally, glottalling used to be heavily stigmatized and until recently in the Southeast, was found almost exclusively in the speech of working-class London's East End speakers. Nowadays, it can be found in the speech of young 'middle-class' speakers, though definitely to a lesser extent than in the speech of socio-economically less privileged groups, with a strong effect of its position in an utterance; for example, in my study of Colchester teenage males (Ryfa 2005: 56–57), /t/ is replaced by a glottal stop, [ʔ], intervocalically in word-internal position 84.74 per cent of the time in the speech of the group with working-class backgrounds and 9.50 per cent of the time with middle-class backgrounds; word-finally between vowels – 95.03 per cent of the time in the former and 65.14 per cent of the time in the latter group. In other contexts and positions in an utterance, T glottalling is a well established feature of contemporary accents of London and the rest of the Southeast, regardless of speakers' social status. Nevertheless, social differentiation is still retained by maintaining differences in frequency and distribution of a glottal stop in different phonetic contexts as several recent studies have demonstrated (Pointner 1996, Williams and Kerswill 1999, Tollfree 1999, Schmid 1999, Altendorf 1999a, b, 2003, Fox 2000, Przedlacka 2002, Ryfa 2005). Altendorf and Watt (2004: 194–195) propose that T glottalling has entered English in three waves, in the following order: in pre-consonantal, pre-pausal and pre-vocalic contexts, and it is the last two waves that in terms of quantities still differentiate the Southeast from the rest of the country.

The description of the consonants in London accents would be incomplete if we did not point to a recent innovation called K-backing, that is, the pronunciation of /k/ in a word-initial position in front of non-high back vowels as a back consonant either [k–] or [q]. Kerswill et al. (2007) and Cheshire et al. (2008) report it to be present in the speech of only young people in inner and outer London. They argue that both in Hackney and Havering, K-backing has become an ethnic marker, which shows statistically significant effects not for ethnicity in isolation but the ethnicity of speakers' friendship networks [ibidem].

To complete the picture of how the T, P and K consonants are pronounced in London, we need to mention that individual speakers, recorded for the *Linguistic Innovators* project use a retroflex stop [ʈ] for initial /t/ (and also [ɖ] for initial /d/). Those speakers do it near-categorically. Retroflex stops are frequently found in South Asian languages, but not in English spoken by White British-heritage adults. The appearance of these sounds can be explained with the fact that in the data they are used by those young people 'who have particularly strong ties with Bangladesh' (Kerswill et al. 2007: 8), which is located in South Asia.

NG

Numerous studies have demonstrated that NG, /ŋ/, in an unstressed position, that is, in the *-ing* suffix in items such as *swimming*, *kicking* or *ceiling*, is a stable variable. It is well established as an indicator of socio-economic class in many speech communities within England, and beyond, and is not undergoing change. In the majority of English dialects within the United Kingdom, NG has two allophonic realizations, a velar nasal, [ŋ], and an alveolar nasal, [n]; in the northwest of England and the Midlands it has yet another variant, [ŋg] (which according to Mathisen 1999 and Watts 2006 is becoming established as a supralocal dialect feature of those regions, distinguishing them from the south of the country). In London and other towns of the Southeast of England, a velar nasal, [ŋ], and an alveolar nasal, [n], variants are well-known markers of socio-economic status, with the former, standard variant, being characteristic of the speech of middle classes, and the latter, non-standard variant, in broad speech of working classes in the area (Pointner 1996: 80–81, Tollfree 1999: 172, Ryfa 2005: 58–59). Regardless of speakers' backgrounds, apart from the two variants, another one, [ŋk], may emerge in lexical items containing the morpheme *-thing*; thus, *something, anything* and *nothing* can be pronounced with [ɪŋk] rather than [ŋ] or [n] at the end of those words (Cruttenden 2001: 199, Hughes et al. 2005: 74).

Grammatical Features

The present review of grammatical variation in the Southeast of England is very tentative, as although several contributions to the knowledge of the grammar of the Englishes of the Southeast have been made, no systematic large-scale study of contemporary recorded spontaneous data has to date been conducted. Where no specific reference is made to London English, it should be assumed that either there is no difference between Southeastern British English and London English with respect to the particular grammatical features discussed in the chapter or such systematic differences have not yet been demonstrated. The reader must also realize that many of those (non-standard) features are not unique to the Southeast of England, but are part of more universal trends existing elsewhere in the country. It must also be remembered that individual speakers within the Southeast may use the features described in the chapter alongside those existing in Standard English. Examples presented in this chapter labelled as 'J.R. 2005', are derived from the author's corpus of recordings of Colchester teenage males (Ryfa 2005). The other illustrations of specific grammatical issues have been borrowed from the existing literature concerning the region.

Nouns

Nouns of measurement

Many non-standard dialects of English, including southeastern varieties, do not have plural marking for certain measurement nouns, such as 'mile', 'foot', 'pound', 'quid', etc. That means that the -s ending denoting a plural is not added to the basic form of the noun, or in the case of the irregular noun 'foot', its plural equivalent 'feet' is not used; instead, a singular form of the noun is used (Examples 1–3). Edwards (1993: 234) points to the semantic redundancy of the plural marking, and Anderwald (2004: 182) reminds us that units of measurement which do not have a plural marking in non-standard Englishes now, did not have it in Standard English historically either, and that the *-s* ending was added to the particular measurement nouns at different times.

(1) Look at the size of this bloke. This is my mate fucking Jamie, and Jack. Jamie's about fucking *eight foot* something, because he's a fucking giant. (J.R. 2005)
(2) And the second job is painter and decorator. That's a *hundred quid* a week, though, a hundred, a *hundred quid* a week, a *hundred pound.* (J.R. 2005)
(3) An eighth for a puff, yeh, over an eighth for puff or over an eighth for weed, or *ten bag* of weed is not persy. That's what dealers do. (J.R. 2005)

On the other hand, in the FRED corpus investigated by Anderwald (2004: 182), the nouns 'inch', 'ounce', 'yard', 'day', 'week' and 'month' behave like other regular nouns, and take the plural ending; thus, we have 'inches', 'ounces', 'yards', 'days', 'weeks' and 'months'. In the same vein, Hughes and Trudgill (1987: 20) and Edwards et al. (1984) find no instances of unmarked plural for 'inches'; yet, Cheshire et al. (1993: 67) report the appearance of 'three inch' in 43.7 per cent of schools taking part in a survey questionnaire.

Pronouns

Personal pronouns

Standard English differentiates personal pronouns according to their position and function in a sentence – and so there are subject personal pronouns, *I, you, he, she, it, we, you, they,* and object personal pronouns, *me, you, him, her, it, us, you, them.* In the non-standard dialects of the Southeast of England, subject personal pronouns may take the same form as standard object personal pronouns (Examples 4–5).

(4) Oi! Oi! Listen to this! Listen to this, oh, you girls and boys! One day I was down the institute, yeh, and *me* and Jamie nearly got in a fight with each other – my step sister stabbed him in the leg! [laughter] (J.R. 2005)
(5) *Him* and *her* are the ones you should pick. (Edwards 1993: 229)

Edwards (1993: 229) claims that such a use of non-subject personal pronouns may serve an emphatic function; however, this suggestion has not been supported by any systematic study.

Anderwald (2004: 178) and Edwards (1993: 230) point to the use of the plural first person object personal pronoun *us* for its singular equivalent *me* (Example 6), but not the corresponding *we* for *I.* This use of *us* is not unique to the Southeast of England, and may be more a matter of a colloquial style rather than dialect, as Edwards (1993: 231) remarks.

(6) He says, give *us* a fiver for it, Ted, and you can have it. (Anderwald 2004: 178)

Anderwald (2004: 178) claims that the standard first person plural object personal pronoun *us* is also frequently found in subject position when it is followed by a plural noun phrase apposition (Example 7).

(7) *Us kids* used to pinch the sweets like hell. (Anderwald 2004: 178)

In addition, the Bergen Corpus of London Teenager Language (COLT) contains instances of *youse* instead of *you* as the second person plural personal pronoun (Stenström et al. 2002).

Reflexive pronouns

In Standard English, the reflexive pronoun system is formed by adding endings *-self* in the singular and *-selves* in the plural to the possessive pronouns *my, your* and *our,* and the object personal pronouns *him, her, it* and *them.* In the Southeast and some other regions of England, the system of reflexive pronouns has been regularized, and all of them are formed by adding *-self* or *-selves* to the possessive adjectives (Cheshire et al. 1993, Edwards 1993, Stenström et al. 2002, Anderwald 2004); hence, we have *meself, yourself, hisself, herself, itself, ourselves, yourselves, theirselves* (Table 2.1, Examples 8–10).

(8) I had ten bob. Two bob for *meself* and eight bob for the board and lodging. (Anderwald 2004: 177)
(9) He builded that boat *hisself.* (Edwards 1993: 230)
(10) They want it for *theirselves.* (Edwards 1993: 230)

Nevertheless, even within this rather regular system, variation exists, which consists in the interchangeable use of the endings *-self* and *-selves* in the plural (Examples 10–12). The third person plural is even more variable, as *-self* may alternate with *-selves,* and *their-* with *them-* (Examples 10, 12–13), resulting in four different combinations *theirselves, theirself, themselves, themself* (Table 2.1).

Table 2.1 Reflexive pronouns in the Southeast of England

	SINGULAR	PLURAL
1st person	meself	ourselves/ourself
2nd person	yourself	yourselves
3rd person	hisself	theirselves/theirself/themself/themselves
	herself	
	itself	

(11) [We] used to have to stand in this copper and bath *ourself*, wash our hair and all. (Anderwald 2004: 177)
(12) They wouldn't come round to make *theirself* a nuisance. (Anderwald 2004: 177)
(13) They would've never forgiven *themself* for allowing me out on the deck. (Anderwald 2004: 177)

In the many non-standard English dialects, including those of the Southeast, the possessive adjective *my* is reduced to a weak form *me* (Example 14); hence, when we discuss the system of reflexive pronouns, we must not assume that the form *meself* (Example 8) is derived from an object personal pronoun *me*, but from the weak form of the possessive *my*, that is, *me*, which can be [mi], [mə], [mɑ], etc.

(14) I give it to *me* brother. (Edwards 1993: 230)

Demonstrative pronouns

In Standard English, the system of demonstrative pronouns is marked for number and distance, so that when a single object/event is close to the speaker (regarding distance in time or space), *this* is used, whereas when it is distant, *that* is used; with multiple objects, demonstratives *these* and *those* are used, respectively. In Southeastern Englishes, and other regional varieties, the system of demonstrative pronouns is more complex (Table 2.2). In the singular, either the same forms as in Standard English are used, or those same forms can be followed by *here* and *there*; thus, *this here* and *that there*. In the plural, close objects/events are referred to by using *these* or *these here*, and distant objects/events by using *them* or *them there* (Examples 15–17). *Them* as a demonstrative pronoun is indeed widely reported in the Southeast (Cheshire 1982, Edwards 1993, Anderwald 2004), including London (Stenström et al. 2002).

(15) *This here* jacket cost a bomb. (Edwards 1993: 233)
(16) What's *them things* called with the paint codes on you're looking at to get all the paint up ...? (J.R. 2005)
(17) They don't realize, mate, my cousins are coming down from London just to get *them boys*, and they don't realize that they're all gonna die, they're all gonna get shot. (J.R. 2005)

Table 2.2 Demonstrative pronouns in the Southeast of England

	SINGULAR	PLURAL
close	this/this here	these/these here
distant	that/that there	them/them there

Relative pronouns

In Standard English, the system of relative pronouns consists of five entries: 'who', with people, 'which', with things, 'that', with people and things, 'whom', as animate object of a sentence, and 'whose', to show possession. When the relative pronoun acts as the object of the relative clause, it can be omitted, so utterances such as 'the car I was driving' are perfectly standard. In the South-east the situation is once more much more complex – the relative pronouns used in Standard English co-occur with 'what' and 'as' used with both animate and inanimate nouns (Examples 18–20).

(18) The girl *what*'s coming over (Edwards 1993: 228)
(19) The car *what* I saw (Edwards 1993: 228)
(20) The boy *as* I asked (Edwards 1993: 229)

Subject zero relatives, that is, no relative pronoun, are used in dialect speech not only in object position but also in subject position (Examples 21–23).

(21) There's a train Ø goes through without stopping. (Edwards 1993: 229)
(22) It ain't the best ones Ø finish first. (Edwards 1993: 229)
(23) There's one single house Ø stands right against the school gates. (Anderwald 2004: 189)

There are linguistic and social constraints on the use of particular relative pronouns, such as type of antecedent (animate vs. inanimate), the syntactic function of the relative marker in the relative clause, length of the relative clause, educational background, sex and age, but space restrictions prevent these being discussed in this general chapter (for details, see Cheshire et al. 1993, Edwards 1993, Stenström et al. 2002, Herrmann 2003, Anderwald 2004, Levey 2006).

Verbs

Present tense verb forms

Variation in the present tense forms is substantial, and several trends can be observed within the verb systems of present-day English. Although in the past, Standard English verbs were inflected for number and person, nowadays the only inflected verb form in Standard English remains in the third person singular. However, the generalization of third person *-s* to other persons is still present, though perhaps declining (Edwards et al. 1984: 18; Edwards 1993: 222–224; Anderwald 2004: 185) in other dialects, including those of the South of England.

(24) So I *goes*, oh clear off. (Cheshire 1982: 43)
(25) We fucking *chins* them with bottles. (Cheshire 1982: 43)

It is not present any more in all places in the Southeast though; in fact, it seems that the more to the east of the Southeast, the less frequent the practice – while in Reading (which is in the west of the Southeast) non-standard speech, it is quite common (Examples 24–25), in London it is almost absent, as it is in the traditional dialects of the Essex area (Trudgill 1990: 94), and even in the modern dialect of young people in Colchester, Essex, see Examples 26–28. That should not be very surprising though, as in the South West, *-s* is present throughout the present tense paradigm (Edwards et al. 1984: 18; Trudgill 1990: 98), and in East Anglia, verb endings have completely disappeared (Trudgill 1990: 98; Edwards 1993: 222). However, both systems are used variably in those regions. The type of subject does not seem to affect the form of the verb; for instance, in the speech of young working-class males, loss of present tense marking is apparent in all persons of main verbs, including third person singular, with both nouns (Examples 26–27) and pronouns (Example 30).

(26) Everyone, *everyone respect* me, really, don't they? (J.R. 2005)
(27) The minute I got in trouble with the police once, any, every, any *copper* that *recognize* me from getting arrested that night, *pull* me over, *stop*, *search* me. (J.R. 2005)
(28) One boy, *he wear* gold pins in his nuts. Schizophrenic, innit? (J.R. 2005)

The lack of subject-verb concord is apparent in the case of third person singular auxiliary 'do', where the *-es* ending is missing as well (Cheshire 1982, Cheshire et al. 1993, Stenström et al. 2002, Anderwald 2004; Examples 29–30).

(29) J: Why do you think she's a bitch? B: Because *she don't* do fuck all for this country, mate! (J.R. 2005)
(30) We know nothing else but to follow people that are getting somewhere if you know what I mean, but sometimes *it don't* work out right if you know what I mean. Sometimes you follow the wrong people and that's why you get yourself into trouble. (J.R. 2005)

PRESENT TENSE 'BE'

The generalization of the third person singular verb BE, 'is', to other persons and numbers is not infrequent in the Southeast (Examples 31–33).

(31) I only beat people, I won't go around trying to find people, but if anyone gives it, then obviously they're getting it down, but, just *grungers is* different. (J.R. 2005)
(32) Where*'s* all these *people* coming from? (J.R. 2005)
(33) Proper chavs, mate, think they're from fucking London town. They think *they is* the bollocks. (J.R. 2005)

Such extension of present tense singular verb BE, 'is', to plural contexts with existential 'there' is indeed extremely common in the Southeast and in many dialects across the English-speaking world (Examples 34–36), to the extent that it is no longer regarded as being non-standard.

(34) *There's* lots of museums. (Cheshire 1999: 135)
(35) There, there, don't get me wrong, *there has been* a few rapes happen in Colchester, but *there is* not as many as London, Manchester, big cities. (J.R. 2005)
(36) There's no false ceiling, *there's* no columns. (Anderwald 2004: 183)

Past tenses

In Standard English the form of the verb depends on its nature – weak verbs add the *-ed/-d* ending to the infinitive to form the Simple Past tense and the Present Perfect tense, and strong verbs form the Past and Present Perfect tense by changing the vowel of the verb stem (some of those strong verbs are marked for different tenses in such a way that there exist three different forms of them – the infinitive, the Simple Past and the Present Perfect). The weak verbs outnumber the strong verbs. In the dialects of the Southeast there is a good deal of variation in the past tenses. The following three patterns persist:

A. Strong verbs with identical present, preterit and past participle forms; thus *give – give – give* and *come – come – come* (Example 37).

(37) I was standing looking at a chap working, and he *come up* to me and wanted to know ... (Anderwald 2004: 180).

B. Strong verbs with identical preterit and past participle forms, for example, *do – done – done* (only when 'do' is a full verb; when it is an auxiliary, it can be *do – did – did*), *drive – drove – drove, forget – forgot – forgot, take – took – took,* etc. (Examples 38–39).

(38) She *done* it, *didn't* she? (Cheshire 1982: 48)
(39) I take speed, I'*ve took* coke, I'*ve took* pills, I'*ve took* speed today! I've been drinking, I'*ve took* speed, oops! I, I have been drinking today! I *have took* speed today! I don't take speed all the time. But my auntie, she *done* hero-ine for two years and, err, she overdosed on crack, and then she was in hospital for three months. (J.R. 2005)

Such a two-way pattern is quite commonly cited as a feature of London's Cockney (Matthews 1938 [1972]), but it is also very common in the non-standard dialects of the rest of the Southeast (Cheshire 1982: 48, Cheshire et al. 1993: 78, Edwards 1993: 221, Anderwald 2004: 184–185).

C. Verbs which are strong in Standard English but weak in the non-standard dialects of the Southeast, for example, *grow – growed – growed* or *build – builded – builded* (Edwards 1993: 220).

With the Past Progressive tense in the Southeast, some verb forms are created by using the past participle rather than the present participle (Example 40).

(40) He *was sat.* (Edwards et al. 1984: 19)

PAST TENSE 'BE'

In the non-standard dialects of the Southeast, the past tense of the verb BE may also follow three different patterns.

A. It may be levelled to 'was' across the whole paradigm, regardless of the person, number and polarity (Cheshire 1982: 44, Edwards et al. 1984: 20, Trudgill 1990: 98, Anderwald 2001: 8 and 2004: 182, Cheshire and Fox 2006a, b, 2009, Cheshire et al. 2011); thus combinations such as *we was/we wasn't, you was/you wasn't* or *they was/they wasn't* are widespread (Examples 41–42).

(41) This is the sort of stuff we got offered when *we was* like six, seven years old on the estate we live in. (J.R. 2005)
(42) It ended up *we wasn't* talking to each other for about two weeks. (Levey 2007)

B. Another, less frequent, pattern involves a generalization to 'were' across the whole paradigm in both positive (Example 43) and negative contexts. Anderwald (2001: 11, 2004: 182–183) reports instances of regularized standard plural 'were' to the singular in both polarity contexts for the dialects of London and Middlesex (now part of Greater London).

(43) Interviewer: Was it easy to get into trouble there? Informant: *It were* easy. Yeah, very easy. (Anderwald 2004: 182)

C. A vast number of the non-standard dialects of the Southeast have 'was' in the positive and 'were' in the negative context across the whole paradigm as in Examples 44–45 (Edwards 1993: 223, Anderwald 2001: 11–12 and 2004:183, Cheshire and Fox 2006a, b, 2009, Cheshire et al. 2011, Levey 2007).

(44) *It was* still good, *weren't it?* (Cheshire and Fox 2006a, b)
(45) My *brother was* saying *it weren't* his fault. (Levey 2007)

Interestingly, Edwards et al. (1984: 20) mention yet another kind of levelling, dependent on whether the subject was singular or plural. This pattern used to be found in traditional Cockney, the dialect of the working classes of London's East End, where 'were' was generalized to the singular and 'was' to the plural persons (Edwards et al. 1984: 20), hence we could have *I were* but *they was*. Recent evidence from the East End of London does not mention this permutation.

Quantitative analyses of non-standard 'was' and 'were' levelling strategies in London reveal distributional differences in the use of the two kinds according to speakers' age, gender and ethnicity, as well as the grammatical person and type of the sentence subject (noun phrase vs. pronoun). However, space restrictions prevent these being discussed here (for details, see Anderwald 2001, Cheshire and Fox 2006a, b, 2009, Cheshire et al. 2011, Levey 2007).

With existential 'there', as in the present tense, the standard singular form, 'was' is extended to plural contexts indeed extremely frequently in many dialects of the Southeast and beyond (Examples 46–47).

(46) Yeh, he was up the top there, and I had a joint, and *there was* two policemen down there, and [name of one informant] started squealing like a pig, like a pig does. (J.R. 2005)
(47) *There was* some papers wanted urgently. (Anderwald 2004: 18)

The irregular verbs HAVE and DO

In the non-standard dialects of the Southeast, the forms of the verbs 'have' and 'do' are dependent on person, number and the grammatical functions they serve.

As a full/main verb in some dialects of English, for example, Reading, Berkshire, 'have' can take the form 'has' with all persons (Examples 48–49), but the non-concord forms are not reported when 'have' acts as an auxiliary verb (Cheshire 1982: 32).

(48) *We has* a muck around in there. (Cheshire 1982: 32)
(49) *I has* the answer for that. (Edwards 1993: 225)

Together with person and number, the grammatical function plays a significant role in the variation concerning the forms of the verb 'do', at least in some dialects of the Southeast. For instance, again in Reading, the standard 'do' co-exists with three non-standard 'do' uses. When 'do' acts as a full verb, it takes the form 'does' [dʌz] with all persons and numbers but the third person singular (Example 50), where it takes the form 'dos' [duːz] (Example 51).

(50) That's what *I does*, anyway, I just ignores them. (Cheshire 1982: 34)
(51) *One bloke* stays at home and *dos* the house-cleaning and all that. (Cheshire 1982: 35)

On the other hand, when 'do' serves the auxiliary function, it may have an invariant form 'do' for all persons and numbers. Except in the Reading study

(Cheshire 1982), in the Southeast 'do' has not been very well investigated, particularly as a full verb. However, there are various reports confirming its non-concord forms for the auxiliary (Example 52).

(52) It hurts my dad more than *it do* her. (Cheshire 1982: 34)

The invariant form is especially common across the negative paradigm; thus, 'don't' is found also for the third person singular (Examples 29–30, 53–54).

(53) All you have to do is go down the college and apply. *It don't* take two seconds to walk down there. (J.R. 2005)
(54) *He don't* have to pay, *he don't* have to pay nothing for them. (J.R. 2005)

Multiple negation

A very widespread way of expressing negation is through the use of more than one negative incorporated within one clause, called 'negative concord' or 'multiple negation' (or double negation if two negatives are involved). The most frequent first element of the negation is the sentence negator *not* attached to an auxiliary or a modal verb, combined with other negating elements, for example, *nothing* and *nowhere* (Examples 54–57).

(55) I only think that she is a wanker because she *don't* do *nothing* for us. (J.R. 2005)
(56) They go into that and then they get nowhere in life because over here, in England, bricklaying, building and roofing, you *can't* get *nowhere*, innit, basically. (J.R. 2005)
(57) They *can't* do you *nothing*. (J.R. 2005)

Other frequent first elements are *never* and *no-one* (Examples 58–59).

(58) He *never* got *no* supper. (Anderwald 2004: 188)
(59) *No-one* would *never* take much offence. (Anderwald 2004: 188)

Multiple negation may also be combined with the use of non-standard *ain't* discussed in pages 78–79; therefore, sentences such as 'I *ain't* done *nothing*' are common.

It is worth noting that Standard English is the only British dialect of English which does not express negation by means of multiple negatives, and the current 'stigma' attached to negative concord, at least in formal contexts, such as in the school setting, is fairly recent – as some sources state such a negative attitude to multiple negation has been present in England for about two hundred years. Tentative quantitative comparisons of the frequency of occurrence of the multiple negation in the non-standard dialects suggest that it is three times more common in the Southeast of England than in the North of England, and also much more common than in the Midlands (Cheshire et al. 1993: 76; Anderwald 2002: 109–114).

'Ain't'/'in't'/'en't' and 'innit'

AIN'T/IN'T/EN'T

One of the most characteristic indicators of non-standard dialects in North America and the United Kingdom, though not in Scotland or Ireland, is the use of a secondary contraction of negative contracted forms to *ain't*. Literature concerning the Southeast of England states that *ain't* is a contracted negative form of the present tense verb BE, both copular, full verb (Examples 60–61) and auxiliary (Examples 62–63), as well as present tense auxiliary HAVE (Examples 64–66), but not full verb HAVE.

(60) The worst drug I've ever taken is probably speed and coke; pills *ain't* really that bad, are they? (J.R. 2005)
(61) And she's a real daddy's girl, you know what I mean? *Ain't* you, darling? *Ain't* she lovely? (J.R. 2005)
(62) How come that *ain't* working? (Cheshire 1982: 51)
(63) And he said no, I *ain't* going. (Anderwald 2004: 186)
(64) Oh, you *ain't* practised, mate! (J.R. 2005)
(65) I *ain't* seen her. (Edwards 1993: 227)
(66) B.: How much dole have you got? J.: I *ain't* got none. (J.R. 2005)

No records of *ain't* for present tense auxiliary DO are mentioned, yet again, instances of such uses of *ain't* can be observed, though perhaps on account of their less frequent occurrence, not documented (Example 67).

(67) I *ain't* get paid till Thursday. (J.R. 2005)

The use of *ain't* with all persons and numbers for present tense copular BE and auxiliary BE and HAVE in London and the rest of the Southeast have been reported in various dialect surveys, including the SED (Cheshire 1982, 1997, Cheshire et al. 1993, Edwards 1993, Stenström et al. 2002, Anderwald 2002, 2004); therefore, we know that the contraction *ain't* appears in a number of forms, most frequently spelt as *ain't*, *in't* and *en't* with phonetic forms /eɪnt, ɪnt, ent/, respectively. Of these forms, *in't* is most frequently reported to appear in tag questions derived from copular BE, as in Examples 68–69, but also from HAVE (Example 70). Cheshire (1997: 195–196) suggests that in the non-standard dialect of Reading, Berkshire, the use of *in't* in what she calls 'unconventional tags' serves a specific discourse function, namely it conveys assertion or perhaps even aggression, instead of mere request for information confirmation, and the person uttering them usually expects a specific answer.

(68) Yeh, the dog's bollocks, mate! That's me, I am the dog's bollocks! ... I am though, *I am* the bollocks, *in't* I? (J.R. 2005)
(69) *You're* a fucking hard nut, *in't* you. (Cheshire 1982: 58)
(70) They'll be sitting and going, 'under the desk can swipe, one second', get the, like, receipt, cause *they've got* a copy of the receipt, *in't they*? They sit there and write down on a bit of paper and go, 'Thank you, please' (J.R. 2005).

INNIT

Typical of London adolescent speech and a fast spreading phenomenon in the Southeast is an invariant tag 'innit', which is supposedly derived from London's multicultural, especially Jamaican community (Andersen 2001: 171). It is assumed that 'innit' has grammaticalized from 'isn't it' and can be used with all persons and verbs, for example, various forms of copular BE (Examples 71–72), content verbs (Examples 73–74) or modal verbs (Example 75–76).

(71) If you smoke crack, crack's addictive, *innit*? Really addictive. (J.R. 2005)
(72) Proper chavs speak like that because they're all, all wannabes, *innit*? (J.R. 2005)
(73) They come with loads of money, *innit*? (J.R. 2005)
(74) She looks like me, not you, *innit*? (J.R. 2005)
(75) Just to practice, I might, like, get every single dancing on so that I can learn, like, different dance styles to always use different ones or become like a choreographer, for example, and then make loads of money of the music videos, *innit*? (J.R. 2005)
(76) You can go with your Mum then, *innit*? (Andersen 2001: 171)

'Innit' can be observed to be used by both genders and various age groups. However, Stenström et al. (2002) find 'innit' to be used mostly by working-class, ethnic-minority young women in the COLT; they also report regional variation within London, with 'innit' most frequently used in Hackney. The author's recordings of young males from Colchester (Ryfa 2005) and some recordings of female teenagers may suggest that the tag is used by people of working-class backgrounds only. However, such a distribution may not be representative of the whole of the Southeast.

Never

In Standard English, *never* implies that an action that it refers to does not take or has not taken place on any occasion, as in 'He's never smoked cigarettes'. In dialects of the Southeast, and other English dialects, *never* (+ past simple) can be used as a past negative to refer to a single event in the past, and can be equated with *didn't* (+ verb infinitive) (Examples 77–78); often context is crucial in disambiguating the meaning of *never*.

(77) I *never went* to school today. (Cheshire 1982: 67)
(78) and, uh, he, he never done a lot of schooling. And he come running out of a, his house one day. And a kid swore black and blue he's nicked a ten bob note off him. He was gonna get some errands. They turned him over, the boy, *never* found no ten bob note. And then when they f- the school report, that was it. It convinced him. (Anderwald 2004: 188)

Modal verbs

The discussion of verbs in Southeastern non-standard dialects would not be complete without mentioning the 'emerging modals' (Krug 2000). Anderwald (2004: 181) speculates that although the contracted forms *gonna* (Example 79), *wonna* (Example 80), *gotta* and *hafta* of BE GOING TO, WANT TO, HAVE GOT TO and HAVE TO, respectively, are found all over Britain, the regional differences in the frequency of their use noted in British National Corpus, may indicate their first emergence in the English Southeast. However, we would need more evidence from spontaneous, non-standard speech from all over the country to be able to verify this tentative suggestion.

(79) There's some chavs that will wake up in the morning and think: 'Right, I'll phone up my boys. Today we're just *gonna* go and pick up some random person' (J.R. 2005).
(80) I was a sheep, I followed, I followed, I started smoking cigarettes, I started smoking cannabis, started smoking weed, then I went on to pills, coke, speed, and err, I stopped doing all that as I *wanna* ho-, hold down my job, and I *wanna* do well, and I *wanna* own my own business, I *wanna* have nice cars, and I *wanna* have a nice girlfriend and be able to go on holiday. (J.R. 2005)

Poplack and Tagliamonte (1996), Krug (2000) and Anderwald (2004) present evidence for a shift in the meaning of the most popular of those 'new modals', where *gonna* is becoming a simple future marker (Example 81) and *wonna* seems to express obligation (Example 82).

(81) Girl 1: Oh, fuck, just do it here for once, just for this once. Why? You're scared you won't pop it? Girl 2: No! Joanna: Don't force her. Girl 1: She, she, no, she's *gonna* do it. She just doesn't wanna do it here. (J.R. 2005)
(82) You've got toothache? You *wanna* see a dentist! (Krug 2000: 147)

Verb particles and prepositions

The grammar of the Southeast of England is, among others, characterized by considerable variation in the use of verb particles and prepositions.

Where Standard English has complex verb particles, non-standard dialects may have ones consisting of single words (Example 83); the converse is also noted – where Standard English verb particles consist of single words, non-standard dialects may have complex ones (Examples 84–85).

(83) I told him to *get out* the house. (Edwards 1993: 233)
(84) Some people *hallucinate off of* it, innit – I don't, it don't really affect me any more, err ... (J.R. 2005)
(85) We *got off of* the bus. (Edwards 1993: 233)

The use of prepositions may be incompatible with the Standard English system. Nevertheless, despite the fact that non-standard dialects have their own grammars and are rule-governed, the literature does not discuss the use of prepositions in those dialects in greater detail (but see a discussion on the frequent use of the verb particle *off of* by Hackney Anglo females in Kerswill's et al. 2007: 10 report); therefore, we do not know the constraints on the use of prepositions in the Englishes of the Southeast.

Adjectives and adverbs

Comparatives and superlatives of adjectives

In Standard English, comparatives and superlatives of adjectives are formed by adding the suffixes *-er/-est* to the basic form of monosyllabic adjectives or using the words *more/most* before polysyllabic adjectives; disyllabic adjectives follow either of these rules, for example, *nice – nicer – nicest, interesting – more interesting – most interesting, happy – happier – happiest* or *awful – more awful – most awful.* This regularization/simplification is relatively recent, as traditional, non-standard dialects, including those of the Southeast, have formed comparatives and superlatives by using the suffixes *-er/-est* in conjunction with the words *more/most,* for example, *fast – more faster – most fastest* (Examples 86–87). Such forms are not uncommon in contemporary varieties (Edwards 1993, Stenström et al. 2002).

(86) I couldn't have asked for a *more nicer* friend. (Edwards 1993: 232)
(87) That was the *most horriblest* experience of my life. (Edwards 1993: 232)

The adjective 'bad' is reported to display variation too – forms such as *bad – badder – baddest* and *bad – worser – worsest* exist alongside the standard set *bad – worse – worst.*

Formation of adverbs

Standard English forms adverbs of manner by adding the suffix *-ly* to the basic form of adjectives, for example, *slow – slowly, terrible – terribly* and *happy – happily.*

In London and the rest of the Southeast of England, and in other regions of the country, the rule does operate alongside the non-standard way of forming adverbs by using the exact basic forms of adjectives without adding any suffixes (Cheshire 1982, Cheshire et al. 1993, Edwards 1993, Stenström et al. 2002, Anderwald 2004; Examples 88–89). Similarly, the irregular adjective *good,* can also serve the function of the adverb (in Standard English the adverb is *well*) (Example 90).

(88) I swum me way out of it *quick.* (Anderwald 2004: 189)
(89) We went on *terrible.* (Edwards et al. 1984: 24)
(90) He done it *good.* (Edwards 1993: 231)

Intensifiers 'well', 'real', 'right' and 'fucking'

A rather recent trend among young people in the Southeast is the use of 'well' serving the function of an adjective intensifier. The use of 'well' has not been well documented to date, but it seems to be gaining popularity in the speech of working-class teenage males in the Southeast as can be deduced from internet sources and from speech recordings, such as the author's Colchester teenage males corpus, where instances of 'well' acting as an adjective intensifier (Examples 91–93) are found. To put it simply, before adjectives, 'well' may be equated to 'very'.

(91) 'The bollocks' means 'the tits', '*well good*', mate. (J.R. 2005)
(92) D'you know what's *well painful*? (J.R. 2005)
(93) Speed is a powdered form. Err, *well hard* to explain it, innit? (J.R. 2005)

Similarly, an investigation of the corpus of recordings made for the *Linguistic Innovators* project reveals 'well' to be frequent, even dominant as an intensifier in outer London Havering (Kerswill et al. 2007). Interestingly, in COLT, 'well' along with 'right' and 'real' (instead of 'really') are predominantly used by London teenagers from middle-class backgrounds (Stenström et al. 2002). Stenström et al. (2002) also report that in the speech of London teenagers, there is no clear distinction between classes in the use of the word 'fucking' as an intensifier. It is also common in the speech of teenagers in Colchester, Essex (Example 94); however, to date no research on the social stratification of its occurrence is available.

(94) I said I fucking just put this plug in this morning, I put this plug in, yeh? And, shut up, mate, I'd never hit my head so hard in a *fucking* long time. (J.R. 2005)

Articles

In the Standard English article system, the indefinite article 'a' (/ə/) is used before a singular noun beginning with a consonant, for example, *a day* /ə 'deɪ/, and 'an' (/ən/) before a singular noun beginning with a vowel, for example, *an apple* /ən 'æpl/. The indefinite article 'the' is pronounced with a reduced central vowel 'schwa', /ə/, that is, /ðə/, before a singular noun beginning with a consonant, for example, *the day* /ðə 'deɪ/, and with an unreduced high front vowel, /iː/, that is, /ðiː/, for example, *the apple* /ðiː 'æpl/.

Certain tendencies in the 'traditional' homeland of 'Cockney' suggesting a change in progress are reported by Fox (2006a), who demonstrates allomorphic variation in the article system in the speech of adolescents of London's East End borough of Tower Hamlets. The aforementioned articles 'an' and 'the' (the latter pronounced as /ðiː/) before singular nouns beginning with vowels, e.g. *an apple* /ən 'æpl/ and *the apple* /ðiː 'æpl/ co-exist with the articles 'a' and 'the' (the latter pronounced as /ðə/) in the same context; thus, *a apple* /ə'æpl/ and *the apple* /ðə 'æpl/. To avoid hiatus between the reduced central vowel and the initial vowel of the following noun, speakers tend to insert a glottal stop, /ʔ/ (to find out more about avoiding hiatus in southern British English, see Britain and Fox 2006, 2008, 2009). In Tower Hamlets, in the lead of the change towards the use of the prevocalic 'a' and 'the' /ðə/, are boys of Bangladeshi origin, followed by boys of white heritage and then white-heritage girls. Fox (2006a) suggests that this change may be contact-driven as her study of the use of articles among friendship groups indicates – it has to be mentioned that Tower Hamlets nowadays is populated with residents of non-white heritage, in particular of Bangladeshi origins, and it is those Bangladeshi migrants and their descendants who constitute around 33 per cent of the total population of the borough, and around 90 per cent of some of the neighbourhoods within.

We know of similar developments in the article systems from other sources concerning grammatical variation in England and beyond, for example, in a 'multiethnolect' termed 'Multicultural London English' (MLE) (for further details regarding lack of allomorphy in the indefinite article system in MLE, see Gabrielatos et al. 2010), Bedford Italian English (Guzzo et al. 2007) and New Zealand English; however, the extent to which the phenomenon is rooted or spread into the Southeast of England is yet to be investigated.

'Estuary English' and Dialect Levelling in the Southeast

In an ongoing debate concerning linguistic features of the Englishes of the Southeast, considerable attention has been given to so-called 'Estuary English', evident in linguistics and the media since David Rosewarne coined the term in 1984, and defined it as an 'intermediate' variety which amalgamates the features of RP (non-localized standard British English accent usually associated with the privileged stratum of the English society) and Cockney (working-class London's East End speech). Rosewarne suggests that this variety reflects a set of changes leading British society towards a more democratic system with blurred class barriers; therefore, 'Estuary English' speakers can be placed on a continuum of accents between RP and Cockney. Indeed, since World War II the Southeast has been affected by heavy migration out of London to new, overspill towns and the surrounding rural areas, and as Basildon research demonstrates, Cockney features have been transplanted there together with its speakers (Fox 2000). Also, for the last few decades, the Southeast has been receiving a great influx of people from other regions of Great Britain, as well as facing high levels of internal socio-geographical mobility, related to economic development, employment growth and improvements in public transport. Such demographic changes and socio-economic situations constitute a breeding ground for dialect contact resulting in the creation of 'new', or modification of existing, dialects. In this case, a less socially marked, regional south-eastern koine appears to have emerged (though not yet focused), and although there is no agreement in the academic world about the exact origins and alleged spread of 'Estuary English', let alone its nature or even the legitimacy of its name (see Ryfa 2003: 9–19), it seems justifiable to associate it with the widespread, within the Southeast, process of dialect levelling, leading to the linguistic convergence of the varieties involved.

The descriptions of 'Estuary English' are made with reference to Standard English and Cockney, and appear at the phonological, grammatical and lexical level; however, the most commented on are pronunciation features. As far as vowels are concerned, Wells (1997 and elsewhere) points to the occurrence of happY-tensing, mentioned hereinbefore. Other vowel phenomena allegedly characteristic of 'Estuary English' are the Diphthong Shift, particularly in the case of the FACE, PRICE and GOAT vowels, and the allophony in GOAT (see pages 58–59). With respect to consonants, L Vocalization, T Glottalling and Yod Palatalization/Coalescence, discussed in pages 61–62, 64–67, are observed (ibidem). Features typical of Cockney, but excluded from the phonetic make-up of 'Estuary English' are monophthongal realizations of the MOUTH vowel, H Dropping, intervocalic word-internal glottal replacement of T and TH Fronting (though, as discussed in this chapter, the latter two are spreading into the accents of younger 'middle-class' speakers in the Southeast and indeed beyond, which questions the validity of the exclusion of TH Fronting or intervocalic word-internal glottal replacement of T from the phonetic make-up of EE). The use of none of those features in isolation makes a person a speaker of 'Estuary English', hence media reports of 'Estuary English' 'sweeping away' other accents are a gross exaggeration, especially that journalists adduce features, for example, T Glottalling, which have been present in the varieties 'threatened' by 'Estuary English' long before the term came into existence. There is also hard empirical evidence disproving the media's claims (for details see Ryfa 2003: 31–38). The prosodic features and lexical items cited in the discussions of 'Estuary English' are largely ignored in research as they are believed to be a matter of style of speech rather than dialect markers. Furthermore, the grammar parallels that of other dialects of the Southeast; therefore, it does not help distinguish 'Estuary English' from other varieties. In fact, determining the exact boundary-marking features of this pseudo-variety seems more and more difficult if not impossible, and it can be concluded from research findings that they are as fuzzy as the region boundaries themselves. The fast advancing process of dialect levelling is causing dialects of the Southeast to be losing their distinctiveness. On the other hand, researchers (Schmid 1999; Altendorf 1999a, b, 2003; Przedlacka 2001, 2002; Ryfa 2005) demonstrate that there is no complete uniformity of speech, even among those who fulfil the necessary criteria to be classified as 'Estuary English' speakers – the differences being mostly quantitative rather than qualitative (although those exist too as can be found in the present chapter); therefore, we can talk of a range, or continuum, of accents covered by an umbrella term of 'Estuary English'. Traces of local varieties do exist within the Southeast as well – as Britain explains, 'partly because the southeastern regional mix is still focusing, partly because distinct local dialects form part of the mix that has engendered the regiolect in different places ... and partly because of particular local, social and demographic factors ...' (2005: 998).

Rosewarne (1984, 1994) anticipated the possibility of 'Estuary English' exerting a strong influence on RP and becoming the pronunciation of the future also in the context of teaching English as a foreign language, yet empirical research does not confirm foreign students' willingness to learn it on account of its rather low comprehensibility, nor does it support claims that it might become the means of business communication (for details, see Ryfa 2003: 50–54). It is therefore doubtful whether 'Estuary English' will ever become anything more than a regional southeastern koine created as a result of complex socio-economic and perhaps also political changes taking place in the Southeast (for a discussion, see Trudgill 2001: 177–179, Przedlacka 2001: 36).

Notes

[1] Bangladeshi girls are excluded from the analysis on account of them not attending a youth club where the data for the research were collected.

[2] For a detailed discussion on the linguistic constraints on the use of the particular realizations, as well as effects of age, ethnicity and friendship groups, see Fox 2007.

Acknowledgements

I wish to express my deep gratitude to all those who helped me complete this chapter by providing invaluable comments or supplying me with additional materials, that is, Prof. David J. Britain, Phillip Tipton, Susan Fox, Jenny Amos, Catharine Carfoot and Heather Grainger.

Bibliography

Altendorf, U. (1999a), 'Es(h)tuary English: is English going Cockney?', *Moderna Språk*, Vol. XCIII, 1, pp. 1–11.

—. (1999b), 'Approaching the notion of "Estuary English": /t/-glottalling and /l/-vocalisation by the Thames Estuary', in C. Paradis (ed.), *Recent Trends in the Pronunciation of English: Social, Regional and Attitudinal Aspects,* pp. 15–31, Stockholm: Almqvist and Wiksell.

—. (2003), *Estuary English: Levelling at the Interface of RP and South-Eastern British English,* Tübingen: Gunter Narr Verlag.

Altendorf, U. and Watt, D. (2004), 'The dialects in the South of England: phonology', in B. Kortmann, E. W. Schneider, K. Burridge, R. Mesthrie, and C. Upton (eds), *A Handbook of Varieties of English: A Multimedia Reference Tool,* Vol. 1, pp. 178–203, *Phonology,* Berlin: Mouton de Gruyter.

Amos, J. (2006), *Yod Dropping on Mersea Island,* Unpublished BA LG405 Project Dissertation, Colchester: University of Essex. <http://privatewww.essex.ac.uk/~jamos/index.html>.

Andersen, G. (2001), *Pragmatic Markers and Sociolinguistic Variation,* (Pragmatics and Beyond 84), Amsterdam/Philadelphia: Benjamins.

Anderwald, L. (2001), 'Was/Were variation in non-standard British English today', *English World-Wide,* 22(1), 1–21.

—. (2002), *Negation in Non-Standard British English: Gaps, Regularizations, Asymmetries,* (Studies in German Linguistics 8), London & New York: Routledge.

—. (2004), 'The varieties of English in the Southeast of England: morphology and syntax', in B. Kortmann and E. W. Schneider (eds), *A Handbook of Varieties of English: A Multimedia Reference Tool,* Vol. 2, pp. 175–195, *Morphology and Syntax,* Berlin: Mouton de Gruyter.

Bailey, R. W. (1996), *Nineteenth-Century English,* Ann Arbor: University of Michigan Press.

Baker, S. (2007), 'Right, do interactional functions constrain phonological variation? Well, maybe not always', An Investigation of the Interactional Constraints of the Discourse Particles Right and Well on Language Variation, Ph.D. thesis, University of Essex, Colchester.

Beaken, M. A. (1971), A study of phonological development in a primary school population of East London, Ph.D. thesis, University of London, London.

Bowyer, R. (1973), A Study of Social Accents in a South London Suburb, M.Phil. Dissertation, University of Leeds: Leeds.

Britain, D. (2002), 'The British history of New Zealand English?', *Essex Research Reports in Linguistics*, 41, 1–41.
—. (2005), 'Innovation diffusion, "Estuary English" and local dialect differentiation: the survival of Fenland Englishes', *Linguistics*, 43(5), 995–1022.
Britain, D. and Fox, S. (2006), 'Vernacular universality, allomorphic simplification and language contact: the regularisation of hiatus avoidance strategies in English non-standard accents', Workshop on World Englishes: Vernacular Universals vs. Contact-Induced Change, Mekrijärvi Research Station, Joensuu University, Finland.
—. (2008), 'Vernacular universals and the regularisation of hiatus resolution', *Essex Research Reports in Linguistics*, 57(3), 1–42.
—. (2009), 'The regularization of the hiatus resolution system in British English: A contact-induced 'vernacular universal'?', in M. Filppula, J. Klemola and H. Paulasto (eds), *Vernacular Universals and Language Contacts: Evidence from Varieties of English and Beyond*, pp. 177–205, London: Routledge.
Britain, D. and Johnson, W. (2004/5), *LG405 Lecture handout*, Colchester: University of Essex.
Carfoot, C. (2004), An investigation of the sociophonology of the fronting of the FOOT vowel in three locations in England, MA dissertation, University of Essex: Colchester.
Cheshire, J. (1982), *Variation in an English Dialect: A Sociolinguistic Study*, (Cambridge Studies in Linguistics 37), Cambridge: Cambridge University Press.
—. (1997), 'Linguistic variation and social function', in N. Coupland and A. Jaworski (eds), *Sociolinguistics: A Reader and Coursebook*, pp. 185–198, Basingstoke: Palgrave.
—. (1999), 'Spoken standard English', in T. Bex and R. Watts (eds), *Standard English: The Widening Debate*, pp. 129–148, London: Routledge.
Cheshire, J., Edwards, V. and Whittle, P. (1993), 'Non-StE and dialect levelling', in J. Milroy and L. Milroy (eds), *Real English: The Grammar of English Dialects in the British Isles* (Real Language Series), pp. 52–96, London: Longman.
Cheshire, J., Fox, S., Kerswill, P. and Torgersen, E. N. (2005), 'Reversing "drift": changes in the London diphthong system', Paper presented at UKLVC5, University of Aberdeen, September 2005.
—. (2008), 'Ethnicity, friendship network and social practices as the motor of dialect change: Linguistic innovation in London', *Sociolinguistica*, 22, 1–23.
—. (2011), 'Contact, the feature pool and the speech community: The emergence of Multicultural London English', *Journal of Sociolinguistics*, 15(2), 151–196.
Cheshire, J. and Fox, S. (2006a), 'A new look at was/were: the perspective from London', Paper presented at Sociolinguistics Symposium 16, Limerick, July 2006.
—. (2006b), 'New perspectives on was/were variation in London', Paper presented at NWAV35, Columbus, OH, November 2006.
—. (2009), '*Was/were* variation: a perspective from London', *Language Variation and Change*, 21, 1–23.
Cruttenden, A. (2001), *Gimson's Pronunciation of English*, 6th ed, London: Arnold.
Edwards, V. (1993), 'The grammar of Southern British English', in J. Milroy and L. Milroy (eds), *Real English: The Grammar of English Dialects in the British Isles* (Real Language Series), pp. 214–238, London: Longman.

Edwards, V., Trudgill, P. and Weltens, B. (1984), The grammar of english dialect: a survey of research, A report to the ESRC Education and Human Development Committee.

Ellis, A. (1889), *On Early English Pronunciation*, Vol. 5, London: Trübner.

Eustace, S. (1969), 'The meaning of palaeotype in A. J. Ellis's On Early English Pronunciation', *Transactions of the Philological Society*, 67, 31–79.

Foulkes, P. and Docherty, G. J. (eds) (1999), *Urban Voices: Accent Studies in the British Isles*, London: Arnold.

Foulkes, P. and Docherty, G. J. (2000), 'Another chapter in the story of /r/: "labio-dental" variants in British English', *Journal of Sociolinguistics*, 4, 30–59.

Fox, S. (2000), Basildon Project 1999/2000, Research paper, Colchester: University of Essex, <http://sociolinguistics.w.interia.pl/PDF/Sue_Fox.Basildon.pdf>.

—. (2003), 'Linguistic and sociocultural contact in London's East End: the Bangladeshi presence', Paper presented at the conference on *Consequences of Mobility: Linguistic and Sociocultural Contact Zones*, Roskilde, 23–24 May 2003.

—. (2006a), 'A new sociolinguistic variable? Allomorphic variation in the English article system among East London adolescents', Paper presented at SociolinguistEssex XI, University of Essex, 31 May 2006.

—. (2006b), 'London's East End – Language change', Paper presented at Villiers Park, 30 January–3 February 2006.

—. (2007), The demise of Cockneys? Language change among adolescents in the 'traditional' east end of London, Ph.D. thesis, University of Essex, Colchester.

Fox, S., Khan, A. and Torgersen, E. (2011), 'The emergence and diffusion of Multicultural English', in F. Kern and M. Selting (eds) *Pan-ethnic styles of speaking in European metropolitan areas*, pp. 19–44, Amsterdam: Benjamins.

Gabrielatos, C., Torgersen, E., Hoffmann, S. and Fox, S. (2010), 'A corpus-based sociolinguistic study of indefinite article forms in London English', *Journal of English Linguistics*, 38(4), 297–334.

Gimson, A. C. (1962), *An Introduction to the Pronunciation of English*, London: Arnold.

—. (1984), 'The RP accent', in P. Trudgill (ed.), *Language in the British Isles*, pp. 45–54, Cambridge: Cambridge University Press.

Guzzo, S., Britain, D. and Fox, S. (2007). 'From L2 to ethnic dialect: hiatus resolution strategies across the generations in Bedford Italian English', Paper presented at IAWE-2007, Regensburg, Germany.

Harris, J. (1990), 'Derived phonological contrasts', in S. Ramsaran (ed.), *Studies in the Pronunciation of English: A Commemorative Volume in Honour of A.C. Gimson*, pp. 87–105, London: Routledge.

Herrmann, T. (2003), Relative clauses in dialects of English: a typological approach, Ph.D. thesis, Albert-Ludwigs-Universität, Freiburg.

Hudson, R. A. and Holloway, A. F. (1977), *Variation in London English, Mimeo, Department of Phonetics and Linguistics*, University College, London.

Hughes, A. and Trudgill, P. (1987[1994]), *English Accents and Dialects: An Introduction to Social and Regional Varieties of English in the British Isles*, 2nd ed., London: Edward Arnold.

Hughes, A., Trudgill, P. and Watt, D. (2005), *English Accents and Dialects: An Introduction to Social and Regional Varieties of English in the British Isles*, 4th ed., London: Hodder Arnold.

Hurford, J. (1967), The speech of one family: A phonetic comparison of the speech of three generations in a family of East Londoners, Ph.D. thesis, University College London, London.

Johnson, W. and Britain, D. (2003), 'L vocalisation as a natural phenomenon', *Essex Research Reports in Linguistics*, 44, 1–37.

—. (2007), 'L-vocalisation as a natural phenomenon: explorations in sociophonology', *Language Science*, 29, 294–315.

Kamata, M. (2006), 'A sociophonetic study of the DRESS, TRAP and STRUT vowels in London English', Leeds Working Papers in Linguistics, Vol. 11.

Kerswill, P. (2003), 'Dialect levelling and geographical diffusion in British English', in D. Britain and J. Cheshire (eds), *Social Dialectology. In Honour of Peter Trudgill*, pp. 223–243, Amsterdam: Benjamins.

Kerswill, P., Cheshire, J., Fox, S. and Torgersen, E. (2007), 'Linguistic Innovators: The English of Adolescents in London', Full Research Report ESRC End of Award Report, RES-000-23-0680, Swindon: ESRC.

Kerswill, P., Torgersen, E. N. and Fox, S. (2005), 'Endogenous linguistic change in inner-London teenage speech as the generator of innovations: implications for models of innovation, leveling and diffusion', Paper presented at NWAV 34, New York University, October 2005.

—. (2006), 'Innovation in Inner-London teenage speech', Paper presented at NWAV35, Columbus, Ohio State University, November 2006.

—. (2008), 'Reversing "drift": Innovation and diffusion in the London diphthong system', *Language Variation and Change*, 20(3), 451–491.

Kerswill, P. and Williams, A. (1994), 'A new dialect in a new city: children's and adults' speech in Milton Keynes', Final report presented to the Economic and Social Research Council, July 1994.

Kjederqvist, J. (1903), The Dialect of Pewsey (Wiltshire). *Transactions of the Philological Society 1903–1906*, London: Kegan Paul.

Krug, M. (2000), *Emerging English Modals: A Corpus-Based Study of Grammaticalization*, Berlin & New York: Mouton de Gruyter.

Kurath, H. and Lowman, G. S. (1970), *The Dialectal Structure of Southern England: Phonological Evidence*, Publication of the American Dialect Society No. 54, Tuscaloosa: University of Alabama Press.

Labov, W. (1994), *Principles of Linguistic Change*, Vol. 1, *Internal Factors*. Oxford: Blackwell Publishing.

Laver, M. (1995), A study into the use of the variable (ʊ) among pupils from different schools in Hampshire and Suffolk, MS dissertation, University of Essex, Colchester.

Levey, S. (2006), 'Visiting London relatives', *English World-Wide*, 27(1), 45–70.

—. (2007), A sociolinguistic analysis of variation in the speech of some London Preadolescents, Unpublished Ph.D. thesis, London: Department of Linguistics, Queen Mary, University of London.

MacMahon, A. M. S. (1994), *Understanding Language Change*, Cambridge: Cambridge University Press.

Mathisen, A. G. (1999), 'Sandwell, West Midlands: ambiguous perspectives on gender patterns and models of change', in P. Foulkes and G. Docherty (eds), *Urban Voices: Accent Studies in the British Isles*, pp. 107–123, London: Arnold.

Matthews, W. (1938[1972]), *Cockney Past and Present: A Short History of the Dialect of London*, 2nd ed., London/Boston: Routledge and Kegan Paul.

Meuter, A. (2002), L-vocalisation and labiodental variants of /r/ in the speech of Colchester Primary School children – the Acquisition of a Sound Change? MA dissertation, University of Essex, Colchester.

Mugglestone, L. (2003), *Talking Proper: The Rise of Accent as Social Symbol*, Oxford: Clarendon Press.

Orton, H. and Wakelin, M. F. (1967), *The Survey of English Dialects*, Vol. 4, The Southern Counties, Leeds: Arnold.

Pointner, F. E. (1996), *Cockney Glottalling: A Study on the Phonetics of Contemporary London Speech*, Essen: Verlag die Blaue Eule.

Poplack, S. and Tagliamonte, S. (1996), 'The grammaticization of *gonna* in five varieties of English: A cross-linguistic comparison', Paper presented at *25th Conference on New Ways of Analyzing Variation*, University of Nevada, October 1996.

Przedlacka, J. (2001), 'Estuary English and RP: some recent findings', *Studia Anglica Posnaniensia*, 36, 35–50.

—. (2002), *Estuary English? A Sociophonetic Study of Teenage Speech in the Home Counties*, Frankfurt am Main: Peter Lang.

Rosewarne, D. (1984), 'Estuary English', *The Times Educational Supplement*, 19 October 1984.

—. (1994), 'Estuary English: tomorrow's RP?', *English Today*, 37, 3–8.

Ryfa, J. (2003), Estuary English: a controversial issue?, Post-graduate diploma paper, Poznan: Adam Mickiewicz University, <http://www.universalteacher.org.uk/lang/joanna-ryfa-estuary.pdf>.

Ryfa, J. (2005), Chavs and Grungers: The creation of distinct speech styles by two hostile communities of practice in Colchester, Essex, M.A. dissertation, University of Essex, Colchester. <http://sociolinguistics.w.interia.pl/PDF/Joanna_Ryfa_MA_Essex.pdf>.

Schmid, C. (1999), Estuary English – a socio-phonological description into a new accent in the Southeast of England, M.A. dissertation, University of Vienna, Vienna. <http://www.phon.ucl.ac.uk/home/estuary/schmid.pdf>.

Sivertsen, E. (1960), *Cockney Phonology*, Oslo: Oslo University Press; New York: Humanities Press.

Spero, M. (1996), L vocalisation in South-Eastern Britain, M.A. dissertation, University of Essex, Colchester.

Stenström, A-B., Andersen, G. and Hasund, I. (2002), *Trends in Teenage Talk. Corpus Compilation, Analysis and Findings* (Studies in Corpus Linguistics 8), Amsterdam: John Benjamins.

Tollfree, L. (1999), 'South East London English: discrete versus continuous modelling of consonantal reduction', in P. Foulkes and G. Docherty (eds), *Urban Voices: Accent Studies in the British Isles*, pp. 163–184, London: Arnold.

Torgersen, E. N. (1997), Some phonological innovations in Southeastern British English, MA dissertation, University of Bergen, Bergen.

—. (2002), 'Phonological distribution of the FOOT vowel, /ʊ/, in young people's speech in south-eastern British English', *Reading Working Papers in Linguistics*, 6, 25–38.

—. (2006), 'Innovation in Inner-London teenage speech', EAP lecture 2, September 2006.

Torgersen, E. N. and Kerswill, P. (2004), 'Internal and external motivation in phonetic change: dialect leveling outcomes for an English vowel shift', *Journal of Sociolinguistics*, 8, 23–53.

Torgersen, E. N., Kerswill, P. and Fox, S. (2006), 'Ethnicity as a source of changes in the London vowel system', in F. Hinskens (ed.), *Papers from the Third International Conference on Language Variation in Europe*, Amsterdam, June 2005.

Trudgill, P. (1986), *Dialects in Contact*, Oxford: Basil Blackwell.

—. (1990), *The Dialects of England*, Oxford: Blackwell Publishing.

—. (1999), 'Norwich: endogenous and exogenous linguistic changes', in P. Foulkes and G. Docherty (eds), *Urban Voices: Accent Studies in the British Isles*, pp. 124–140, London: Arnold.

—. (2001), *Sociolinguistic Variation and Change*, Washington, DC: Georgetown University Press.

—. (2004), *New Dialect Formation: The Inevitability of Colonial Englishes*, Edinburgh: Edinburgh University Press.

Watts, E. (2006), Mobility-induced dialect contact: A sociolinguistic investigation of speech variation in Wilmslow, Cheshire, Ph.D. thesis, University of Essex, Colchester.

Wells, J. C. (1982), *Accents of English*, Cambridge: Cambridge University Press.

—. (1997), 'What is Estuary English?', *English Teaching Professional*, 3, 46–47.

Williams, A. and Kerswill, P. (1999), 'Dialect levelling: change and continuity in Milton Keynes, Reading and Hull', in P. Foulkes and G. Docherty (eds), *Urban Voices: Accent Studies in the British Isles*, pp. 141–162, London: Arnold.

Wright, J. (1905), *The English Dialect Grammar*, Oxford: Henry Frowde.

Wright, P. (1981), *Cockney Dialect and Slang*, London: Batsford.

Yorkshire

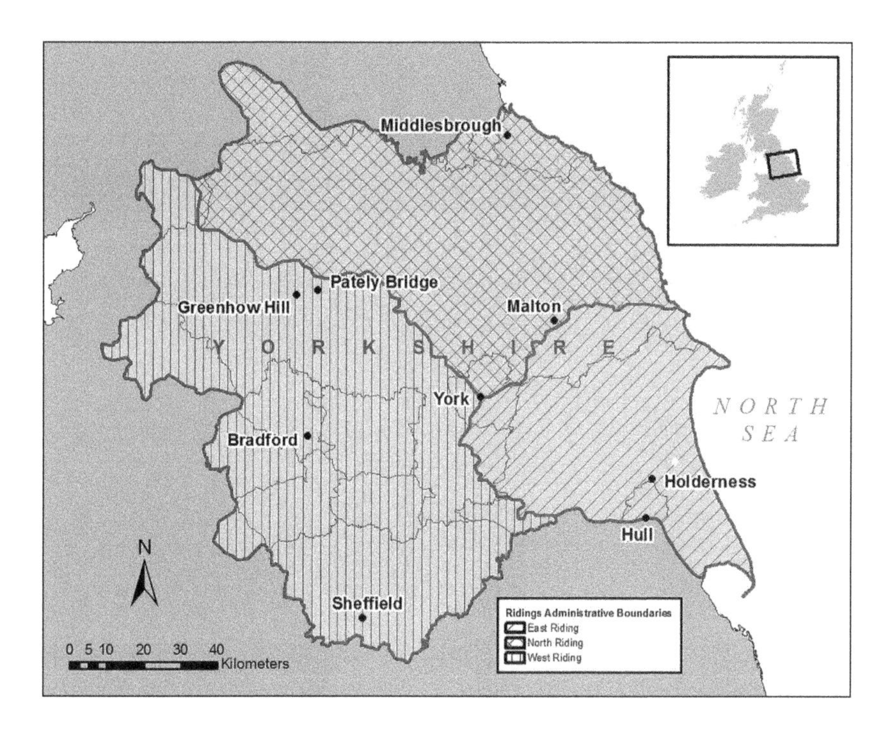
Middlesbrough
Pately Bridge
Greenhow Hill
Malton
Y O R K S H I R E
York
NORTH SEA
Bradford
Holderness
Hull
N
Sheffield
Ridings Administrative Boundaries
East Riding
North Riding
West Riding
0 5 10 20 30 40
Kilometers

Chapter 3

Yorkshire English

Barry J. H. Rawling

Dialectically English may be viewed as falling into four categories: urban, rural, modern and traditional. The 'traditional' dialects[1] offer a greater diversity and richness than their modern counterparts. For this reason, the main focus in this chapter is traditional Yorkshire English. Stanley Ellis (1992: 14) refers to the 'great dialectal gulf that separates Yorkshiremen in the North and East Ridings from the more industrial West Riding'. It is because of this linguistic dichotomy that the dialects are discussed below in terms of these ancient divisions rather than those of the present-day administrative areas (i.e. North Yorkshire, South Yorkshire, etc.). Accordingly, for the purposes of this chapter, locations falling outside the present borders of Yorkshire, as a result of the 1974 reorganization of Local Government, are regarded as still being part of the county. For example, although Middlesbrough is located in present-day Cleveland, it is treated as still being part of the North Riding. Additionally, the conventions of the Yorkshire Dialect Society are employed. Thus the North, East and West Ridings are frequently abbreviated to NR, ER and WR. Where the North and East Ridings are referred to simultaneously the abbreviation employed is NER.

Geographical Position and Demographic Data

Yorkshire, described by Singleton and Rawnsley (1986: 7) as 'the county of broad acres', is the largest county in England. Situated in the north of the country, it borders on Lancashire and Greater Manchester to the west, the North Sea to the east, Derbyshire, Nottinghamshire and Lincolnshire to the south and Cumbria and Durham to the north. Geographically it can be broken down into the western uplands of the Pennines, the Wolds in the east and the North York Moors. In the centre is the great plain (or Vale) of York that runs from the county's northern border to its southern extremities. The other lowlands of note are the Vale of Pickering and the Plain of Holderness. In total, the county covers around 6,000 square miles (15,000 km) and has a population of approximately 4,700,000.[2]

Historical Background

Prior to 1974, when the Local Government Act of 1972 was implemented, the borders of Yorkshire equated approximately to those of the old Danish kingdom of York and the administrative arrangement of the three Ridings had remained virtually undisturbed for over a millennium. The word Riding has its origins in the Old Norse *þriðjungr*, 'a third part' but the history of Yorkshire begins long before the arrival of the Scandinavians.

Although Yorkshire has been inhabited for about 10,000 years, after groups of hunter-gatherers moved into the area during one of the milder inter-glacial periods, for the most part, it is only the advent of the Brittonic Celts, Angles, Scandinavians and Normans that has any relevance to the development of the Yorkshire dialect. It could be said that, to all intents and purposes, the Conquest was the last major incursion to have any great impact on Yorkshire English. However, this is not to say that the people of Yorkshire thereafter lived in a state of isolation.

In the thirteenth century, German labour and expertise was brought in from the continent to assist in mining and the development of England's mineral resources. Strong trading links with Holland from the eleventh century onwards also meant some contact with the Dutch. Furthermore, during the Industrial Revolution, Yorkshiremen were also exposed to other dialects as large numbers of labourers moved into the West Riding from, for example, East Anglia, Lincolnshire and areas where local industries had collapsed. All these events contributed, in one way or another, to the development of Yorkshire English.

Sociocultural and Linguistic Background

Like any language or dialect, Yorkshire English has been shaped by its history and has gradually evolved out of the linguistic diversity that existed among the various settlers, invaders and migrant workers from the time of the Iron Age onwards.

The Britons

The earliest linguistic contribution was lexical and consisted of words taken from the Brittonic language of the Iron Age Britons. Nevertheless, as mentioned in an earlier chapter, such borrowings were minimal. However, in relation to Yorkshire English, Witty (1927: 45) claims that the celebrated sheep scoring numerals (so called because they run from one to twenty) are also a legacy of Yorkshire's British forebears. He reaches this conclusion having found that the Welsh *pimp* and *dic* ('five' and 'ten') bear a close resemblance to the equivalent scoring numerals. The scores vary according to geographical location and the version illustrated in Table 3.1 is associated with Wensleydale.

Although Witty was convinced that the scores are genuinely of Celtic origin and that they have been in existence for over 1500 years, not everyone shares his views.

Barry (1967: 25ff), for example, claims that there is a noticeable lack of evidence to support the existence of the scores prior to 1745 and attempts to find anyone who uses or has used this method of counting have proved unsuccessful. Furthermore, having reviewed all the written material relating to these numbering systems, Barry found that none of the data had been obtained first hand. Thus some doubts are raised concerning the true origins of these methods of counting.

One explanation offered by Barry is that the scores are a corrupted form Welsh. Some landowners had estates both in Yorkshire and in Wales and there is the possibility that, in the post-medieval period, labour moved between the two. It is thus conceivable that the scores may be the result of communication between migratory Welsh and Yorkshire agriculture workers. Alternatively, linguistic contact may have been made following the movement of Welsh labour into the woollen mills of the West Riding and the Yorkshire mines during the eighteenth and nineteenth centuries. Barry argues that this notion of Welsh influence does receive some support from the fact that the scores associated with Pately Bridge (WR) and Greenhow Hill (WR) do display some resemblance to that language.

It is clear that further investigation is required before any firm conclusions can be drawn regarding the linguistic origins of these counting systems. Notwithstanding, it could be argued that, if they are indeed a corrupted form of Welsh, and as that language is a direct descendant of Brittonic, then these strange numerals are indeed a bequest of Yorkshire's British ancestors.

Table 3.1 Sheep scoring numerals found in Wensleydale.

one	*yan*	eleven	*yan-dick*
two	*tean*	twelve	*tean-dick*
three	*tither*	thirteen	*tither-dick*
four	*mither*	fourteen	*mither-dick*
five	*pip*	fifteen	*bumper*
six	*teaser*	sixteen	*yan-a-bum*
seven	*leaser*	seventeen	*tean-a-bum*
eight	*catra*	eighteen	*tither-a-bum*
nine	*horna*	nineteen	*mither-a-bum*
ten	*dick*	twenty	*jigger*

The Angles

The Old English of the Angles was made up of two dialects, Mercian and Northumbrian. Crystal demonstrates some of the differences between the two using the first line of the Lord's Prayer (Table 3.2).

Table 3.2 An illustration of some differences between the two dialects of Old English spoken by the Angles, Crystal (1995:29).

Mercian:	*feder ure þu eart in heofenum*
Northumbrian:	*fader urer ðu art in heofnu(m)*

These two distinct speech forms were separated by a border that ran from the River Mersey in the west across to the River Humber in the east. Northumbrian was spoken to the north of this line and Mercian to the south. Originally, only the Northumbrian dialect was spoken in Yorkshire, but there was an eventual encroachment of Mercian into the southern parts of the county. This is considered to be, in part, the origin of the variations between the speech of the NER and that of the WR.

In contrast to the limited lexical contribution of Brittonic, the Old English (henceforth OE) of the Anglian settlers lives on in Yorkshire dialect not only in its pronunciation but also in its grammar and vocabulary.

The maintenance of OE sounds in Yorkshire English arose out of northern linguistic conservatism, that is, the people of Yorkshire failed to adopt sound changes which occurred during this period in the south of the England. For example, when southern short /o/ in words such as *long, strong* and *wrong* developed from the OE short /a/, the original forms *lang, strang* and *wrang* were retained in Yorkshire and the North. Similarly, the OE short /ɪ/ diphthongized to /ʌɪ/ in, for example, *blind, find* and *climb,* but in the northern areas of the country the pronunciations continued to be [blɪnd, fɪnd, clɪmb].

The preservation of OE grammatical features is still evident in plurals, pronouns and in verbal past tenses. For example, plural forms in *–n* are seen in *shoon* 'shoes' and *een* 'eyes' while OE vowel mutation still exists in dialectal *kye* 'cows' (< OE cȳ). The Yorkshire pronoun *yon* for 'that over there' is derived from *ʒeon* 'that' and, though not confined solely to Yorkshire dialect, the OE third person objective plural *hem* 'them' still survives as *'em* (e.g. *give 'em the money*). The OE ancestry of some dialectal past tenses can be seen in the use of *drunk* (< OE *druncon*) for *drank, begun* (< OE *begunnon*) instead of *began* and *rid* (< OE *ridon*) in place of *rode.*

As can be seen, the link between dialect forms and the OE source words are clearly recognizable. Further examples of this relationship between the traditional vocabulary of Yorkshire and that of OE are given in Table 3.3.

Table 3.3 Further examples of the relationship between the traditional vocabulary of Yorkshire and that of Old English.

Dialect	Standard English	Old English
nobbut	'only'	*nānbūtan 'none but'*
oxter	'armpit'	*ōxta, ōcusta*
greet	'to cry'	*grēotan* 'to cry, to lament'
spurrins	'marriage banns'	*spyrian* 'to inquire, to investigate'
dree	'to endure; to undergo; to suffer; to bear'	*drēȝoan* 'to do, to work, to perform'
clemmed	'thirsty, starving'	*beclemman* 'bind, enclose'
beet	'to repair'	*bētan* 'make good, repair'
baht	'without'	*būtan*

The Scandinavians

Although the Scandinavians may have had some impact on English phonologically (Wakelin 1977: 130) their main contribution to the English language as a whole was in the sphere of word stock and, to some extent, grammar. In terms of the lexicon, a large number of Old Norse (ON) words passed into mainstream English (e.g. *sky, egg, take*) but many now remain only in dialect. Table 3.4 contains examples of common Yorkshire words that owe their existence to the Danish and Norwegian invaders.

However, some words of Scandinavian origin are scattered and do not occur in all parts of Yorkshire. For example, *feal* 'to hide' (< ON *fela*) appears only in some northern areas, while *carr* 'low lying land' (< ON *kjarr*) occurs in a number of locations in the east of the county. *Haver* 'oats' (< ON *hafre*) is peculiar to some western localities. Furthermore, an Old English word was sometimes replaced by its Old Norse equivalent. For instance, ON *taka* 'take' was adopted

Table 3.4 Examples of common Yorkshire words that owe their existence to the Danish and Norwegian invaders.

Dialect	Standard English	Old Norse
ket	'carrion, offal, rubbish'	*kjöt* 'meat, flesh'
gowk	'cuckoo'	*gaukr* 'cuckoo'
how	'hill, hillock'	*haugr* 'mound, caim'
sackless	'foolish, simple, stupid'	*saklauss* 'innocent'
nay	'no'	*nei*
agate	'on the way (e.g. *get agate!* "get on your way!")'	*gata* 'way, street'
clegg	'a horsefly'	*kleggi*
blather	'to chatter inanely'	*blaðra* 'to talk nonsense'
ettle	'to aim, to attempt; to intend'	*etla* 'to think, conjecture'
deg	'to sprinkle'	*döggva* 'to bedew'

in place of OE *niman* and ON *kettil* 'kettle' superseded OE *citil*. In a number of cases, however, the OE word remained only in standard English while the ON version continued to exist in dialect, for example, *slippery* (< OE *slipor*) and *slape* (< ON *sleipr*) and *must* (< OE *mōste*) and *mun* (< ON *mun*).

With regard to grammar, there is one aspect, peculiar to Yorkshire English, which may also be attributable to the influence of the Scandinavians. Trudgill (1999: 107) draws attention to the first person present indicative of the verb *to be* that, in 1950s Yorkshire, took the regular form of *I am* in the eastern part of the county but occurred as the variant *I is* in the west. Wakelin (1977: 135) suggests that the latter has its origins in the Old Norse *ek es* (an older form of *ek er*) 'I am'.

The Normans

The adoption of French vocabulary into the English language in the years following the Norman Conquest has already been discussed in an earlier chapter. However it is notable that a number of these French loans now only exist in dialect (Table 3.5).

The linguistic impact of French on the language as a whole was striking. The century following the arrival of the Normans saw the demise of the purely Germanic Old English and the birth of the hybrid Middle English.

Middle English

The Middle English period was a time of great innovation and change that impacted on all components of the English dialects. In relation to phonology, although some phonemes of medieval Yorkshire English either mutated as a pure vowel or remained unaffected, a number of vowels were transformed into diphthongs (Table 3.6).

However, phonological remodelling was not confined to vowels alone. For example, towards the end of the Middle English period the uvular fricative /χ/

Table 3.5 Examples of French loans which now exist only in dialect.

Dialect	Standard English	Old French
arran	'spider; spider's web'	*araigne*
bar	'except'	*barre (n) barrer (v)*
douce	'gentle, pleasant'	*dous, douce* 'sweet'
fashion	'to bring oneself to do something' e.g. *'e couldn't fashion ti tell 'er t'bad news.*	*fashion, façon* 'to make'
caffle	'to quarrel, to argue'	*caviller* 'to mock, to rail'
urchin	'hedgehog'	*heriçon*
bezzle	'to eat or drink greedily; to squander'	*beziller*, 'to ravage, to lay waste'
spice	'sweets'	*espice*

Table 3.6 Vowels of Yorkshire English that were transformed into diphthongs.

Middle English	Change	Dialectal realization
ē	/i:/	*dead* [di:d], *eye* [i:]
u	none	*pound* [pund]*, *ground* [gɹund]*
ǭ	In some cases /ɪ(:)/ but generally /ɪə/ (NER) and /ʊɪ/ (WR)	*to* [tɪ], *do* [dɪ:] *fool* [fɪəl, fʊɪl] *spoon* [spɪən, spʊɪn]
ǭ	/ʊa/ and /ʊə/ in southern and western parts of Yorkshire	*road* [rʊad, rʊəd] *stone* [stʊan, stʊən]
ā	/ɪə/, /ɪa/ and /ea/ in northern and eastern parts of Yorkshire.	*road* [rɪəd, rɪad, read] *stone* [stɪən, stɪan, stean]
ou	/aʊ/	*grow* [gɹaʊ] *four* [faʊə]

* but [pa:nd] and [gɹa:nd] in southern parts of the WR
(Wakelin 1977: 88ff; Griffiths 1999: 50ff)

was replaced by the labiodental /f/ in some northern dialects (Strang 1974: 167) which may well account for the rendering of *dough* and *plough* as [dʊf/dʊəf] and [plʊf/plɪəf] in some parts of Yorkshire.

It was during this time frame that the phenomenon of definite article reduction (DAR) emerged in the northern dialects. There are a number of theories concerning its history, but the one which, according to Jones (2002: 326ff), has received the most support proposes that DAR has its origins in the progressive assimilation of Middle English *þe*, that is, that the fricative became a plosive when immediately preceded by /t/ or/ð/. The resulting form *te*, which is well attested in a number of Middle English texts, is generally considered to be the initial stage in the development of the reduced article.

Jones (2002: 343), however, referring to the present-day allomorphic variations, cites the orthographic convention of Cawley's (1959) *Yorkshire Dialogue*, a dialect poem, written by George Meriton and published in 1683, depicting various conversations between members of a Yorkshire farming family. He draws attention to the fact that all the variants consist of combinations of three basic sounds [t, θ, ʔ]. He argues that, because of the known cross-linguistic mutations [θ > t] and [t > ʔ], it is these sounds that are the source of DAR.

Nevertheless, he considers that current theories regarding the genesis of DAR are inconclusive and that the subject would benefit from further investigation. The situation with regard to grammar is not so open to question.

During the Middle English period, some nouns (e.g. *ȝer* 'years' and *siþe* 'times') had no plural endings when following a numeral, thus *þre ȝer* 'three years'. A number of genitive forms were similarly uninflected and possessives such as *sister sunes* 'sister's sons' were the norm (Burrow and Turville-Petre 1996: 39ff).

The Survey of English Dialects (SED) highlighted the fact that both these features were still extant in the mid-twentieth century, for example, *five pound* and *my brother boots.* Other instances of grammatical forms from this period are found in the following line from a verse fragment dated 1272 found in York (cited by Leith 1996: 124): *wel qwa sal thir hornes blau* ('alas, who shall these horns blow'). Both *sal* [sal] (which according to the Linguistic Atlas of Late Middle English is a form found predominantly in the North) and the plural demonstrative adjective *thir* [ðɪr] are attested in the SED (IX. 4. 2/3. and IX. 10 5.). The dialectal reflexive suffixes of *-sel, -sen, -seln, -sens etc.* (e.g. *missen* 'myself' *theirsens* 'themselves' etc.) also originate from this period, being derived from ME *seluen* 'self'.

Phonological innovation and grammatical relics are, however, not the only legacy of these times. A host of new words were absorbed into the English dialects some of which are still familiar to the present-day inhabitants of Yorkshire (Table 3.7).

It is also possible that the celebrated cautionary *Ey up*! [ɛɪ ʊp] 'look out!' has its origins in Middle English *ee* or *egh up* 'eye up' (cf. modern Norwegian *se opp,* literally 'see up').

German and Dutch

Reference has been made to the fact that, historically, the people of Yorkshire were exposed to both German and Dutch through the import of labour from, and trade with, the European continent. German is believed to be the source of a number of coal-mining terms like, for example, *toadstone* that is used to refer to a fossilized object and which is possibly derived from *todtes gestein* 'dead stone'. Similarly, *loch,* an unfilled cavity in a vein, is supposed to have its origins in *loch* 'hole'. A steel bucket, used during the process of sinking a shaft, is called a *kibble* and is said to be an Anglicized form of *kübel* 'bucket'. Middle Dutch is the source of words like *clomp* (< *clumpe* 'a wooden shoe'), meaning to 'tread heavily' or 'walk noisily' and *groop* (< *groepe*) denoting a 'drain'. *Korf* 'basket' has given us *corve* or *corf,* a container that is used for keeping live fish or for moving coal in the mines.

Table 3.7 The new words absorbed into the English dialects and which are familiar to the present-day inhabitants of Yorkshire.

Dialect	Standard English	Middle English
clout	'blow'	*cloute*
morn	'morning'	*mor(o)wen*
close	'field'	*clos*
yond	'that person'	*ȝond*
childer	'children'	*childer*
lad	'boy, youth'	*ladde* 'fellow'
mowdiwarp	'mole'	*molde-warpe* 'earth-thrower'
ower	'over'	*ower, ouer*

Modern English

The late eighteenth century saw the development of some phonological characteristics that today distinguish the northern dialects from their southern counterparts. According to Wales (2002: 49) it became fashionable in London society to lengthen /a/ to /ɑ:/ in words such as *path, fast* and *laugh.* Similarly /ʊ/ was centralized to /ʌ/ in, for example, *cup, but* and *rub.* Wales suggests that the north retained the original phonemes of /a/ and /ʊ/ because large centres of population in which these fashionable pronunciations may have been adopted did not exist. Barber (1993: 193) draws attention to a further innovation that materialized around 1800, that is, the diphthongization of the vowel [e] in words such as *dame* and *bake* to /eɪ/. This transformation also failed to completely take root in Yorkshire and the original monophthong can be heard to this day.

The Linguistic Description of the Components of Yorkshire English

Much of the following material and some of the examples, particularly in relation to phonology and grammar, are drawn from Upton et al. (1994) and the Survey of English Dialects.

Phonology

The SED records a number of different realizations in relation to vowels, diphthongs and triphthongs, but it is only the more common or contrasting variants that are reviewed here. The properties of some Yorkshire consonants are also explored and an appraisal is made of the occurrence of DAR within the region.

Vowels, diphthongs and triphthongs

The realization of these speech sounds in Yorkshire English is not always consistent and some variation can occur according to geographical location. Table 3.8 contains examples of those vowels that are common across the region.

Some of the main variations of pronunciation are evinced by the phonological differences that exist between the WR and the NER (Table 3.9).

As can be seen, some monophthongs are subject to diphthongization but this process is occasionally reversed with diphthongs and triphthongs being transformed into a single vowel. For example, medial /eɪ/ in words like *take* and *make* is rendered as /ɛ/ [tɛk, mɛk] though in word-final position, can be either /ə/ or /ɪ/. Thus, for instance, *Monday* and *yesterday* might be realized, respectively, as ['mʊndə] and ['jɪstədɪ]. The fact that /ʌɪ/ can occur as /ɪ/ in words such as *blind* and *find* has already been mentioned, but it may also be articulated as /i:/ or even /ɛɪ/. Accordingly words like *tonight, light, fight* and *height* could be pronounced as, for example, [tə 'ni:t, li:t, fɛɪt, ɛɪt]. These combinations, like the vowels mentioned above, are also prone to diversification according to geographical location (Table 3.10).

Table 3.8 Examples of vowels that are common across the region.

RP	Dialect	Examples
/ɑ/	/a/*	grass [gɹas] branch [bɹantʃ]
/ɛ/	/ɪə/	lead [lɪəd] head [ɪəd]
/ɒ/	/a/	wasp [wasp] wrong [ɹaŋ]
/ʌ/	/ʊ/	suck [sʊk] duck [dʊk]
/i/ (word-final)	/ɪ/	city ['sɪtɪ] quarry ['kwɒɹɪ]

* but see Table 3.9 regarding the pronunciation of *afternoon*

Table 3.9 The phonological differences that exist between the West Riding and the North and East Ridings.

RP	WR	NER	Examples
/ɑ/	/a/	/ɛ/	afternoon [aftə 'ʊɪn], [ɛftə 'nɪən]
/ɔ/	/ʊə/	/ɪə/	door [dʊə], [dɪə]
/u:/	/ʊɪ/	/ɪə/	fool [fʊɪl], [fɪəl]
/ə:/	/ə/	/ɒ/	church. [tʃətʃ], [tʃɒtʃ]

Table 3.10 The combinations prone to diversification according to geographical location.

RP	WR	NER	Examples
/əʊ/	/ʊə/	/ɪə/	toes [tʊəz] clothes [klɪəz]
	/ɔɪ/	/ʊə/	coal [kɔɪl] foal [fʊəl]
/aʊ/	/aʊ/ or /a:/*	/u:/	mouse [ma:s] out [u:t]
/ʌɪə/	/ɑ:/*	/aɪə/	fire [fɑ:] tire [taɪə]
/aʊə/	/aʊə/	/ʊə/	flower [flaʊə] hour [ʊə]

* in southern parts of the WR

Consonants

The pronunciation of Yorkshire consonants can also be either uniform across the region or confined to a particular area. For instance, the elision of word final /g/ in words like *fishing, shooting etc.* [ˈfɪʃɪn, ˈʃu:tɪn] and the omission of initial /h/ from such as *hat* [at], *head* [ɪəd], *etc.* are fairly commonplace. Neither is it unusual for intervocalic /t/ to be replaced by /ɹ/, for example, *what about it* [wɒɹ ə ˈbu:t ɪt] and *get off my foot* [gɛɹ ɒf mɪ fʊɪt]. Two exceptions to this commonality of articulation are the pronunciation of /ɹ/ and the devoicing of voiced consonants.

According to Trudgill (1999: 27ff), the sounding of /ɹ/ is partially retained[3] in some eastern areas of the county, for example, when following the /ə:/ vowel as in *bird.* Furthermore, French (1986: 30f) reports that, in spite of the fact that word-final /ɹ/ (e.g. in words such as *better, four* and *star*) has not been pronounced in Standard English for at least three hundred years, it is nevertheless still heard in the speech of the Malton district, notably an area that extends into both the East and North Ridings. He goes on to say that, within this area, there is also a tendency for it to be pronounced by some retired agricultural workers when it precedes a short pause, for example, *after dinner – I went to church* [ˈɛftə dɪnə:ɹ a: wɪənt tə tʃɒtʃ]. French proposes that this signals to the listener that, although the speakers would be hesitating, they nevertheless intended to continue speaking.

On the subject of devoicing, this is associated particularly with the WR[4] and relates to the phenomenon whereby voiced consonants such as *b,g,d,* become *p, k, t,* when they immediately precede a voiceless one. Thus, for example, *dig coal* in WR speech is rendered as [dɪk kɔɪl].

Definite Article Reduction

The reduced form of the definite article is often symbolized in dialect literature as *t'* or *th'* as can be seen from the following extract from *Wuthering Heights*: '*T' maister's down i' t' fowld. Go round by th' end ot' laith, if ye want to spake to him*' (Brontë 1847: 24; cited by Jones, 1998). However, this representation is an oversimplification of the situation. For instance, *t'* has a number of phonetically related allomorphs, for example, [d], [t̥], [ʔ], [ʔt] etc. Also more than one variant, including the standard *the*, occurs in most locations in the county (Jones 1998: 103ff). The question arises as to what triggers the selection of a particular allomorph.

There is a consensus (e.g. Wright 1905, Jones 1998, Barry 1972) that the choice is governed by the phonological environment. Barry (1972: 167ff), for example, found that [t] preceding a vowel is predominant throughout most of Yorkshire and that the pronunciation of *the other* as [tʊðə][5] is similarly a common feature of the dialect. The variant [t] is also the phoneme of choice when the article occurs before an initial consonant, but where that consonant happens to be <t> a glottalized form (e.g. [ʔ] or [tʔ]) is employed instead. Jones (2004: 19) also identifies the use of [ʔ] before initial <l> , <s> , and <r> and draws attention to the fact that, in some areas, the variants [ʔ], [t] and [θ] alternate. The following map summarizes the overall situation with regard to the geographical distribution of the variant allomorphs. Note the zero form in the Holderness region of the East Riding.

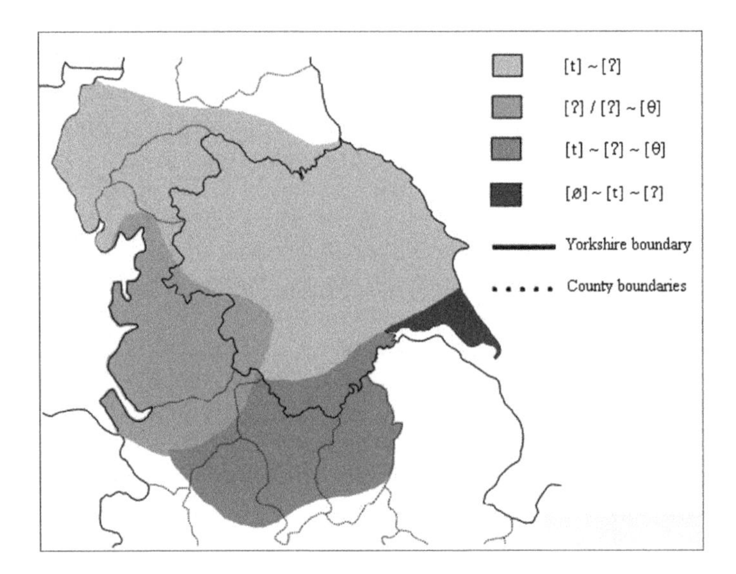

After Jones 2004,1998: 114

Notwithstanding the above, the phonological environment may not be the only determinant of DAR usage. Rupp and Page-Verhoeff (2005: 340) have detected a pattern that suggests that the frequency of the occurrence of DAR increases when reference is made to something:

- in the immediate environment, *Jenny's in* ***t' kitchen***
- directly referred to anaphorically, *he was riding his* ***bike*** *along a path and when he hit a bump he fell off* ***t' bike*** *and hurt his wrist,*
- of which both speaker and hearer have shared knowledge, ***t' post office*** *was robbed this morning.*

Nonetheless, it seems that before any firm conclusions can be formed regarding DAR, much more data are required. The question arises whether any organization or institution would be willing to provide the manpower or funding for a large-scale survey.

Grammar

Some features of Yorkshire grammar, such as unmarked plurality (*ten pound, four week*) and uninflected possessives (*my father farm, our Joe girl* and *two week hard graft* 'two weeks hard work'), have already been examined in relation to their historical origins and therefore, with the exception of reflexive pronouns, are not mentioned below.

Demonstrative adjectives and adverbs

Standard English demonstratives are not always the first choice of speakers of Yorkshire English and *these here* might therefore be employed instead of 'these', *them* in place of 'those', and *yon* for 'that' or 'those'. The last is also employed as a pronoun indicating 'that over there' although if reference is made to 'that person over there' the word *yond* is used instead. The meaning of some adverbs employed as intensifiers may be equally obscure. For instance, 'too' is expressed by *over,* [ɒvə, ɒwə], 'very' is *right* [ɹi:t, ɹɛɪt] and 'really, completely' are *fair.* Thus a Yorkshire person might be heard to say: *this 'ere 'ammer's over big; them cakes are right tasty* and *'e were fair flummoxed* ('he was completely confused').

Pronouns

Unlike Standard English, Yorkshire dialect has retained the second person singular forms of *thou* [ðu:, ða, ta], *thee* [ðɪ], *thy* [ðɪ] and *thine* [ðaɪn, ða:n] for use when conversing with family members or close friends. Some examples are *thou'll cop it when thy father gets home* and *he's got his brass and thou's got thine.* (In these contexts *cop* means 'catch' and *brass* refers to 'money'.) The standard forms *you* and *yours* are employed in all other circumstances.

Archaic forms of the third person singular feminine and the nominative singular neuter pronouns are also still in evidence. Feminine *she,* although generally occurring as [ʃə] or [ʃɪ], is found as *hoo* [u:] (<OE heo) or *shoo* [ʃu:] (<ME s(c)ho) in the south-western area of the WR. Neuter *it* may occur in a contracted form reminiscent of the Early Modern English period; for example, *how is 't* and *'t is three o'clock.* Its employment may also be entirely otiose; for instance, *yon sow, it's picked a litter* ('that sow over there has given birth prematurely').

In Yorkshire, two meanings are attributed to the first person objective plural *us.* In one sense, which is fairly widespread across the English dialects, it translates as 'me', thus *give us a cig* ('give me a cigarette'). In the WR it is employed in place of the possessive *our.* Accordingly, 'we're going to catch our bus' is expressed as *we're bound to catch us bus.* Note the use of *bound to* [ba:n tə] to indicate the future. According to Kellett (1992: 36), the equivalent form in the NE Ridings is *off to,* for example, *she's off to cook my dinner* [ʃəz ɒf tə ku:k mɪ 'dɪnə].

Concerning relative pronouns, there is a greater variety of choice in the dialect than is the case in Standard English. For example, *who* can be replaced by either *what* [wat, wɒt] or *at* [ət] (the latter presumably being a reduced form of 'that') and *that* can be either *what* or *as* [əz]. 'I know the girl who lives in that house over there' might thus be communicated variously as *I knows the lass* ***what /at/ as*** *lives in yon house.*

Reflexives pronouns have already been mentioned in relation to the historical development of their suffixes, but the stem can also be irregular, for example, ***hissen*** 'himself', ***ussels*** 'ourselves' and ***theirsens*** 'themselves'. It is perhaps worth mentioning that the second person singular and plural forms are also employed in imperatives, for example, *sit thissel down* or *oss thissens* ('try').

Prepositions

Yorkshire prepositions are more diverse in form and, occasionally, in meaning compared to those of Standard English. For example, in addition to 'between' there are the options of *atween, atwixt* and *betwixt,* 'above' is *aboon,* 'opposite' is *anenst* and 'behind' is *ahint.* When speakers of Yorkshire English use *while* they do so in the sense of 'till' so visitors to their home might be *staying* ***while*** *Saturday.* 'Of' can be either expressed as *on* or omitted altogether, thus *in front* ***on*** *it* and *plenty brass* 'a lot of money'.

Verbs

A number of verbs carry inflections and have variations not seen in Standard English. The following are examples found in the SED: *thou sees, burglars steals them, they stops in.* Occasionally there is the more unusual *they looken* and *they washen.* Non-standard inflections are also present in the past tense, for example, *he cem* 'came', *he spack* 'spoke' and *I rid* 'rode'. Other forms include *they growed, I creeped, etc* although these variations are fairly common throughout the English dialects. Additionally, both the *–ed* and *–en* inflections are used to form past participles (e.g. *catched, creeped, getten/gotten* and *cutten*) although not all such participles are as readily recognizable, for example, *rocken* 'reached', *brussen* 'burst' and *spacken* 'spoke'.

Yet another interesting feature is that which Upton et al. (1994) term 'anomalous conjugation'. Using the verb *to be,* this is exemplified in the present tense by *I is, thou is, hoo/shoo is,* and *they is* and in the past tense by *I were, shoo were* and *thou/we/they was.* The modals *shall* and *must* are also dialectically variable and the following forms are recorded in the SED, *we sal, I sl, he mun* and *they mun't.* As can be seen from the last example, negatives are generally constructed in the normal way but there are some idiosyncratic forms, for example, *I ammet* 'I am not', *he disn't* 'he does not', *we han't/hannot* 'we have not' and *I'm none* 'I am not'. (Note the use of 'none' [nɪən/nʊən] in place of 'not' [nʊt].) Moreover, double negations such as *we ain't done nowt* and *nobody's had no time to go home* are not infrequent.

Finally, there are a number of phrasal verbs, the meaning of which may not be immediately clear to the uninformed: *give over!* 'stop it!', *let on* 'tell, reveal', *wait on* 'wait', *think on* 'remember', *get shut on* 'get rid of', *take off* 'imitate', *take on* 'make a fuss' and *happen on* 'come across, discover'.

Numerals

Numerals can be expressed in a manner reminiscent of the Middle English period. In effect, the numbers are reversed so that the higher one follows the lower. Consequently, 'twenty four' might be rendered as *four and twenty*.

Lexicon

The word stock of Traditional Yorkshire Dialect is both rich and diverse. Many words are widely used and recognized across the county (e.g. *bairn* 'child', *badly* 'ill', *gob* 'mouth' and *brass* 'money') but others are confined to a geographical location. 'Sweets', for example, are *spice* or *spogs* in the West Riding but *goodies* in the North and East Ridings. In the latter you might be *gannin'* or 'going' somewhere but in the West Riding you would be *bound* [ba:n]. While residents of the West Riding speak of an *arran* ('cobweb'), a *twinge* ('earwig') and being *crammocky* ('awkward, unsteady') those in the North and East Ridings refer to a *musweb*, a *forkin'-robin*, and are *crammely*. On the other hand there are a number of homonyms that could be a source of confusion to those having no knowledge of the dialect. For instance, in the West Riding *cob* means 'to pick clean', *hull* is used to refer to 'a grinding shop', *to paddle* is 'to mess about', *chats* are 'small potatoes' and *weak* means 'cowardly'. In the North and East Ridings, however, these words respectively denote 'to strike', 'a pigsty', 'to walk slowly', 'catkins' and 'foolish'.

The specialist vocabularies of Yorkshire's industries may also be thought of as being a facet of Yorkshire dialect and examples of the nomenclature are given in Table 3.11.

Unfortunately, just as the mechanization of agricultural methods and the depopulation of the rural areas have contributed to the erosion of rural vocabulary, the decline of these industries is likely to be accompanied by further lexical attrition.

Of course vocabulary is more than just single words and Yorkshire English has a wealth of interesting phrases and sayings. For instance, 'a year' is *a twelve month*, 'the autumn' is referred to as *'t' back end*, and 'hello!' may be expressed as *now then!* One can be *as wick as a lop* ('as lively as a flea'), *as deeaf as a yat stowp* ('as deaf as a gate post') or *as common as muck* ('dirt'). If Yorkshire people feel they've been treated unfavourably they might consider that it's *nut jannock* ('not fair') and *reckon nowt to it* ('not think much of it'). More examples of Yorkshire idiom are found in Table 3.12.

Table 3.11 Examples of the nomenclature.

Industry	Dialect word	Standard English
Coal-mining	pog	'miner's work allotment'
	stall	'working place at the coal face'
Quarrying	delf-hole	'quarry'
	ashlar	'deepest working layer'
Steel	codder	'leader of a press forging team'
	skelp	'strips of steel out of which tubing is made'
Wool	beam-mate	'a person working on the other side of a loom'
	doddins	'pieces of wool'
Fishing	chat	'a small haddock'
	dowly	'dull, gloomy or overcast weather'

Table 3.12 More examples of Yorkshire idiom.

Yorkshire Dialect	Standard English
To be 'ard on	'To be fast asleep'
Allus at t' last push	'Always at the last minute'
All of a fullock	'In a big rush'
Livin' ower t'brush	'Living together out of wedlock'
All ower t'shop	'All over the place'
Tek a good likeness	'To be photogenic'
Choose 'ow tha does it	'No matter how you do it'
Nobbut a mention	'Just a small amount'

After Kellett (1992: 64)

Yorkshire English Usage within the Region Today

Although recent evidence suggests that non-standard varieties are beginning to have an increasingly larger influence on the processes of variation and change, for some considerable time it has been Standard English and RP that have impacted on the Yorkshire vernacular. This, coupled with geographical and social mobility, has resulted in both the loss of many traditional characteristics and the general urbanization of speech in the agricultural communities. Large numbers of the rural population now favour the speech habits of local towns and cities over those of the countryside. These 'Mainstream Modern Non-standard Dialects' as Trudgill (1999: 5-6) calls them, are closer to Standard English but still retain certain local features. This is the situation with Yorkshire English.

Despite the extensive erosion of the word stock a number of the long-standing grammatical features, mentioned earlier in an historical context, are still employed. For example, *them* continues to be used in place of *those, what* still assumes the role of *that,* and the omission of plural markings is still in evidence (Cheshire and Edwards 1997). Moreover, Tagliamonte (1998) identifies the ongoing variation between *was* and *were* and, additionally, attests to the continuation of a similar alternation between *come* and *came (*Tagliamonte 2001). Multiple negation and the use of *ain't* still endure (Kerswill 2001: 3) and *thee* and *thou* remain as familiar forms of address (Wales 2002: 64). According to Jones (2004: 18) DAR appears to be secure for the foreseeable future and, from personal experience, the forms *I is, yon, hissen etc.* and possessive *us* remain alive and well. The grammar therefore appears to be relatively stable and, although phonological changes are in progress (see below), it is still possible to distinguish between the accent of the West Riding and that of the North and East Ridings, for example, *about* [ə'ba:t, ə'bu:t], *right* [ɹɛɪt, ɹi:t], *school* [skʊɪl, skɪəl].

Media Use of Yorkshire English

The dialect featured in programmes such as Emmerdale, Heartbeat and Last of the Summer Wine is for the most part a modern urbanized type of speech with only a limited number of traditional features. The same is true of dialect prose such as that found in publications like the Dalesman, a monthly magazine featuring stories about the people and places of Yorkshire; James Herriot's series of books based on his life as a vet in the Yorkshire Dales; and the stories of Gervaise Phinn, an ex-schoolteacher and school inspector, recalling his experiences with Yorkshire school children. Furthermore, the employment of the Yorkshire vernacular in these publications is intended more to elicit a humorous response than to promote its use. The same can be said about newspaper articles. One such, entitled *Ay up doc, am feelin' a bit dowly!,* appeared in the local Gazette and Herald (4 April 2000) which reported the issue of a special 1000 word dictionary to a group of Austrian doctors working in Yorkshire to help them to understand such words as *jiggered* ('tired'), *roaring* ('crying'), *manky* ('infected') and, of course, *dowly* ('poorly, ill').

A more serious approach to Yorkshire English, especially the traditional form, is taken by such organizations as the Yorkshire Dialect Society and the East Riding Dialect Society whose publications examine, discuss and foster the use of traditional features. Additionally, there are internet websites that are devoted to the analysis and study of the dialect. For instance, there is the Yorkshire Dialect website (www.yorkshiredialect.com) and the British Library's sound archive (www.bl.uk/learning/langlit/sounds) that contains more than six hundred sound recordings of various dialects (including that of Yorkshire) drawn from the SED and the Millennium Memory Bank archive.

Current Trends

It has already been noted that Yorkshire grammar is relatively stable in comparison to the traditional word stock. The latter is in a state of attrition owing mainly to changes in agricultural working practices and rural depopulation.[6] This depopulation is the result of increased geographical mobility that, together with social mobility, has not only caused the breakdown of close-knit social networks (essential to the maintenance of traditional dialect forms), but has also brought individuals into contact with speakers of other vernaculars. The result, claims Kerswill (2002: 187f), has been geographical diffusion and dialect levelling,[7] the affects of which are ongoing. The broadcast media may be a vehicle for the first of these processes.

Williams and Kerswill (1999: 162) observe that programmes aimed at the young tend to employ 'an informal and non-standard register'. Moreover, a survey of viewing and listening habits of youngsters aged sixteen and over has revealed that, on average, they spend around fifty percent of their spare time listening to the radio or watching television. As such, they are likely to hear more non-local speech than their own vernacular (Foulkes and Docherty 1999: 15). Because a large number of these programmes emanate from the South, northern youngsters are being exposed to varieties of southern speech that are fast coming to be associated with youth culture and the younger generation (Williams and Kerswill 1999: 162).

As mentioned earlier, such non-standard varieties of speech appear to be replacing RP and Standard English as linguistic models. It is certainly true that the replacement of /t/ by /ʔ/, both word-medially and word-finally (e.g. *butter* [bʊʔə], *what* [wɒʔ]) now appears to be widespread and that the glottalling of the plosives /p/ and /k/ are similarly commonplace. The occurrence of these phonemes has been identified in Sheffield (WR) by Stoddart et al (1999: 73f), in Hull (ER) by Williams and Kerswill (1999: 157) and in Middlebrough (NR) by Llamas (2000: 124ff). Llamas also refers to the phenomenon of glottalization, the realization of /p/, /t/ and /k/ as a double articulation, that is, [ʔp, ʔt, ʔk] or [pʔ, tʔ, kʔ]. This is a prominent feature of Newcastle and Tyneside English that is now being adopted in Middlesbrough. This suggests to Llamas that Middlesbrough English is, to some degree, not only moving away from Standard English but from the Yorkshire vernacular as well.

Other research has revealed even more phonological innovations in progress. For instance, in Bradford (WR) Watt and Tillotson (2001: 296) have identified the fronting of [o] to [ɵ], while in Sheffield Stoddart et al (1999: 77) have observed, inter alia, the apparent transition of [a] to [ɑ:] in words such as *bath* and the replacement of [in] by [ɪŋ] in, for example, participles. The fronting of [ð] and [θ] to [v] and [f] (e.g. *feather* ['fɛvə] and *three* [fɹi:]) is also beginning to emerge in many locations regionally.

The Future of Yorkshire English

So what does the future hold for Yorkshire English? It seems likely that the erosion of the vocabulary will be ongoing under the continuing pressures of the social forces mentioned above. However, it is still possible that individual local words may survive. For example, despite the fact that eighty variants of *left-handed* found in the SED have been replaced by *cack-handed*,[8] a form now well established in Yorkshire, *gawky*, *gocky* and *keggy-handed* are still in active use in the county (Paynter et al., 1997: 12).

There is no doubt that phonological innovations will also continue to materialize, but this has ever been the case. It does not necessarily mean that local distinctions of pronunciation will disappear entirely. Language, after all, is part of an individual's social identity and speaking with a local accent and employing local expressions are ways of relating to, and showing solidarity with, one's peers, neighbourhood, city or region. If Rawnsley (2000: 3; cited by Wales 2002) is correct in claiming that 'the North of England evokes a greater sense of identity than any other region of the country', then the survival of local accents is a strong possibility.

The stability of Yorkshire grammar has already been noted. Nevertheless, much has been made of the impact of educational policy fostering the use of Standard English within our schools and the question arises whether this stability can be maintained. Research by Cheshire and Edwards (1997: 67ff) suggests that the policy of correcting frequently used non-standard speech forms has been largely counterproductive and has resulted in either hypercorrection or in linguistic forms that, as they say, 'could not be attributed to standard English', for example, *Can you please borrow me a pen?* It is their opinion that today's teachers are likely to be no more successful in eradicating the non-standard speech forms than their predecessors.

Overall, based on the above, although it appears that the future of Yorkshire vocabulary is somewhat bleak, it is possible that at least some of the distinctive features of Yorkshire English will persist for some time yet, albeit only in grammar and pronunciation.

Notes

1 Traditional dialects are described by Hughes and Trudgill (1996: 30) as those varieties of English spoken 'in relatively isolated rural areas by certain older speakers'.
2 Estimated figure for 2006 from the UK Office of National Statistics.
3 By 'partial retention' Trudgill means that /ɹ/ is vocalized 'in certain words and positions but not in others'.
4 Devoicing has been found to occur in locations as far away as York and beyond.
5 It seems that a number of SED informants considered *t' other* to be a single word.

[6] Statistics show that, in the second quarter of the nineteenth century, 66% of the population lived in rural areas whereas by the closing decade of the twentieth century only 10% remained. Of these only just over a tenth were employed in agriculture (Kerswill 2001: 7).

[7] Kerswill (2002: 187f) describes geographical diffusion as a process whereby linguistic features progress outwards from influential and densely populated areas and are adopted for various reasons by members of other centres of population. Dialect levelling on the other hand refers to the loss of marked variants, that is, those forms which are uncommon or small in number.

[8] *Cack-handed* was once more likely to be found in the southeast of England.

Bibliography

Barber, C. (1993), *The English Language – A Historical Introduction*, Cambridge: Cambridge University Press.

Barry, M. V. (1967), 'Yorkshire sheep-scoring numerals', in *Transactions of the Yorkshire Dialect Society*, Vol. XII, 67, 21.

—. (1972), 'The morphemic distribution of the definite article in contemporary regional English', in M. F. Wakelin (ed.), *Patterns in the Folk Speech of the British Isles*, pp. 165–181, London: The Athlone Press.

Brontë, E. (1847), *Wuthering Heights*, Penguin Classics Edition, 1994.

Burrow, A. and Turville-Petre, T. (1996), *A Book of Middle English*, 2nd ed, Oxford: Blackwell.

Cawley, A. C. (ed.) (1959), George Meriton's 'A Yorkshire Dialogue, 1683', Yorkshire Dialect Society reprint 2.

Cheshire, J. and Edwards, V. (1997), 'Lessons from a survey of British dialect grammar', in *Links and Letters*, Vol. 5, 1998, 61–73.

Crystal, D. (1995), *The Cambridge Encyclopaedia of the English Language*, Cambridge: Cambridge University Press.

Ellis, S. (1992), '40 Years on: Is dialect dead?', in *Transactions of the Yorkshire Dialect Society*, Vol. XVIII, 92, 6.

Foulkes, P. and Docherty, G. (eds) (1999), *Urban Voices – Accent Studies in the British Isles*, London: Arnold.

French, P. with Miller, S. Cade, V. and Hunt, C. (1986), 'Documenting language change in East Yorkshire', in *Transactions of the Yorkshire Dialect Society*, Vol. XVI, 86, 29.

Griffiths, B. (1999), *North East Dialect: Survey and Word List*, Newcastle upon Tyne: The Centre for Northern Studies, Department of Historical and Critical Studies, University of Northumbria.

Hughes, A. and Trudgill, P. (1996), *English Accents and Dialects*, Third Edition, London: Arnold.

Jones, M. J. (1998), 'The phonology of definite article reduction', in C. Upton and K. Wales (eds), *Dialectal Variation in English: Proceedings of the Harold Orton Centenary Conference 1998*, Vol. XXX, 103–122, Leeds Studies in English.

—. (2002), 'The origin of definite article reduction in northern English dialects: evidence from dialect allomorphy', *English Language and Linguistics*, 6, 325–345.

—. (2004), The phonetics and phonology of definite article reduction in northern English dialects, Unpublished Ph.D. dissertation, University of Cambridge.

Kellett, A. (1992), *Basic Broad Yorkshire,* Revised Edition, Otley: Smith Settle.

Kerswill, P. (2001), 'Mobility, meritocracy and dialect levelling: the fading (and phasing) out of received pronunciation', in P. Rajame (ed.), *British Studies in the New Millennium: Challenge of the Grassroots. Proceedings of the 3rd Tartu Conference of British Studies,* University of Tartu, Estonia, August 2001.

—. (2002), 'Models of linguistic change and diffusion: new evidence form dialect levelling in British English', in *Reading Working Papers in Linguistics,* 6, 187–216.

Kerswill, P. and Williams, A. (2000), 'Mobility versus social class in dialect levelling; evidence from new and old towns in England', in K. Mattheier (ed.), *Dialect and migration in changing Europe,* pp. 1–13, Frankfurt: Peter Lang.

Leith, D. (1996), The origins of English, in D. Graddol, D. Leith and J. Swann. (eds), *English History, Diversity and Change,* New York: Routledge.

Llamas, C. (2000), 'Middlesbrough English: convergent and divergent trends in a "part of Britain with no identity"', in D. Nelson and P. Foulkes (eds), *Leeds Working Papers in Linguistics,* 8, 123–148.

Orton, H. and Halliday, W. J. (1963), *Survey of English Dialects: The Basic Material,* Vol. 1, Parts 1–3, Leeds: Arnold.

Paynter, D., Upton, C. and Widdowson, J. D. A. (1997), *Yorkshire Words Today: A Glossary of Regional Dialect,* Sheffield: The Yorkshire Dialect Society, The National Centre for English Cultural Tradition and The University of Sheffield.

Rawnsley, S. (2000), 'Constructing "The North": space and sense of place', in N. Kirk (ed.), *Northern Identities,* pp. 3–22, Aldershot: Ashgate.

Rupp, L. and Page-Verhoeff, J. S. (2005), 'Pragmatic and historical aspects of definite article reduction in northern English dialects', *English World-Wide,* 26, 325–346.

Singleton, F. B. and Rawnsley, S. R. (1986), *A History of Yorkshire,* Chichester: Phillimore and Co. Ltd.

Stoddart, J., Upton, C. and Widdowson, J. D. A. (1999), 'Sheffield dialect in the 1990s: revisiting the concept of NORMs', in *Urban Voices – Accent Studies in the British Isles,* pp. 72–89, London: Arnold.

Strang, B. (1974), *A History of English,* London: Methuen and Co Ltd.

Sykes, D. R. (1955) 'Dialect in the Quarries at Crosland Hill, near Huddersfield, in the West Riding', in *Transactions of the Yorkshire Dialect Society,* Vol. IX, 54, 26.

Tagliamonte, S. (1998), 'Was/were variation across the generations: view from the city of York', *Language Variation and Change,* Vol. 10, 2, pp. 153–191, Cambridge University Press (Printed in USA).

—. (2001), 'Come/came variation in English dialects', *American Speech,* 76(1), 42–61.

Trudgill, P. (1999), *The Dialects of England,* 2nd ed, Oxford: Blackwell.

Upton, C., Parry, D. and Widdowson, J. D. A. (1994), *Survey of English Dialects: The Dictionary and the Grammar,* London: Routledge.

Wakelin, M. F. (1977), *English Dialects: An Introduction,* Revised Edition, London: The Athlone Press, University of London.

Wales, K. (2002), 'A Cultural History of Northern English (from 1700)', in R. Watts and P. Trudgill (eds), *Alternative Histories of English.* London: Routledge.

Watt, D. and Tillotson, A. (2001), 'A spectrograph analysis of vowel fronting in Bradford English', *English World-Wide*, 22(2), 269–302.

Widdowson, J. D. A. (1966) 'The Dialect of Filey – A Selection of Terms Concerning Fishing and the Sea', in *Transactions of the Yorkshire Dialect Society*, Vol. XII, 66, 28.

Williams, A. and Kerswill, P. (1999), 'Dialect levelling: change and continuity in Milton Keynes, Reading and Hull', in P. Foulkes and G. Docherty (eds), *Urban Voices – Accent Studies in the British Isles*, pp. 141–162, London: Arnold.

Witty, J. R. (1927), 'Sheep and sheep-scoring', in *Transactions of the Yorkshire Dialect Society*, Vol. IV, 28, 41.

Wright, J. (1905), *English dialect Grammar*, Oxford: Oxford University Press.

North East

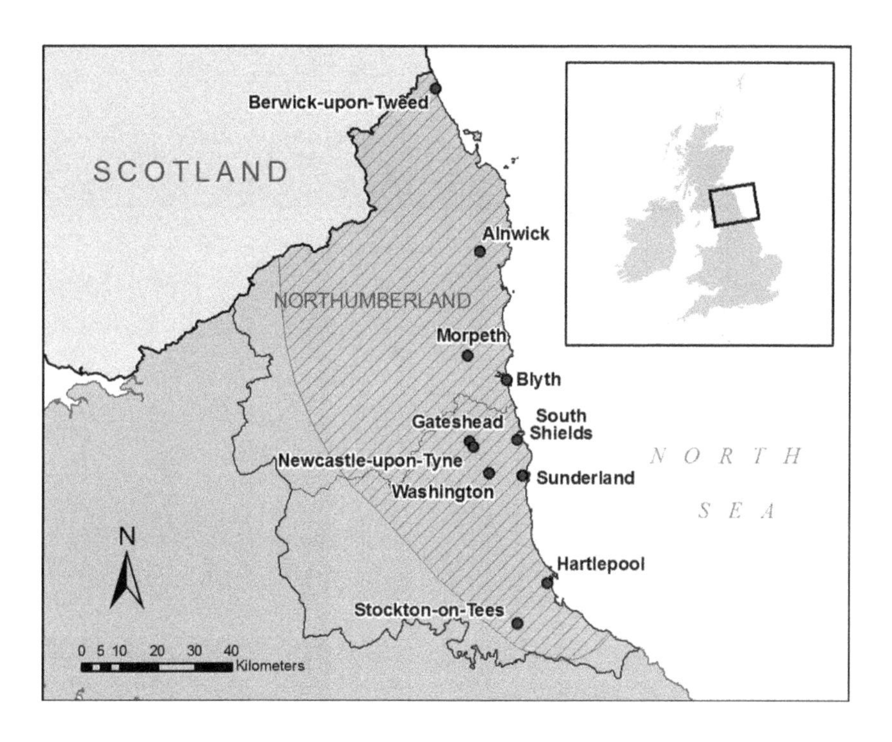

Berwick-upon-Tweed
SCOTLAND
Alnwick
NORTHUMBERLAND
Morpeth
Blyth
South Shields
Gateshead
Newcastle-upon-Tyne
Washington
Sunderland
NORTH SEA
Hartlepool
Stockton-on-Tees
N
0 5 10 20 30 40
Kilometers

Chapter 4

North East Dialect

The late Bill Griffiths

Introduction

Though the concept of a North East region is a twentieth-century one, there are good reasons for studying the language east of the Pennines, from the Tweed to the Tees, as a unity from the late seventeenth century, not least the homogenizing influence of the Great North Coalfield as it became fully developed. As a segment of the east coast, the sparsely settled and historically turbulent lands of North Northumberland, and in the south the non-mining belt between Trimdon/Sedgefield and the Tees, have helped delineate the region. Industry served to make a single North East of the two historical counties of Northumberland and Durham, and the concentration of population in conurbations like Tyneside and Wearside acted to promote dialect rather than erode it.

There is, still, a sense of the value of dialect in the region that continues to resist the pressures and inroads of (inter)national usage, at both a popular and an informed level . The publications of Harker (1972, 1985) have brought a wealth of nineteenth-century dialect poetry into the public domain, which would otherwise have remained difficult to access in out-of-print books and manuscripts. Websites from the BBC and British Library use sound excerpts to demonstrate regional dialects, and attest a renewed interest in and respect for the local language. At the immediate level, interesting personal word lists have been published that illuminate less well-known aspects of the region's dialect, for example, Teward (2003) on Teesdale.

Academic interest has tended to sideline lexis, perhaps in the belief that the great *English Dialect Dictionary (EDD; Wright* 1898–1905) was the final word in that line; recent studies (e.g. at Newcastle University, Aberdeen University) have concentrated on the phonology of the dialect, where traditional /u/, short front /a/ and diphthongized long /a/ persist, or can be studied as changing, along with variations in the glottal stop for intervocalic /t/. The rather beautiful intonation and its rising emphasis remain distinctive, and with the vowel sounds provides immediate identity for the North East voice,[1] along with a handful of easily recognized words like 'canny' and 'dunch' – but this apparent continuity belies a state of flux (and largely loss) in the traditional vocabulary of the region.

A simple survey carried out in 2001 by the Durham & Tyneside Dialect Group provided a check view of the state of the lexis. A much wider variety of dialect was found to be recollected, if not regularly used, than is supposed by a largely indifferent media; strategies of survival became clear, like doubling up to explain meaning (e.g. *guissie-pig, hacky-dorty, mell-hammer*); other traditional terms were adapted to new contexts (e.g. *dut* from 'bowler hat' to 'ski hat'; *sneck* from an old-fashioned 'latch' to the latch on a 'Yale' lock); other words that sounded well were used indiscriminately to represent violence: 'I'll ploat yeh', 'I'll stot yeh' and the like. Many beautiful (and useful) words did not make it, for example, *sark* (shirt), *ettle* (to intend), *lowse* (to release).

A significant number of neologisms emerged (e.g. *cuddy* 'chewing gum', *croggy*, 'the share of a bike-ride'); and subtle differences in local usage were reported, probably dating from the twentieth century, for example, the synonyms *bait* (traditional), *tommy* (Hartlepool), *scran* (general) for 'food' or *forkytail* (Tyneside) and *twitchybell* (East Durham) for 'an earwig'. One strangely antique survival was the distinction between *spelk* and *spell* (both meaning 'splinter'): the former from Old English (*spelca*) is standard in Co.Durham, the latter from Old Norse (*spella*), on Teesside, a rare example of preference according to ancient settlement patterns.

Language, of course, is not a genetic feature but a cultural one; and despite the legend of an Anglian Northumberland, free of Viking intrusion, dialect north of the Tyne is just as likely to contain Old Norse-based words as dialect south of the Tyne. The count of ON-based words is slightly higher in Upper Teesdale, but whether from conservatism of language or early Viking influence is not clear.

The Emergence of the Modern North East Dialect

The roots of this modern dialect lie in the later seventeenth century, when a concept of dialect emerged as a reaction to the rising strength of 'National' English and political centralization of London. Bishop Kennet's manuscript dictionary of dialect words of the 1690s first distinguishes a few words as proper to Co.Durham, where previous commentators had been satisfied with the label 'Northern'. One of the first 'edited' dialect texts as such is George Meriton's (1683) *A Yorkshire dialogue*, which includes a 'clavis' or lexical key, showing an awareness of a new audience, possibly neither local nor dialect-apt.

The seventeenth century also marks the rise of the coal trade and the economic prominence of Newcastle-upon-Tyne. It was a Newcastle schoolmaster, Edward Chicken, who composed the first text with samples of miners' speech in dialect included, ca. 1720. His *Collier's Wedding* features the pitman Tom, his intended bride, Jenny, and her mother. Direct speech of the pitman and mother is given in dialect form, though Jenny's is given in a more modest standard English (like the pure rhyming couplets of the body of the poem). Here, Jenny's mother expresses her irritation at being visited late at night by Tom, who has come to ask for Jenny's hand in marriage:

Lass, ***whe's*** that with ye? Whe shou'd it be?	who
Sit still, says *Tom*, 'tis none but me;	
I came to have a little ***Clash***:	chat
Hout Lad, get Hame, ye're nought but ***Fash***:	trouble
My Pipe's just out, then we'll to Bed;	
So, *Jenny*, come and loose my ***Head***,	hair
And get some Coals, and mend the Fire,	
And lay my ***Cods*** a little higher;	cushions
And, *Tom*, be sure that ye get Hame,	
And give my Service to your ***Dame***:	mother
De'il scratch your Arse, what brought you here;	
Ye've kept our Daughter up I fear.	
Tom rose and came where *Bessy* sat,	
And fann'd the Fire with his Hat;	
Play'd with her Pipe till it was broke,	
And grinn'd and laugh'd, and then he spoke:	
Your *Jenny* is my Heart's Delight;	
De'il rive their Sark gangs Hame to Night:	Devil rip their shirt
I'll have her, had she not a Smock . . .	

(*The Collier's Wedding*, 2nd ed., Newcastle 1764)

The implication of Chicken's satire is that the educated citizens of Newcastle were at one with 'civilised' English and regarded the talk of pitmen and their families, settling e.g. at Benwell just west of Newcastle, as curious, unmetropolitan and impolite. Where did the pitmen come from? The wedding customs described by Chicken are noted elsewhere as common to both Northumberland and Durham,[2] so the answer seems to be this is native or country talk coming to town.

They bring non-standard words from Old English (*hame*), Old Norse (*cod, rive, sark*) and French (*fash, dame*) in a mix that would surely go back to Middle English North. From OE, the North East arguably retained some features of Old Northumbrian vocabulary such as *bairn* for 'child' and *gang* for 'go' (though both these are confirmed in their role by similar forms in Old Norse); *snook* for headland may well be another example, and *piner* for 'sharp wind'. Whether the North East received a special input from Medieval French is hard to assess – there being so few (English) texts that can be specifically attributed to the area from that time. *Wulliemot* for 'guillemot', and the high frequency of the use of *warrant* as a verb may suggest a special impact in the early years of the Conquest, as opposed to later French forms in /gu-/. The fourteenth century was a turbulent time in the border counties, and the fondness for up-to-date French in Southern England may have had less impact further north. There is also less room for the adoption of words from Latin and Greek that typify the South in the sixteenth century and later (thus the North East preferred *likeness* to 'photograph', *wheezes* to 'bronchitis', etc.). While there is a special inheritance from Old Norse across the whole North of England, the pattern that begins to mark out the North East is a regional one of word retention, word preference (i.e. high frequency use) and word rejection – in comparison to the South – and ultimately to other sections of the North.

The Loan Word Factor

Another and a major factor is the presence of new (loan) words that begin to set NE dialect increasingly apart by ca. 1800. What is 'new' is hard to assess, with few if any local texts for the sixteenth and seventeenth centuries (except the Border Ballads, whose exact location and date, however, are elusive, and whose descent and editing may obscure original features). A considerable body of printed dialect songs exists from Newcastle from the 1790s on, and it is these that give the best evidence of the special word use of the North East, along with a number of early dictionaries – notably Bell (1815) and Brockett (1829). Two dominant sources for loans are Scots (Lowland) and Dutch, though both assertions need clarification.

Some Scots words in the NE dialect could arguably go back to a common OE origin; but non-English forms like *eggtaggle* ('triviality') and *howdy* ('midwife') are unlikely to qualify. Other examples, not readily attested in the NE before ca.1820, are similarly suspect. The process of loan from Scots does not seem to be a gradual drifting of words from North to South, for there was relatively little reason for Scotsmen to settle in the borderlands, but many chances for direct employment on Tyneside. Scots are noted as prominent among the keelmen working on the Tyne, and Scots surnames are common to this day in North East mining villages.

Putative loan-words from Dutch might similarly be attributed to common Germanic origin. One criterion is again, non-appearance in pre-1800 texts and word lists. The justification lies in the frequent contacts between Newcastle and Amsterdam in the coal trade; and between the North East and Holland in general regarding North Sea fishing (including whaling?), and perhaps smuggling (itself a word from Dutch).

Dutch may be the earlier of the two influences, from the late medieval period onwards – consistent with the idea of a special maritime culture across the North Sea.

There was a significant export trade in the later Middle Ages from Newcastle to the ports of Flanders, Holland, Zeeland, France, and the Baltic, where coal served to dry madder and smoke fish, as well as to burn lime and work iron (Hatcher 1993:26)

We will examine that influence first ...

Dutch

FOZY - of dry soft unsound vegetables
1821, cf. Du. *voos*, Norw. *fos* 'spongey'

GROVE/GROOVE – 'mine or pit'
A seventeenth-century introduction, possibly linked to OE *grafan* 'to dig', but compare early Mod.Du. *groeve* 'excavation'

HOY – 'to throw'

In the NE *hoy* means 'to throw, lob, chuck'. There are problems in tracing this to the Scots word *hoy* 'to shout hoy! to urge on, incite, drive forward with cries' 1786, 1787 etc., which is only used with a person as direct object; the meaning 'to heave up (a heavy object), to throw or toss up' is only recorded in Scots 1923, 1937, 1957 and likely derived from the NE verb.

Another possibility is a back formation from *hoise* as a form of *hoist* (thus Border Ballads C15–16), 'they hoysed their sails' and elsewhere[3] but the simplest source is the Dutch word *gooien*, which in pronunciation and meaning is close to the NE verb.

Its poor record in NE texts is an added indicator of a new formation: first noted in Brockett (1829) (to heave or throw, as a stone), and common in modern usage (e.g. *hoyin-oot* for 'closing time in a pub'!), it is not found in the Metrical Cuthbert (where *cast* is the standard Northern verb), Ray (1674), Meriton (1683), Kennet (1690s), Grose (1787), Wilson (1790s) (Gateshead), Bailey (1810), Bell (1815), Luckley (1870s) (Alnwick).

HARRING – 'herring'
Harring – Tyneside ca.1800. OE. *hæ'ring, héring* gives rise to the standard form *herring*, but Tyneside *harring* could well be influenced by MDu *harinc*, Du *haring*.

MIZZLE – 'to drizzle'
First recorded in English in 1483, likely derived from Du dialect *miezelen*

PEA-JACKET – 'sailor's coat'
First noted 1741 – compare Du *pij-jakker.*

PLOAT – 'to pluck'
First recorded in 1825 (Brockett, Newcastle) – compare Flem. and Du. *ploten* 'to pluck'.

STOT 'to bounce'

This is not an OE word, though *stot* meaning 'young bullock or steer' from ON is well attested in the North East, for example, Raine MS XXXX, Ray 1674, Grose 1787, Dinsdale 1849 (mid-Tees), Atkinson 1868 (Cleveland), etc.

In the *Scottish National Dictionary* the first occurrences (intrans.) are 1782, 1790, 1792 etc., (trans.) 1885 etc. It is not found in Burns' poems however.

In the NE *stot* is not present in the Border Ballads (Bewick 1790; **(Tyne)** Wilson 1790; Bell 1815); its first appearance is in Brockett (1829) (trans and intrans.).

The possible key to this pattern is the Dutch verb *stoten* (Compare the usage in South Africa, where 'the small antelope with its characteristic bounding run (known as pronking or stotting) is standard fare'). (*Guardian* 2006).

Introduction from Dutch to Scots and the NE in the late eighteenth century, or to Scots and thence to NE in the early nineteenth century is a feasible profile.[4]

(i) Also possibly from Dutch, but attested in England before the modern period are:

Blare ('to cry') ca.1440 – compare MDu *blaren*

Bully ('friend, mate') C16 – compare Du. *boel* (lover, brother)

Corf / corve ('basket') 1391 – compare MDu. korf, ON. korfr

Cracket – 1635, 1643. This and the parallel form *cricket* do not appear in English before the seventeenth century. A *krakk* or 'stool' is recorded in Norwegian, and so possibly in ON; but a more modern link would be with Du (Low German) *kruk-stool,* 'a movable seat'.

Cranky – 'tottering' – likely from Du *krengd,* of a ship laid or lying over on its side.[5]

Cranky ('ill') – C16 as vagabonds' cant – but ultimately from Du. or Ger. *krank* sick, ill; *Cranky* – jolly – this variant, found in Brockett and the *EDD,* is unaccounted for, and appears in contrast to the above.

Dike (hedge, earth or stone wall) 1450s – OE. *díc* 'ditch' seems to retain the original meaning of an excavation and therefore a watercourse, pond. By extension, the meaning 'wall formed by throwing up earth' emerges in OFr, MDu, Dan, but probably comes into English from Dutch *dijk* 'dam'. That in Yorkshire *dike* equals 'a pond or ditch' and in Durham 'hedge, stone wall' argues against an ON origin for the word in the sense of 'wall'.

Elsin ('awl'), ca.1440 – apparently from MDu. *elssene* (later *elzen(e),* mod.Du. *els*):

Geck – 'to scorn', 1583. compare MDu *ghecken,* Du *gekken.*

Haar – 'mist, fine rain', 1662 – compare MDu. *hare* (Du. *haere*) keen cold wind.

Hack ('pick-like tool') – 'a heavy agricultural tool' *Michigan University Dictionary* (1333), either as cognate with MHG. and Ger. *hacke,* 'mattock, hoe', or introduced from Du. *hak* 'hoe, mattock'. The word is not found in OE., nor in ON.

Kit ('tub'), 1362, apparently from MDu. *kitte* 'a wooden vessel made of hooped staves' (Du. *kit* tankard).

(*ii*) Less certain are:

Cavil ('a lot', in apportioning by chance) – Du *kavel* ('lot'), but also ON *kafli* ('piece, bit'). Its early use in the *Cursor Mundi* ca. 1300 ('þan kest þai cauel' line 18907) suggests an early derivation from ON, perhaps reinforced by comparison with the Dutch.

Clemmed – 'compressed' – Du *klemmen* to pinch, cramp, compress, but also OE compound form *beclemman* 'to restrain, confine, shut in'. That the simplex form of the verb does not appear in English before 1600 may suggest Dutch influence.

Bunch – 'to kick'. The relatively late recording of *bunch* (1362 cf. *punch* 1382) is suspicious, as too late to be OE palatalization of /c/ from some common Germanic root – could it simply be a version of *punch,* for which some origin in French can be deduced? *OED* examples of *bunch* 'to kick' are centred on the North East, but it is doubtful if Du. *bonken* 'to beat, thrash', can be the local source, though it may have influenced usage.

It may reinforce the assumption of loan to note that a fair proportion of the words tested above relate to maritime and mining topics, that is, areas of developing technology where borrowing might be expected. Even everyday words with an early assumed loan date add weight to the idea of the existence of a cross-North Sea culture, which again would be significant for the North East.

Scots

CANNY – 'admirable', etc.

This is reasonably derived from the OE root *cunnan* 'to know how to', with cognate forms in ON – cf. Norw. *kunnig* 'knowing, skilful'. Unlike the Southern meaning of real/normal (implicit in *uncanny*), the Scots adjective has a large range of meanings, for example, 'pleasant' 1733, 'gentle, quiet, steady' 1762; the word itself goes back in Scots to at least 1592. These provide a reasonable origin for the NE sense of 'moderate, careful, admirable', for example, 'it's a canny way'. It is one of a number of forms in –/y/ that are common in NE and Scots, for example, *Santy* for Santa, *footy* for football, *slippy* rather than slippery, etc.

HOWDIE – 'midwife'

This is not an OE form, but is common in Scots where *howdie* 'midwife' is recorded in 1725, 1786, 1815, etc. It might be a 'cant or nick-name', devised in Edinburgh (suggested by the *Scottish National Dictionary*), then popularized by Burns. Its first recorded use in NE is in Bewick's tale 'The howdy and the upgetting' (published in 1850 but referring back to the 1790s). It became a common NE term for 'midwife'.

DIVVENT – 'don't'/DIV – 'do'

A likely source is Scots, where 'Diven ye ken' is noted, Banffshire 1872, 'Div I ken . . .?' in Walter Scott's poem (1816) 'O Mortality'. Another early example is its use in George MacDonald's (1882) novel *Castle Warlock* which in its dialect surely looks back to MacDonald's own childhood in the Aberdeen area (1830s). It is not found in Burns' poems. As to origin, the *Scottish National Dictionary* says, 'the form *div* is used emphatically . . . the /v/ is due to anology with *hiv*, emphatic form of *hae*, 'have'.

It is first noted on Tyneside in Brockett (1829) (as *div*) but is absent from Border Ballads, the Metrical Cuthbert, Ray (1674), Kennet (1690s), Grose (1787), Wilson (1790s), and never seems to have caught on far from Tyneside itself, for example, not mentioned in Palgrave (1896) (Hetton-le-Hole), Teward (2003) (Teesdale), Egglestone (1870s) (Weardale). *Div/ divvent* contrast markedly with the Durham forms *Aa dee* and *Aa dinnut.*

The evidence is tantalizing and equivocal, but sufficient, I think, to point to the introduction of an interesting range of distinctive words, coming into everyday use in the North East by 1800–1820, but not typical of earlier local usage, and probably deriving from Scots by migration or Dutch by maritime contact, with the further tantalizing possibility of a community of words developing on the North East coast because of North Sea contacts, north-south and east-west.

Dispersal and Publication

Central to the process of amalgamation would be the workers on the Tyne – the sailors and the keelmen, in the heavily populated quayside areas of Sandgate and the like. The vocabulary moved into the mining community either by imitation, or because after the strike of 1844, there were fewer jobs for keelmen; while the old crowded housing of Newcastle quayside burned down in 1854, aiding dispersal of communities and language. The switch from maritime to mining is noticed in 1842:

> Half of the pitmen at this colliery [Percy Main] have been at one time soldiers and sailors, mostly sailors. Many of them have been brought up pitmen, have then gone to sea, and at last returned to the pit again.
>
> *Parliamentary Papers* 1842:.585

Also, typically skilled rather than unskilled workers, Scotsmen soon found a direct place in the mining industry. Thence, a relatively small step to circulate around the Great North Coalfield, considering the high mobility of the workforce in especially the first half of the nineteenth century (and later as deep mines opened in East Durham). The process of assimilation was not complete or consistent: local word usage persisted and the adoption of Tyneside terms was partial at best. Thus *divvent* and 'tek the ghee' have never spread far from Tyneside itself (Co.Durham equivalents *dinnut* and *fashed* or *tewed*). A further study of the dates and geography of new pits in the region might even provide tracks of dispersal, replacing the old dependence on market towns as centres of contact and the ecclesiastical dominance of Durham City.

It is not surprising that the fast growing conurbation of Tyneside should forge itself a distinctive version of NE dialect, nor that the usage of Newcastle, the centre of the coal trade and of entertainment, should influence the rest of the coalfield. What perhaps is curious is that this dialect of mining owed little to the lead mines of the Pennines or elsewhere, in commercial operation from the sixteenth century; for example, a mine in the Pennines was *a groove*.

If we look at Heslop's wordlist for Newcastle and Northumberland in the 1890s there is a large contingency of words no longer in use, not easily traceable to historic roots, and not found elsewhere in the region, for example, *gellfish* 'flighty', *ghent* 'a tall person', *gib* 'a crochet hook', *gifty* 'prolific', etc. These seem to be transient newisms, faithfully noted down by Heslop, but in effect little more than passing slang. They do indicate that word invention was an important element in this dialect; but those terms that found wider currency in the coalfield were of an earlier vintage, for example, introduced by ca.1820.

A positive factor in the moulding of nineteenth-century dialect could be the printed form itself (which in turn has certain Scottish conventions e.g. /aw/ for the long /a/ vowel), so that Tyneside dialect – the most printed – turns up in some odd places. Here is part of a letter from the *South Durham Herald* of 23 Mar 1867, supposedly from a 'Retiort Keelmin'.

Tawkin' fornent lock-oots an' torn-oots, what de ye think o' the Hartlepeul Torn Ups, mistor? A varry *doolar-is* iccount has been forridid te me biv a Hertlepeul Toon Coonsillor . . . consarnin' the goold an' silver mine thit's been fund on the beech thair, sor. Too half-rockt layborrors gan dandorrin' illang be the sea side, the tuthor day, happind te drop on tiv a peety reef o' rocks, an' the doddil [tobacco remnant] o' won o' the cheps pipes teuk intiv it's heed te fawl on te this seaweed gardin. Tommy stoopt down te pick the doddil up, when he seed what te him leukt like a black penny lyin' close te the reekin' [smoking] baccy.

Tommy picks her up, rubs her a bit, finds oot she's silvor, an' cawls on his meyt that was wawkin' on iffore him te cum back. Annuther, an' annuther, an' still lots iv uthors, torns up thor black bellies fra the peet . . .

This is an unusual editorial mix – with *silvor* for the expected *sillor, down* for *doon* but *toon* for *town, doddil* for *dottle* . . . The dialect of the Tyne has become almost a literary staple and the tension between its authentic and satirical usage has arguably energized rather than weakened the status of dialect in print, given a receptive, non-critical audience.

Printing may also have helped regularize the morphology and syntax. As innovations like simplifying case endings and word order in Middle English were pioneered in the North, the gap between NE dialect and standard English in point of grammar is surprisingly narrow. A special use of conjuctions like *at* ('that', from ON?), *till* and *while* is notable, and the tendency to level the present of the verb 'to be' to *is* – for example, *we'se, I'se, ye'se* – but the present participle in -/in'/ is surely a reduction of the standard -/ing/ not a relic of the OE –/ende/ form. Modal verbs vary somewhat: *have* fulfills the role of *must* or *ought*: 'ye hevn't te dee that'; while *must* sometimes has the force of *cannot*: 'they mustn't have valued it'. High frequency tags include ending a statement in *man* (applied to man, woman and child, in the OE fashion), and statement and question often end in an extra, rising 'like?' As against these minor points, it is the special range of vocabulary that distinguishes NE dialect, and while visitors from the South still like to pretend they cannot understand much that is said in the North East, a century or two ago that would indeed have been very much the case.

In the Twentieth Century

Unlike the continuance of accent and intonation, the erosion of dialect vocabulary in the twentieth century (and arguably from much earlier, since modern dialect is in itself a compromise between local and national forms) has been dramatic, and is difficult to account for. Is it a natural death or has dialect been 'pushed'?

Fred Wade (1976), local historian and dialect collector in Annfield Plain, in northwest Co.Durham, identifies over-zealous schooling as a main source:

> Children at school then were compelled to drop the dialect and to speak in the manner dictated to them by their masters. Some scholars found it very hard to drop the dialect altogether, and these children were helped to overcome speaking dialect in school by a liberal application of the stick which was then the universal remedy for any short comings of the scholars . . .
>
> Outside the school we never used anything else than the dialect except we were addressed by someone whom we knew was better educated and spoke in the manner we were compelled to use in school, but among ourselves and our parents there was no feeling of guilt or shame because we conversed in the same manner as our ancestors had done for hundreds of years.
>
> Wade MS, intro (1976)

Newcastle City Council recently fell into the same 'big stick' category when it was detected advising staff not to use familiar dialect to its 'clients' – including traditional forms of address like 'pet' and 'hinny' and some common phrases.[6]

But besides the intervention of authority we must take into account the economic despair of the inter-war years; the rise of the Labour Party (with national rather than local allegiances and aspirations), the reaction against tradition among the youth in the 1960s and the turn to American pop culture, the drive for 'modernism' in the 1960s when many traditional colliery rows were demolished and much of central Newcastle reshaped and the decline of heavy industry since Word War 2 must all play a part. The 1960s was also, arguably, the heyday of the English 'O' level exam. (Few schools today care to remember dialect, and the National Curriculum is regrettably restrictive.)

Into this cultural uncertainty, Scott Dobson's *Larn yersell Geordie* of 1969 came as something of a revelation: himself part of the 'aware' set of Newcastle, he championed dialect, gave it new life and identity (as 'Geordie') and focused on the traditional mining village as the touchstone of speech and manners (rejecting the excesses of modern planning and art fashions). His inventive humour did much to reinvigorate Tyneside's image of itself and his many booklets of the 1970s remain as popular and enjoyable as ever. Dobson it was who suggested opening a letter to your local councillor with the respectful 'Esteemed Hinny ...'

The loss of the region's coal mines by the early 1990s (and by a parallel trend, the end of much of its shipbuilding tradition) was part of a disruption and remobilization of society that still has not ended. Villages and seaside towns have tended to become high-value housing; council estates reduced and privatized; the block manual labour dispersed. Dialect implies not only a society or cohesive group within society, but a *reality;* it conveys reassurance of world view. It is that reality which has been fractured, and the subtending belief that has been removed.

Dialect, used with affection by older people still, has become something of a specialist area, encouraged north of the Tyne by the Northumbrian Language Society and to the south by the Durham & Tyneside Dialect Group. They promote research and new writing in dialect, but without more support from schools and the media, can have only marginal impact. The rejection, by referendum, of the call for a regional assembly in 2005, and the unexpected defeat of Newcastle in its bid for the title of European City of Culture 2008, have underlined the lack of progress towards a recognition of regional cohesion and achievement.

For the young, newisms and Americanisms are preferred, but surprisingly, some of what appeals as new is old enough in its way: the twenty-first century 'Charver' terminology on Tyneside, chronicled in Marshall Hall's magazine *Newcastle Stuff,* is largely based on Romany, re-emerging from the council estates around Newcastle: for example, *chaw* 'to steal', *ken* 'home', *lowie* 'money'. If *different* is the motive, then a vast store of dialect words lies dormant, just waiting to be redeployed!

For all the debate about the status of dialect, the compositions in North East dialect are arguably the finest among the English dialect literatures (second only, in a wider frame of 'English', to that of Lowlands Scots, whose creative vigour Tyneside in some sense inherited at the beginning of the nineteenth century). The poems of Thomas Wilson, and songs of Tommy Armstrong and Alexander Barrass are true literary treasures, alongside a host of smaller songmakers, humorists and prosists. Only a fraction of this is appreciated outside the region. Here, as a fitting conclusion, is a Tommy Armstrong (1987) poem with its typical blending of seriousness and humour ...

'The Sheel Raw Flud'
'S lang as aw live awl nivor forget
One Setorday wen it was se wet,
Ivory body wis nearly ***bet*** overwhelmed
Fra th' Setorday till th' Sunda', O!
The ducks did quack an' the cocks did craw,
For wat wis up thae diddent naw,
It neerly droon[d]ed awl Sheel Raw,
That nasty Sunda' mornin', O!

Mall Jonson tiv hor husbind sais:
"Reech me ma stockens en ma stais,
For God' suaik let me heh ma stais,
Or else aw will be droonded, O!"
"Tha clais," said he, "thor ***guain we*** mine, gone with
Like ***Boyd*** an' ***Elliott***, up the Tyne; (professional rowers)
Aw've leukt fra five, an' noo its nine,
This nasty Sunda' mornin', O!"

On the bed she began to rowl,
An' flung hor airms aroond th' powl,
Sa'en, "Lord heh marcy on maw sowl
This nasty Sunda' mornin', O!"
Th' vary cats thae ran up staires,
Thinkin' thae wor gon ***for fairs*** for real
That nasty Sunda' morning', O!

Aw wis sorry for Sally Clark,
Th' fire wis oot, an' awl wis dark,
She gat oot i' bed wi nowt but hor ***sark***, shift
That nasty Sunda' mornin', O!
She muaid a splash we sic a ***clattor***, row, noise
Thit Bob cried oot, "Sal, wat's th' mattor?"
She sais, "Aw's up to me eyes i' wattor,
It must be a nasty mornin', O!"

Bob jump'd oot of he's bed an' awl,
He went where ivor he heerd hor squal,
But th' wattor wis alwis shiften Sal,
That nasty Sunda' mornin', O!
At last th' wattor brust opin th' dor,

An' weshed away buaith Bob an' hor,
At ***Tinmith*** they wer wesh't ashore, Tynemouth
That nasty Sunda' mornin', O!

Notes

[1] We may notice briefly here that the Vowel Shift of Southern England took a different turn in the North where /u/ retained its traditional value, and likewise /o/ (though long /o/ broke to /iu/ e.g. *biuts* ('boots'); long /e/ fronted to /i/ as in the South; but long /a/ broke to give /i + a/ in contrast to Southern /a + i/). Long /i/ resisted (in the eighteenth century 'Colliers Rant' – *neit* rhymes with *feet*) but has now broken to approximate to the Southern form, and long /o/ has smoothed or conformed, though in a longer form of the vowel than in the South (*coook, boook,* as it were). *Stane* or *styen* for 'stone' and *keuk* for 'cook' are no longer standard. A few fossil forms, like a short /i/ in *finnd, blinnd,* survive in set phrases. Transition continues, and surely justifies current studies in North East phonology. See further Smith (1996), especially ch. 5.

[2] So Brockett (1829) assures us in his dictionary (s.v. 'bride-ale'), cf. Heslop 1893–4 (p.xvi); but Wilson (1790s), writing of Gateshead speaks of similar customs his side of the river in *The Pitman's Pay,* part 3.

[3] For example, to hoist [variant MSS: hoise, hoyse] – 'when they would haul up anything into the ship with a tackle or with a dead rope, or get up a yard, they call it hoisting'. The Seaman's Dictionary (Mainwaring 1620s).

[4] An extra dimension to this word comes from some possible ME parallels: – the Middle English poem *Parlement of the Thre Ages* has: 'And he stotayde and stelkett and starede full brode' – 'and he [the stag] ?—ed and stalked and stared all round'. The *Michigan University Middle English Dictionary* gives two verbs: *stot* (with a short /o/) meaning 'to pause in bewilderment' – which fits the above context well, and derives from OFr *estotier*; and *stot* with a long /o/, similar, but also capable of meaning 'stumble, stagger', from MDu *stoten.* On reflection, neither need influence our verb 'stot' (to bounce) brought into popular usage ca.1800.

[5] 'We say a ship is crank-sided when she will bear but small sail, and will lie down very much with little wind' [i.e. tends to keel over] *The Seaman's Dictionary* (Mainwaring 1620s).

[6] See articles in *The Independent* and *The Times,* 17 Aug 2.

Bibliography

Armstrong, T. (1987), in R. Forbes (ed.), *Polisses and Candymen: The Complete Works of Tommy Amstrong, The Pitman Poet Composed in the 1880s, 1890s,* Consett: The Tommy Armstrong Trust.

Atkinson, J. C. (1868), *A Glossary of the Cleveland Dialect,* London: John Russell.

Bailey, J. (1810), *General View of the Agriculture of the County of Durham,* London: Richard Phillips.

Barrass, A. (1897), *The Pitman's Social Neet,* Consett: J. Dent.
Beattie, W. (ed.) (1952), *Border Ballads,* Harmondsworth: Penguin.
Bell, M. S. (1815), *Bell-White MS 12,* New Castle: Newcastle University.
Bewick, T. (1790s), *The Howdy and the Upgetting – Two Tales of Sixty Years Sin Seyne, as related by the late Thomas Bewick of Newcastle, in The Tyne Side Dialect,* London: printed for the admirers of native merit, 1850.
Brockett, J. T. (1829), *A Glossary of North Country Words in Use,* 2nd ed, Newcastle: T & J. Hodgson.
Chicken, E. (1764), *The Collier's wedding,* 2nd ed, Newcastle. [Written 1720s re miners at Benwell].
Cuthbert, M. (1891), *The Life or St Cuthbert in English Verse c. AD 1450,* Durham: Surtees Society, Vol. 87.
Dinsdale, F. T. (1849), *A Glossary of Provincial Words used in Teesdale in the County of Durham,* London, 'The area covered is from Middleton in Teesdale to Darlington and north of the Tees for 9 or 10 miles along this route'.
Dobson, S. (1969),*Larn Yersel' Geordie,* Newcastle: F. Graham.
Egglestone, W. (1877), *Betty Podkin's Visit to Auckland Flower Show* (Stanhope, 1876) and *Betty Podkin's Letter Ted Queen on Cleopatra's Needle,* (London, 1877).
Green, J. (1879), *Tales and Ballads of Wearside,* Sunderland.
Griffiths, B. (2000), *North East Dialect: The Texts,* Newcastle: Centre for Northern Studies.
—. (2004), *A Dictionary of North East Dialect,* Newcastle: Northumbria University Press.
Grose, F. G. (1787), *A Provincial Glossary,* London: S. Hooper.
Guardian, 10 April 2006, pp. 20
Hall, M. (2000–2002), *Contributions to Newcastle Stuff,* the magazine edited by M. Hall.
Harker, D. (ed.) (1972), *Allan's Illustrated Edition of Tyneside Songs* (1891), Newcastle-upon-Tyne.
—. (ed.) (1985), *Songs From the Manuscript Collection of John Bell,* Surtees Society, Vol. 196.
Hatcher, J. (1993), *The History of the British Coal Industry,* Oxford: Clarendon.
Hay, J. (2003), *Spider and Other Tales of Pit Village Life,* Seaham: Amra Imprint. [Relates to Ushaw Moor, early Twentieth Century.]
Heslop, R. O. (1893–1894), *Northumberland Words: A Glossary of Words Used in the County of Northumberland and on the Tyneside,* 2 vols, English Dialect Society.
Kennet, B. (1690s), 'Etymological collections of English words and Provincial Expressions', British Library MS Lansdowne 1033, Vol. 99, Bishop Kennet's Collection.
Kennington, F. (2006), *As Spoken in Berwick,* Stockport: F. L. Kennington.
Luckley, J. L. (1870s), *The Alnwick Language,* Newcastle Central Library.
MacDonald, G. (1882), *Castle Warlock,* London: Sampson Low.
Mainwaring, Sir H. (1620s), 'The Seaman's Dictionary', in *The Life and Works of Sir Henry Mainwaring,* Vol. 2, pp. 69–260. (Publications of the Navy Records Soc, Vol. 56, 1922).
Meriton, G. (1683), *A Yorkshire Dialogue,* repr. Yorks Dialect Soc, 1959.
Michigan University Middle English Dictionary – online edition. Available at <http://quod.lib.umich.edu/m/med/>.

OED (Oxford English Dictionary), 2nd ed (disk version), Oxford: Oxford University Press.

Palgrave, F. M. T. (1896), *A List of Words and Phrases in Everyday Use by the Natives of Hetton-le-Hole in the County of Durham,* English Dialect Society, Vol. 74.

Parliamentary Papers, 1842 Commissioners Reports, Vol. 16, pp. 585.

Philip, W. M. (1872), *It 'ill A' Come Richt: A Scottish Story of Thirty Years Ago,* pp. 176–178, Aberdeen: John Adam.

Raine, J. (1835), MS BL MS Egerton 2868 *Wills and inventories illustrative of the history of the northern counties of England* [uses wills of the Diocese of Durham, wills of the Diocese of York, and records of trials held in York Castle, plus some early printed books and diaries] Edited for the Surtees Society.

Ray, J. (1674), *Collection of English words, Not Generally Used,* London: Trübner 1874.

Robson, J. P. (1849), *Songs of the Bards of the Tyne* (Newcastle).

Scottish National Dictionary (1952), in W. Grant and D. Murison (eds), Edinburgh.

Smith, J. (1996), *An Historical Study of English: Function, Form and Change,* London: Routledge, see especially Chapter 5.

—. (2004), 'Phonological space and the actuation of the Great Vowel Shift in Scotland and Northern England', in M. Dossena and R. Lass (eds), *Methods and Data in English Historical Dialectology,* pp. 309–328, Bern: Lang.

Teward, K. (2003), *Teisdal' en how twas spok'n,* Teesdale.

Wade, F. (1976), *Glossary of Stanley and Annfield Plain.* (Wade MS manuscript supplied by the author's daughter, Jenny Wade.)

Wilson, T. (1790s), 'Pitman's Pay', *The Newcastle Magazine,* 1826, 1828, 1830. [A 'collected' edition, with glossary, was issued with an introduction by the author, in 1843; the work relates to Gateshead in the 1790s.]

Wright, J. (ed.) (1898–1905), *English Dialect Dictionary,* 6 Vols, Oxford.

West Midlands Region

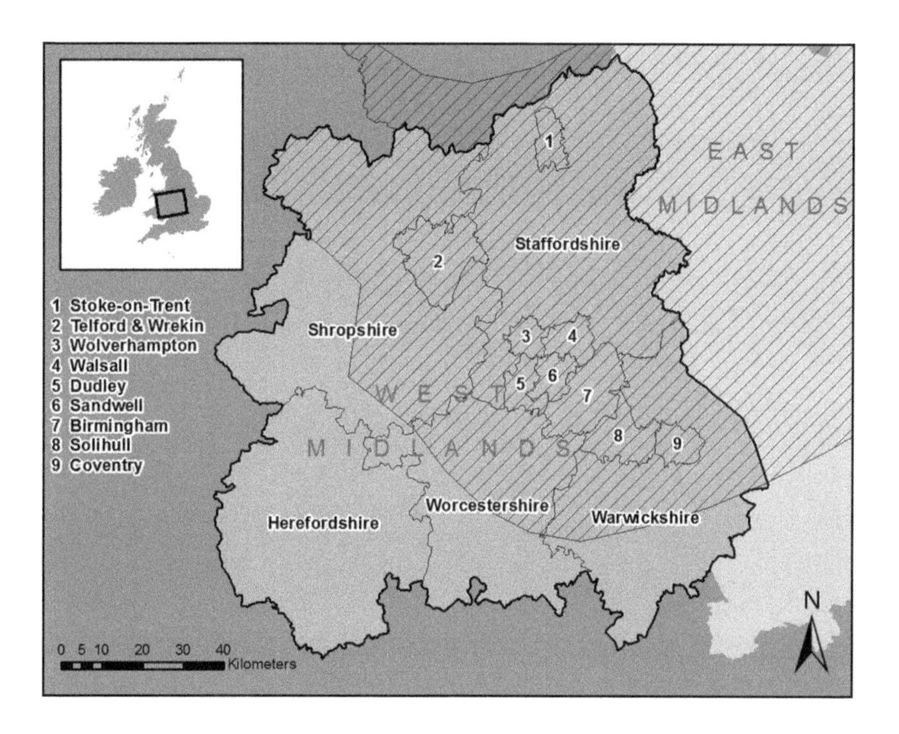

Chapter 5

West Midlands English

Steve Thorne

The Place

The area of central England known today as the Midlands roughly corresponds to the Anglo-Saxon kingdom of Mercia and consists of the traditional counties of Derbyshire, Herefordshire, Leicestershire, Lincolnshire, Northamptonshire, Nottinghamshire, Rutland, Shropshire, Staffordshire, Warwickshire and Worcestershire. Norfolk, Suffolk and Cambridgeshire were also included in the 2001 UK census (ONS 2007), but these are generally considered part of East Anglia. The Midlands is divided into two regions: the East Midlands and the West Midlands. The West Midlands county, consisting of the cities of Birmingham, Coventry and Wolverhampton, as well as the Black Country[1] and the metropolitan borough of Solihull, was created in 1974 when the 1972 Local Government Act came into effect, but its county council was abolished by the Local Government Act of 1985. The West Midlands county has now been superseded by the West Midlands region, although the county still exists in a limited respect as a legal entity.

The West Midlands region comprises the counties of Herefordshire, Shropshire, Staffordshire, Warwickshire and Worcestershire, the cities of Birmingham, Coventry and Wolverhampton, and the metropolitan boroughs of Dudley, Sandwell, Solihull and Walsall. It covers an area of 12,998 square kilometres from Stoke-on-Trent in the north to Hereford and Evesham in the south, from Shrewsbury in the west to Rugby and Burton-on-Trent in the east.

The West Midlands is at the centre of the UK's road and rail network, with motorways linking the North with the South East and South West meeting in Birmingham and Coventry. The main west coast railway line between London and the North West of England and Scotland also passes through Birmingham and Coventry. Contrary to popular belief, the West Midlands is not entirely urban. An area roughly equivalent to three quarters of the region is rural and includes five Areas of Outstanding Natural Beauty as well as part of the Peak District National Park.

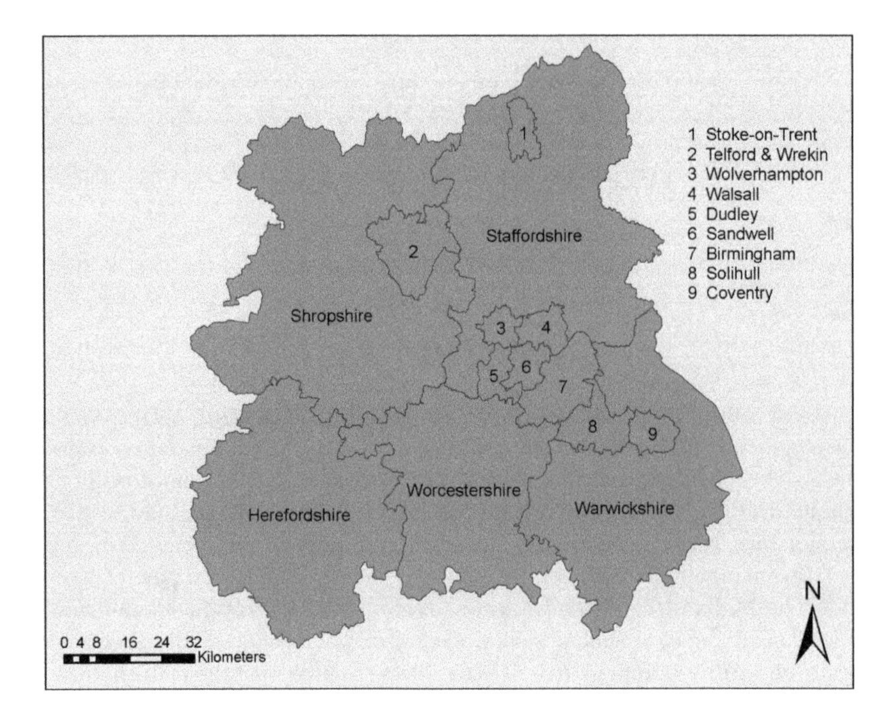

There are 38 local authorities in the West Midlands region: 3 unitary authorities, 4 counties, 7 metropolitan district authorities and 24 district councils. The official representative body of the region is the West Midlands Regional Assembly, which has limited administrative functions such as regional planning and economic development. The assembly is not an elected body, but is made up of members appointed from local councils across the region and members of environmental and regional interest groups.

The People

The population of the West Midlands is currently around 5.27 million (9 per cent of the total UK population), 49.1 per cent of which is male and 50.9 per cent female. Average life expectancy at birth is 75.6 years for males and 80.4 years for females. Of the people living in the region, 19.5 per cent are aged 0–14 years, 64.5 per cent are aged 15–64 and 16.0 per cent are aged over 65.

More than half of the region's population lives in urban areas. Birmingham, the United Kingdom's second largest city, for example, has a population of over 1 million. The greatest growth in population, however, has occurred in the urban areas outside the cities, while the cities themselves have recently seen a slight decrease in population.

	Population	Change since 1991
West Midlands Region	5,266,308	+6.1%
Herefordshire	174,871	+13.7%
Shropshire	283,173	+10.5%
Staffordshire	806,744	+5.8%
Stoke-on-Trent	240,636	+0.9%
Telford & Wrekin	158,325	+17.2%
Warwickshire	505,860	+8.7%
Birmingham, Coventry, Solihull & The Black Country	2,555,592	+0.4%
Worcestershire	541,107	+8.4%

Source: Advantage West Midlands (2007).

According to the West Midlands Regional Observatory (2007), most people leaving the region moved to the East Midlands and the South-West of England, while most of those arriving came from the South-East.

The ethnic minority population is slightly higher in the West Midlands than the national average and within this there are significant sub-regional variations and local concentrations of particular ethnic minority groups: 11.26 per cent of the population of the West Midlands is non-white compared with 9.08 per cent of the population nationally; 2.93 per cent of the population is of Pakistani descent compared with 1.44 per cent nationally and 3.39 per cent is of Indian descent compared with 2.09 per cent nationally. Conversely, the region has a smaller percentage of its population from black ethnic minority groups than the national average. By far the highest concentrations of ethnic minority groups are in and around the cities of Birmingham, Coventry, Wolverhampton and Stoke-on-Trent.

There were 2,309,561 jobs based in the West Midlands in 2003 with 18 per cent of these within the manufacturing sector and around 70 per cent in the service sector.

According to the Office for National Statistics (ONS 2007), the economic activity rate in the region in the spring of 2003 was 78.6 per cent compared with 78.8 per cent nationally.

Although there is a strong sense of national identity, with 61 per cent of the population describing themselves as English compared with a 57 per cent figure for England as a whole,[2] a significant proportion of those living in the West Midlands are unaware of the region's boundaries and, consequently, do not have a strong sense of regional identity. The region also suffers from some negative perceptions, primarily relating to parts of the main urban areas such as Birmingham and the Black Country. This, in turn, has a negative effect upon the way in which the language of the region is perceived by people from other parts of the United Kingdom (see Thorne 2003).

	Workplaces	Employees
Agriculture & Fishing	588	4,269
Energy & Water	342	14,554
Manufacturing	20,129	418,347
Construction	17,552	100,804
Distribution, Hotels & Restaurants	58,103	553,293
Transport & Communications	9,410	129,596
Banking, Finance & Insurance	49,456	382,889
Public Administration, Education & Health	15,892	594,948
Other Services	15,170	110,861

Source: Annual Business Inquiry (2003).

The Past

The first and perhaps most important point to bear in mind regarding the history and language of the West Midlands is that the region is the most central and landlocked in England. Since the history of the United Kingdom is one of successive waves of immigration by sea, the native dialects of coastal areas were often the first to be affected. Any sociocultural or linguistic transitions taking place elsewhere in the country thus took a relatively long time to seep through to the heartlands, and it is no accident that West Midlands English, as we shall see, has retained many of the features of previous ages of English. The second point to bear in mind is that the West Midlands was perfectly situated to become the birthplace of the industrial age. 'If a beneficent Creator had laid out a geological palette specifically so that man could 'bring forth' the Industrial Revolution', remarks Skipp (1980: 17), 'he could hardly have done better', and the influx of people from all over the United Kingdom and often much further afield who came to the West Midlands to find work during the eighteenth, nineteenth and twentieth centuries was to have an enduring influence on its language.

There is evidence of human activity in the West Midlands dating back to Lower Palaeolithic times. Archaeological finds have indicated the presence of Mesolithic hunter-gatherers in the region, as well as human habitation throughout the late Stone Age and early Bronze Age. There is little evidence of any extensive settlement during the Iron Age, and the region appears to have encompassed the territories of three native British tribes: the Cornovi to the north west, the Corieltauvi to the north east and the Dobunni to the south. The Brythonic/Celtic language spoken by these native British tribes has left its mark on a few place names in the region. During the Roman occupation of Britain (c. 43–450AD), each of these former tribal territories boasted a 'civitas' (city-state): Wroxeter (in present-day Shropshire), Leicester and Cirencester (in present-day Gloucestershire), and a handful of Romano-British place names survive.

It was the Germanic invaders of Britain, however, who were to leave the most significant mark on the place names and language of the West Midlands. From c. 450AD, according to Bede's (c. 731) *Ecclesiastical History of the English People*, large numbers of Saxons, Jutes, Angles and Frisians migrated from their homelands in Denmark and the Low Countries and began to settle in the south and east of England, gradually extending their conquered territories to include the Midlands. Not much is known about the arrival of Anglo-Saxons in the West Midlands, but it is believed that the region was first settled by Angles in the middle of the sixth century.

An Anglian tribe under the leadership of Beorma was among the first to colonize the region. His people (ingas) set up a homestead (ham) which was later to become known as Birmingham (Beorma + ingas + ham). One of the main bands of Anglians were the Mierce, the boundary people or 'Lords of the March', whose heartland was in and around Lichfield and Tamworth just to the north of Birmingham. Under a ruler of the Mierce called Penda, these scattered tribes of Anglians were brought together to form the kingdom of Mercia, which extended deep into the Midlands and covered much of the present-day counties of Staffordshire, Leicestershire, Nottinghamshire, Derbyshire and Warwickshire.

Under King Aethelbald (716–57) and King Offa (757–96), Mercia became the most powerful kingdom in Anglo-Saxon England. Any remaining Britons had been assimilated into Anglo-Saxon culture by this time, and the Celtic language was no longer spoken. The dominance of Old English in the West Midlands is reflected in both the rarity of Celtic and Romano-British place names and the abundance of those of Anglo-Saxon origin. The 'don' in Breedon and many other West Midlands place names, for example, is the Old English for 'hill'. Early Old English (c. 450–850), however, was by no means a uniform language, and had four distinguishable dialects: Northumbrian, Mercian, West Saxon and Kentish. Northumbrian (spoken north of the Humber) and Mercian (spoken between the Humber and Thames), as Baugh and Cable (1996: 51) explain, were similar in some respects: 'They possess certain features in common and are sometimes known collectively as Anglian', but 'each possess certain distinctive features as well'. Following the death of Offa, Wessex became the dominant Anglo-Saxon kingdom, and its dialect became the variant used by Old English scribes, though many West Saxon texts indicate a Mercian influence, probably because Mercian scribes were employed by King Alfred of Wessex (848–99AD) to assist in the revival of learning, which he championed.

The period between 850 and 1100 saw extensive invasion and settlement from Scandinavia. In 873, Danish Viking forces gained control of north eastern

Mercia, but, after years of continuous war, were prevented from further gains by King Alfred. The Danelaw treaty restricted the Danes to the territories east of a line running roughly from Chester to London. Since the West Midlands lies largely west of this line, there are very few place names of Norse origin in the area, and the language of the Danish invaders does not appear to have had anything like the major impact that it had further north and east. Freeborn (1998) determines the extent of Danish and Norwegian Viking settlements in Britain by mapping place names ending in the Norse –by (town), –thorp(e) (village), –thwaite (piece of land) or –toft (ditto), but in the English-held west Mercian kingdom, the overwhelming majority of place names end in the Old English –ham (homestead), –leah (woodland clearing or glade), –worth (enclosure), –halh (hall), –burh (fortification) or –grene (grassland).

After the Norman conquest in 1066, French became the official language in England, but many great works of literature were written in the various dialects of Middle English (c. 1100–1450): Northern, which covered the same area as the Old English kingdom of Northumbria, Southern, which covered the former kingdom of Wessex, Kentish in the south east, East Midland, stretching from the Thames to the Humber and covering much of the old Danelaw territory, and West Midland or West Central, covering Lancashire, Cheshire, Shropshire, Herefordshire, Warwickshire, Worcestershire and Staffordshire. Since there was still no standard English dialect, scribes attempted to represent sounds orthographically, and texts written in the West Midland dialect, such as the *Brut* (c. 1200), *Ancrene Wisse* (c. 1230) and *St Katherine* (c. 1230), therefore give us a clear picture of the kind of language spoken in the region during this period. Baugh and Cable (1996: 406–407) list 'the appearance of OE ă + nasal as *on, om: wone*' and 'the feminine pronoun *ha, heo* for *she*' in *St Katherine* as 'significant West Midlands characteristics', both of which are still produced by people living in the region.

Laȝamon's *Brut*, a chronicle history of Britain, was written by the parish priest of Areley Kings in Worcestershire, and *Ancrene Wisse*, a book of devotional advice, was written by the canon of Wigmore Abbey in northern Hertfordshire, but by far the two most important texts written in the Middle English West Midland dialect are *Sir Gawain and the Green Knight* (c. 1360) and *The Vision of Piers Plowman* (c. 1370). The anonymous *Sir Gawain and the Green Knight*, an Arthurian romance, was composed in a northern West Midland dialect by someone who may have come from the borders of Cheshire and Staffordshire. The poem is written in what is known as the alliterative long line, a style which was extremely out of date at the time and which harks back to the (by then) archaic Old English style of rhythmic and alliterative poetic metre instead of the fashionable courtly rhyming form which had been introduced by the Normans. *The Vision of Piers Plowman*, a social allegory also in alliterative verse, was written by William Langland, who probably lived either in the Malvern Hills in Worcestershire or the Clee Hills in Shropshire. Over fifty manuscripts of the poem have survived, and it appears to have been the most well known and widely read of the Middle English alliterative poems. The Middle English West Midland dialect is also immortalized in many place names. Rea, the name of a Birmingham river, for example, is derived from the Middle English 'atter ee', meaning 'at the water'.

As Crystal (1995: 41) points out in his discussion of the manuscripts in the Early Chancery Proceedings, the language of the Central Midland dialect area during the Middle English period played a much more significant role in the shaping of modern standard English than was traditionally thought to be the case. The 'Chancery hand' (developed in Italy in the thirteenth century and spread to London via France), according to Crystal, fostered the standardization of English. The orthographic and grammatical order which the Chancery scribes imposed upon their texts, moreover, did not derive 'from the language and style found in the works of Chaucer and Gower', as was previously thought, but from the dialects spoken in the West Midlands during the fourteenth century: 'the main influence on the standard language was the Central Midlands area, several of whose linguistic features eventually influenced the shape of Chancery Standard'.

The reason the West and East Midland dialects could exert such a powerful influence is that they appeared to act as a communication bridge between the northern and southern dialect areas, as John of Trevisa explains in his translation of Ranulph Higden's *Polychronicon* (c. 1385):

> þerfore it is þat Mercii, þat beeþ men of myddel Engelond, as it were parteners of þe endes, vnderstondeþ bettre þe side langages, norþerne and souþerne, þan norþerne and souþerne vnderstondeþ eiþer oþer
>
> (Therefore it is that Mercians, who are men of Middle England, as it were partners of the extremes, understand better the languages on either side, Northern and Southern, than Northerners and Southerners understand each other.)

It therefore made perfect sense to favour 'myddel speche' over that of the 'souþ' and 'norþ contray', and the West Midlands dialect area still bridges the gap between north and south.

Although the West Midlands region was not officially recognized until the late twentieth century, the various settlements of the West Midlands have long been important centres of commerce and industry. Coventry was one of England's most important cities during the Middle Ages, with its prosperity built upon wool and cloth manufacture. Birmingham and Wolverhampton have a tradition of industry dating back to the sixteenth century when small metal working industries developed. Birmingham was known for its manufacture of small arms, whereas Wolverhampton became a centre of lock manufacture and brass working. The coal and iron ore deposits of the Black Country provided a ready source of raw material. The area grew rapidly during the industrial revolution, and by the twentieth century had grown into one large conurbation. Coventry was slower to develop, but by the early twentieth century had become an important centre of bicycle and car manufacture. Stoke-on-Trent has been almost exclusively known for its industrial-scale pottery manufacturing since the seventeenth century, but other industries such as coal mining and iron and steel making have also contributed to the development of the city.

According to surviving eighteenth-century hearth tax returns, most of the migrants who moved into the West Midlands during the early stages of the industrial revolution came from neighbouring regions, but by the nineteenth century the West Midlands had become a magnet for people from Cornwall, Wales, Ireland and Scotland. During the late nineteenth and early twentieth centuries there were also significant migrations of people from parts of Europe such as Germany, Italy, Switzerland, Turkey, Cyprus, Serbia, Greece and Poland. Yet another seismic shift in the population and language of the West Midlands occurred shortly after World War II, when thousands of immigrants from the Caribbean, India, Pakistan, Kashmir, Bangladesh, Yemen and China settled in redeveloped urbanized areas of the region. Like the scores of economic migrants before them, they came to find work in the region's many industries, and their native speech also had a considerable impact on West Midlands English.

Hughes and Trudgill (1979) and Trudgill (1999) suggest that the various dialects of the region are sufficiently similar to warrant being known collectively as 'the West Midlands dialect', and other sociolinguists have even gone so far as to suggest that the same dialect is spoken by people from other parts of the Midlands. It is clear that dialects within the West Midlands have more in common with each other than they do with the dialects of other parts of the United Kingdom, but this is perhaps a necessary and understandable simplification of a much more complex reality. 'The West Midlands dialect' is an umbrella term, and it is important to note that West Midlands English has a significant number of observable internal variations. Not only are there a considerable number of lexical, grammatical and phonological differences between Birmingham and Black Country Englishes, but there are also 'fierce arguments as to where the boundaries [between the two areas] lie' (Don 2001). To confuse the two is, in fact, one of the cardinal sins of the locality: 'One insult that no Blackcountryman will tolerate is to be mistaken for a Brummie[3]' (Drabble 1952: 36); 'The greatest insult that can be levelled at a Brummie is to equate him with a Black Countryman' (Bird 1974: 6).

Some commentators have claimed that the language of Birmingham has begun to spread into neighbouring areas of the West Midlands. In *The Adventure of English* (2002), Bragg suggests that the dialect of Shakespeare's Stratford-on-Avon in Warwickshire is now 'more influenced by nearby Birmingham'. Trudgill (1999), furthermore, predicts the survival of 'the West Midlands dialect' focused on Birmingham. The fact is that there are still major differences between dialect districts within the West Midlands. The same dialect, moreover, is not spoken uniformly by people from all over the region. There is a dialect continuum running through the West Midlands, as there is on a much larger scale throughout the rest of the United Kingdom: 'What you have is a continuum of dialects sequentially arranged over space: A, B, C, D' (Wardhaugh 1993: 42). Dialect A has much more in common with dialect B than it does with dialects C and D, dialect B has much more in common with dialects A and C than it does with dialect D, and so on.

It is not even possible to talk about Birmingham English as if it were an unadulterated and homogeneous entity. Linguistic boundaries (if, indeed, there are such things) seldom correspond with geographical boundaries, and there are significant differences between various dialects within the city. The dialect in the north of the city is different from that spoken in the south, the dialect of working-class Brummies is different from that of middle-class Brummies, the dialect of older Brummies is different from that of younger Brummies, the dialect of Asian Brummies is different from that of white Brummies, ad infinitum. The task facing anyone wishing to characterize West Midlands English is therefore a difficult one, but despite this complex internal diversity, variants of West Midlands English have more shared than differing characteristics, and those in which they agree (phonological, syntactic, lexical, etc.) serve as the defining core. It is precisely by picking out these shared features that we will define contemporary West Midlands English.

The Present

Middle-class West Midlands English conforms by and large to the UK standard in both accent and dialect (lower-middle-class speakers, however, generally tend to have some form of local accent), whereas working-class West Midlands English is characterized by non-standard segmental, suprasegmental, syntactic and lexical forms. The following account of these non-standard variants draws heavily on recorded data but is by no means exhaustive. The dialectal features discussed here, furthermore, are much more common in the speech of older generations of West Midlands speakers. Increasingly, it is only the distinctive accents of younger speakers which identify them as being from the West Midlands. Due to greater social mobility, educational reforms and improvements in communication, the non-standard syntactic, morphological and lexical features peculiar to West Midlands English appear to be on the wane. It should therefore be noted that what is true of the dialect of middle-aged and older working-class speakers is not necessarily true of all varieties of working-class West Midlands English.

Segmental and suprasegmental variables in West Midlands English

Wells (1982: xviii) uses keywords ‘intended to be unmistakable no matter what accent one says them in’ which have become a standard frame of reference in descriptive dialectology. The full set as transcribed for Received Pronunciation (RP),[4] and modified slightly by Foulkes and Docherty (1999), is employed in the following description of segmental variables in West Midlands English.

KIT [ɪ̣]	LOT [ɒ]	FACE [æɪ]
horsEs [ɪ̣]	FLEECE [ɜi]	PRICE [ɔɪ] > [oɪ]
TRAP [æ̣]	happY [ɜi] > [iː]	CHOICE [ɔɪ]
BATH [æ̣]	GOOSE [ɛʊ] > [ɜu]	GOAT [ʌʊ]
commA [æ̣] > [ɛ]	NURSE [ɜ̣ː]	MOUTH [ɛʊ] > [ɜu]
lettER [æ̣] > [ɛ]	PALM [ɑː]	CURE [jɜuæ̣] > [jʊæ̣] > [jʊə] > [jɔː]
STRUT [ʊ]	START [ɑː]	SQUARE [ɜː]
FOOT [ʊ]	THOUGHT [ɔː]	NEAR [ɜiæ̣]
DRESS [ẹ] > [ɛ̣]	FORCE [ɔː]	
CLOTH [ɒ]	NORTH [ɔː]	

Segmental variables in West Midlands English, after Wells (1982)

(A single transcription indicates that little or no variation has been identified in the regional pronunciation, whereas a number of transcriptions indicate significant internal variation.) The following description of suprasegmental variables in West Midlands English utilizes a modified version of the descriptive framework originally proposed by Brazil (1978, 1985 and 1997) and Brazil *et al* (1980), and further developed by Bradford (1988).

Monophthong vowel sounds

West Midlands articulation of /ɪ/, such as that occurring in words like ‘f**i**t’, ‘s**y**mbol’, ‘c**i**t**ie**s’ and ‘v**i**ll**a**ge’, is perhaps the most salient and instantly recognizable feature of the accent associated with the region, having a less centralized and much closer quality (= [ɪ̣]) than any other UK variant. The West Midlands accent also differs from other varieties in that the audible level of closeness and frontedness of /ɪ/ remains constant, whether in word-initial or word-medial position, and seldom seems to be affected by word stress or intonational falls or rises, for example, ‘She always minded er own business (= [bɪ̣znɪ̣s])’. It should also be noted that ‘seen’ and ‘sin’, and ‘been’ and ‘bin’ are homophonous pairs in Birmingham speech, the vowel sound in each word being realized as [ɪ], whereas RP speakers generally tend to lengthen the vowel sound in 'seen' and 'been' to [iː].

West Midlands /æ/ can be categorized as northern in that it is commonly realized as [æ̞] and seldom veers towards its closer southern pronunciation. The West Midlands accent also differs from most southern UK variants in that [æ̞] typically occurs in words where unvoiced fricative consonantal sounds follow the vowel, such as 'f***a***st', 'l***a***st', 'm***a***sk', 'p***a***ss', 'gr***a***ss', 'p***a***th', 'b***a***th', 'd***a***ft', '***a***fter', and also in words where a voiced alveolar nasal consonantal sound follows the vowel, such as 'ch***a***nce', 'd***a***nce' and 'comm***a***nd'. Whereas southern speakers tend to pronounce each of these words with a lengthened *C*[ɑ] (=[fɑːst], [lɑːst], [mɑːsk], [pɑːs], [ɡɹɑːs], [pɑːθ], [bɑːθ], [dɑːft], [ɑːftə], [tʃɑːns], [dɑːns], [kəmɑːnd]), in the West Midlands, as well as in northern UK dialect areas, there is generally no attempt made to differentiate between this and the vowel sound in words such as 'l***a***nd', 's***a***t' or 'b***a***g'. It should be noted, however, that there are certain ways in which West Midlands realizations of the BATH vowel differ from northern realizations. For example, 'half', 'aunt', 'laugh' and 'laughter', unlike their northern versions (=[*(h)æf*], [ænt], [læf], [læftə]), are realized as [*(h)ɑːf*], [ɑːnt], [lɑːf] and [lɑːftæ̞], that is, with a lengthened *C*[ɑ]; –er (e.g. 'moth***er***', 'comput***er***', 'wat***er***', 'Christoph***er***'), –re (e.g. 'mit***re***'), –or (e.g. 'doct***or***', 'raz***or***'), –ar (e.g. 'coll***ar***', 'sug***ar***', 'pill***ar***'), –ure (e.g. 'pict***ure***', 'mixt***ure***'), –ur (e.g. 'sulph***ur***'), –our (e.g. 'col***our***'), –eur (e.g. 'amat***eur***'), as well as –a (e.g. 'Chin***a***', 'dog***ma***') word terminations invariably have a far less neutralized lip position in West Midlands speech than in RP, being realized as [ɛ] or [æ̞] in most instances, for example, 'The best thing I can remember (= [ɹ̝ɪmembæ̞]) about your grandfather (=[ɡɹæ̞nfɑːðæ̞])', whereas the influence of a more centralized RP [ə] ending is noticeable in the speech of middle-class West Midlands speakers. Mathisen (1999: 110) observes a similar quality in Black Country speech: 'The unstressed vowel is frequently less central than schwa'. To this extent, West Midlands accents appear to share something in common with southern variants. The word-initial and word-final vowel sounds in '***a***noth***er***' are both realized as a close- to open-mid unrounded central vowel (= [ənʌðə]) in RP, whereas West Midlands speakers of all ages produce a more open and fronted sound in both positions.

The unrounded Cardinal Vowel /ʌ/ is virtually non-existent in West Midlands English, [ʊ] being the common realization in most cases and with very little internal variation. Minimal pairs such as 'putt' and 'put', 'cud' and 'could', 'tuck' and 'took', 'luck' and 'look', and 'stud' and 'stood' are therefore homophonous. West Midlands articulation differs from some northern UK English accents (particularly those in the North West) in that words like 'h***oo***f', 'r***oo***f' and 'sp***oo***n' are pronounced with a vowel sound approximating a lengthened [uː] rather than [ʊ], but the way in which a rounded [ʊ] occurs in West Midlands English where an unrounded *C*[ʌ] is usually articulated in southern varieties must nevertheless be viewed as a northern characteristic.

A more open type of /e/ approaching *C*[ɛ] is common in the West Midlands. Whereas RP and southern varieties of UK English have much closer varieties, often with added glides (see Gimson and Cruttenden 1994: 102), the West Midlands articulation of this vowel sound appears to bear more in relation with the open type of /e/ used in northern UK varieties, and has variants ranging through [e̝] to [ɛ̝], for example, 'I was erm a member (= [mɛ̝mbæ̝]) of the CP'. The typical Black Country realization of this vowel is [ɛ].

Comparisons of the limited amount of available references to the subject indicate that there has been considerable confusion among phoneticians regarding the way in which the /iː/ vowel is articulated in the West Midlands. Wells (1982: 363), for instance, suggests that variants such as [ɪi] and [əi] are common, whereas Crystal (1995: 240) states that there is a 'noticeable glide [əɪ] in several UK accents' (e.g. Liverpool, Birmingham, London), although this is 'shorter in Scots'. Hughes and Trudgill (1979: 54) assert that '/iː/ is [ɜi]', unless in word-final position, 'in which case it is [iː]', and Gimson and Cruttenden (1994: 98) describe Liverpool and Birmingham realizations as 'dialectal' glides 'of the type /ɨi/'. Most of the speakers in the recorded data, however, appear to realize the vowel sound occurring in words such as 'n*ee*d', 'th*e*se', 'dis*ea*se', 'p*ie*ce', 'rec*ei*ve', 'k*ey*', 'q*uay*', 'p*eo*ple' and 'mach*i*ne' as a diphthongized glide [ɜi], rather than a lengthened monophthong, beginning in the close-mid central area and moving out towards *C*[i], for example, 'I 'ad six brothers and me (= [mɜi]) that's seven'. Black Country variants range from [iː] through [ɪi] to [əi] (Mathisen 1999).

Cardinal Vowel 8, lengthened in RP to [uː] for the vowel sound in words such as 'd*o*', 'm*oo*d', 'r*u*de', 'gr*ou*p', 'fl*ew*', 'sh*oe*', 'j*ui*ce' and 'bl*ue*', is diphthongized in West Midlands articulation. Having, as its starting point, a close-mid to open-mid centralized position slightly lower than that for /iː/, and then moving in the direction of *C*[u], it is typically realized as [ɜu], for example, [dɜu], [mɜud], [ɹɜud], [gɾɜup], [flɜu], [ʃɜu], [dʒɜus], [blɜu]. Wells (1982: 363) states that another variant, [ʊu], is also common in Birmingham speech.

The most common realization of the vowel sound in words such as 'h*er*', 's*ur*f', 'b*ir*th', 'w*or*st', '*ear*th' and 'adj*our*n' is [ɜ̝ː] in West Midlands speech, being of a closer quality than most other Englishes. Fairly close and centralized variants approximating [ə̝] or [ə̝] are common in the Black Country dialect. RP variants tend to be relatively open (= [ɜ̞ː]), whereas r-colouring [ɝ] is a characteristic of South West English articulation (as well as rural varieties in southern areas of the West Midlands), and a more rounded and fronted variety (=[œ]) is common in Liverpool. Accents spoken in the southern hemisphere, such as Australian, South African and Zimbabwean, are perhaps the only varieties of English with a vowel sound similar to that in Birmingham pronunciation, also being realized as [ɜ̝ː] in the words listed above.

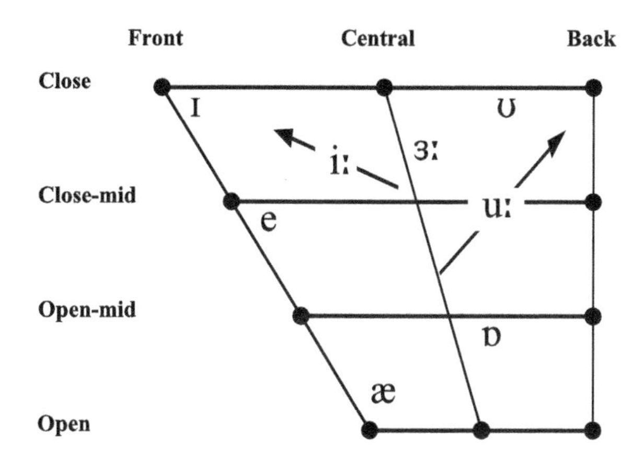

Typical realizations of monophthong vowels in West Midlands English

Diphthong vowel sounds

Whereas RP realizations of the diphthong vowel glide in words such as 'br***ea***k', 'w***a***ke', 'w***ay***', 'w***ai***st' and 'w***ei***ght' have starting points ranging from anywhere in the region of *C*[e] through to *C*[ɛ], depending, it seems, upon the age of the speaker, and monophthongal (=[eː]) or centralized (=[eə]) variants are usual in most northern UK English varieties, the West Midlands and South East accents are similar in that realizations generally tend to have a comparatively more open starting point (=[æɪ]) than most other UK English dialects. Mathisen (1999: 109) notes a similar realization in Black Country English, but incorrectly suggests that Birmingham articulation typically starts further back: 'A wide diphthong with a very open and front starting point, *day* [dæi], *cake* [kæik] versus [kʌik] in Birmingham. For elderly speakers also [ɛi]'. One phonological feature which does appear to disaffiliate the two, however, is the way in which older Black Country speakers occasionally tend to triphthongize this vowel sound: 'Some realizations may be classed as triphthongs, as in *age* [æiədʒ], *sale* [sæiəᵐ] or *days* [dæiəz], where [ə] or [ə̧] is more noticeable than as a mere glide-off. [æiə] may even be disyllabic in [dæi əz]' (Mathisen, ibid.). This seldom occurs in other areas of the West Midlands.

West Midlands English has variants of /aɪ/ ranging from [oɪ] in close-mid position to [ɔɪ]; the most common starting point being somewhere just below *C*[ɔ] in open-mid position (=[ɔ̧]) and moving in the general direction of /ɪ/, for example, 'I didn't like (=[lɔ̧ɪk]) it'. A starting point nearer to *C*[o] is characteristic of Black Country speech. Mathisen (1999: 109) has [aɪ], [ɑi] and [ɔɪ]. Since RP, southern and most northern varieties of UK English have starting points extending from front to back in a fully open position, the West Midlands dialect appears to have the closest starting point of all. For speakers in some areas of the West Midlands, furthermore, a phonemic merger between /aɪ/ and /ɔɪ/ often results in there being virtually no audible difference between the vowel sound occurring in words such as 'f***i***ve' and 'n***oi***se'. Minimal pairs in RP such as 'line' and 'loin', 'file' and 'foil', and 'tie' and 'toy' can therefore be homophonous.

The diphthong vowel glide in words like 'l***o***ne', 'sh***ow***', 'w***oe***', 't***oa***d' and 'th***ough***' (usually quite wide in West Midlands speech, with greater lip rounding for the first element than most other UK English variants) is commonly realized as [ʌʊ]; beginning in an open-mid back position and moving in the direction of /ʊ/. RP realizations generally tend to have centralized starting points between the close-mid and open-mid positions, whereas some southern realizations begin in the region of /æ/ for the first element, and most northern (as well as Scottish) variants have 'a relatively pure vowel around *C*[o]' (Gimson and Cruttenden 1994: 126). As Gimson and Cruttenden (1994: 125) point out, in each 'the lips are neutral for the first element', so the comparatively rounded quality of West Midlands realizations appears to be unique in this respect.

West Midlands realizations of the vowel sound occurring in words such as 'c***ow***', 'h***ou***se' and 'pl***ough***' generally tend to have a slightly less open starting point (=[ɛʊ]) than RP realizations (=[aʊ] > [aɪ]). Some realizations may also have a very close termination. Black Country realizations are similar, but Mathisen (1999: 109–110) notes that triphthongization (e.g. 'town' = [tɛuən]) and even closer starting points (=[eʊ]) are also common, particularly among working-class males in Sandwell. It should also be noted that in some varieties of West Midlands English, the vowel sound in 'l***oo***se', diphthongized in West Midlands articulation to [ɜu], may be similar enough to that in 'l***ou***se' to cause them to become homophonous.

The centring (/ʊə/) CURE vowel sound has more variants than any other in West Midlands English. Realizations of /ʊə/ range from [ɔː] through [ʊə] and [ʊæ̞] to [ɜuæ̞], depending, so it seems, upon the lexical choice, age, gender, ethnicity and social status of the speaker. Although 'Shaw' and 'shore' are homophonous in the articulation of working-class and older West Midlands speakers (both being realized as [ʃɔː]), the vowel sound in *sure*, as in a number of other words like 'poor', 'cure' and 'tour', is quite commonly realized as [ʊæ̞] or, as is the case in some variants, triphthongized to [ɜuæ̞], with both realizations having much more open and fronted second elements, for example, 'Poor (=[pɜuæ̞]) as bleedin' church mice'. Typical Black Country realizations are either [ʊə] or [əuːə], having 'a very close, back and rounded starting point; sometimes a close central starting point' (Mathisen 1999: 110).

The centring diphthong vowel glide occurring in most southern British English realizations of words such as 'squ***are***', 'l***air***', 'th***ere***' and 'p***ear***' (= [skweə], [leə], [ðeə], [peə]) is generally realized in West Midlands speech as a long monophthongized central vowel (=[ɜː]), for example, [skwɜː], [lɜː], [ðɜː], [pɜː]. Although, as Gimson and Cruttenden (1994: 133) remark: 'a long monophthong [ɛː] is a completely acceptable alternative in General RP', relatively few northern British English accents appear to favour a diphthongized pronunciation. (Scottish and Liverpool realizations of /eə/, e.g. are [eː] and [ɛː] respectively, whereas those of RP and the dialects of South East England are [æə̜] and [e̞ə].) To this extent, the West Midlands [ɜː] variant can be classified as yet another principally northern characteristic.

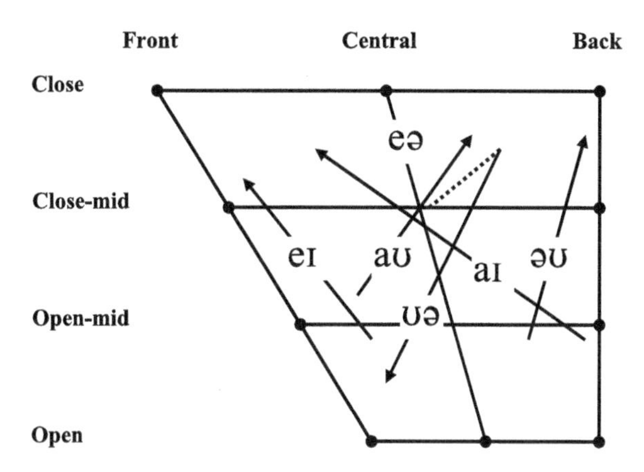

Typical realizations of diphthong vowels in West Midlands English

Consonantal sounds

The aitch sound, whether a voiceless glottal fricative (=/h/) in word-initial position (e.g. '***h***appy', '***h***orse', '***h***ill', '***wh***o', '***h***ome'), a voiceless glottal fricative in word-medial position (e.g. 'ab***h***or', 'any***h***ow', 'be***h***ave', 'man***h***ood', 'per***h***aps'), or a voiced glottal fricative (=/ɦ/) in word-medial position (e.g. 'be***h***ind') for RP realizations, is largely absent in working-class West Midlands English. This phenomenon, known as 'h-dropping' or 'h-deletion' (Trudgill 1983: 76–77), is also a feature of many other UK English accents.

The word-initial consonant sound in words like '***n***o' and '***n***ame', in word-medial position in 'mo***n***ey' and 'spa***nn***er', and in word-final position in 'me***n***' and 'colo***n***' is realized as a voiced alveolar nasal (=[n]) with no significant social or regional variation throughout the United Kingdom. There is, however, a good deal of difference between realizations of words where in writing an 'n' is followed by a letter denoting either a voiced (e.g. 'wi***ng***') or unvoiced velar plosive (e.g. 'wi***nk***'), and the West Midlands variant is one of its most prominent characteristics. When in word-medial position (e.g. 's***ing***er', 'f***ing***er'), –ing– is realized as [ɪŋg] in Birmingham and Black Country speech, as it also appears to be in the north-west Midlands areas of

Staffordshire, Derbyshire, and Cheshire, whereas –ing word terminations have variants ranging from [ɪ̣ŋg] through [ɪ̣ŋ] to [ɪ̣n] (e.g. 'singer' = [sɪ̣ŋgæ̣], 'singing' = [sɪ̣ŋgɪ̣ŋg], [sɪ̣ŋgɪ̣ŋ] or [sɪ̣ŋgɪ̣n]) depending on the social status of the speaker. [ŋ] appears to be the variant favoured by middle-class West Midlands speakers, whereas both [ŋg] and [ɪ̣n], occasionally also [ŋk], for example, 'I'd never done costume makin' or anythink (= [ɛ̣nɜiθɪ̣ŋk])', appear to be favoured by working-class speakers.

There are relatively few glottal stops in the speech of elderly and middle-aged West Midlands speakers; the words 'daugh*te*r' and 'bu*tt*er' (=[dɔʊ/ə] and [bʌ/ə] in London), for example, both being invariably realized with voiceless alveolar plosives in word-medial position, for example, [dɔːtæ̣], [bʊtæ̣]. The same also appears to apply when /t/ is in word-final position (e.g. 'i*t*', 'fee*t*', 'tha*t*'), and when in word-final position preceding a word-initial consonant (e.g. 'ge*t* me', 'we haven'*t* won'). The speech of younger working-class West Midlands speakers, however, is very different. In the recorded data, glottal stops are frequent in all three positions, for example, 'daughter' = [dɔː/æ̣], 'feet' = [fɜi/], 'get me' = [gẹ/ mɜi], 'I've got a little (= [lɪ̣/ʊᵐ]) bit of (= [bɪ̣/əv]) a substance that I (= [ðæ̣/ɔ̣ɪ]) always use'. Mathisen (1999: 110) notices a similar pattern in Black Country speech: 'The glottal stop is very frequent in teenage speech and also variably in young adult (30 years) speech, especially in MC [middle-class], but very infrequent in the speech of the elderly . . . Glottalisation in general, as a boundary marker or in emphatic speech, is more common for teenage and young adult groups than the elderly'.

The English of rural areas of the West Midlands, particularly Herefordshire, Shropshire, Worcestershire and Warwickshire, is predominantly rhotic and the 'r' in words such as 'ca*rd*', 'ca*rt*', and 'ca*rs*' is pronounced, whereas the English of urban areas such as Birmingham, Wolverhampton, Coventry and the Black Country is non-rhotic. In continuous speech, however, the linking r (e.g. 'for him' = [fəɹɪ̣m]; 'car exhaust' = [kɑːɹɛ̣gzɔːst]) and intrusive r (e.g. 'saw edge' = [sɔːɹɛ̣dʒ]; 'law and order' = [lɔːɹənɔːdæ̣]; 'drawing' = [dɹɔːɹɪ̣ŋg]) are categorical.

West Midlands speakers regularly produce the voiced alveolar tap (/ɾ/) in disyllabic words such as 'ma*rry*' (=[mæɾɜi]), 've*ry*' (=[veɾɜi]), 'so*rry*' (=[sɒɾɜi]), 'wo*rry*' (=[wʊɾɜi]), 'pe*r*haps' (=[pəɾæps]) and 'al*r*ight' (=[ɔːɾɔɪt]), where /ɹ/ is in word-medial position and is preceded by a monophthong. In most cases, taps of this kind replace /ɹ/ when in initial position for the second syllable, but can also be found in monosyllabic words like 'b*r*ight' (=[bɾɔɪt]), 'p*r*int' (=[pɾɪnt]), 'g*r*eat' (=[gɾæɪt]) and 'c*r*eam' (=[kɾɜim]), where /ɹ/ follows a word-initial consonant (especially if either a velar or bilabial plosive), for example, 'An' it was greasy (=[gɾɜisɜi])'. [ɾ] seldom occurs when an alveolar plosive (e.g. '*tr*ain', '*dr*own') is in word-initial position, possibly because these sounds are so similar and, therefore, difficult to produce in tandem. It should also be noted that the production of [ɾ] among West

Midlands speakers is by no means uniform and can vary considerably from speaker to speaker (even among those of the same age, gender, social class and/or ethnicity) and can sometimes be adopted and dropped within the space of a single utterance.

Nasalization

In West Midlands accents, as in Liverpool, Manchester, London, American, Canadian, Australian, West Indian, Asian and French English accents, vowels following nasalized consonants ('miss' = [mɪ̰̃s]; 'nick' = [nɪ̰̃k]) can have a nasal formant present. (Fujimura (1962) describes this quality as a 'nasal murmur'.) In some West Midlands varieties, nasalization may also occur independently of nasalized consonants ('kiss' = [kɪ̰̃s]). Typical West Midlands realizations of 'singer' (= [sɪ̰̃ŋgæ̰̃]) would have a greater nasal airflow during the second vowel than would normally be the case in RP accents (= [sɪ̃ŋə]), for example, 'We used to 'ave to go on coal lorries singin' (= [sɪ̰̃ŋgɪ̰̃n])', 'If old lady Carey was doin' one of er bakings (=[bæɪkɪ̰̃ŋgz])'. The phenomenon of nasal consonants affecting adjacent vowel sounds in such a way is known as coarticulation, and occurs right across the spectrum of working-class West Midlands speech, regardless of sex, age or ethnicity.

Intonation

Cruttenden (1986: 138–139) asserts that by far 'the most noticeable variation within British English is the more extensive use of rising tones in many northern cities. This phenomenon is reported for Birmingham, Liverpool, Glasgow, Belfast, and Tyneside, and something very similar is reported for Welsh English. It is not reported for rural areas of England or Scotland, nor does it occur in Edinburgh'. He goes on to suggest that the use of rising intonation in these areas is due to a 'strong Celtic influence' – a direct influence in the case of Wales (where many speak a Celtic language), an indirect influence in the case of Belfast (where most do not speak a Celtic language), and an even more indirect influence in other cases, 'where the influence is dependent on an influx of people from Ireland and Scotland'. As noted above, Irish, Welsh and Scottish migrants have had a major impact on the dialect of Birmingham, so Cruttenden's suggestion that the more extensive use of rising intonation in and around the city is due to an indirect 'Celtic influence' appears to be correct. There are, however, a number of differences between the characteristic intonation patterns of the West Midlands and most other areas of the United Kingdom.

The use of rising or 'referring' tones (*r*) where proclaiming tones (*p*) would be expected in most other varieties of UK English is a prominent characteristic of West Midlands English. Whereas RP and most southern UK English speakers have two choices open to them (*p* and *p* +), West Midlands speakers have four (*p*, *p* + , *r* and *r* +):

tone	West Midlands realizations	RP realizations
proclaiming	*p*, *p* + , *r*, *r* +	*p*, *p* +
referring	*r*, *r* + , *p*	*r*, *r* +

West Midlands and RP realizations of proclaiming and referring tones

The type of referring tone common in West Midlands English, moreover, is different from that occurring in other dialect areas. In words with three syllables, the tonic movement could perhaps best be described as a 'rise-plateau-rise' (beginning with a rise rather than a 'jump-up' on the tonic syllable, levelling out for the second syllable in the enclitic segment, and rising again for the third, but also common in words with four syllables). The tonic movement which occurs in words with two syllables in West Midlands English could perhaps best be described as a 'slight curve down then high rise'. It appears that Type 1 (*r* + realized as a 'rise-plateau-rise') and Type 2 (*r* realized as a 'slight curve down then high rise') tonic movements are interchangeable and can occur in any given position without causing a change in meaning, but since there are few genuine examples of free variation (see McArthur 1992: 416), it is more likely that the recorded data is not large enough to have unearthed what conditions the variability.

Syntactic and lexical variables in West Midlands English

Syntax

One of the most prominent syntactic variants in West Midlands English is negative concord, for example, 'I don't want to marry nobody', 'I won't 'ave no cotter with 'em no more'. This also occurs in other non-standard UK dialects, though its 'syntactic distribution often varies' (Cheshire 1982: 63). Labov (1972) and Trudgill (1983) point out that a number of English dialects allow syntactic constructions of the type: 'I don't want none', 'He hadn't got no shoes', and 'I can't find none nowhere', whereas the following can only be found in some: 'She hadn't got hardly any', 'They stood there without no shoes on', 'We haven't got only one', 'It ain't no cat can't get in no coop'. The first five types are all common in West Midlands English.

Adjectives which are normally inflected to produce comparative or superlative forms in the standard UK dialect may take a syntactic or 'periphrastic' form in West Midlands English, for example, ''E was more cuter than me, you see', 'Them was the most baddest rough-houses in the street'. Northall (1896: xvi) lists non-standard comparatives such as 'badder' (worse) and 'worser' (worse), and superlatives such as 'worsest' and 'worstest' (worst), each of which are still produced in West Midlands English, as examples of inflected forms in the Warwickshire dialect ('bestest' is also regularly produced in West Midlands English), although none of these occur in the recorded data.

As in other non-standard UK dialects, 'them' is often used in West Midlands English as the plural demonstrative denoting distance, for example, 'You did get them people in them days who was good to what they called the poor'. The West Midlands demonstrative system differs from that of many other dialects, however, in that 'thisn' is often used for the singular demonstrative indicating nearness, and 'thatn' is occasionally used for the plural, for example, 'Which one yo arter? Thisn' (Chinn and Thorne 2001: 155), 'That'n, That'ns. In that manner. This'n, This'ns. In this manner'. (Northall 1896: xviii), although both are much more common in rural areas of the West Midlands.

'Up' is often used prepositionally in West Midlands English instead of 'to', for example, 'He went up the pub half an hour ago' (McArthur 1992: 130), 'off' is frequently used instead of 'from', for example, 'I got a letter off our brother this mornin'', and 'on' is commonly used in place of 'of', for example, 'Not one on 'em knowed what they was a-doin', I swear' (Chinn and Thorne 2001: 70). The use of 'of a' in place of the prepositions 'on', 'in' or 'at', for example, 'They used to come in of a Christmas mornin'', although widespread in the West Midlands, is common in other dialect areas. There is evidence to suggest, however, that 'a' was widely used in the Warwickshire dialect as a substitute for the preposition 'to', for example, 'You have not been abed, then?' (Shakespeare, *Othello*, Act III, Scene I). In *The Vision of Piers Plowman* by William Langland, there is the line 'Tho was Peres proude and pott hem alle a-werk'. Older West Midlands English speakers still say that they are going 'a-work' rather than 'to work', and Northall (1896) lists 'a-wum' (at home), 'a-foot' (on foot) and 'a-doors' (of doors, e.g. 'out a-doors') as further examples of similar 'prepositional prefixes'.

The regularization of standard English irregular verbs is widespread in West Midlands English, for example, 'Ar, I knowed [knew] 'im a lung time agoo' (Rhodes 1950: 27), 'I've knowed [known] 'er since 'er was a nipper' (Chinn and Thorne 2001: 110). Although non-standard dialect speakers from other regions also tend to regularize irregular verbs, West Midlands English appears to be unique in the way that irregular verbs can sometimes take a whole range of alternative irregular forms, for example, 'When 'er seed [saw] me a-comin', 'er was that tekken [taken] a-back' (Rhodes 1950: 6), 'Better a belly bost [burst] than a good thing lost' (Northall 1896: 187), 'The cut's froz [frozen]' (Skeat 1876: 56).

Other non-standard verb forms frequently heard in the West Midlands include the use of past participles in place of the past simple: 'The reason that they done [did] that was because if they 'ad a win', and the use of the present simple in place of the past participle: 'And if I'd 'ave give [given] up my 'ome I couldn't take anything of my own with me'. The use of 'was' (the first and third person singular of the past tense of the verb 'to be') in place of the plural 'were' is also common: 'They wasn't allowed to stay', as is the use of 'says' or 'goes' as the present historic: 'I says to the missis, I goes what's up with yo?' The verb 'to learn', moreover, is frequently used in West Midlands English with the meaning 'to teach', for example, 'They don't learn yer anything'. Shakespeare uses it in this way in *The Tempest* when Caliban says: 'The red plague rid you for learning me your language'.

Another syntactic peculiarity of West Midlands English is the way in which the present tense of the verb 'to be' is formed. West Midlands speakers occasionally produce 'bin' rather than 'are' for the third person plural, as in this example from an anonymous inscription reproduced in Palmer (1976: 7): 'Man, it behoves thee oft to have in minde/That thou dealest with the hand that shalt thou find:/Children bin sloathful, and wives bin unkind,/Executors bin covetous and keep all they find'. 'Theym', however, is perhaps the more commonly heard variant nowadays, for example, 'Theym born but not buried' (Chinn and Thorne, 2001: 198). 'We am' (or 'we'm') is used for the first person plural in the present tense, for example, 'If yer expectin' us to do a wick's work fer two-three fardins, yer must think we'm fools above the shoulders' (Chinn and Thorne, 2001: 160), and it should also be noted that 'bist' (as in the German 'du bist' – 'you are'), for example, "Ow bist yer? [How are you?]', is the second person singular form of the present tense in Black Country speech.

The letter 'a', having phonological variants ranging from [æ̧] to [ə], is regularly added as a prefix by older West Midlands English speakers to the present participle of verbs such as 'go', 'come', 'walk', 'play', 'stand', 'tell' and 'knock' when in the past or present continuous tenses, for example, 'You en't a-tellin' me what to have!' Jackson (1879: 33) suggests that its use 'represents the Anglo-Saxon æt, at, or on, used in composition for 'in', 'on', 'upon', and Morris (1882) appears to support this theory. 'A' is also regularly pressed into service as a contracted form of the verb 'have' in the present perfect tense, for example, 'I wun't a known it'.

The use of 'don't' in place of the standard negated form of the present tense of 'do' for the third person singular, for example, 'It don't [doesn't] worry me', is common practice in most non-standard Englishes, but West Midlands English possesses its own unique set of verb negations. 'Nare' (or 'ne'er') is regularly used as a variant of 'never', for example, 'I told yous 'e'd nare do no good' (Rhodes, 1950: 51), and 'nare-a' is 'not', for example, 'Nare-a one of 'em was any good' (Ainsworth, 1989: 31). 'Never' can also occur as a negative preterite, for example, 'I came back to Brum and I never contacted anyone', as well as on its own in a verbless clause, for example, 'I never'. 'Dain't' is the negated past tense form of the verb 'do', for example, 'We used ter play in the road, dain't we?' 'Dai', as in 'I dai do it', is the shorter form more commonly heard in the Black Country dialect.

'Wun't', with a short vowel sound ([wʊnt]), is the West Midlands variant of 'will not', whereas 'worn't' ([wɔːnt]) is the West Midlands equivalent of 'wasn't', the negated past tense form of the first and third person singular and plural of the verb 'to be', for example, 'She worn't like the rest of 'em'. 'Am not', in West Midlands English, is 'bain't', the negated form of the first person singular of the verb 'to be', for example, 'I bain't a-gooin' to work nex'wick' (Northall, 1896: 209). Although now mainly used by speakers from the Black Country and the north-westerly parts of the region, 'bain't' is still in widespread use among older generations of West Midlands speakers and its similarity to the German form of the verb 'to be' in the first person singular ('bin') suggests a possible Germanic/ Anglo-Saxon root.

Whereas 'ain't' is common in most other urban working-class dialect areas, variants of 'haven't' ranging from 'in't' through 'en't' to 'ain't' are regularly produced by West Midlands speakers of all age groups, for example, 'I in't done nothing wrong' (Chinn and Thorne, 2001: 64). 'Mon't' and 'daresn't' (Northall (1896: vii) lists 'dare-no' and 'dussn't' as older Warwickshire dialect variants) are further examples of verb negations which appear to be unique to the region. 'Mon't' is the negated form of the auxiliary verb 'must', for example, 'I told er er mon't play in the 'oss-road', and 'daresn't' is the negated form of the verb 'dare', for example, 'Er daresn't go back to er mother's'. 'Cor' is also used in some parts of the West Midlands in place of 'can't'.

A morphological peculiarity of West Midlands English is the way in which some plural nouns and adjectives are often marked with an –en inflection. Old English plurals, as Freeborn (1998: 105) points out, 'were marked with a variety of different inflections, <–as, –u, –ru, –a, –an >, or with a zero inflection, or by a change of vowel. Today almost all plural nouns take the <–s> suffix, from the OE [Old English] <–as>. A few take <–en>, from the very common OE <–an> plurals, and a small set, including *goose/geese*, are irregular, where a change of vowel signals plural number. The OE plural of *cild* was *cildru*, which became ME [Middle English] *childre* or *childer*. In one dialect *childer* was given an additional <–en> suffix – *childeren* – which has become the Standard English *children*'. A few other examples of this exist in the present day standard UK dialect plural forms of ox (oxen) and brother (brethren), but the historical process of regularization has resulted in most –en inflections being lost. West Midlands English seems unique, however, in that, for older speakers at least, plural nouns (such as 'housen' [houses] and 'easen' [eves]) have survived. According to Skeat (1876: 27), the use of 'this old Anglo-Saxon plural' was much more widespread up until the mid-nineteenth century, though no other examples are given. There is also ample evidence to suggest that –en inflections on adjectives have survived. For example, 'bostin' (not listed in the OED), which is derived from the Anglo-Saxon 'bosten', meaning 'something to boast about', is a term used throughout the region for anything 'great'. Again, this feature appears to be a left-over from a much earlier period of English, but is steadily falling out of use.

'Yous' is the West Midlands second person plural pronoun in the nominative, accusative and dative cases, and 'yourn' is the genitive possessive pronoun for the second person singular and plural, for example, 'It must feel like 'e's yourn'. '(H)isn', the 'h' being frequently dropped, is the masculine third person singular possessive pronoun in West Midlands English, for example, 'Them illnesses of 'isn backened 'im at 'is schoolin' (Rhodes, 1950: 51). Up until the early modern English period, the possessive pronoun was often formed by adding an 'n' sound to the end of the pronoun, for example, 'thy book – that book is thine'. This is continued today, but only in the first person singular, for example, 'my book – that book is mine'. In the second and third person singular in contemporary English the 'n' sound has been replaced by an 's', and we have 'your book – that book is yours', and 'his book – that book is his'. But in West Midlands English, we hear 'your book – that book is yourn', and 'his book – that book is hisn'. Most of the other West Midlands possessive pronouns terminate in a similar fashion: 'ern' is the feminine third person singular, 'ourn' is the plural first person and 'theirn' is commonly used as the third person plural.

'Er' is commonly used in place of 'she'; the feminine pronoun for the third person in the nominative case, for example, 'Er was a little older than me'. Rhodes (1950: 3) states that 'er' is 'not 'her', as is generally supposed, but a corruption of the Anglo-Saxon 'heo' (she)', for example, 'He hire hand nam and heo sona aras: *he took her hand and she at once arose*' (Bosworth and Toller 1898: 7). In *Sir Gawain and the Green Knight*, 'hir' or 'her' appears as the accusative, dative and genitive (possessive adjective) of the feminine third person singular, as it does in contemporary West Midlands English. According to Upton et al. (1987), the dominant form now considered to be 'standard' did not emerge until medieval times, so West Midlands English appears to have retained the older form. Whereas 'e' and 'im' (common in many other urban working-class dialects due to the prominence of h-dropping) are merely pronunciation variants of 'he' and 'him', not so 'er', 'ern' or 'erself'.

Although strictly speaking a phonological variable, the West Midlands realization of the second person singular pronoun 'you' in the nominative case needs to be discussed here if we are to formulate an accurate picture of the complete pronominal system. 'You' is articulated in West Midlands English as 'yo' ([jʌʊ]), as in 'Where yo' bin?' (Skeat 1876: 42). 'Yow' ([jaʊ]) is the variant more commonly heard in the Black Country dialect. In a letter to William Allingham (dated 8 March 1877), George Eliot points out that '*yer*, without any sound of the *r*' was commonly used by Warwickshire dialect speakers for the second person singular in the accusative case, as indeed it still is today in West Midlands speech, though this is also used in the dative case, for example, 'As I was sayin' to yer'. A pronunciation of 'your' approximating [joə] (perhaps from the Anglo-Saxon 'eower') can still be detected in the speech of older residents of the West Midlands, though this is also more of a Black Country dialect feature.

A complete table of personal pronouns can therefore be presented as follows (brackets are used to signify that certain sounds are commonly dropped):

	Nominative (Subject)	**Accusative (Object)**	**Dative (Indirect object)**	**Genitive (Possessive)**	
SINGULAR				(adj.)	(pron.)
First person	I	us/me	us/me	me/ma	mine
Second person	yo/you	yer/you	yer/you	your	yourn
Third person	(h)e	(h)im	(h)im	(h)is	(h)isn
	er	er	er	er	ern
	it	it	it	its	its
PLURAL					
First person	we	us	us	our/us	ourn
Second person	yous/you	yous/you	yous/you	your	yourn
Third person	they	(th)em	(th)em	their	theirn

The pronominal system in West Midlands English

Northall (1896: xvii) lists the following as characteristics of the old Warwickshire dialect area: 'Shisn [shizn]. Hers…Tharn. Theirs…The nominative case and the accusative are perpetually confounded in such phrases as "They ought to have spoken to we; he told she so; us won't be hurt". [These remarks might be applied, with equal propriety to the folk-speech of Glouc., Leic., Worc., and other Midland shires.]' Although h-dropping, the use of 'us' for the first person singular in the accusative and dative cases, the possessive adjective 'me', for example, 'I'd got two black mincers you know and they- nearly shut me eyes was', and the retention of –n inflections in possessive pronouns occur in some other non-standard UK dialects, the pronominal system outlined above appears to be unique to West Midlands English alone.

Lexis

As could also be said of other non-standard UK dialects, the West Midlands dialect has many localized lexical variables. For a full account of these, see Skeat (1876), Jackson (1879), Poole (1880), Tomkinson (1893), Northall (1896), Wright (1898–1905), Shaw (1930), Hughes and Trudgill (1979), Upton and Widdowson (1996) Trudgill (1999) and Chinn and Thorne (2001), but among the most common are 'miskin' (from the Old English 'mixen' meaning 'dung') for 'dustbin', 'suff' (not listed in the OED) for 'drain', 'yampy' (not listed in the OED) for 'mad', 'kaylied' (not listed in the OED) for 'drunk', 'pikelet' (described in the OED as a Midlands word for 'a round teacake with small holes, to be buttered and toasted; but in other districts it seems to be sticky unsweetened crumpet or else a muffin'), 'out-door' (not listed in the OED) for 'off-licence', 'um' for 'home', 'donnies' (not listed in the OED) for 'hands', 'ax' (= /æks/) for 'ask' (derived from the Anglo-Saxon 'axian', and much older than the present standardized form), and 'ar' (not listed in the OED) for the affirmative adverb expressing approval, acceptance or compliance.

What is remarkable about these lexical items is not only that so few of them are listed correctly or listed at all in the OED, but that so many of them are derived from Anglo-Saxon. This clearly shows the major impact that the early Anglian settlers in the West Midlands had on the language of the region. For example, 'wassin' (not listed in the OED), the West Midlands word for 'throat', derives from the Anglo-Saxon 'wasend' meaning 'gullet'. 'To blart' (derived from 'blaetan', the Anglo-Saxon word for the bleating of sheep), is an intransitive verb meaning 'to cry'. 'Lezzer', a contraction of 'leasowe' (field), derives from the Anglo-Saxon 'læswian', but is described in the OED as restricted to the Scots and Northumbrian dialects. 'Clemmed', again questionably described in the OED as confined to northern parts of England and therefore 'of Norse origin', is the West Midlands word for 'hungry'. It has an Anglo-Saxon root, and bears more than just a passing resemblance to the modern German 'klemmen' (to pinch).

'Mom' is the diminutive form for 'mother' used throughout the West Midlands: 'And our mom used to mek us'. On the Births, Deaths and Marriages pages of West Midlands newspapers, it is rare to find the word 'mum'. In Wales, Ireland and much of northern England, the diminutive is 'mam', but in the West Midlands the /æ/ monophthong is often realized as /ɒ/ when it occurs in word-medial position immediately before the nasalized consonants /m/ or /n/, and the orthography is often altered to reflect this. As with 'mam' and 'mom', so too with 'man' and 'mon', for example, 'They used to put yer in-between the old gal and the old mon'. There is also a much earlier record of this variant. When a giant enters King Arthur's hall early in *Sir Gawain and the Green Knight,* he is stared at in slack-jawed amazement, 'for each mon had marvelled at what it might mean'. An /ɒ/ sound can also appear in the West Midlands pronunciation of words such as 'land' (lond), 'hand' (hond) and 'hammer' ('ommer), particularly in more rural areas of the region.

West Midlands English therefore appears to have retained the Old English variant despite the steady process of standardization in other dialectal areas of the United Kingdom, as Freeborn (1998: 114–115) explains: 'OE spelling and pronunciation of the low back vowel before [n] varied between *an* and *on.* In late OE it was *an* except in the West Midlands dialect, which is that of the *Brut.* Chaucer, in the late fourteenth century, has *lond,* like the *Brut,* but *land* eventually became standard'.

This explains why, as McArthur (1992: 926) notes, 'Early editions of Shakespeare spelled the vowel in *band* and *bond* indifferently' – these spellings were attempts to represent the pronunciation orthographically. It should also be noted that the OE and ME West Midlands pronunciation of other words such as 'wrang' (*wrong*) and 'lang' (*long*), for example, 'I haue lyued in londe, quod Y, my name is Longe Wille...' (i.e. William Langland, the author of *Piers Plowman*),

	OE	Brut	standard MnE
[an] – [ɔnd]			
	hwanon/ hwonon	**wonene**	*whence*
	anc/onc	**onke**	= *thought, favour*
[and] – [ɔnd]			
	land/lond	**lond/londe**	*land*
	mann/monn	**mon/monne**	*man*

Old English [ɑ] before a nasal consonant, after Freeborn (1998)

eventually became the standard British English pronunciation, and, as Freeborn (1998: 114) points out, 'busy' and 'bury' today have the West Midland spelling.

Conclusion

Dialects do not belong to clearly defined areas, and attempts to label segmental, suprasegmental syntactic and lexical features as specifically West Midlands are frustrated further by the fact that many are restricted to areas (or isoglosses) within or overlapping the geographical boundaries of the region. Considering its geographical position, it is perfectly natural for West Midlands English to waver, as we have seen, between northern and southern variables, tending towards the one or the other in those areas lying nearer to the adjacent dialects, and the convergence of northern and southern isoglosses in the West Midlands places the region midway in the dialect continuum between northern and southern varieties as a transition zone between the two. Not only is West Midlands English a mixture of northern and southern varieties of UK English, however, but it is also a hybrid of rural and urban varieties: a mixture of the Herefordshire, Shropshire, Staffordshire, Warwickshire and Worcestershire traditional dialects with the accents, dialects and languages of the many immigrant speech communities which settled in the region during and after the Industrial Revolution. The language of the West Midlands thus reflects its current multicultural population, although its roots can be traced back as far as the early Old English period.

Notes

[1] A formerly heavily industrialized area west of the M6, with Dudley at its centre and Wolverhampton marking its north-western corner, Walsall to the north-east, Stourbridge to the south-west and Halesowen to the south-east.

[2] This strong sense of identity did not extend to being British, with only 48% of people describing themselves as such in the 2001 census.
[3] A native of the city of Birmingham.
[4] A term widely used for the standard UK accent and often subdivided into 'marked', 'refined' or 'upper-class' (U-RP), and 'unmarked' or 'general' (non-U) variants which, like the standard UK dialect, has high status and is notoriously difficult to pin down geographically. The U-RP variant is also popularly known as 'upper-crust', 'public school' or 'the Queen's English', whereas non-U forms of RP are commonly referred to as 'BBC' or 'university-educated English'.

Bibliography

Advantage West Midlands (2007), *The West Midlands Region*, Advantage West Midlands [accessed 2 January 2007], available from <http://www.advantagewm.co.uk/>.
Ainsworth, B. (1989), 'Brumspeak', in *The Birmingham Historian*, Vol. 4, pp. 23–26.
Annual Business Inquiry (2003), *Annual Business Inquiry 2003*, Office for National Statistics [accessed 2 January 2007], available from < http://www.statistics.gov.uk/abi/>.
Anonymous, (1977), St. Katherine. Paris: Société d'Edition.
—. (1987), Sir Gawain and the Green Knight. Hammondsworth: Penguin.
—. (2006), Ancrene Wisse. Oxford: Oxford University Press.
Baugh, A. C. and Cable, T. (1996), *A History of the English Language*, London: Routledge.
Bede, (1969), *Ecclesiastical History of the English People*. Oxford: Clarendon Press.
Bede, the Venerable. (1935), *The Ecclesiastical History of the English People*, London: Burns, Oates and Washbourne.
Bird, V. (1974), *Portrait of Birmingham*, Birmingham: Robert Hale.
Bosworth, J. and Toller, T. N. (1898), *An Anglo-Saxon Dictionary*, Oxford: Oxford University Press.
Bradford, B. (1988), *Intonation in Context*, Cambridge: Cambridge University Press.
Bragg, M. (2002), *The Adventure of English*, London: Hodder and Stoughton.
Brazil, D. (1978), 'Discourse Intonation II', in *Discourse Analysis Monographs*, Vol. 2, pp. 27–41.
—. (1985), *The Communicative Value of Intonation in English*, Birmingham: University of Birmingham English Language Research.
—. (1997), *The Communicative Value of Intonation in English*, 2nd ed, Cambridge: Cambridge University Press.
Brazil, D., Coulthard, R. M. and Johns, C. (1980), *Discourse Intonation and Language Teaching*, London: Longman.
Cheshire, J. (1982), *Variation in an English Dialect: A Sociolinguistic Study*, Cambridge: Cambridge University Press.
Chinn, C. and Thorne, S. (2001), *Proper Brummie: A Dictionary of Birmingham Words and Phrases*, Studley: Brewin Books.
Cruttenden, A. (1986), *Intonation*, Cambridge: Cambridge University Press.

Crystal, D. (1995), *The Cambridge Encyclopaedia of the English Language*, Cambridge: Cambridge University Press.
Don, M. (2001), 'To the manor born', in *The Observer*, 6 May, p. 6.
Drabble, P. (1952), *Black Country*, Birmingham: Robert Hale.
Foulkes, P. and Docherty, G. (eds) (1999), *Urban Voices: Accent Studies in the British Isles*, London: Arnold.
Freeborn, D. (1998), *From Old English to Standard English*, Basingstoke: Macmillan.
Fujimura, O. (1962), 'Analysis of nasal consonants' *Journal of the Acoustic Society of America*, 62, 1865–1875.
Gimson, A. C., and Cruttenden, A. (1994), *Gimson's Pronunciation of English*, London: Edward Arnold.
Higden, R. (1865), *Polychronicon*. London: Longman.
—. (2004), *Polychronicon*. Heidelberg: Winter.
Hughes, A. and Trudgill, P. (1979) *English Accents and Dialects*, London: Edward Arnold.
Jackson, G. F. (1879), *Shropshire Word-Book: A Glossary of Archaic and Provincial Words Used in the County*, London: Trübner.
Labov, W. (1972), *Sociolinguistic Patterns*, Philadelphia: University of Pennsylvania Press.
Langland, W. (1995), *The Vision of Piers Plowman*. London: Everyman.
—. (2009), *The Vision of Piers Plowman*. Oxford: Oxford World Classics.
Layamon, (1847), Brut. London: Society of Antiquaries of London.
—. (1963), Brut. Oxford: Oxford University Press.
Mathisen, A. (1999), 'Sandwell, West Midlands: ambiguous perspectives on gender patterns and models of change', in P. Foulkes and G. Docherty (eds), *Urban Voices: Accent Studies in the British Isles*, London: Arnold.
McArthur, T. (ed.) (1992), *The Oxford Companion to the English Language*, Oxford: Oxford University Press.
Morris, R. (1882), *Specimens of Early English*. Oxford: Clarendon Press.
Northall, G. F. (1896), *A Warwickshire Wordbook*, London: Henry Frowde for the English Dialect Society.
ONS (2007) *2001 UK Census Online*, Office for National Statistics, accessed 2 January 2007, available from <http://www.statistics.gov.uk/census/>.
Palmer, R. (1976), *The Folklore of Warwickshire*, London: B. T. Batsford.
Poole, C. H. (1880), *Glossary of Archaic and Provincial Words of Staffordshire*, London: Henry Frowde for the English Dialect Society.
Rhodes, R. C. (1950), *A Birmingham Glossary*, Unpublished manuscript held at Birmingham Reference Library.
Shakespeare, W. (1969), *The Tempest*. London: Edward Arnold.
—. (1994), *The Tempest*. New York: Washington Square Press.
Shaw, T. (1930), *A Glossary of Black Country Words and Phrases*, Birmingham: Cornish Brothers.
Skeat, W. (ed.) (1876), *Original Glossaries*, London: Trubner and Co. for the English Dialect Society.
Skipp, V. (1980), *A History of Greater Birmingham*, Birmingham: Victor Skipp.
Thorne, S. (2003), *Birmingham English: A Sociolinguistic Study*, Ph.D. thesis, University of Birmingham.

Tomkinson, K. (1893), *Words of Old Worcestershire*, London: Tomkinson Ltd.
Trudgill, P. (1983), *On Dialect: Social and Geographical Perspectives*, Oxford: Blackwell.
—. (1999), *The Dialects of England*, Oxford: Blackwell.
Unknown. (1999), *St Katherine*, Kalamazoo: Medieval Institute Publications, Western Michigan University.
Unknown. (2000), *Ancrene Wisse*, Kalamazoo: Medieval Institute Publications, Western Michigan University.
Unknown. (2007), *Sir Gawain and the Green Knight*, London: Faber.
Upton, C. and Widdowson, J. (1996), *An Atlas of English Dialects*, Oxford: Oxford University Press.
Upton, C. Sanderson, S. and Widdowson, J. (1987), *Word Maps: A Dialect Atlas of England*, London: Croom Helm.
Wardhaugh, R. (1993), *An Introduction to Sociolinguistics*, Oxford: Blackwell.
Wells, J. C. (1982), *Accents of English*, Cambridge: Cambridge University Press.
West Midlands Regional Observatory (2007), *West Midlands Regional Observatory: State of the Region Update Reports*, West Midlands Regional Observatory accessed 2 January 2007. Available from: <http://www.wmro.org/standardTemplate.aspx/Home/OurResearch>.
Wright, J. (1898–1905), *The English Dialect Dictionary*, 6 vols, London: Henry Frowde for the English Dialect Society.

South West England, Counties and Administrative Areas

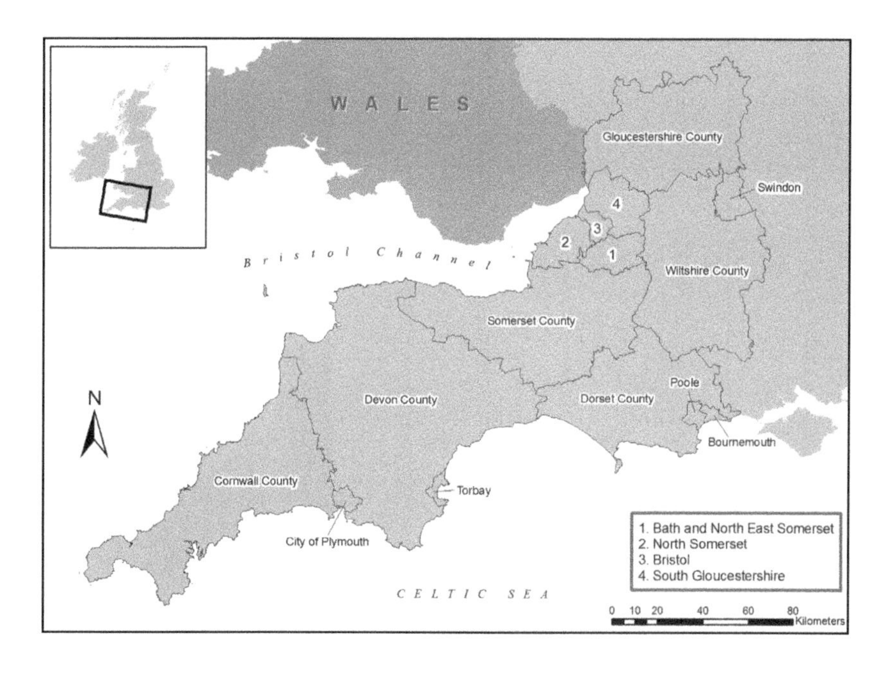

Chapter 6

South West English

Susanne Wagner

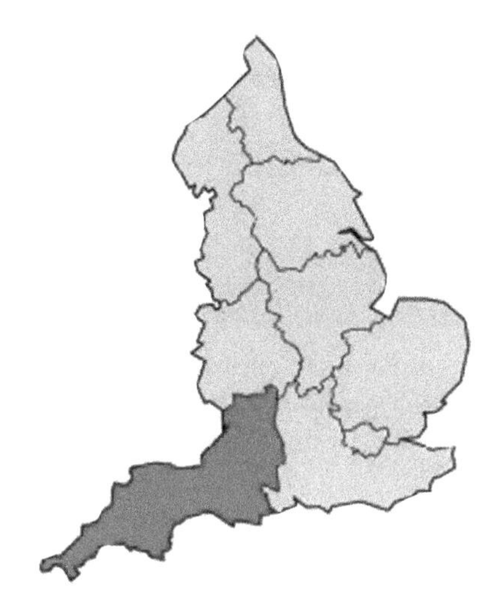

Map 1: South West England

The Region

South West England is one of the nine regions[1] of England. At approximately 24,000 km, it occupies the largest area, but ranks only seventh in population with about 5 million inhabitants. Its administrative headquarters are located in Bristol and Plymouth. The region had originally been divided into Avon, Cornwall, Devon, Dorset, Gloucestershire, Somerset and Wiltshire. Restructuring has led to a number of changes: Avon no longer exists, and a number of urban districts are now unitary authorities (mainly Bath, Bristol, Swindon, Poole, Bournemouth, Torbay, Plymouth; cf. Maps 1 and 2)[2].

Somerset
- 1. Bath and North East Somerset (Unitary)
- 2. North Somerset (Unitary)
- 11. Somerset (Shire)

Bristol
- 3. Bristol (Unitary)

Gloucestershire
- 4. South Gloucestershire (Unitary)
- 5. Gloucestershire (Shire)

Wiltshire
- 6. Swindon (Unitary)
- 7. Wiltshire (Shire)

Dorset
- 8. Dorset (Shire)
- 9. Poole (Unitary)
- 10. Bournemouth (Unitary)

Devon
- 12. Devon (Shire)
- 13. Torbay (Unitary)
- 14. Plymouth (Unitary)

Cornwall
- 15. Cornwall (Shire)

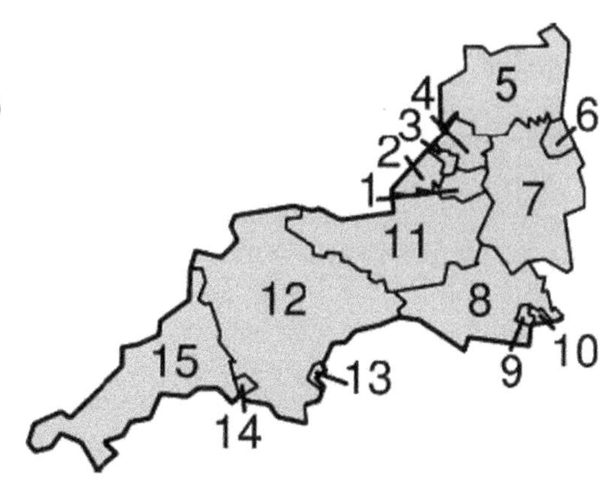

Map 2: Counties and administrative areas

What is called South West England or 'The South West' is largely identical with what is known as the West Country and much of the Anglo-Saxon kingdom of Wessex.[3] Within the region, a special position is occupied by Cornwall on historical and cultural grounds. There are even proposals for Cornwall to form a separate region,[4] which have failed so far.

The South West is a largely rural area where nowadays tourism and agriculture play major roles; dairy farms occupying vales are typical sights. The highest point of the region is the highest hill in Dartmoor at some 600 metres. The landscape is granite moorland in the west, while chalk and limestone downland as well as clay vales dominate in the east. Historically, tin mining (particularly in Cornwall) and fishing provided major sources of income. For decades, the port of Poole, Dorset, served as the major port of embarkation for the summer fishery in Newfoundland.

The South West as a linguistic region

The Rural South West

The South West has always been recognized as a separate linguistic region, usually contrasting South West and South East which together form 'the South' (traditionally excluding East Anglia). To the North, the South West is bordered by the Midlands.

The major criteria for differentiating between South West and non-South West varieties from a linguistic point of view include the following: Typical of a South West accent to the present day is what is known as the West Country burr, which is caused by two different linguistic phenomena. On the one hand, South West English is rhotic, contrasting with its non-rhotic neighbours both to the East (South East English) and North (Midlands English). On the other hand, the phoneme [r] is generally realized as a retroflex in the South West, with retroflex colouring often extending to the phonetic environment as well. Another accent feature traditionally mentioned about the South West is the voicing of initial fricatives so that *finger* sounds like *vinger*, a feature that is no longer part of the modern varieties of South West England.

As for morphosyntactic features, the South West English dialect to the present day maintains one of the richest inventories of vernacular features of all regional Englishes. Although different constructions and features can be found in different parts of the region, and not all are present in all counties to the same extent, the overall picture is one of homogeneity within the region, which contrasts starkly with neighbouring dialects. Major differences that survive to the present day can be found in the pronominal and verbal systems (see below).

Varieties of the South West dialects were among the most popular in studies in the nineteenth century, only surpassed by the prominence of Northern dialects (cf. Ihalainen 1994: 231–232). Among the publications of the *English Dialect Society* (EDS), which formed the basis of the *English Dialect Dictionary*

(Wright 1898–1905), are a number on the South West that are unsurpassed in detail to the present day. No other region has been covered as extensively by the EDS as the South West, which is largely thanks to Frederic Elworthy's publications (cf. Elworthy 1965a, 1965b, 1965c, but see also Chope 1965, Couch 1965, Courtney 1965). Different from most other EDS publications, which generally focused on phonology and lexicon, Elworthy's work contains detailed descriptions of the morphosyntax of the variety (West Somerset) as well.

When fieldworkers began their work on the *Survey of English Dialects* (SED) in the 1950s, the focus of dialectology was still on accent and lexical features. The morphology and grammar section of the SED questionnaire, about 15 per cent of the total of more than 1300 questions, focuses on high-frequency features such as agreement and forms of personal pronouns, with several questions about irregular verb paradigms.[5] Unsurpassed in its width of coverage (311 localities all over England with 7 in Cornwall, 11 in Devon, 5 in Dorset, 13 in Somerset, 9 in Wiltshire), the SED to the present day is an important, if not the major source on (traditional) dialects. Modern studies are often quite restricted regionally in focusing on just one community or even village. Thus, when cross-dialect or even cross-country comparisons are attempted, these are often done with material that is about 2 generations or almost 60 years removed from the present – the SED data.

Within the South West, it is often mentioned that the region of West Cornwall should be ascribed special status. It is the region with the shortest history of English in the area, as Cornish, a Celtic language closely related to Welsh and Breton, was spoken until the eighteenth century. Traditionally, it is assumed that (a) a dialect of English did not have the same time to develop as the dialects of the neighbouring regions and that (b) English as the language of the higher classes and the medium of instruction at school was acquired in a form closer to Standard English (StE) than the local varieties of the other South West counties.

> [S]peakers of Cornish in the Modern Cornish period would learn not the ancient Wessex dialect of east Cornwall, Devon and Somerset . . . , but a version of English taught them in schools and by the upper classes and better-educated (note that it was the gentry who gave up Cornish and spoke English first), an English deliberately acquired, as distinct from a regional dialect passed on from generation to generation. (Wakelin 1975: 100).

It is thus assumed that West Cornwall to the present day is 'less dialectal' than East Cornwall or the neighbouring counties. However, data from West Cornwall in FRED[6] show that traditional South West features can indeed be found there. Detailed linguistic studies of English in Cornwall are not available; it is possible that the West East contrasts have to be reevaluated, at least in part (cf. Wagner 2004a, 2005).

Judging by the number of publications, the South West was still intriguing both laymen and experts in the 1970s and later. Martyn Wakelin, who had already been involved in the SED project, continued to work on dialects of the South West for the next decades, largely using SED material (cf. Wakelin 1970, 1975, 1984, 1986). Ossi Ihalainen studied two peculiarities of the South West in particular, namely periphrastic *do* and gendered pronouns (cf. e.g. Ihalainen 1976, 1985a, 1985b, 1991a, 1991b), but was also involved in the construction of a computerized corpus of dialect texts, reporting on technical and contextual difficulties arising (cf. e.g. Ihalainen 1988, 1990, 1994).

The Urban South West

Although many studies with traditional methodologies and aims were published in the twentieth century, the shift from traditional to modern dialectology has not (yet) reached the South West. To the present author's knowledge, there are no studies available (yet) on urban varieties in the South West proper. A PhD thesis is currently being prepared by Kate Wallace at the University of Leeds (see Wallace 2007), focusing on the city of Southampton in Hampshire, which has been labelled as South West and South East in the past.

Recent research undertaken by Wallace in the Southampton area, which encompasses the city of Southampton and the neighbouring borough of Eastleigh, reveals a similar variety of opinions among its inhabitants regarding the location of the area. When asked to say where Southampton is geographically, ME, an 83-year-old female from Southampton, replies:

> South. I'm a bit confused about that because sometimes we're put in the South West and sometimes we're put in the South East. We're basically bang in the middle [...]. Because I don't really feel aligned to the South West, although I think it's a lovely part of the country, because it is more rural basically. It's different altogether to the South East which is just South of London with all that [*sic*] problems.

Though Wallace finds that informants appear to be unsure as to whether Southampton lies in the South East or the South West (witnessed by statements such as 'I don't know really which one we're in'), the reality seems to be that they do not believe the Southampton area to be in either. In the opinion of Wallace's informants, it is 'central South', 'bang in the middle', its inhabitants 'slap-bang Southerners' without 'any great affinity to either [the South East or the South West]'. RW, a 69-year-old male from Eastleigh Borough argues that 'we live in the South, not in the South East or the South West, because we are virtually in the middle'. These informants do not appear to identify with the South East or the South West. MG, a 22-year-old female from Eastleigh Borough, states, 'I don't really class myself as South East or South West [...] I'm Southern'.

Despite the fact that some of Wallace's speakers are reluctant to place the Southampton area in either the South East or the South West, and that many instead feel Southern, nearly half of the speakers interviewed for the

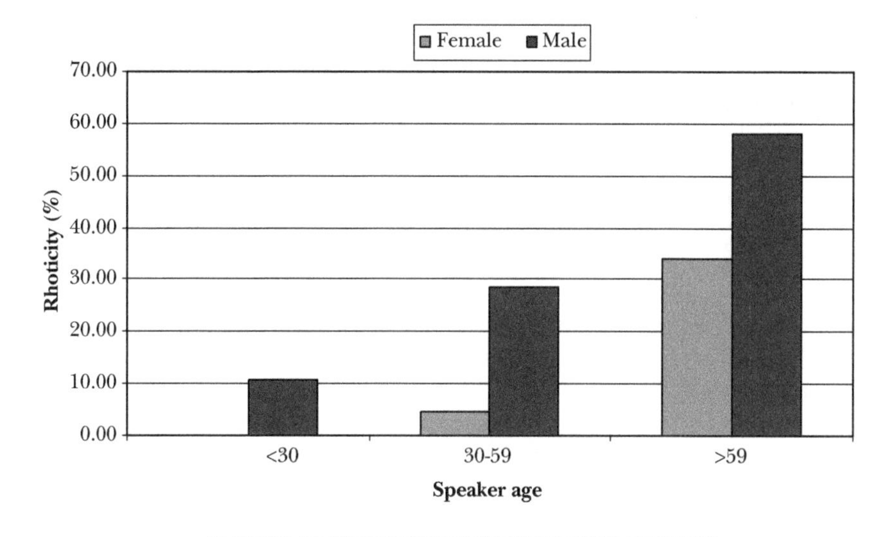

	Rhoticity	
Speaker Age	**Female**	**Male**
< 30	0.00% [n = 0/150]	10.67% [n = 16/150]
30–59	4.67% [n = 7/150]	28.67% [n = 43/150]
> 59	34.00% [n = 51/150]	58.00% [n = 87/150]

Figure 6.1 Rhoticity in the Southampton area according to speaker age and sex.

Southampton area study are variably rhotic (also see section 3 below). Figure 6.1 shows rhoticity in the speech of the sixty Southampton area informants (ten in each of the six speaker cells) during relatively casual interviews, according to speaker age and sex (all data from Wallace 2007).

On this evidence, it would appear that rhoticity is on the decline in the Southampton area, since it is most frequently found in the speech of those aged 60 and above. Since the Southampton study is an apparent-time one, however, it is not possible to say this categorically. Rhoticity in the Southampton area is also subject to sex variation, being more common in men than in women.

Another feature of South Western speech (Wells 1982: 345–346) found in the Southampton area is /aː/ in the BATH lexical set. According to Wallace's findings, /aː/ is most commonly found in the speech of older informants and among the working class, while RP /ɑː/ is found in the speech of the middle class. Informants aged 60 and above also retain the historical /l/ in the word *palm*, another feature of Western speech (Wells 1982: 346).

It is not simply phonological features traditionally associated with the South West which are found in Southampton. L vocalization, which Wells (1982: 259) states has its origins in 'the local accent of London and the surrounding counties', is widely used by speakers in the Southampton area. Sex-based variation in the use of this feature is minimal but age-based variation is clear. Of the tokens of [ɫ] collected from Southampton area speakers under the age of 30, 78.33 per cent are realized as a vocoid, compared to 75.33 per cent of tokens collected from those aged 30 to 59, and 46.33 per cent of tokens from speakers aged 60 and above.

In conclusion, the Southampton area accent includes a mixture of typically South Eastern and South Western features. Though sometimes placed in the South West by linguists, Southampton's inhabitants express a degree of uncertainty regarding its location and many state that they are from the South as opposed to the South East or the South West. That said, when asked to whom they feel closer, people from the South East, the South West or neither, eighteen informants in the Southampton area study replied that they feel closer to people from the South West, compared to only seven who said people from the South East. Thirty-five out of sixty, however, said that they do not feel close to either. Llamas (2000: 123), discussing Berwick-upon-Tweed and Middlesbrough, comments that 'a "border town" status [...] can entail a problematic construction of identity'. It is clear that this comment could well be applied to the Southampton area in its central position on the Southern coast.

The South West?

The discussion of the 'border town' Southampton already illustrates that the South West is by no means a homogeneous dialect area. This can also be seen in the publications of the EDS when Elworthy focuses on West Somerset, stating that East Somerset is already very different, or when Chope says something similar about the dialect of Hartland in Northwest Devon, which, despite bordering Cornwall, is much closer to West Somerset than to Cornwall (1965: 2).

Basing studies on SED material is also not unproblematic. Somerset, for example, proved to be rather tricky in a study of gendered pronouns (cf. Wagner 2005) in that these were much more frequent in the other counties and even in West Cornwall. Detailed analyses of distributional patterns in the South West show that these generally do not pattern neatly (cf. e.g. Klemola 1996, Wagner 2001, 2005). From a modern point of view, many of these discrepancies between traditional and modern studies can be explained quite easily: while work on dialects and particularly morphosyntactic features traditionally puts the spotlight on their presence or absence (type: Does feature X exist in this region?), modern studies usually emphasize quantity rather than quality (type: How frequent is feature X in this region?). As a result of these differences in emphasis or focus over time, features that are mentioned in traditional studies might be over-emphasized as modern readers tend to equate the mentioning (which in fact only means that the feature does occur in the region) with 'is very common' or even 'is the norm'.

Pronunciation

Probably the best-known feature associated with West Country pronunciation to the present day is its rhoticity, that is the presence of /r/ in all positions.[7] Since /r/ is often realized as a retroflex, it is also responsible for the distinctive West Country burr that many people, visitors and natives alike, name as the most distinguishing characteristic of modern West Country English. Examples (1a) to (1c) from the SED fieldworker notebooks from Cornwall also show that a retroflex /r/ very often leads to a retroflex realization of the preceding and / or following sound. Hyper-rhoticity, the realization of an /r/ not present in spelling, does also occur (cf. ˈnɔʳːʈ *naught* in 1b.). As with other types of hyper-correction, it is assumed that speakers of West Country accents insert an /r/ because similar words have /r/ in the same position.

1. a. ˈiː ad ə ˈbaʳːɽaɪɚː ˈɖɽuːv ˈɽæːʈ ˈɖɽʊː ən
   he 'ad a bar iron drove right through en
   it had a bar of iron driven right through it (SED FN Co1)

   b. ˈnɛvɚː ˈjɚːd ən kɔːɫd ˈnɔʳːʈ ˈɛɫs
   never heard en called naught else
   never heard it called anything else (SED FN Co2)

   c. ˈðas wɒt də kɫɒɪm ˈɛnɪwɚːɽ ɒn ˈwɔːɫz ən ˈʈɽiːz
   that's what do climb anywhere on walls an' trees
   that's what climbs anywhere on walls and trees (SED FN Co5)

Another feature of traditional West Country accents is the voicing of initial fricatives so that *finger* becomes *vinger*, *say* becomes *zay*. The Dorset poet William Barnes used spellings like these in his publications, for example:

Ov all the birds upon the wing
Between the zunny show'rs o' spring, –
Vor all the lark, a-swingèn high,
Mid zing below a cloudless sky,
An' sparrows, clust'rèn roun' the bough,
Mid chatter to the men at plough, –
The blackbird, whisslèn in among
The boughs, do zing the gaÿest zong.

(from *The Blackbird*, Barnes 1844: 3)

Voiced initial fricatives are already used as a South Western stereotype in Shakespeare's *King Lear* (cf. e.g. McArthur 1992: 1112) and can still be found in the SED (cf. 2), but have since receded to some rural areas and older speakers. It is more than likely that the feature will disappear with that generation.

2. ˈzoːk əm vɚː ˈgɪt æʊt ðə ˈsteːnz
   zoak 'em for get out the stains
   soak them to get out the stains (SED FN Co3)

Vowels

Diphthongs are often realized as monophthongs in the South West (particularly FACE and GOAT vowels, see *soak* and *stains* in example 2), thus still realizing these sound sequences as if the Great Vowel Shift had not happened. The MOUTH-diphthong tends to be /æʊ/ rather than /aʊ/, and the GOAT-diphthong can vary between /oː/, /ɔː/ or /æʊ/. The diphthong in PRICE is generally a monophthong somewhere between /aː/ ~ /ɑː/ ~ /æː/. On the other hand, West Country accents also tend to diphthongize certain monophthongs, e.g. /klɛɪn/ *clean* (SED FN Co5) or /gɪən/ *again* (SED FN Co1), with the latter a possible example of metathesis.

Consonants

Rhoticity and the generally retroflex realization of /r/ as well as the voicing of initial fricatives has already been mentioned above. Another feature separating the South West from the South East and Midlands accents is the realization of /l/ as dark in most and sometimes all positions.

Overall, traditional West Country accents are very conservative. Old pronunciations such as /æ/ for /a/ as in /æːftɚːɽ/ *after* (SED FN Co7) or monophthongal realizations of diphthongs are preserved, as are such features as rhoticity. Given such a high degree of conservativeness and with realizations such as /ɒ/ for /ɑ/ in the LOT vowel, West Country accents particularly of the traditional type probably sound much more like American than British English to a lay person or non-native speaker of English.

Morphology and Syntax

The South West of England is one of the few regions in England which, in addition to a distinct accent, also features a number of morphosyntactic forms different enough from StE to be noticed even by the non-linguist. Most noteworthy to the present day are features that have survived from the days of the traditional West Country dialect. Among those that are restricted to the South West exclusively (or at least predominantly) are pronoun exchange, gendered pronouns (for both see sections on personal pronouns and periphrastic *do*).

The following sections first discuss features found in the noun phrase and verb phrase respectively, with later sections focusing on other areas. Both traditional features that are often disappearing nowadays or have already disappeared and more general features also frequently found in other varieties of English around the world are mentioned.

The noun phrase

Articles, number and adjective formation

Rogers (1979) mentions that – different from StE – the definite article is used with some nouns in West Country dialect: referring to diseases, 'one has "the chicken pox"', and its 'the both' (1979: 31). Given the settlement history and links between the regions, this is a possible candidate for substrate influence from Celtic Englishes. In Irish English, the over-use of the definite article is a well-known feature (cf. e.g. Filpulla 2004: 90–92). The indefinite article is usually invariable *a*, even where a vowel follows. Examples from FRED include the ones in (3).

3. a. *I went in* ***the*** *Musgrove Hospital in 1979.* (FRED Som_032)
   b. *...we had to walk a mile to* ***the school*** *and back.* (FRED Som_012)
   c. [Interviewer: *Did you take any exam? For example, did you take a scholarship exam to the County School?*] *Yes, I took it two years following, and failed* ***the both*** *of them.* (FRED Con_007)
   d. *...but I stayed on until* ***the Christmas.*** (FRED Con_008)
   e. *If* ***a end*** *comes off he automatically stops, see.* (FRED Wil_001)
   f. *A journeyman is* ***a apprentice*** *that has served his apprenticeship . . .* (FRED Dev_002)

Number is generally not marked overtly on nouns if they are preceded by units of measurement (cf. e.g. Rogers 1979: 33, Barnes 1970: 20). This is one of the most widespread features in varieties of English world-wide. Typical examples are *forty mile, ten ton* or *four pound.* Traditionally, the plural allomorph [ɪz] was employed as a means of consonant cluster simplification in nouns ending in [st], resulting in plurals such as *ghostes* or *beastes* (cf. Rogers 1979: 33). Although it has long died out in the South West, it can still be found in traditional dialects of Newfoundland, which was settled by people from the West Country to a large extent (cf. e.g. *savage beastes* and *by God 'tis ghostes here* from Halpert and Widdowson 1996).

Another feature that seems to have survived longer in Newfoundland than in the West Country is the use of the suffix *-en* to form an adjective with the meaning 'made of' (e.g. *wooden*). Figuring prominently in the folktales published by

Halpert and Widdowson (1996) is a *glassen pole* (i.e. made of glass). Irregular comparatives and superlatives (e.g. double marking as in *worser* or *most beautifullest*) do occur, but are relatively rare nowadays.

Personal pronouns

As already mentioned, two of the three features most noteworthy in the morphosyntax of South West English dialects can be found in the pronominal domain or more exactly that of personal pronouns, namely pronoun exchange and gendered pronouns. In addition, both the domains of reflexive pronouns and demonstrative pronouns show forms and uses different from StE. From a formal point of view, one form has to be mentioned that is distinctive of West Country English and varieties derived from it such as Newfoundland English: The object form of the third person masculine pronoun is [ən], usually spelt *un* or *en*, a form that is said to be a remnant from Old English form *hine*.

Pronoun exchange

The term 'pronoun exchange' is probably Ossi Ihalainen's (cf. Ihalainen 1991a, but see also Wakelin 1981: 114). It describes a rule for the use of case-marked pronominal forms (i.e. *I* vs. *me*, *he/she* vs. *him/her*, *we* vs. *us* and *they* vs. *them*) that is completely different from that of StE. While in StE the case of the pronoun depends on grammatical requirements, that is, basically the question whether the form is in subject position or not, West Country dialects are said to use subject forms (i.e. *I, he, she, we, they*) in emphatic positions, while the oblique forms (*me, him, her, us, them*) are used in non-emphatic contexts.

As a result, two scenarios are possible: (a) the occurrence of subject forms in oblique slots – for example, *give it to I* or *he gave I the book* and (b) the occurrence of oblique forms in subject slots – for example, *her's a coward, us always call it X*. It should be noted that the phenomenon in (a) is the rule for pronoun exchange, while the possibility in (b) is rather restricted. Discussions of pronoun exchange can be found in Elworthy (1965b: 35–38), Kruisinga (1905: 35–36) and Wright (1905: 271), to name just a few. Examples from the SED and FRED can be found in (4).

4. a. *I did give I did give* ***she*** *a 'and and she did give* ***I*** *a 'and and we did 'elp one another.* (FRED Wil_011)
   b. *Well, if I didn't know* ***they****, they knowed* ***I****.* (FRED Wil_009)
   c. *they always called* ***I*** *Willie, see.* (FRED Som_009)
   d. *Uncle Willy, they used to call him, you remember* ***he?*** (FRED Con_006)
   e. *Never had no fault at all with* ***she****.* (FRED Som_005)
   f. ***Us*** *never keeped any pigeons.* (SED FN Co1)
   g. ***'er*** *is, idn'* ***'er?*** (SED FN Co3)

An analysis of pronoun exchange based on FRED and data from the SED field-worker notebooks reveals that the phenomenon is highly complex. Certain regions seem to favour certain forms (e.g. *us* in subject position is incredibly frequent in Devon in the SED, but almost absent from e.g. Somerset), certain forms only occur in certain syntactic environments (e.g. *them* or rather *'em* occurs in subject position only in tags, e.g. *They wouldn' know thicky word, would 'em?* SED FN Co1), and overall, pronoun exchange is very rare in more modern data – in FRED, for example, only about 1 per cent of all pronominal forms in the South West material are 'exchanged'. However, it is unclear if the phenomenon ever was more frequent than this.

Some overall tendencies can be summarized from the investigation of some 1200 'exchanged' pronominal forms found in the SED. First, as already mentioned above, subject forms in object slots are the more frequent exchange scenario. While more than half of all possible exchanged forms do indeed occur in these contexts, this is true for only about 20 per cent of all subject forms. Second, there seems to be a direct relation between the two exchange scenarios in that a region with a high frequency for scenario A (subject forms in non-subject slots) will almost certainly show comparatively low frequencies for scenario B (object forms in non-object slots). That is to say, a person who says *Give it to she* is rather unlikely to say *Her don't need it.* Third, the West Country is split in two parts as to its use of exchanged pronouns. While more easterly locations (and particularly Wiltshire) seem to favour subject-for-object forms, the West Country proper uses mainly object-for-subject forms. West Cornwall patterns with the East rather than the West here. And fourth, the SED evidence suggests that pronoun exchange was already on the retreat, even in its homeland, in the late nineteenth and early twentieth centuries. The only domains where we find pseudo-pronoun exchange in modern StE are those where a general confusion about case marking helps advance such misuses as *between you and I.* This should not be confused with the dialect phenomenon described here.

Gendered pronouns

In addition to pronoun exchange, the personal pronoun paradigm of the South West features another interesting discrepancy from StE. The examples in (5) illustrate a phenomenon for which experts have not yet found a common name:

5. a. *Lovely church that is if you've ever seen '**im. He**'s worth looking at.* (FRED Som_036)
   b. *We call **en*** [n̩] *a peeth* [*well*]. (SED FN Co6)
   c. *... press them like that and you'd see your thumb mark in them or any other apple really when **he**'s ripe, wadn't it, but when **he**'s not ripe **he**'s hard, isn't **he** ...* (FRED Som_001)

The distribution of these gendered pronouns used to follow a simple rule in the traditional dialects: count nouns are *he*, mass nouns are *it*; only humans can also be *she*. Because of the pressure of StE on dialects in general and since non-standard uses of *she* can also be found in spoken English world-wide (cf. e.g. MacKay and Konishi 1980; Mathiot and Roberts 1979; Morris 1991), the modern system of gender assignment in the South West is far more complex. Things that would have been *he* in traditional dialect can now be *she* (spoken Standard) and *it* (StE) – not an easy puzzle to solve. An extensive discussion of pronominal gender assignment in varieties of South West England as well as Newfoundland can be found in Wagner (2003) and (2005). Siemund (2007) discusses the phenomenon from a typological point of view.

Gendered pronouns are interesting for a number of reasons. One is that they are not, or at least not as openly, stigmatized as many other morphosyntactic dialect features. Endless discussions can be held by native speakers about why their car is a *she* or why in certain contexts almost everything can be *she*. However, as with pronoun exchange, these modern uses are only reminiscent of the dialect phenomenon proper but in fact have nothing to do with it historically. Although some researchers have looked into these modern uses (e.g. MacKay and Konishi 1980; Mathiot and Roberts 1979; Morris 1991; Pawley 2004), they are far from being understood.

In the modern South West, gendered pronouns are losing ground to the spoken Standard and StE forms. The loss of the traditional system seems to follow the path outlined by Ihalainen (1985b, 1991a): The standard forms invade the system from the less accessible positions in the Noun Phrase Accessibility Hierarchy (cf. Keenan and Comrie 1977). As a result, utterances like the following can be encountered: *when I saw the plough nobody valued it, if he had been kept dry he would have been good now* (FRED Som_015); *So, therefore, if they had to use a stone jar they used to get the basket maker to put some wicker around it, so if he had a bump he wouldn't break* (FRED Som_024). In both examples, gendered pronouns are still used in subject position, while the object slots have been taken over by StE *it*. A detailed investigation of the Ihalainen's Accessibility Hypothesis can be found in Wagner (2004b).

Possessives

South West speakers tend to avoid neuter *its*, which is generally substituted by the analytic *of it*. It has not yet been investigated whether this is the only remnant of a more general avoidance of possessive pronouns postulated by Barnes (1994: 129–130), Elworthy (1965b: 13), Hancock (1994: 105), Rogers (1979: 32) and Wakelin (1986: 38), giving preference to such phrases as *the father of un* over *his father*. It can be assumed that the avoidance of *its* is not a feature of West Country dialect, but rather a tendency to be found in spoken

English in general. The examples in (6) illustrate that the use of the analytic *of it* may even result in two adjoining *of*-phrases (6b, 6c).

6. a. *the owner* ***of her;*** *the captain* ***of her*** (FRED Som_028)
   b. *then you've got a chance to run out of the way* ***of him*** (FRED Som_005)
   c. *I had an idea of the price* ***of it*** (FRED Con_009)
   d. *you couldn't really see the colour* ***of it*** (FRED Wil_002)
   e. *Sherford was the name* ***of it,*** *that's right* (FRED Dev_001)

Demonstratives

It is argued by some of the nineteenth-century authors (cf. e.g. Barnes 1844: 130; 1970: 17–18; Elworthy 1965a: 23; 1965b: 29) that traditional West Country dialect used to distinguish mass and count forms not only in the domain of personal pronouns (cf. above, gendered pronouns), but also in demonstratives. This supposedly resulted in a system which contrasted *thick* (count) with *this* (mass), both with an optional *here*, in the 'close' domain, and *thick* with *that* (plus an optional *there*) in the 'distant' domain. While examples of the forms as such can still be found in the SED and FRED (see examples in 7 below), lacking a larger data pool the contrast can no longer be established. A close-distant-remote system as occasionally postulated for South Western dialects in modern studies (e.g. Trudgill 1999: 86; Harris 1991; Trudgill and Chambers 1991: 10) cannot be established from either traditional accounts or corpus data, as examples of a threefold distinction are non-existent.

Another difference of the demonstrative system in non-standard varieties generally is the use of *they* or *them* where StE employs *those*. While examples of *them* are ubiquitous in many English dialects, *they* is not found as frequently.

7. a. *they had* ***this here*** *place on the racecourse* (FRED Dev_004)
   b. *Well, like* ***thick*** *one what 's in there now, ehr, for killing all* ***they*** *women.* (FRED Som_005)
   c. *That's what all* ***them*** *old buildings are.* (FRED Con_006)
   d. *when you come to* ***that there*** *corner, that's called Tugrushen corner.* (FRED Som_014)
   e. *In* 'ðɪk kʊ̃ntrɪ *in this district;* 'ðɪk 'bʊʃ *this bush;* 'ðat ðɛə 'mɪɫks 'gɒn *that there milk's gone;* 'ðiːz jər 'kʊp *this here cup* (SED FN So Montacute)

Reflexives

The StE reflexive pronoun paradigm is irregular in employing a mixture of forms: the possessive pronoun is used to form the first and second person singular as well as plural forms. In the third person, however, personal pronouns + *self/selves* are used. Naturally, many varieties of English world-wide regularize these irregularities. As a result, the possessive pronoun is used for all forms, that is, *hisself* is used where StE has *himself* and *theirselves* substitutes StE *themselves.* Plural marking tends to be optional where the possessive pronoun already gives that information – thus, *ourself* and *theirself* is possible, *yourself* is singular, *yourselves* is plural.

Relative markers

The traditional relative pronouns, that is, the *wh*-forms, are only rarely used in most non-standard varieties, which is also due to the fact that contact clauses or zero relatives are used (a) much more frequently than in StE and (b) also when the relative pronoun is the subject of the relative clause which is not allowed in StE (cf. 8b.–d.).

Rather than relative pronouns, which are traditionally marked for case (*who – whose – whom*) and animacy (*who/whose/whom* vs. *which*), the invariant relative particle *that* is used universally, both for things and human beings. In the South West, the particles *as* (traditional) and the more innovative *what* also occur. For a detailed study on relativization strategies in British English dialects, see Herrmann (2005).

Non-restrictive relative clauses, which in StE require a *wh*-form, are only rarely used in spoken language generally. Dialects usually avoid them altogether by using co-ordination rather than subordination as in *he's a nice guy – I didn't know that before* being the spoken alternative to a written *he's a nice guy which I didn't know before.*

8. a. *my dear sister* ***as*** *is dead and gone …* (FRED Wil_005)
   b. *There's a pair of blocks down there* **Ø** *was made when I was apprentice.* (FRED Som_016)
   c. *I know a man* **Ø** *'ll do it for 'ee.* (SED FN Co4)
   d. *you had a barrow* **Ø** *runs from there straight across like that* (FRED Som_001)
   e. *we had a big churn* ***what****'d hold forty gallons* (FRED Som_011)
   f. (gap 'name '), *you know* ***what*** *was boss* (FRED Som_009)
   g. *and there were a man in there* ***and he*** *were a dowser* (FRED Wil_001)

The verb phrase

Concord with forms of be

As the most frequently used verb of the English language, *be* shows a degree of variation that is highly uncommon. The StE paradigm distinguishes the forms *be, am, are, is, was* and *were,* with agreement rules that are different from any other verbal paradigm. It is thus not very surprising that dialects tend to regularize and reduce this highly complex paradigm. Forms occurring traditionally in the South West include the use of invariant *be* throughout the present tense paradigm (*I be, you be, he/she/it be, we be, you be, they be*), the extension of *am* to the plural (*we'm, you'm* and *they'm*), the use of *was* where StE uses *were* and vice versa (e.g. *you was, they was, he were* etc.).

Regularized irregular verbs

Irregular verbal paradigms are usually regularized and/or reduced in many spoken varieties of English. Analogy plays a major role in these regularization processes. Two major strategies are employed: Paradigms with three different forms (present – past – past participle) are generally reduced to two forms, with identical past and past participle forms. As a result, the paradigms look as if either the past or the past participle form is used to cover the other function as well (e.g. *take – took – took; do – done – done*). Another regularization strategy is the weakening of strong verbs, that is, the *-ed* ending of the weak verbs paradigm is added to verbs which are strong in StE (e.g. *run – runned; catch – catched*). Examples from the South West can be found in (9).

9. a. *which **catched** my knee* (FRED Som_032)
   b. *he **knowed** how to get 'em* (FRED Wil_010)
   c. *that chap was **took** to hospital* (FRED Som_020)
   d. *he **done** all that plastering* (FRED Dev_007)
   e. *he **throwed** un* (FRED Con_003)

Negative concord

The StE rule that two minuses equal one plus is not valid in most spoken varieties. As a result, double or multiple negation is still negation, no matter how many negative forms are included in an utterance. West Country dialect is no exception in this respect, as the examples in (10) show.

10. a. *I was **never no** footballer* (FRED Con_005)
    b. *You **can't** alter them **no** way* (FRED Wil_001)
    c. *he **wouldn't** go **no** further* (FRED Dev_008)
    d. *No that **ain't no** use now* (FRED Dev_002)
    e. *Mother **never** had **no** trouble with **none** of we* (FRED Som_005)

Auxiliary versus full verb distinction of the primary verbs

The traditional dialects of South West England distinguish between the full verb and auxiliary uses of the primary verbs *do, have* and *be*. While the base form is used in the auxiliary uses, an *-s* ending is added in all full verb functions. Moreover, the past tense of auxiliary *do* is *did*, while it is *done* in main verb function.

11. a. *he* ***do*** *fly around here and* ***have*** *a look* (FRED Wil_011)
    b. [Interviewer: *It makes a messier cheese – was it now –*] *It* ***do****.* (FRED Som_025)
    c. *and they* ***has*** *these long trousers tucked up like this* (FRED Som_022)
    d. *perhaps it might be a good idea if I* ***has*** *a bit of insight in case mother was taken ill* (FRED Som_011)
    e. *and in they days the ladies didn't ride straddle like they* ***do's*** *today, they used to ride side-saddle*. (FRED Wil_001)
    f. ðat 'av bɪn sɛd *that has been said* (SED FN So Monacute)

Periphrastic do

Periphrastic *do* refers to the use of a non-emphatic form of *do* followed by the bare infinitive of a full verb. In South Western varieties, periphrastic *do* seems to serve two functions, namely to signal habituality and to serve as a simple tense carrier, although uses of the latter are rare in more modern material. Examples from the SED and FRED are given in (12).

12. a. *As I* ***do*** *say to my niece, I say, you know, you're far better off, I said, than what we were, I said* (FRED Wil_012)
    b. *…she* ***did*** *do a lot of needlework, …* (FRED Wil_018)
    c. *William, my son,* ***do*** *live down there* (FRED Con_005)
    d. *But they* ***did*** *work 'til quarter to six at night, that was their normal time and as I say, the hooter* ***did*** *blow at the finish and all machines* ***did*** *shut down they were gone within about five minutes. It didn't take long to do it. They* ***did*** *sweep round the machines before they left, they always do that when the machines are running* (FRED Wil_006)
    e. 'apɫ biːz 'wi də kɔːɫ əm
       apple bees we do call 'em
       apple bees we call them (SED FN Co4)
    f. 'ðas wɒd 'aɪ də duː
       that's what I do do
       that's what I do (SED FN Co4)
    g. 'sʌm də 'kiːp ət ən 'sʌm də 'spɛnd ət
       some do keep it an' some do spend it
       some keep it and some spend it (SED FN Co6)

The most detailed study on periphrastic *do* is Klemola (1996), mostly based on material from the SED Basic Material and fieldworker notebooks. Kortmann

(2004) discusses *do* as a tense and aspect marker in a wider range of languages and dialects. It is important to note that periphrastic *do* is not distributed homogeneously throughout the West Country. Although it is almost impossible to reconstruct the distribution in the nineteenth and early twentieth centuries, it can be shown that periphrastic *do* was more frequent in some and probably non-existent in other counties (cf. Wagner 2007).

Verbal -s

Newfoundland English to the present day is known for one feature that must have been inherited from its West Country donor dialects: verbal *-s*, that is the use of an *-s* ending on all persons of the present tense verb paradigm. It is generally agreed that the *-s* marks habituality (cf. e.g. Clarke 1997, 1999). Examples of verbal *-s* can be found in (13).

13. a. *So I **goes** back with him* (FRED Dev_005)
    b. *None of these posh sandwiches like you **gets** now mind!* (FRED Wil_009)
    c. *we **wants** to pull it* (FRED Som_004)
    d. *they **gives** certificates every week* (FRED Wil_001)
    e. *No I **thinks** no* (FRED Oxf_001)

Although some researchers have investigated verbal *-s* in the South West (cf. e.g. Jones and Tagliamonte 2004, Klemola 1996), any interaction between it and periphrastic *do* remains unclear. Elworthy (1965c: xlvi) mentions a shift in the aspectual paradigm of West Somerset towards the end of the nineteenth century:

> Another advance apparently connected with increasing instruction is the more common use of the inflection *us* in the intransitive and frequentative form of verbs instead of the periphrastic *do* with the inflected *pres. infin. I workus to factory*, is now the usual form, whereas up to a recent period the same person would have said, *I do workey to factory*. An old undergardener, speaking of different qualities of fuel for his use, said, *The stone coal* lee·ustus (*lasts*) *zo much longer, and gees morey it too* – that is, does not burn so quickly – Feb. 2, 1888. He certainly would have said a few years ago –*The stone coal* du lee·ustee (*do lasty*) *zo much longer*. This form is also superseding the old form *eth*, which latter is now becoming rare in the Vale of West Somerset.

Prepositions

Traditional West Country dialect tends to substitute certain prepositions for others, with generally geographical explanations. Thus, anything in the East is *up* and West is *down*, following the sun's path in the Northern hemisphere (cf. Rogers 1979: 41). StE would generally use *to* and *at* in the same contexts.

Rogers (1979: 41) also mentions another phenomenon occurring rather frequently in FRED (about 60 examples). An 'otiose *of*' is used in front of a direct object following a progressive verb form. As an extension, the same construction is used after gerunds. This results in phrases of the type *the doing of it* meaning *doing it*. Examples from FRED can be found in (14). Elworthy (1965b: 87–95) lists other peculiarities with regard to prepositional use in the South West.

14. a. *we never carried a hammer for* ***chipping of 'em*** (FRED Som_011)
    b. *or you weren't* ***doing of it*** *right* (FRED Wil_009)
    c. *what they used to have for the* ***milling of it*** (FRED Con_011)
    d. *I don't mind* ***doing of it*** (FRED Som_002)

Adverbs

There is a tendency even in spoken StE to use the adjective rather than the adverb in slots which traditionally require the use of the adverbial form (regular form: adjective + *-ly*; many irregular ones such as suppletive *good-well*). Utterances of the type *He's real nice* or *they're driving good* are no longer considered dialectal, but merely colloquial. It can be assumed that these forms survived the prescriptivist phase in the dialects as witnessed by examples from the 1950s (ɪts ˈtərbɫ ˈbad *it's terribly bad*; ˈsoː əz juː kən ˈgɛt əm aʊt ˈiːzɪ *so as you can get them out easily;* SED FN So Montacute).

Former features

In addition to the features mentioned here, there are a number of very traditional features which are no longer common in the modern South West. Among them is the use of an *a*-prefix on present progressive and past participle forms (e.g. *a-changing, a-been*), purposive clauses introduced by *for* or *for to* (e.g. wɒdˈɪvɚɽ ˈɛɪɫd iː vɚː ˈdu ət *whatever ailed you to do it* SED FN Co1; fə tə ˈkiːp ðə ˈkɒrn frəm ˈgɛtɪn bɪˈɔɪnd ðə ˈbɫeːd *to keep the corn from getting behind the blade* SED FN So Montacute; *Always the evenings for to get the men for to do it* FRED Som_025), and the distinction of transitive and intransitive infinitives of transitive verbs (thus, *I do dig the garden*, but *Every day, I do diggy for three hours*; cf. Rogers 1979: 37). This construction can occasionally be found in the SED fieldworker notebooks, but seems to have been rare then already (wiː də ˈbɽɪŋ æʊɽ ˈʃiːp ɪn ˈɫami *we bring our sheep in to lamb* SED FN Co6; aɪ gɒt ˈbɽeːv ɫɒt ˈduː jənɔː ˈpɪgz teːmeːt ən ˈkæʊz tə ˈmɪɫki *I've got a lot to do today, you know; pigs to feed and cows to milk* SED FN Co4, illustrating that the *-y* is dropped before a vowel, cf. Rogers 1979: 37). Other forms no longer in use include the once famous *utch* corresponding to StE *I* (e.g. ˈʊtʃ biː

gɔɪn ðɛər *I am going there* SED FN So Montacute) and the form *bain't* which was used widely as the negative of *be* (e.g. ˈbeənt əs *arent't we* SED FN So Montacute, *They bain't like they used to be, be 'em?* SED FN Co2).

Conclusion

To the present day, South West English is one of the most distinctive varieties of English English. Although many of its traditional features are currently being or already have been lost, it maintains others that are unique to the region. Interestingly, the most distinguishing characteristics of the variety cannot be found in pronunciation, although the West Country burr is quite exceptional, but in morphosyntax. With pronoun exchange and a unique system of gender assignment resulting in gendered pronouns, the personal pronoun paradigm shows idiosyncrasies which are only found in other varieties of English if their origins can be traced to the South West, as is the case with Newfoundland English. And although periphrastic *do* might be rarer today than it used to be, it can still be found even in recent interviews, suggesting that the semantic distinction it illustrates is still recognized by locals. Despite the pressure from the often more standard neighbouring South Eastern varieties, the wealth of features found in varieties of South West England distinguishing them from their neighbouring lects is not likely to disappear completely in the near future.

Notes

1 The Government Office Region is currently the highest local government entity in England.
2 Map 1 and 2 are taken from Wikipedia *q.v.* 'South West England'.
3 The present-day counties of Hampshire, Wiltshire, Dorset, Somerset and Berkshire were considered to form the heartland of traditional Wessex, extending northwards as far as the river Thames. The modern South West is thus located further to the West than the old kingdom. The labels *West Country* and *South West* will be used as synonyms here.
4 See, for example, http://www.publications.parliament.uk/pa/cm200304/cmselect/cmodpm/972/972we33.htm.
5 Of the 1322 questions of the SED questionnaire, 730 (55 per cent) concern lexical items, 387 (29 per cent) investigate phonological issues.
6 More details on FRED, the Freiburg English Dialect Corpus, can be found http://www.anglistik.unifreiburg.de/institut/lskortmann/FRED.
7 The linguistically correct formulation would be that postvocalic /r/ is preserved in syllable-final pre-pausal and pre-consonantal position in rhotic accents, but is not realized in these positions in non-rhotic accents. Wells (1982) is still the most comprehensive overview of English accents. The following paragraphs will only mention certain peculiarities.

Bibliography

Barnes, W. (1844), *Selected Poems*, Hardmondsworth: Penguin, Ed. A. Motion, 1994.

—. ([1886]1970), *A Glossary of the Dorset Dialect with a Grammar*, Guernsey/St. Peter Port: Toucan Press.

Chope, R. P. ([1891]1965), *The Dialect of Hartland, Devonshire*, Vaduz: Kraus Reprint Ltd. [Publications of the English Dialect Society 65.]

Clarke, S. (1997), 'English verbal *-s* revisited: the evidence from Newfoundland', *American Speech*, 72, 227–259.

—. (1999), 'The search for origins. Habitual aspect and Newfoundland Vernacular English', *Journal of English Linguistics*, 27, 328–340.

Couch, T. Q. (1965), *Glossary of Words in Use in Cornwall – East Cornwall*, Vaduz: Kraus Reprint Ltd. [Publications of the English Dialect Society 27.]

Courtney, M. A. (1965), *Glossary of Words in Use in Cornwall – West Cornwall*, Vaduz: Kraus Reprint Ltd. [Publications of the English Dialect Society 27.]

Elworthy, F. T. ([1875]1965a), *The Dialect of West Somerset*, London: Trübner. [Publications of the English Dialect Society 7; Vaduz: Kraus Reprint Ltd., 1965.]

—. ([1877]1965b), *An Outline of the Grammar of the Dialect of West Somerset*, London: Trübner & Co. [Publications of the English Dialect Society 19; Vaduz: Kraus Reprint Ltd., 1965.]

—. ([1886]1965c), *The West Somerset Word-Book*, London: Trübner & Co. [Publications of the English Dialect Society 50; Vaduz: Kraus Reprint Ltd., 1965.]

Filppula, M. (2004), 'Irish English: morphology and syntax', in B. Kortmann and E. W. Schneider (eds), *A Handbook of Varieties of English Vol. II: Morphology and Syntax*, pp. 73–101, Berlin/New York: Mouton de Gruyter.

Hancock, I. F. (1994), 'Componentiality and the creole matrix: The southwest English contribution', in Montgomery, Michael (ed.), *The Crucible of Carolina. Essays in the Development of Gullah Language and Culture*, pp. 95–114, Athens/London: University of Georgia Press.

Halpert, H. and John D. A. W. 1996, *Folktales of Newfoundland – The Resilience of the Oral Tradition*, St. John's: Breakwater.

Harris, M. B. (1991), Demonstrative pronouns and adjectives in a Devonshire dialect', in P. Trudgill and J. K. Chambers (eds), *Dialects of English. Studies in Grammatical Variation*, pp. 20–28, London/New York: Longman.

Herrmann, T. (2005), 'Relative clauses in English dialects of the British Isles', in B. Kortmann, T. Herrmann, L. Pietsch and S. Wagner, *A Comparative Grammar of English Dialects: Agreement, Gender, Relative Clauses*, pp. 21–123. Berlin/New York: Mouton de Gruyter.

Ihalainen, O. (1976), 'Periphrastic do in affirmative sentences in the dialect of East Somerset', *Neuphilologische Mitteilungen*, 77, 608–622.

—. (1985a), 'He took the bootle and put 'n in his pocket: the object pronoun *it* in present-day Somerset', in W. Viereck (ed.), *Focus on: England and Wales*, pp. 153–161, Amsterdam: Benjamins.

—. (1985b), 'Synchronic variation and linguistic change: evidence from British English dialects', in R. Eaton, O. Fischer, W. Koopman and F. v. d. Leek (eds), *Papers from the 4th International Conference on English Historical Linguistics, Amsterdam, 10–13 April 1985*, pp. 61–72, Amsterdam: Benjamins.

—. (1988), 'Creating linguistic databases from machine-readable dialect texts', in A. R. Thomas (ed.), *Methods in Dialectology*, pp. 569–584, Clevedon: Multilingual Matters.

—. (1990), 'Methodological preliminaries to the study of linguistic change in dialectal English: evaluating the grammars of Barnes and Elworthy as sources of linguistic evidence', in S. Adamson et al. (eds), *Papers from the 5th International Conference on English Historical Linguistics, Cambridge, 6–9 April 1987*, pp. 189–204, Amsterdam: Benjamins.

—. (1991a), 'On grammatical diffusion in Somerset folk speech', in P. Trudgill and J. K. Chambers (eds), *Dialects of English. Studies in grammatical variation*, pp. 104–119, London/New York: Longman.

—. (1991b), 'A point of verb syntax in south-western British English: an analysis of a dialect continuum', in K. Aijmer and B. Altenberg (eds), *English Corpus Linguistics. Studies in Honour of Jan Svartvik*, pp. 290–302, London: Longman.

—. (1994), 'The dialects of England since 1776', in R. Burchfield (ed.), *The Cambridge History of the English Language, Vol. V: English Language in Britain and Overseas. Origins and Developments*, pp. 197–274, Cambridge: CUP.

Jones, Megan & Tagliamonte, Sali, (2004), 'From Somerset to Saman: Preverbal did in the voyage of English', *Language Variation & Change*, 16, 93–126.

Keenan, E. L. and B. Comrie (1977), 'Noun phrase accessibility and Universal Grammar', *Linguistic Inquiry*, 8, 63–99.

Klemola, J. (1996), Non-standard periphrastic do: a study in variation and change, Ph.D. thesis, Department of Language and Linguistics, University of Essex.

Kortmann, B. (2004), '*Do* as a tense and aspect marker in varieties of English', in B. Kortmann (ed.), *Dialectology meets Typology: Dialect Grammar from a Cross-Linguistic Perspective*, pp. 245–275, Berlin/New York: Mouton de Gruyter.

Kruisinga, E. (1905), *A Grammar of the Dialect of West Somersetshire: Descriptive and Historical*, Bonn. [Bonner Beiträge zur Anglistik, Heft 18.]

Llamas, C. (2000), 'Middlesbrough English: convergent and divergent trends in a part of Britain with no identity', *Leeds Working Papers in Linguistics and Phonetics*, 8, 123–148.

MacKay, D. G. and Konishi T. (1980), 'Personification and the pronoun problem', *Women's Studies International Quarterly*, 3, 149–163.

Mathiot, M. and Roberts M. (1979), 'Sex roles as revealed through referential gender in American English', in M. Mathiot (ed.), *Ethnolinguistics: Boas, Sapir and Whorf Revisited*, pp. 1–47, The Hague: Mouton.

McArthur, T. (ed.) (1992), *The Oxford Companion to the English Language*, Oxford: OUP.

Morris, L. (1991), Gender in modern English: the system and its uses, Ph.D. thesis, Université Laval, Quebec.

Pawley, A. (2004), 'Australian Vernacular English: some grammatical characteristics', in B. Kortmann and E. W. Schneider (eds), *A Handbook of Varieties of English Vol. II: Morphology and Syntax*, pp. 611–642, Berlin/New York: Mouton de Gruyter.

Rogers, N. (1979), *Wessex Dialect*, Bradford-on-Avon: Moonraker.

Siemund, P. (2007), *Pronominal Gender in English: A Study of English Varieties from a Cross-Linguistic Perspective*, London: Routledge.

Trudgill, P. (1999), *The Dialects of England*, Oxford: Blackwell.

Trudgill, P. and Chambers J. K. (1991), 'Pronouns and pronominal systems in English dialects', in P. Trudgill and J. K. Chambers (eds), *Dialects of English. Studies in grammatical variation*, pp. 7–10, London/New York: Longman.
Wagner, S. (2002), *Pronoun Exchange – A Feature of English Dialects?*, manuscript, Universität Freiburg. Available from http://www.tu-chemnitz.de/phil/english/ling/staff_wagner.php.
—. (2003), Gender in English pronouns – myth and reality, Ph.D. dissertation, Englisches Seminar, Universität Freiburg, http://www.freidok.unifreiburg.de/volltexte/1412.
—. (2004a), English in Cornwall – a re-evaluation, Paper presented at the *15th Sociolinguistics Symposium*, Newcastle upon Tyne, 1–4 April 2004.
—. (2004b), '"Gendered" pronouns in English dialects – a typological perspective', in B. Kortmann (ed.), *Dialectology meets Typology: Dialect Grammar from a Cross-Linguistic Perspective*, pp. 479–496, Berlin/New York: Mouton de Gruyter.
—. (2005), 'Gender in English pronouns: South West England', in B. Kortmann, L. Pietsch, T. Herrmann and S. Wagner, *A Comparative Grammar of British English Dialects. Agreement, Gender, Relative Clauses*, pp. 211–367, Berlin/New York: Mouton de Gruyter.
Wagner, S. (2007), 'Unstressed Periphrastic *do* from Southwest England to Newfoundland?', *English World-Wide*, 28(3), 249–278.
Wakelin, M. F. (1970), 'Names for the cow-house in Devon and Cornwall', *Studia Neophilologica*, 42, 348–352.
—. (1975), *Language and History in Cornwall*, Leicester: Leicester University Press.
—. (1981), *English Dialects: An introduction*, London: Athlone Press.
—. (1984), 'Rural dialects in England', in P. Trudgill (ed.), *Language in the British Isles*, pp. 70–93, Cambridge: CUP.
—. (1986), *The South West of England*, Amsterdam: Benjamins.
Wallace, K. E. (2007), Social Variation in the English of the Southampton Area, Ph.D. thesis, School of English, University of Leeds. http://etheses.whiterose.ac.uk/408/1/uk_bl_ethos_446497.pdf (last accessed 11.09.2011)
Wells, J. C. (1982), *Accents of English*, Cambridge: CUP.
Wright, J. (1898–1905), *The English Dialect Dictionary*, Oxford etc.: Henry Frowde.
—. (1905), *The English Dialect Grammar*, Oxford etc.: Henry Frowde.

Scotland

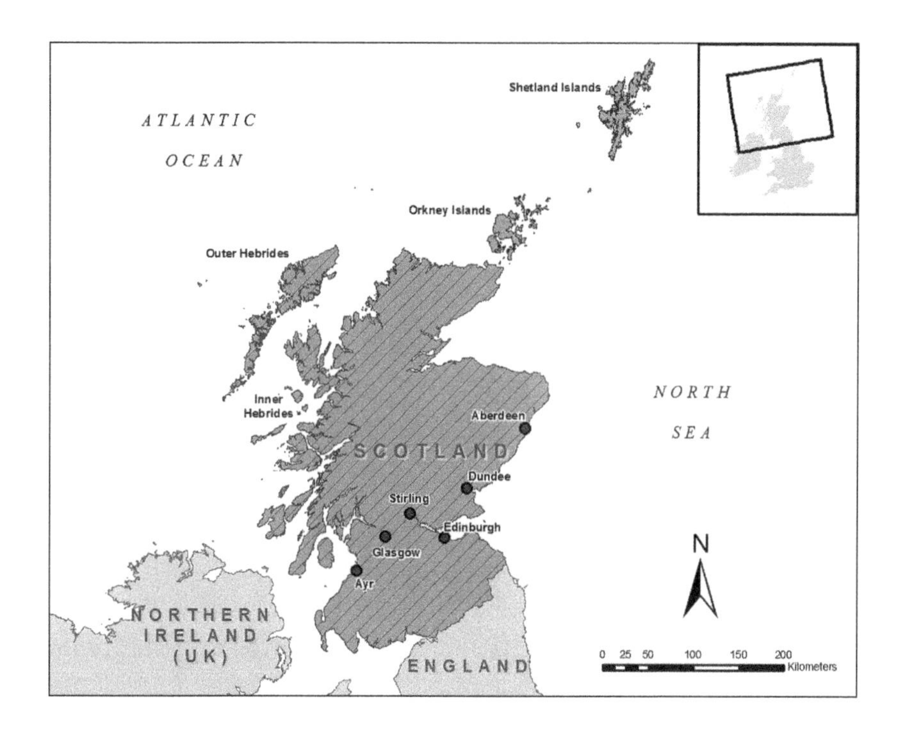

Shetland Islands
ATLANTIC
OCEAN
Orkney Islands
Outer Hebrides
Inner
Hebrides
NORTH
SEA
Aberdeen
SCOTLAND
Dundee
Stirling
Edinburgh
Glasgow
Ayr
N
NORTHERN
IRELAND
(UK)
ENGLAND
0 25 50 100 150 200
Kilometers

Chapter 7

English in Scotland

John Corbett and Jane Stuart-Smith

Introduction

English in Scotland has a history stretching back to the eighth century. A northern variety of English eventually developed as a medium of spoken and written communication in lowland Scotland, and, by the sixteenth century, the name 'Scots' began to be applied to this distinctive national language. Scots differed from southern English largely in terms of its vocabulary, which was comparatively Norse-influenced, its pronunciation, and in certain surface grammatical features, including past-tense and participial inflexions. By the middle of the sixteenth century, Scots was the main medium of speech in lowland Scotland, and it was widely used in poetry and non-literary prose in the form of histories, treatises, laws and letters.

The Reformation (1560), the Union of the Crowns (1603) and the Act of Union (1707) all forged closer political ties between England and Scotland, and Scottish Standard English grew out of interaction between southern English and Scots. Southern English was adopted as a written standard, and the speech of the upper class, and to a lesser extent the middle class, moved towards a 'polite' southern English model. While the developing varieties of the rural working classes maintained some traces of traditional Scots, that of the new urban working classes was subject to much greater innovation and change, mainly as a result of immigration and language contact. From the eighteenth century onwards, cultural movements have popularized literary written Scots, latterly utilizing a denser and more obscure vocabulary than is normally found in everyday speech. Some of this literary Scots is based on the speech forms of particular areas of Scotland, while other literary texts 'synthesise' the varieties spoken and written in different places and times, in order to produce a non-regional, national literary medium.

Today's English in Scotland continues to be a product of different developing and interacting systems, including what is left of traditional Scots, and standard and non-standard Englishes elsewhere. While largely subject to dialect levelling and erosion, English in Scotland continues to have distinctive pronunciation, and to maintain distinctive lexical, syntactical and semantic features.

Background, Including Demographic and Geographical Information

Geographical information, including maps

There is considerable debate about the position and appropriate terminology for the varieties of language which are currently spoken in Scotland and which ultimately share a common historical derivation from Old English (e.g. McClure 1988 on defining Scots). We adopt an admittedly over-simplistic stance: we describe Scottish English in terms of an essentially bipolar linguistic continuum (e.g. Aitken 1979, 1984), with broad Scots at one end, and Scottish Standard English at the other. Scots is generally, but not always, spoken by the working classes, while Scottish Standard English is typical of educated middle class speakers. Following Aitken's model, speakers of Scottish English either switch discretely between points on the continuum (style/dialect-switching), which is more common in rural varieties, or drift back and forth along the continuum (style/dialect-drifting), which is more characteristic of the urban dialects of the central belt. Throughout Scotland, spoken Scots is increasingly becoming limited to certain domains, for example, among family and friends; more 'formal' occasions tend to involve the use of Scottish Standard English. Of course the boundaries between Scots and Scottish Standard English, and Southern English, spoken by a small percentage of the population, are not discrete, but fuzzy and overlapping.

Scottish Standard English, here taken as a variety differing from Southern Standard English in accent, and only in occasional lexical and grammatical usage, is a possible variety for the majority of speakers across Scotland, depending on social context. There are slight differences in Scottish Standard English across the country. Highland English is a particular form of Scottish Standard English spoken in the mountains of the north and west of the country (for more details, see e.g. Shuken 1984).

The Scottish National Dictionary recognizes four main dialect divisions of Lowland Scots: Mid or Central Scots (CSc), Southern or Border Scots (SSc), Northern Scots (NSc) and Insular Scots (ISc -Shetland and Orkney). Central Scots, which is spoken by the majority of the Scottish population who live in the Scottish central belt, is again divided into East Central, West Central and South Central Scots (Ulster Scots spoken in Northern Ireland is from West and South Central Scots; Montgomery and Gregg 1997; Montgomery 2003). Urban Scots of the industrial central belt (e.g. Glasgow, Edinburgh) is historically derived from forms of Central Scots. Northern Scots, particularly the variety spoken around Aberdeen, is often called the Doric (McClure 2002).

Alongside spoken Scots, there also exists Lallans (='Lowlands Scots'). Lallans is a mainly literary form of Scots, which was popularized in the 1920s by Hugh MacDiarmid and other writers. It is a highly 'dense' variety of Scots

(McClure 1979, 2003), synthesizing features from various regional dialects with a number of resurrected archaic terms. In some respects Lallans meets the need for a written standard for literary Scots, and to a lesser extent, for a written standard for wider public uses. In practice, Lallans is used very infrequently for non-literary purposes and is even more rarely spoken, though the return of a Scottish Parliament in 1997 has seen a limited revival of Scots used for political and other purposes.

Brief History

A detailed survey of the early history of Scots is given in the introduction to the twelfth and final volume of the *Dictionary of the Older Scottish Tongue* (Macafee and Aitken 2002). Before the Anglian invasions of the seventh century AD, Scotland was predominately Celtic-speaking. The invaders introduced a northern variety of Anglo-Saxon ('Anglian') into a pocket of south-east Scotland. A century and half later, the southern borders of Scotland were invaded again by Vikings, who also assailed the far north of the country. At the time of the Norman Conquest, most people in Scotland still spoke one or another Celtic language; present-day Scots Gaelic is derived from one of these Celtic varieties. During the same period, Anglian was spoken in the south-east, and Old Norse was used in the far north and in the borders.

From the perspective of English in Scotland, then, the period until 1100 can be termed the 'Old English' period. The following, 'Older Scots', period runs from 1100 to 1700. Various political developments in England and Scotland during the late eleventh and early twelfth centuries led to an influx of Northern English speakers into Scotland. Refugees from the aftermath of the Norman Conquest in England were followed by settlers who were encouraged by the Normanised David I of Scotland to establish burghs in the lowland counties. As a result, the twelfth to the fourteenth centuries saw the gradual development of a particular variety of English in lowland Scotland which we recognize as Scots, but which was known to its earlier speakers and writers as 'Inglis' (Gaelic was called 'Erse' or 'Irish'). By the fifteenth century, however, the differences between Scots and its southern cognate were so pronounced that some writers, most notably Bishop Gavin Douglas, were beginning to distinguish between 'Inglis' and 'Scots'. The main historical basis of Scots, then, was the language of northern English settlers from 1100 onwards, a language considerably influenced by Norse after the long period of Scandinavian occupation of the north of England. Scotland's independent links with France also meant that the influence of French on Older Scots was distinctive.

Before the first large-scale literary work in Scots, Barbour's *Brus* (1375), preliterary Scots is only scantily attested, for example, in place names and glosses.

In 1398 the Scottish Parliament moved from Latin to Scots as the language of record, and until the Union of the Crowns (1603), Scots flourished as a literary and spoken language. Thereafter, with increasing English influence, particularly after the Act of Union of the English and Scottish parliaments in 1707, the use of written Scots declined beyond specific literary genres (e.g. comedy, satire). Beyond the literary sphere, of Ramsay, Burns and others during the eighteenth century or Lallans in the twentieth, written Scots gave way to a standard variety largely indistinguishable from that developed in England. Since the late twentieth century there has been a limited revival of non-literary Scots prose (Robertson 2002).

While the Modern Scots period, from 1700 onwards, saw the sharp decline of written Scots, spoken Scots remained more vigorous, at least in rural areas, and among the working classes; middle and upper class speakers tended to base their language behaviour on the written standard and prestige pronunciation of metropolitan English. Despite ongoing dialect change, and levelling of Scots towards Scottish Standard English, this linguistic situation still persists. A legacy of industrialization is the relatively recent distinction between 'Good' Scots, that is, traditional and rural varieties, and 'Bad' Scots, that is, 'degenerate' and urban varieties (cf. Aitken 1984: 529; Purves 1997).

Demographic information, including population, numbers of speakers of English and of other languages

It is probably fair to say that the majority of the population of Scotland, now estimated at 5,254,800 at the 2011 Census (www.gro-scotland.gov.uk) are potential speakers of Scottish Standard English. There are no official estimates or census statistics for the number of Scots speakers in Scotland, although Scots is recognized as a 'language' by the European Bureau for Lesser-Used Languages.

Defining the number of speakers of Scots in Scotland is extremely difficult, and cannot be easily resolved by asking speakers (Murdoch 1995; Maté 1996; for discussion, see Macafee 1997b: 515–18). The problem is created and exacerbated by a number of interrelated reasons:

1. the difficulty of recognizing Scots language as linguistically distinct from Scottish English (for both linguists and native speakers);
2. the unresolved difficulty of determining whether Scots is an autonomous language;
3. the negative attitudes held towards Scots, which is often regarded as a degenerate form of speech, synonymous with slang, in urban areas (e.g. Menzies 1991; Macafee 1994);
4. the ongoing development of Scots, including a process of dialect levelling towards English throughout Scotland.

In the wake of the 1991 Census, two studies (Murdoch 1995; Maté 1996) attempted to survey the number of Scots speakers, and at the same time (Maté 1996) to evaluate the feasibility of assessing the Scots-speaking population through a survey tool such as a Census question. The number of self-professed Scots speakers was relatively low in both sample surveys (57 per cent in Murdoch; 30 per cent in Maté). In both cases, older working-class speakers were more likely to classify themselves as speaking Scots.

The conclusions of Maté's research, sponsored by the General Register Office For Scotland, state that the 'inclusion of such a Census question would undoubtedly raise the profile of Scots' (p.2), but at the same time do not argue strongly for the Census as the optimal tool for estimating Scots speakers:

> Adequate estimates of the numbers of people who assess themselves as Scots speakers can be obtained from sample surveys much more cheaply than from a Cesnsus .... A more precise assessment of genuine Scots language ability would require a more in-depth interview survey and may involve asking various questions about the language used in different situations. Such an approach would be inappropriate for a Census. (Maté 1996: 2)

No question on Scots was included in the 2001 Census, despite a campaign in support of one. A further campaign for the 2011 Census was successful; at the time of writing, the outcome is awaited.

A small percentage of the Scottish population are acknowledged to be bilingual in Gaelic. The Census has a question on competence in Scottish Gaelic (Can the person speak, read or write Scottish Gaelic?). In the 2001 Census 92,400 respondents claimed to have at least some general knowledge of Gaelic, approximately 1.9 per cent of the population (www.scrol.gov.uk). Nearly the same percentage of the population (2.01 per cent) were recorded as belonging to an ethnic minority (defined as Pakistani, Indian, Bangladeshi, Chinese, other South Asian, African, Caribbean, Black-Scottish or any other Black background, any mixed background, or any other background: see www.scotpho.org.uk/web/site/home/Populationgroups/Ethnominorities/ethnic_data/ethnic_popcomp.asp). As Verma (1995) points out, any substantial ethnic population also has linguistic implications, leading to 'the recent emergence of a bilingual, and culturally and linguistically diverse, population in schools, where for historical reasons monolingualism was the norm' (p. 120). His analysis of data for ESL provision for the Lothian region reveal 54 languages other than English in primary schools, and 37 in secondary schools, with overall Panjabi and Chinese (Hakka/Cantonese and Mandarin) as most common.

Linguistic background and contacts

Much like the history of English in England, the history of Scots reflects considerable language contact. Scots developed in a country once predominantly

Celtic-speaking, from a variety of northern Middle English, heavily influenced by Norse ('Anglo-Danish'; Aitken 1985: ix). Its formative development took place during the twelfth to early fifteenth centuries, when Scotland had close political and cultural contacts with France, as well as trading contacts with the Netherlands. Until the Reformation (1560), Latin was the language of the church, as well as education and the legal system. As might be expected, Scots has had considerable contact with forms of southern English. This was particularly strong after the Reformation, when Southern English versions of the Bible and Psalter were introduced into Scotland, and especially after the Union of the Crowns and the Act of Union, and the closer political and social relationship with England which followed. The development of Scottish Standard English, the written standard which forms the basis for the spoken variety of middle class Scots, can be seen as the result of interaction between traditional Scots and the increasingly influential Southern Standard English of the seventeenth and eighteenth centuries.

Scots developed from a variety of Northern English. Thus, while showing a distinctive shape resulting from its own particular history, the majority of Scots phonology, morphology and syntax reflect its Anglo-Saxon heritage. In terms of vocabulary, Scots still preserves words which have since been lost from standard Southern English, for example, *blate* 'shy', *gloaming* 'twilight', *greet* 'weep'.

The linguistic imprint of Norse in Scots is considerable (Smith 1994). Historically, this results from Scots being derived from a variety of English already heavily influenced by Norse. All linguistic levels were affected. Phonologically, it seems likely that aspects of the Scots vowel system, including the retention of the long back vowel /u/ in *hoose*, cf. standard English /aʊ/ *house*, reflect linguistic contact between Norse and Northern English. In terms of grammar, the reorganization of the Scots strong verb system may reflect Norse influence, while the Scots present participle forms in *-and*, *-en* /ən/ are from Old Norse *-andi*. The particularly close relationship of Norse and Northern English is reflected in lexical borrowing. Not only are Norse forms found in open class words, for example, *kirk* 'church', *kist* 'chest', *gate* 'road' *lass* 'girl', but also in function words, for example, the prepositions *till* 'to', *frae* 'from', and in Middle Scots, in the pronominal forms *thay* 'they', *scho* 'she'.

The original languages of Scotland were Celtic. Only traces of the first, 'p-Celtic' languages, British, and Pictish, spoken in the north, are found. British elements occur in place names such as *Glasgow* or Edin*burgh*, British *din* eidyn. Pictish occurs in names such as *Pitlochry* and *Pittenween*. Scottish Gaelic, a 'q-Celtic' language, was only introduced into Scotland in the ninth century. Interestingly the amount of Gaelic-derived words in Scots was largely underestimated until recently (McClure 1986; Ó Baoill 1997). Gaelic forms are found in geographical terms, for example, *bog*, *cairn* 'pile of stones', *craig* 'cliff', as well as more generally, *clan* 'family', *ingle* 'fireside', *sonsie* 'pleasant', and in words referring to Highland culture, for example, *claymore*, the broad sword, *whisky* from

Gaelic *usige* 'water'. Sabban (1985) discusses the influence of Gaelic syntax on Highland English, for example, in the use of the non-perfective for the English perfective, in *I was smoking all my life* (for 'I have been smoking ...'). Celtic languages may also have influenced Scots phonology. The incorporation of Gaelic loans with the phoneme /x/ may have helped maintain /x/ in Scots and Scottish Standard English (Wells 1982: 190), and 'Celtic influence' is cited as the reason behind the high rising intonation contour observed in Glasgow, as well as in other northern cities (Cruttenden 1986: 139).

The Romance influence on Scots largely reflects the social prestige of French and Latin during the Middle Ages, as the languages of the nobility, administration, education and the Church. Latin loans are most evident in high-style or 'aureate' literature, in words like *auditoris* 'listeners' or *confortable* 'comfortable'. Latin words were also borrowed, often through French, to express concepts to do with, for example, religious or secular administration, *benefice* 'a church living', or *sessioun* 'a court of justice'. As Scots law ultimately derives from Roman law, Scots legal terminology is also heavily drawn from Latin.

The first wave of French borrowings into Scots dates from the Anglo-Norman period, and includes terms relating to the administration of burgh life, for example, *bailie* 'magistrate', *dyvour* 'bankrupt', *stint* 'tax'. Later, Parisian French continued to be a source of vocabulary, partly because of the political ties between Scotland and France which culminated in the Auld Alliance (1296–1560). During this period a number of words relating to food and domestic life entered Scots from French, for example, *disjune* 'breakfast', *brisket* 'meat from the breast of an animal', *gigot* 'leg of mutton or lamb', *tassie* 'cup' and *serviette* 'napkin'. The last example entered standard English in the eighteenth century, but was regarded by Samuel Johnson as an affected scotticism. Despite a general tendency of French loan words to cluster in the higher registers, some terms do express less refined concepts, for example, *creeshy* 'greasy', *manky* 'filthy' and *stour* 'dust'.

Trading relations with the Netherlands since the fourteenth century, as well as with Flemish craftsmen who settled in Scotland from the twelfth to sixteenth centuries, ensured a stock of Scots words of Dutch origin (Murison,1971). Dutch loan words include various words for the main object of trade, cloth, such as *dornick* 'tablecloth linen', and also more general words still used today, for example, *pinkie* 'little finger' and *golf*.

The influence of southern English on Scots, sometimes referred to as a process of 'anglicization' (e.g. Aitken 1979), has been significant and prolonged. Aitken notes that the incorporation of English elements into Scots was helped by the linguistic similarity of Scots and Midland or south-eastern English, and by the lack of any 'strong linguistic loyalty' towards Scots. Even before the Reformation, writers from England were admired and emulated. Written Scots first shows clear signs of anglicization in the sixteenth century in the adoption of English spelling conventions, for example, <sh> for traditional <sch>. Increased contact with English during the seventeenth century, partly through the reading of southern English religious texts in church, and partly through social contact, led to a widespread assimilation of Scots to the 'more elegant and perfect' English of the South by the Scottish middle and upper classes (Aitken 1979: 92). By the Act of Union the Scottish bourgeoisie tended to write Scottish Standard English. During the eighteenth century this written variety influenced middle-class language, although this was also influenced by Scots, mainly in terms of pronunciation (Aitken, 1979: 95f.). Scottish Standard English became the standard language for administration and education in Scotland, and from this emerged the possibility of bidialectalism in Scots and Scottish Standard English for many speakers, a situation which still continues today.

Phonology

Increasingly phonetic and phonological features alone distinguish Scottish Standard English (SSE) and Scots from other varieties of world English. The differences between the various dialects of Scots (and Scottish Standard English) are also largely phonetic and phonological. What follows is necessarily a very brief overview of Scottish English phonology. For more discussion of the phonology of Scottish Standard English, see Abercrombie (1979), Wells (1982: 393–417), and of Scots, see Grant (1931), Robinson (1985: xx–xxviii); and more recently Johnston (1997), whom we largely follow. For the pronunciation of older forms of Scots, see, for example, Aitken (1977) and Jones (1996).

Consonants

The consonant systems of Scottish Standard English and the Scots dialects are shown in Table 7.1. Overall the systems are very similar. In comparison to many other varieties of English, Scottish English usually shows two extra phonemes, /x/ and /hw/, as in *loch* and *whine* which contrast with *lock* and *wine* respectively. The Doric is unusual in showing /f/ for /hw/, as in *fite* for *white*. Scottish English is rhotic, that is, /r/ is pronounced in all positions in the word, in *red, car* and *card*. The realization of /r/ is variable, but more often an apical tap/approximant as opposed to a trill (Johnston 1997: 510–11); a retroflex pronunciation of /r/ is common in Highland English, and is also typical of middle-class Scottish Standard English in Edinburgh and Glasgow (e.g. Murison 1977: 33). The realization of /l/ tends to be velarized, or dark, in all positions of the word.

One feature that Scots dialects share in contrast to Scottish Standard English are the results of a historical process of l-vocalization of the fifteenth century, which accounts for Scots forms such as *baw, saut, fou,* beside SSE *ball, salt, full.* We note certain variants which are characteristic (though not always exclusively) of regional varieties of Scots (numbers in the text refer to footnote numbers in Table 7.1):

Table 7.1 Consonants of Scottish Standard English and Scots dialects (superscript numbers refer to points of interest noted in the text)

SSE	Central & urban Scots	Southern Scots	Northern Scots	Insular Scots
p	p	p	p	p
b	b	b	b	b
t	t[1]	t	t	t
d	d	d	d	d
k	k	k	k	k[1]
g	g	g	g	g
f	f	f	f	f
v	v	v	v	v
θ	θ, h, f[2]	θ; f[1]	θ	θ, t[2]
ð	ð[3]	ð	ð; d[1]	ð, d
s	s[4]	s	s	s
z	z	z	z	z
ʃ	ʃ	ʃ	ʃ	ʃ
ʒ	ʒ	ʒ	ʒ	ʒ[3]
h	h	h	h	h
x	x[5]	x	x; θ[2]	x
hw	hw[5]	hw	f[3]	hw
tʃ	tʃ	tʃ	tʃ	tʃ, ʃ[4]
dʒ	dʒ	dʒ	dʒ	dʒ
m	m	m	m	m
n	n	n	n; kn, gn[4]	n; kn, gn[5]
ŋ	ŋ	ŋ[2]	ŋ	ŋ
r	r[6]	r	r; vr[5]	r; wr[6]
l	l[7]	l	l	l
w	w	w	w; v[6]	w
j	j	j	j	j

Central and urban Scots: (1) glottal stops for /t/ (also /p k/) in *butter, a lot of,* are common, and spreading throughout Scotland; (2) [h] for /θ/ in *hing,* for *thing,* is traditional Scots; /f/ for /θ/ (e.g. *fing*) is more recent in urban Scots, and may be linked to the Southern English use of /f/ for /θ/; (3) [ɾ] for /ð/ in urban Scots; (4) a 'retracted' articulation, auditorily similar to /ʃ/, is found for /s z/; (5) /x/ and /hw/ tend to be replaced by /k/ and /w/ respectively; (6) vocalization, and hence effective loss, of postvocalic /r/ is becoming common; (7) l-vocalization similar to that of Cockney (to [o ɣ]) is common in Glasgow. Features 5–7 are particularly common in young working-class Scots speakers. (Note that here for convenience we group Central and urban Scots together. For specific details of variation see e.g. Johnston (1997) with references.)

Southern Scots: (1) /f/ for /θ/ in *frae*, CSc *thrae* 'through'; (2) [ɲ] for /ŋ/ in *sing*.

Northern Scots: (1) traditionally /ð/ for /d/ in *fadder*, CSc *faither* 'father', but now recessive; (2) /θ/ for /xt/ in *mith*, for CSc *micht* 'might' is now highly recessive; (3) /f/ for /hw/ in *file* 'while'; (4) initial velars in /kn gn/ are pronounced, in *knee, gnaw*; (5) /vr/ for /wr/ in *vrang*, CSc *rang* 'wrong'; (6) /v/ for /w/ in *shavvin*, CSc *shawin* 'showing' is now recessive.

Insular Scots: (1) word-initial /kw/ is /xw/ in *queen*; (2) /t d/ for /θ ð/ in *tank, feader* for *thank, feather*; (3) /ʒ dʒ/ devoice to /ʃ tʃ/; (4) /ʃ/ for /tʃ/, especially in Shetlandic; (5) /kn gn/ are pronounced in *knee, gnaw*; (6) /w/ in /wr/ in *wrest* 'sprain'.

Vowels

The economy of the Scottish English vowel system as compared to that of RP was noted by Abercrombie (1979). This is partly due to the continued presence of post-vocalic /r/, which was lost with subsequent diphthongization in RP. Scottish English tends to show a phonetic distribution of short and long vowels, which is described by the Scottish Vowel Length Rule (also called Aitken's Law): vowels are phonetically short unless before a voiced fricative, /r/ or a pause, including a morpheme boundary. Thus, the vowels in *grief, bead* and *greed* are short, but are long in *grieve, beer, bee* and *agreed* (= *agree* + past tense *-d*); Wells (1982), 400f. This rule can also account for the distribution of diphthongs, with /ʌi/ in *tide* in 'short' environments and /ae/ in *tied* in 'long' environments.

Table 7.2 compares the vowel systems of Scottish Standard English and the Scots dialects. Points of interest and often-noted variants are indicated in the table, and noted briefly below (numbers in the text refer to footnotes in the table):

Scottish Standard English: (1) /ɛ̈/ is found in a few words, for example, *never, heaven*, in some speakers; (2) some Scottish Standard English speakers show /a ɑ/ for /a/, /ɒ ɔ/ for /ɔ/, /ʊ u/ for /u/ (usually [ʉ]), with a similar, but not identical, distribution to southern English.

Central and urban Scots: (1) /ɪ/ is often realized as [ɛ] or even [ʌ]; (2) /i/ in *heid*, SSE *head*; (3) /ɛ/ in *efter*, SSE *after*; (4) /ɔ/ for /a/ in *hand*; (5) /e/ in *hame*, SSE *home*; (6) /a/ for /ɑ/ [ɔ] in *wrang*, SSE *wrong*; (7) /ɪ/ in *muin*, /e/ in *dae*, beside /u/ in SSE *moon, do*. (The distribution of these two vowels, also SSc /ø e/, corresponds to the 'short' and 'long' environments of the Scottish Vowel Length Rule.) (8) /u/ [ʉ] in *hoose*, SSE *house*.

Southern Scots: (1) /əi/ in *mey*, CSc *me*; (2) /ɛ/ is realized as [æ] in *bad*, CSc *bed*; (3) [ɪə] for /e/ in *beeath*, CSc *baith* 'both', /ji/ for /e/ after /h-/, for

Table 7.2 Vowels of Scottish Standard English and Scots dialects (superscript numbers refer to points of interest noted in the text).

SSE	Central & urban Scots	Southern Scots	Northern Scots	Insular Scots
i	i	i; əi[1]	i; e;[1] əi[2]	i
ɪ	ɪ[1]	ɪ	ɪ	ɪ
e	e	e	e	e
ɛ	ɛ; i[2]	ɛ[2]	ɛ	ɛ; e[1]
ɛ̈[1]	ɪ	ɪ	ɪ	ɪ
a[2]	a; ɛ;[3] ɔ[4]	a	a	a
o	o; e;[5] ɑ	o; e, ɪə, ji;[3] uə[4]	o; i[3]; ɑ[4]	o; i[2]; ɑ[3]
ɔ[2]	o; ɔ; ɑ[6]	o	o; ɑ[4]	o; ɑ[3]
u[2]	u; ɪ, e[7]	u; ø, e[5]	u; i, wi;[5] jʌu[6]	u; ø[4]
ʌ	ʌ	ʌ	ʌ	ʌ
ʌi	ʌi	ʌi	ʌi	ʌi
ae	ae	ae	ae	ae
ɔe	ɔe	ɔe	ɔe	ɔe
ʌu	ʌu; u[8]	ʌu; u[6]	ʌu; u	ʌu; u

Note: For each variety, this table shows the stressed vowels and main variants according to lexical incidence: a sequence such as Central Scots 'ɛ; i' means that Central Scots shows /ɛ/, and also in some words /i/, beside SSE /ɛ/ (examples are given in the text).

example, *hyim*, CSc *hame* 'home', and word-initially, for example, *yin* for north CSc *ane* /en/ 'one'; (4) [uə] for /o/ in *nose*; (5) /ø/ in *mune*, beside CSc /ɪ/ *muin* 'moon'; (6) /u/ is sometimes /ʌu/ in *cow*, CSc *coo* 'cow'.

Northern Scots: (1) /e/ for /i/ in *maet*, CSc *meat*; (2) [əi] in *swyte*, CSc *sweet*; (3) /i/ in *steen*, CSc *stane* 'stone'; (4) [ɑ] in *snaa*, CSc *snaw* 'snow' or *ba*, CSc *baw* 'ball'; (5) /i/ in *meen*, CSc *muin* 'moon' and /wi/ after velars, for example, *gweed*, CSc *guid* 'good'; (6) /jʌu/ in *byowty*, CSc *beauty*.

Insular Scots: (1) /e/ in *hade*, CSc *heid* 'head'; (2) /i/ in *steen*, CSc *stane* 'stone'; (3) [a] or [ɑ] in *snaa*, CSc *snaw* 'snow'; (4) /ø/ in *schön*, CSc *shune* 'shoes'.

Suprasegmentals

As might be expected, there is some variation in the prosodic features of intonation, rhythm and voice quality across Scottish Standard English and the Scots dialects, though little has been documented (see Wells 1982: 414–15). It has been noted that terminal pitch contours of east coast (e.g. Edinburgh) intonation tend to fall, in contrast with a rising pattern in west coast speech (e.g. Glasgow);

Brown et al. (1980), 19–20; Cruttenden (1995). Rhythmically, Abercrombie (1979) notes a tendency for a pattern 'short-long' in Scottish English disyllabic words, for example, *table*. There seems to be systematic differences in voice quality between Scottish Standard English and Scots, at least in the urban contexts of Edinburgh and Glasgow, with Scots speakers tending to show more jaw protrusion, auditory pharyngealization, and harsh, more whispery phonation (Esling 1978a, b; Stuart-Smith 1999).

Vocabulary

The vocabulary of Scots was the focus of the most prolonged and intensive scholarly attention during the twentieth century. The *Scottish National Dictionary* (1931–76), the *Dictionary of the Older Scottish Tongue* (1937–2002) and their successors stand as a monument to the generations of lexicographers who compiled them, and together with the *Linguistic Atlas of Scotland* (1975–86), they remain the primary source of information for more recent extensive surveys of Scots lexis (e.g. Macafee 1997a; Tulloch 1997).

The foundations of Scots vocabulary are northern Old English and Old Norse, supplemented by items from earlier Celtic languages, from Latin, and from the languages of later settlers and trading partners, such as French and Dutch.

Although the same loan words might enter Southern English and Scottish English through patterns of trading and settlement, it is important to note that their histories of adoption might differ. *Serviette*, for example, was established north of the border long before the time is was noted as an affected scotticism by Samuel Johnson in his *Dictionary of the English Language* (1755), and even words common to both Scottish and Southern English can have different meanings in each variety.

Vocabulary items come into Scots by means other than borrowing. For example, McClure (1981) observes that a considerable number of dictionary entries concern imaginative words which have only one or two citations, which suggests a national propensity to create new terms. Examples from the *SND* include *hellyifyoll* (an Orcadian term for 'a storm of words, or severe scolding') and *hig-rig-ma-reel* 'confusedly'. Lallans writers in the twentieth century defended their right to create new words, sometimes in the face of criticism that their synthetic Scots is somehow inauthentic (Young 1947).

Tulloch (1997) gives extensive examples of a number of processes used to create neologisms. These include compounding, as in *himmelsferd* (*himmel* + *ferd*, 'journey to heaven'); derivations by adding prefixes or suffixes, as in *comfarantlike* 'decent', 'becoming', *comflek* 'reflect' and *complowsible* 'reasonable'; reduplication, as in *howdy-towdy* 'tawdry' (an old head-dress); and clipping, as in *gutties* 'gymshoes', from the *gutta-percha* used to make their soles; now extended to include trainers.

In general, the principles of Scots morphology are very largely the same as those of present-day standard English. Certain Scots words and word classes have taken a different route from Old English to the present day: for example, the *n*-plural which English preserves in *children* and *oxen* is further preserved in Scots words like *een* 'eyes' and *shoon* 'shoes'. The past-tense of regular verbs in Older Scots tended to use an *-it* inflexion, which survives into present day usage in some verbs in a reduced form, for example, *tellt* 'told' and *dee't* 'died'. Today, some Scots speakers retain a three-part demonstrative system, *this/that/yon*; although analogy accounts for variation between the distant *yon* (from OE adjective *þeon*) and the more recent innovation *thon* (Macafee 1992–3).

The distribution and currency of Scots vocabulary items are difficult to determine. The *Linguistic Atlas of Scotland* shows that there is considerable variation in the terms used in different parts of Scotland for the same concept; for example, 'head over heels' is *heelster gowdie* in the north-east and *tummle your wulkies* in the south-west, the latter deriving from an Ulster Scots expression, 'tumble the wild cat'. Macafee (1994) charts loss and innovation in vocabulary in the east end of Glasgow: where older terms like *knock* 'clock' are dying out, new items like *swedger* 'sweet' are coined. It is difficult to predict the course of individual items, however. The term *happit* 'wrapped, clothed' is used as the name of a Scottish clothes retailer, although it is questionable how many customers are aware of its meaning. Other terms are revived and disseminated through popular culture. For instance, the success of the Leith-based novel and film *Trainspotting* by Irvine Welsh has increased at least passive knowledge of hitherto localized, Romany-derived thieves' cant, such as *gadgie* 'man', and *radge* 'crazy', throughout Scotland. Although much Scots vocabulary has been lost, much is retained, and much is continually gained and revived (Tulloch 1997: 431). However, as Macafee (1997b: 541) warns, such is the poor state of awareness of Scots among today's Scottish people that their distinctive vocabulary may not be recognized as such, but instead mistaken for slang, or the colourful language of a given locality or subculture.

Syntax

Despite an increase in recent activity and publications, research into the syntax of Scots remains uneven. The older period has been investigated by Devitt (1989), Meurman-Solin (1993), and a short grammar of Older Scots, based on materials in the *Dictionary of the Older Scottish Tongue*, has been compiled by Macafee (1992–3). Area studies of the modern period include those on the southern counties by Murray (1873) and on central Scotland by Wilson (1915, 1923, 1926). Sociolinguistic investigations into the speech of twentieth-century Scots include Macaulay (1977) and Macafee (1983, 1994) on Glasgow; Brown and Miller (1980) on Edinburgh; and Macaulay (1991) on Ayr. Overviews are given by Miller (1993) and Beal (1997); they are much more detailed than is possible here. Purves (1997) offers a short prescriptive grammar based on literary sources, intended for the use of modern writers in Scots.

Scots, like English, has a basic SVO structure. Older Scots had two systems of present-tense SV concord, depending on whether or not the verb was preceded by a personal pronoun. Verbs not preceded by such a pronoun were inflected in all persons and numbers, for example, *the wyfis . . . taks thair parts* 'the wives... take their parts'. When preceded by a personal pronoun, neither the first person singular nor the plural verb is inflected, but the others are, for example, *I mervell; Thay play; thou luikis.* When a personal pronoun governs two verbs, the first is uninflected and the second is inflected; for example, *I renunce . . . and takis* 'I renounce . . . and take' (Macafee, 1992–3: 21). In present-day Scots, plural subject nouns still tend to take *is*, as in *the lambs is oot the field*, and even educated speakers use *is* with the dummy subject *there*: *there's no bottles* (Miller 1993: 109). There is still variation in the Scottish system of concord, but, as Macafee suggests, the general processes involve simplification of the standard English inflection system.

During the eighteenth and nineteenth centuries, one perceived difference between Scots and English in the SVO pattern concerned the position of the direct and indirect object. Murray (1873: 91) identifies the pattern *gie mey them, he toeld them't* as being the Scottish equivalent of 'give them to me, he told it to them'. Later commentators make no mention of this feature, which suggests that other varieties of English have moved towards the pattern once marked as a scotticism (Beal 1997: 364–5). What is and is not marked as a scotticism can vary over time. The periphrastic *do* construction, as in *he did . . . call for ale,* became frequent in Scottish texts in the later sixteenth century, probably owing to southern influence. By the beginning of the eighteenth century, however, *do* periphrasis had declined in English texts, making its continued use north of the border a marked Scottish feature. The same grammatical construction, then, can begin as an indicator of anglicization, but later become a scotticism (Meurman-Solin 1993).

Murray (1873: 196) states that only *that/at* were used as relative markers in Scots speech, and *quhulk/quhilk* was found in speech solely when the antecedent was itself a clause, as in *Hey said 'at hey mæt us onna the muir, quhulk wasna the case.* It is likely that *wh*-marked relative clauses gradually moved from written mode to speech, although there is still a high frequency of *that*-marked clauses in Scots speech (Romaine 1982). Macaulay (1991) observes a lower proportion of *wh*-relative clauses and a higher proportion of zero-marked ones in working-class Scottish speech in comparison with middle-class speakers, leading Beal (1997: 361) to conclude that the process of change is continuing. From Older Scots to the present day, non-finite subordinate clauses expressing purpose have been introduced by *for to*, as in *I'm going for to give youse a prophecy* (Macafee 1983: 84).

At the phrase level, most commentators note the use in Scots of the definite article in nominal phrases where it would be absent in standard English. It is used by middle-class speakers when referring to close relatives (*the father*), with time expressions (*that was the Friday*), and with certain institutions (*into the hospital*). Working-class speakers also used the definite article with tasks, games and pastimes (*the gardening, the bingo*), with certain expressions of quantity (*the half of them*), in expressions of direction (*back the way*) and in some generalizations (*that's the tractors for you*) (Macaulay 1991). Similar uses of the definite article have been observed since Beattie (1787); however, there is some disagreement about exactly when the definite article can be used. Again, variation can be expected. From Beattie (1787) to Beal (1997), commentators have also observed a similar, now possibly fossilized, use of the possessive pronoun in expressions like *I'm away to my bed* and *we were in for wer lunch* 'we were in for our lunch'.

Macaulay (1991) observes different prepositional uses and distributions among his working-class and middle-class speakers; for instance, the use of *fae, to* and *on* by working-class speakers where middle-class speakers would use *from, for* and *to*. His examples include *She came fae Patna, I'm labouring to a bricklayer* and *I'm no waiting on you*. Miller (1993) extends this list, and argues for further research into prepositional usage in Scots.

The use of modal auxiliary verbs varies substantially in most varieties of English, and Scots is no exception. Miller (1993: 116–21) lists the major differences, including the avoidance in Scots of *shall, may* and *ought*. Instead, *will, can* and *should/want* are used, as in *you want to come out and attack right away*. *Must* is used in Scots, but its meaning is often restricted to the deductive meaning, as in *It must be next week that she's arriving*. A sense of obligation is expressed by *have to, need to, supposed to* or *meant to*. Unlike standard English, it is possible to use more than one modal auxiliary in a verb phrase, as in *I'll can do that tomorrow, or she might can get away early*. Double modals with *can* were observed by Murray (1873) and Wilson (1915); Miller (1993) suggests that their use is increasing.

Negation in Scots is achieved by (i) the clitic *-na* attached to the auxiliary verb *dae/do*; (ii) less commonly, *-na* being attached to the lexical verb; and (iii) emphatically, the use of the particle *no/na* after the copula or auxiliary verb, as in *that's no what I'm after*. In middle-class speech cliticized negatives are generally avoided, and *not* is the preferred form, as in *you'll not be thinking of leaving*. Multiple negation is possible, but where Macafee (1983: 47) observed it frequently in Glasgow speech, Macaulay (1991: 54–5) found it relatively seldom used, even among working-class speakers in Ayr.

There are various differences in verb forms marking tense and aspect in Scottish English. Like other varieties of English, simplification of the irregular verb paradigm results in forms such as *I seen*, and *she's went*. In speech, the present participle marking the progressive aspect is *-in*, as in *I'm goin*. This form derives from the Older Scots *-and* participle form, which was until the sixteenth century distinct from the gerund, *-ing*. Unlike standard English, Scots allows expression of 'mental' activities using the progressive aspect, as in *I'm thinking you're wanting your tea*. Progressive aspect can also be used to express habitual states and generalizations in Scottish English (Miller 1993: 121–2).

Semantics

The semantic relationship between Scots and English is extremely complex and little explored. Aitken (1979: 85–7) proposes a model of Scottish speech which attempts to take into account the interactions with English which describe a present Scottish speaker's behaviour. At the Scots end of a continuum are those words which derive from early Scots speech. Here he places items such as *bairn* and *mair*. At the English end of the continuum he puts later borrowings from southern English, such as *child* and *more*. At the centre of the continuum he places 'common core' vocabulary, or those items which have an equally lengthy history in English and Scots, such as *name* and *winter*. As speakers switch from one part of the continuum to the other, or drift along it, they speak more or less 'broad' Scots. Useful though Aitken's continuum is, it nevertheless disguises subtle semantic distinctions between Scots and English vocabulary items.

First of all, the availability of a large number of English synonyms for Scots items increases the connotational richness of a Scottish speaker's repertoire. Although *cowp* and *capsize* or *kenspeckle* and *conspicuous* are denotationally synonymous, they belong to different registers – use of the Scots terms would normally indicate a more intimate, less formal relationship between the speakers than the English terms would. This, however, is less true of scotticisms which denote certain concepts associated with distinctively Scottish institutions like the Church or the Law, for example, the terms *kirk* or *culpable homicide* still belong to official, public registers.

Secondly, there may also be considerable differences in the semantic development of common core items in English and Scots, as a comparison of the *Dictionary of the Older Scottish Tongue* and the *Scottish National Dictionary* with the *Oxford English Dictionary* reveals (see also Tulloch 1997: 406–13). The common core item *croon*, for example, was borrowed into Older Scots from Middle Dutch, and originally meant 'to utter a continued, loud, deep sound' or 'to bellow like a bull'. By the eighteenth century, the meaning had weakened to 'to sing (or speak) in a low murmuring tone', or 'to sing (a song, tune, etc) in a low murmuring undertone'. This meaning was used by Scots poets and writers, such as Galt and Burns, and afterwards the term appears in the works of English novelists including Dickens and George Eliot. The term was popularized widely in English, however, by its application to popular American band singers of the twentieth century, such as Rudy Vallee and Bing Crosby. The verb *croon*, therefore has a much longer history in Scots than in English, and the current English meaning is a development of the early Scots one.

The semantic histories of the verbs *stay* and *doubt* also reflect slightly different usages and developments in the Scots and English meanings of these common core words. The English use of *stay* would normally be in the progressive aspect, *Where are you staying?*, expressing temporary residence. Scots tend to use the term in the simple aspect, *Where do you stay?* to express permanent residence.

In Scots and English, the main early meaning of *doubt* is 'to be wavering or undecided in opinion or belief'. In English, there was originally also the possibility of using *doubt* with an object clause or an infinitive phrase to mean 'to fear, be afraid (that something uncertain will take place or has taken place)'. The *OED* cites one of Shelley's letters (1820) as a late example of this meaning: 'I doubt that they will not contain the latest and most important news'. In standard English this meaning is archaic. In present-day Scots, however, the meaning is still current, alongside the weaker meaning of 'suspect'. The quite different possible meanings of *doubt* in Scots are disambiguated by the following if-clause or that-clause: *I doubt if it's going to rain* (= 'I am uncertain'), versus *I doubt (that) it's going to rain* (= 'I suspect it is').

Scots lexical items, then, enter into complex relations of near-synonymy with their English counterparts, and even common core items can have different semantic histories and slightly different uses. This differentiation between Scots and English also extends to grammatical items. In particular, the different Scots and English uses of the modal auxiliary verbs have long been noted and excited frequent comment (e.g. Sinclair 1782; Murray 1873; Aitken 1979; Miller 1993; Beal, 1997). The eighteenth-century prescriptivists lamented the Scots use of *will* instead of *shall*, indicating that the volitional meaning of *will* was weakened and lost early in Scots, and *will* subsequently replaced *shall* as a simple marker of futurity. This process is now in evidence in standard English. Similarly, in Scots, *can* and *get to* are preferred to *may* when expressing permission: *Can I go now?* and *Are you getting to go to the pictures?* Again, in standard English the use of *may* to express permission is becoming a marked feature of formality, and *can* is being used more widely (Beal 1997: 367).

It is a feature of modernity that the semantic range of Scots as a whole is more limited than that of standard English – although in the Prologue to his translation of Book I of the *Aeneid* (1513), Gavin Douglas also complained about the lack of linguistic resources available to him in Scots, and articulated his need to supplement his Scots vocabulary with borrowings from other tongues, including English. Even so, in Douglas's time, the range of Scots could be extended to encompass all aspects of contemporary life, public and domestic. Today, efforts to create a Scots vocabulary capable of articulating aspects of technology or modern business would meet with ridicule. The *Scots Thesaurus* (1990), although it selects only a sample of Scots vocabulary, nevertheless gives some indication of the semantic coverage of Scots, and those areas which are rich in expression. Unsurprisingly, the prominent categories are to do with the natural world, traditional industries such as fishing, building and farming, food and drink, religion and the law, war and violence, physical and emotional states, and the family and social behaviour. Within these categories, semantic distinctions are as fine and sometimes finer than are found in standard English; for example, different expressions for 'fatigued' include *dirt deen, disjaskit, doilt, dowf, dowless, ergh, fauchled, fendless, forfauchlet, forfochtin, forjidget, fornyawd, fusionless* and *haggit* – to name but a few. While the overall semantic range of Scots might be narrower than standard English, its density in patches can at times be greater.

Media Use of English

The written language of newspapers and magazines printed in Scotland for Scottish readers is largely similar to that of standard Southern English. Some broadsheet newspapers sometimes carry articles written in Scots (Lallans), for example, the writing of Stuart McHardy in the *Herald* (Glasgow), or Robbie Shepherd in the *Aberdeen Press and Journal* (Aberdeen).

Douglas (1997; 2009) is currently working on Scots and Scottish English in the press. Her analysis is based on a database of a range of Scottish and English broadsheet and tabloid newspapers, published during 1995. Her preliminary results (1997) suggested that both Scots and Scottish Standard English are rarely used in the language of the Scottish press, and tend to be confined to certain parts of the newspapers such as feature articles. (Douglas defines portions of text as Scots or Scottish Standard English in terms of the distribution of recognizably Scots lexis.)

Interestingly, Douglas' work indicates differences in the types of Scots lexis found in broadsheet and tabloid newspapers. Broadsheets contain more literary and archaic Scots, tabloids tend to use urban Scots of colloquial speech. Her analysis confirms that sustained dense Scots is generally found in articles which focus on 'discussions of Scots writers, comments on the use of the Scots language, suggestions for Scots spelling reform, or similar Scottish topics' (McClure 1979: 47). Both Scots and Scottish Standard English are used to refer to material culture (e.g. in letters, diaries), and also to express humour.

The Scottish radio and television stations generally broadcast using regional varieties of Scottish Standard English. The speech of many formal television presenters (e.g. newscasters, weather presenters, continuity presenters) is only barely recognizable as Scottish. Intonation and vowel qualities are often closer to those of Southern English presenters, leading to a rather unusual 'hybrid' accent, unlike that of most of their viewers.

Broad Scots is rarely heard on television and radio, other than in programmes specifically designed for educational purposes. Some notable exceptions were the Scots language programmes put together by Billy Kay, such as the television series, *The Mither Tongue* (Kay 1993), and the radio show, *Amang guid company*, as well as the Scots Tongue Week, held from 12–18 October 1996 on BBC Radio Scotland. The *Radio Times* issue for that week also gave the majority of the programme listings in Scots, heading it with a paragraph in Lallans:

> 'Throughout this week, Radio Scotland's programming celebrates the richness and diversity of the Scots spoken word. Fae Scots in the closes tae Scots in the schule an Scots in the kirk, we hear the soun o the nation. Tom Morton's

looking oot for licht herted contributions tae his new Scots wards competition. Robbie Shepherd taks a keek at the Doric Festival, Edi Stark discovers fit wye we a spik that bit different in Scotland, Frieda Morrison stravaigs oot and aboot and Colin Bell speirs aboot the pint o it a. Wi news and wither in Scots on Monday and Mr Anderson giein the Scots wards a birl in the efterneens, Radio Scotland rediscovers the poo'r o the spoken word in Scots. Efter this wik o Radio Scotland, ye'll hae the Scots tongue licked.'

The last sentence perhaps reflects why broad Scots is not used more often in the media. It suggests that many Scottish people find Scots difficult to understand. This is either because it is different from their own local dialect (Murison 1977: 36, observes that the BBC uses West Central Scots as their standard) or, perhaps more likely, because such a form of Scots (Lallans) is in fact a spoken version of a literary creation, drawing on a mixture of dialect forms, which is rarely used as a medium of communication. Douglas (1997) also suspects that even in the written language of the press, Lallans is rarely used in broadsheet, and never in tabloid papers, because it is difficult for many readers to understand.

The incomprehensibility of Lallans was a key motif in an advertising campaign for Grant's whisky run in a series of posters and television advertisements in 1996 (Corbett 1997). A typical Scottish scene was captioned in the posters with a phrase of broad Scots (from Burns), for example, *unco sonsie* 'very pleasant' or *ilka dram a ferlie* 'every measure a wonder'. The coordinated television advertisements showed various Scottish individuals (of different ages and background) puzzling over what the caption meant. The campaign capitalized on the use of Scots to express 'Scottishness' but at the same time acknowledged that the actual medium was not always easily comprehensible. In general, broad Scots and Scottish Standard English are rarely used to advertise Scottish products.

Literature in Scottish English: Oral and Written

Vernacular literature began to appear in Scotland in the late fourteenth century. The earliest surviving work is John Barbour's national epic, *Brus* (1375) which incorporated some historical elements into a romance fashioned on French models. When Scottish authors referred to their language they termed it 'Inglis', and seemed to perceive little or no difference between their northern variety and the southern variety of Chaucer, Lydgate and Gower. Indeed, during the fifteenth and early sixteenth centuries, Chaucer in particular was regarded as a source of inspiration for such Scottish writers in 'Inglis' as King James I, Robert Henryson and William Dunbar, although their concerns and sophistication elevate them well above the role of mere imitators of the English master. Prose in 'Inglis' during this period is largely concerned with chivalric treatises and moral and religious works. By the time of Gavin Douglas's translation of Virgil's *Aeneid* in 1513, some writers had begun to regard the northern and southern varieties as different languages, and renamed the northern form 'Scottis'; however, this attitude was by no means general. Sir David Lindsay of the Mount, author of the play *Ane Satyre of the Thrie Estaitis* (1554) continued to term his language as 'Inglis'.

During the sixteenth century much of the literary production in Scotland centred on the Scottish court, and in the later part of the century James VI was an active poet, translator and patron of a group of writers including Alexander Montgomerie, John Stewart of Baldynneis and William Fowler. They produced sonnet sequences, long narrative poems and prose works such as Fowler's translation of Machiavelli's *Il Principe*. Though evidently Scottish, the literary language of the later sixteenth century was becoming increasingly anglicized. Reasons for this include the relative strength of the printing industry in England, which tended to promote southern features as norms, and the continuing prestige of English literature. When James VI and the Scottish court relocated to London as a consequence of the Union of the Crowns in 1603, the focus of Scottish literary culture also shifted. Seventeenth-century writers like William Drummond of Hawthornden and Thomas Urquhart of Cromarty wrote in a medium largely indistinguishable from that of their English contemporaries, and literature in Scots was mainly confined to the oral tradition of songs and ballads.

The Act of Union of 1707, which absorbed the Scottish state into Great Britain, prompted a political and cultural reaction which included a revival of interest in literature in Scots. Allan Ramsay republished earlier Scots poets along with his own verse, and he was followed by other poets of the Scots revival, most famously Robert Fergusson and Robert Burns. Their poetry alluded strongly to the oral traditions of song, ballad and comic poetry which are still healthy today, as evidenced by the founding in 1951 of the School of Scottish Studies at Edinburgh University, to encourage research into the folklore and oral traditions of Scotland. The poets of the eighteenth-century Scots revival also experimented with more literary forms, such as the Spenserian stanza and the Horatian ode. During the nineteenth century, much of the dynamic experimentalism of this period was blunted by imitation, which focused on the sentimental, rural and comic aspects of Scottish life, although it has been argued that smaller periodical publications kept alive a radical tradition in Scots verse (Leonard 1990).

In the nineteenth century, however, the Scottish novelists, Sir Walter Scott, James Hogg, John Galt and Robert Louis Stevenson incorporated a considerable amount of Scots into their novels and short stories, usually in the form of dialogue spoken by the lower middle classes and peasantry. These novels reached an audience beyond Scotland, as, to a lesser extent, did the sentimental, comic 'kailyard' novels of later writers such as JM Barrie. Within Scotland during the Victorian period, newspapers and local periodicals often included writing in Scots which tackled contemporary themes and political issues (Donaldson 1986).

Political events in the twentieth century again influenced literary trends. The rise of Scottish nationalism in the early decades of the twentieth century can be linked to a renaissance in Scots poetry and prose which again tackled contemporary themes. The landmark works of this period are Hugh MacDiarmid's *A Drunk Man Looks at the Thistle* (1926) and Lewis Grassic Gibbon's trilogy *A Scots Quair* (1932–4). This resurgence of modern Scots writers included poets such as Sydney Goodsir Smith, Robert Garioch, JK Annand, Alexander Scott and Tom Scott; novelists such as Jessie Kesson and Fred Urqhuart; and dramatists such as James Bridie, Joe Corrie, Robert Maclellan and Ena Lamont Stewart. Now, literary Scots is represented by a range of varieties, from the 'high' literary language, sometimes called 'Lallans', employed by MacDiarmid, to specific localized dialects such as the Shetlandic of William Tait or the Aberdonian of Sheena Blackhall. Urban Scots is represented by the 'phonetic' poems of Tom Leonard, the stylized Glaswegian of Edwin Morgan, and the Dundonian of WN Herbert.

Recent writing in Scots has again reached an audience beyond Scotland. James Kelman's *A Disaffection* (1989) won the prestigious Booker Prize for Literature, while Irvine Welsh's *Trainspotting* (1993) achieved international success and notoriety as a novel, a play and a film. Few extended prose works attempt to sustain a dense, literary Scots; a thinner, urban Scots is likely to be used in dialogue and short passages. Broader Scots is now confined largely to drama, poetry and song.

Literature in Scottish English, or Scots, has an independent tradition stretching back over six hundred years. However, literature in Scots is only part of Scottish Literature, which, over the centuries, also includes writing in Gaelic, Latin and English. Although obviously related to literature in England in complex ways, Scottish Literature can be seen to have a separate set of concerns and to have developed to serve the specific needs of the Scottish community. In recognition of the importance of this tradition, the Department of Scottish Literature was founded at Glasgow University in 1971, the first and so far the only university department to offer a full range of courses in Scottish Literature at the undergraduate and postgraduate levels. However, English Studies departments within and beyond Scotland now also offer courses and encourage research into all aspects of literature in Scotland.

Education Policies and Publications

After the Union of the Crowns in 1603, the written language of literate Scots quickly became governed by norms based on the standard variety of English which was developing in England. However, in the first century following the Union of the Crowns, the move towards a standard English written variety did not necessarily stigmatize Scots speech as uneducated: the lawyer and man of letters, Sir George Mackenzie (1630–1714), in an essay on the type of eloquence suited to the bar, argued that while English is fit for 'haranguing', Scots is best for 'pleading'. Only during the eighteenth century, despite the persuasive force of Scots, its revival as a literary medium in poetry and prose, and its function as a marker of national identity, did its general association with speech rather than writing, and eventually with the lower social classes, result in its being widely regarded as an uneducated language variety.

Explicit stigmatization of Scots in schools was also a gradual process. The 1696 Act of the Scottish Parliament finally fulfilled the Scottish reformers' vision of a school in every parish, supervised by the church, and financed partly by local landowners, who provided the schoolhouse and a small salary, which the schoolmaster supplemented with fees. The parish schools of the seventeenth and eighteenth centuries seem at times to have regarded English and Scots as interchangeable – the Stirling Burgh Records of 23 August 1718 seem to use the terms synonymously when referring to the 'Scots or English classe in the gramer school' (cited in Aitken 1992: 894). References to 'English' classes in the 'Statistical Accounts' published in 1790 by Sir John Sinclair usually refer to classes in reading, which was taught separately from writing. Literacy rates in lowland Scotland were relatively high in the eighteenth century, and the prestige accorded to written English as a mark of education probably contributed to the relative decline in the status of Scots over time.

In 1872 the Education (Scotland) Act came into force, making it compulsory for every child between the ages of 5 and 13 to receive education. The Scotch Code of 1878 set standards of examination, which assessed reading and writing in English with particular attention being paid to grammatical analysis and the 'form of composition, spelling, grammar and handwriting to be considered'. Although writing in Scots was not explicitly encouraged, other parts of the curriculum could accommodate the mother tongue: among the songs presented to school inspectors by pupils at Roberton parish school in Lanarkshire in May, 1875, were several by Robert Burns, as well as one entitled 'Nae Luck About the House' (Cooper 1973: 60–1).

The Scottish elements of the school curriculum became a point of contention soon after the passing of the 1872 Act. Despite opposition, early initiatives to prioritize Scottish history were abandoned, and Gaelic and Scots were deemed to be much lower in status than English, though it was granted that they might have their uses: 'But though almost infinitely inferior to English, Gaelic may very usefully be employed by teachers in remote corners to explain their lessons to the children, just as Broad Scotch is employed in several parts of the country': *Committee of Council on Education in Scotland Report 1878–9,* cited in Anderson (1995: 216).

The role of education during the Victorian era was partly to promote British citizenship, and the sidelining of Scottish subjects, including Scots language, prompted a series of patriotic campaigns in the early decades of the twentieth century. In 1907, a Scottish Education Department memorandum acknowledged the value of teaching in the 'mother tongue' of Gaelic and Scots. Later SED pronouncements were not to be so sympathetic. Primary teachers in 1946 were instructed that '...the first duty of the infant teacher and the continuing duty of all primary teachers, is to implant and cultivate fluent speech in standard English' (*Primary Education*, HMSO 1946; cited in CCC/COPE, 1980: 7).

Effectively, the teaching of Scots in schools runs into the basic problem that it has not been used as a full discursive written language since the sixteenth century. Its role in schools has been confined to speech and to the expressive arts – song, poetry, fiction and drama – and even then sometimes its presence has been suffered rather than encouraged. However, after a cautious spell in the middle of the twentieth century, the past few decades have witnessed a series of active interventions by Scottish educationalists to encourage the use of Scots in schools. Most of these interventions came under the umbrella of the Scottish Consultative Council on the Curriculum (or SCCC), an independent advisory body to governments and the teaching profession.

In 1976 one of its committees, the Scottish Central Committee on the Curriculum, published *Scottish Literature in the Secondary School*, which included a chapter by linguist AJ Aitken on 'The Scots Language and the Teacher of English'. This was followed in 1980 with the Committee on Primary Education's *Scottish English: the Language Children Bring to School* (CCC/COPE 1980) – a brief selection of commentaries, discussion points and activities to promote Scots at the elementary stage. The SCCC's recommendations on Scotland's indigenous languages were incorporated into the Scottish Office Education Department's guidelines for *English Language 5–14* (1991). Crucially, these guidelines encourage the use of Scots in the classroom, and provide for its place in the national assessment of pupils. The lack of resources to implement these guidelines was met, at least in part, by *The Kist/A' Chiste* (1996), an extensive anthology of texts in English, Gaelic, and different varieties of Scots, with accompanying tapes and teachers' pack, again aimed at the 5–14 age group. Beyond this level, Scots is also present as an optional element at Higher Still and Advanced Higher levels. The Subject Guides to *English and Communication* (1997) specify performance criteria which involve pupils in the study of the history of Scots and its present-day range of varieties. However, it is fair to say that the new *Curriculum for Excellence* guidelines still tend to marginalize the teaching of Scots in schools [see http://www.ltscotland.org.uk]. To counter this marginalization, between 2002 and 2011, a small publisher called 'Itchy Coo' produced over 30 titles in broad Scots poetry and prose, aimed mainly at younger readers [see http://www.itchy-coo.com/].

Current Trends

The history of Scots and Scottish Standard English is essentially seen as one of dialect levelling, generally towards Scottish Standard English. The popular notion that varieties of Scots throughout Scotland are gradually becoming less distinctive is borne out by the results of recent research (see discussion in Macafee 1997: 541–6). Macafee (1988, 1994) showed evidence of the loss of traditional Scots lexis in the urban Scots of Glasgow, although with variation according to individual speakers. She argues (e.g. 1997: 541f.) that the introduction of slang forms does not compensate for the loss of Scots, and hence that lexical 'erosion' is taking place. More recently, her work with the North East Language Project (NELP) at Aberdeen University has confirmed sharp lexical erosion in younger speakers of the Doric (see McGarrity 1998, 1999; Macafee 1997, 1998).

The reasons for the levelling of Scots are highly complex. Attitudes towards urban Scots tend to be negative (e.g. Menzies 1991; Murdoch 1995); these may account for lexical erosion, but only in part. The NELP study (e.g. Macafee 1998) showed that Doric speakers held generally very positive attitudes towards their local dialect. While there was a correlation between positive attitudes towards participation in the language (e.g. 'The Doric forms an important part of our North-East identity') and measured knowledge of Scots lexis, the high degree of lexical erosion cannot be explained purely in terms of attitudes. Macafee concludes that other factors are at work, such as changes in material culture. The presence of conflicting attitudes towards traditional and national standard varieties may also play a role, that is, that the local dialect is important for local identity, but at the same time that knowledge of Scottish Standard English is more helpful for social and economic success.

Levelling in terms of Scots lexis is also being accompanied by levelling of grammar and syntax, and also accent. Preliminary results from a socially stratified dataset of urban speech, collected in 1997 in Glasgow, have indicated grammatical and syntactic levelling of children's urban Scots towards non-standard Southern English. Some aspects of pronunciation also seem to be similar to non-standard Southern English, such as /f/ for <th> in *think, tooth* (Stuart-Smith, 1999). Such changes in accent may be part of a long-term process of levelling. However as long as other features remain (e.g. Scottish vowel quality) we should probably regard them as signs of accent change for urban Scots. Such evidence suggests that the current emphasis on the levelling of Scots should perhaps be adjusted to recognize an alternative ongoing process in English in Scotland – one of language change.

The Future

The future of Scots is notoriously difficult to predict. In the past, reports of its demise have been greatly exaggerated, and current discussions of dialect levelling and language death continue that gloomy tradition. Despite the observations of Tulloch (1997) that Scots or Scottish English has the power to coin new expressions and revive old ones, there is still a powerful sense of loss when the distinctive speech of one generation is succeeded by that of the next. Macafee (1994, 1997) worries that, while new Scottish English words are evidently being coined, they tend to remain in the lower registers, effectively contributing to the stereotype of Scots as colourful slang. Even so, as long as a community requires its speech variety to do more than a standard language can, English in Scotland will continue to have its distinctive character. Moreover, it is significant that, over the centuries, an appetite for some form of literature in Scots – whether songs, poetry, novels or plays – has remained steady, and it is likely that some form of cultural production, from poems in Lallans to novels and films in urban Scots, will be maintained.

It is difficult to foresee the long-term effects of the most recent educational developments, as they attempt to counter five centuries of educational practice in which broad Scots has been deliberately or unconsciously marginalized and stigmatized – despite consistent pockets of resistance. The promotion of Scots in education is still problematical, given the continuing expansion of English as a global language, and the growth of a multicultural Scotland, in which Punjabi or Urdu are as likely to feature as minority languages in some schools as Gaelic or broad Scots. Furthermore, those who promote the use of Scots in education have themselves a mixed agenda. Some wish to supplement or even displace standard English with a Scots standard, capable of expressing a distinctive national identity across the full range of linguistic functions. Others wish to value rather than denigrate the language children bring to school, in order to raise their self-esteem and so enrich their experience of education. A range of viewpoints is presented in *The Scots Language: Its Place in Education* edited by Liz Niven and Robin Jackson (1998). Whatever the long-term results of present curricular changes may be, it is clear that Scots is better placed than it has ever been to move out of the margins and at least some way towards the centre of education in Scotland. It is unlikely, however, that a standard Scots will develop to replace standard English as the everyday written language of the public domain.

Like any language, the particularly Scottish variety of English has the ability to signal an individual's group affiliations, whether these are perceived in terms of nationality, regional identity, social class, age group or gender. If Scottish English suffers from an identity crisis – signified in part by the proliferation of names given to the variety, such as Scots, Doric, Lallans and the Patter – it is because the Scottish people construct their identities in different ways: as independent Scots, as North Britons, as city or country dwellers. While one set of speakers might regard the 'Scottish' aspects of their speech as signalling national identity, others might regard them as signalling primarily class or regional identity. Yet others might regard such features as simply 'bad English'. The future status of English in Scotland is therefore tied to a developing sense of Scottish national identity, and that has taken various twists and turns over the centuries.

At the turn of the millennium, the future of Scottish English looks brighter than it has done for some time. The subject is gaining a firmer foothold in the curricula of Scottish schools and universities, and the devolved Scottish parliament promises to give an institutional focus to a renewed sense of shared nationhood. The characteristics of Scottish English, or Scots, will doubtless continue to change and adapt, but the status accorded to the variety should rise in parallel with the self-esteem of its speakers.

Bibliography

Abercrombie, D. (1979), 'The accents of Standard English in Scotland', in A. J. Aitken and T. McArthur (eds), pp. 68–84.

Aitken, A. J. (1977), 'How to pronounce Older Scots', in A. J. Aitken (ed.), *Bards and Makars,* pp. 1–21, Glasgow: University of Glasgow Press.

—. (1979), 'Scottish speech: A historical view with special reference to the Standard English of Scotland', in A. J. Aitken and T. McArthur (eds), pp. 85–118.

—. (1984), 'Scots and English in Scotland', in P. Trudgill (ed.), pp. 517–32.

—. (1985), 'A history of Scots', in M. Robinson (ed.), pp. ix–xvi.

—. (1992), 'Scots', in T. McArthur (ed.), *The Oxford Companion to the English Language,* pp. 893–9, Oxford: Oxford University Press.

Aitken, A. J. and T. McArthur (eds) (1979), *The Languages of Scotland,* Edinburgh: Chambers.

Anderson, R. D. (1995), *Education and the Scottish People 1750–1918,* Oxford: Clarendon Press.

Beal, J. (1997), 'Syntax and morphology' in C. Jones (ed.), pp. 335–77.

Beattie, J. (1787), *Scoticisms Arranged in Alphabetical Order,* Edinburgh.

Brown, E. K. and J. E. Miller (1980), *Scottish English,* End of Grant Report to the Social Science Research Council.

Brown, G., K. Currie and J. Kenworthy (1980), *Questions of Intonation,* London: Croom Helm.

CCC/COPE (1980), *Scottish English: The Language Children Bring to School,* Edinburgh: Consultative Council on the Curriculum/Committee on Primary Education.

Clark, M. M. and P. Munn (eds) (1997), *Education in Scotland: Policy and Practice from Pre-school to Secondary,* London: Routledge.

Cooper, S. (1973), *The 1872 Education Act in Lanarkshire,* Hamilton: Hamilton College of Education.

Corbett, J. (1997), 'But Grannie, what does "unco sonsie" mean?', Paper presented at PALA, Nottingham, July 1997.

—. (1999), *Written in the Language of the Scottish Nation: A History of Literary Translation into Scots,* Clevedon: Multilingual Matters.

Craigie, W. et al. (1937), *A Dictionary of the Older Scottish Tongue,* 8 vols, Chicago: University of Chicago Press; London: Oxford University Press.

Cruttenden, A. (1986), *Intonation,* Cambridge: Cambridge University Press.

—. (1995), 'Rises in English', in J. Windsor-Lewis (ed.), *Studies in General and English Phonetics,* pp. 155–73, London: Routledge.

Devitt, A. J. (1989), *Standardising Written English: Diffusion in the Case of Scotland 1520–1659,* Cambridge: Cambridge University Press.

Donaldson, W. (1986), *Popular Literature in Victorian Scotland: Language, Fiction and the Press,* Aberdeen: Aberdeen University Press.

Douglas, F. (1997), 'The construction of "Scottish English" in Scotland's press', Paper presented at *Fifth International Conference on the Languages of Scotland and Ulster*, University of Aberdeen, 1–5 August, 1997.
—. (2009), '*Scottish Newspapers, Language and Identity*, Edinburgh: Edinburgh University Press.
Esling, J. H. (1978a), 'Voice quality in Edinburgh: A sociolinguistic and phonetic study', Ph.D. Dissertation, University of Edinburgh.
—. (1978b), 'The identification of features of voice quality in social groups', *Journal of the International Phonetic Association*, 7, 18–23.
Grant, W. (1931), 'Introduction', in *The Scottish National Dictionary*, Vol. 1, Edinburgh: Scottish National Dictionary Association.
Grant, W. and D. Murison (eds) (1931–76), *Scottish National Dictionary*, 10 vols, Edinburgh: Scottish National Dictionary Association.
Henderson, H. (1992), *Alias McAlias: Writings on Song, Folk and Literature*, Edinburgh: Polygon.
HMSO (1946), *Primary Education*, Edinburgh: HMSO.
—. (1993), 1991 *Census: Report for Scotland*, 2 vols, Edinburgh: HMSO.
—. (1994), *1991 Census – Cunntas-sluaigh 1991: Gaelic language – A' Ghaidhlig, Scotland – Alba*, Edinburgh: HMSO.
Jack, R. D. S., A. Hook, D. Gifford and C. Craig (eds) (1987–8), *The History of Scottish Literature*, 4 vols, Aberdeen: Aberdeen University Press.
Johnston, P. (1997), 'Regional Variation', in C. Jones (ed.), pp. 433–513.
Jones, C. (1996), *A Language Suppressed: The Pronunciation of the Scots Language in the Eighteenth Century*, Edinburgh: John Donald.
—. (ed.) (1997), *The Edinburgh History of the Scots Language*, Edinburgh: Edinburgh University Press.
Kay, B. (1993), *The Mither Tongue*, Ayrshire: Alloway.
Leonard, T. (1990), *Radical Renfrew*, Edinburgh: Polygon.
Macafee, C. I. (1983), *Varieties of English Around the World: Glasgow*, Amsterdam: Benjamins.
—. (1988), 'Some studies in the Glasgow vernacular', Ph.D. Dissertation, University of Glasgow.
—. (1992–3), 'A short grammar of Older Scots', *Scottish Language*, 11–12, 10–36.
—. (1994), *Traditional Dialect in the Modern World: A Glasgow Case Study*, Frankfurt: Lang.
—. (1997a), 'Older Scots lexis', in C. Jones (ed.), pp. 182–212.
—. (1997b), 'Ongoing change in modern Scots: The social dimension', in C. Jones (ed.), pp. 514–48.
—. (1998), 'Scots language attitudes and language maintenance', Paper presented at the *Harold Orton Centenary Conference*, University of Leeds, 24–6 March 1998.
Macafee, C. and B. McGarrity. (1999), 'Scots Language Attitudes and Language Maintenance', *Leeds Studies in English*, n.s. 30, 165–79.
Macaulay, R. K. S. (1977), *Language, Social Class and Education: A Glasgow Study*, Edinburgh: Edinburgh University Press.
—. (1991), *Locating Dialect in Discourse: The Language of Honest Men and Bonny Lasses in Ayr*, New York: Oxford University Press.
Mackenzie, Sir G. (1711), *An Idea of the Modern Eloquence of the Bar*, Edinburgh: M. Robert Freebairn.

Macleod, I. et al. (eds) (1990), *The Scots Thesaurus,* Aberdeen: Aberdeen University Press.
Maté, I. (1996), *Scots Language: A Report on the Scots Language Research Carried Out by the General Register Office for Scotland in 1996,* Edinburgh: General Register Office.
Mather, J. Y. and H. H. Speitel (1975–86), *The Linguistic Atlas of Scotland,* 3 vols, London: Croom Helm.
McClure, J. D. (1979) 'Scots, its range of uses', in A. J. Aitken and T. McArthur (eds), pp. 26–48.
—. (1981), 'The Synthesisers of Scots', in E. Haugen, J. D. McClure, and D. Thomson (eds) *Minority Languages Today,* Edinburgh: Edinburgh University Press. pp. 91–9.
—. (1986), 'What Scots Owes to Gaelic', *Scottish Language,* Vol. 5, pp. 85–98.
—. (1988), *Why Scots matters,* Edinburgh: Saltire Society.
McGarrity, B. (1998), 'A sociolinguistic study of attitudes towards and proficiency in the Doric dialect in Aberdeen', M.Phil. Dissertation, University of Aberdeen.
McMillan, D. and D. Gifford (eds) (1997), *The History of Scottish Women's Writing,* Edinburgh: Edinburgh University Press.
Menzies, J. (1991), 'An investigation of attitudes to Scots and Glasgow dialect among secondary school pupils', *Scottish Language,* 10, 30–46.
Meurman-Solin, A (1993), *Variation and Change in Early Scottish Prose: Studies Based on the Helsinki Corpus of Older Scots,* Helsinki: Suomalainen Tiedeakatemia.
Miller, J. E. (1993), 'The Grammar of Scottish English', in J. Milroy and L. Milroy (eds), *Real English: The Grammar of English Dialects in the British Isles,* pp. 99–138, Harlow: Longman.
Montgomery, M. B. and R. J. Gregg (1997), 'The Scots language in Ulster', in C. Jones (ed.), pp. 569–622.
Murdoch, S. (1995), *Language Politics in Scotland,* Aberdeen: Aiberdeen Univairsitie Scots Leid Quorum.
Murison, D. (1971), 'The Dutch Element in the Vocabulary of Scots', in A. J. Aitken, A. Macintosh, and H. Pálsson (eds), *Edinburgh Studies in English and Scots,* pp. 159–76, London: Longman.
—. (1977), *The Guid Scots Tongue,* Edinburgh: Blackwood.
Murray, J. A. H. (1873), *The Dialect of the Southern Counties of Scotland,* London: The Philological Society.
Niven, L. and R. Jackson (1998), *The Scots Language: Its Place in Education,* Dundee: Northern College.
Ó Baoill, C. (1997), 'The Scots-Gaelic Interface' in C. Jones, pp. 551–68.
Purves, D. (1997), *A Scots Grammar: Scots Grammar and Usage,* Edinburgh: Saltire Society.
Robertson, R. et al. (1996), *The Kist/A' Chiste,* Edinburgh: SCCC/Nelson Blackie.
Robinson, M. (1985), *The Concise Scots Dictionary,* Aberdeen: Aberdeen University Press.
Romaine, S. (1982), 'The English Language in Scotland', in R. W. Bailey and M. Görlach (eds), *English as a World Language,* Amsterdam: Benjamins.
Sabban, A. (1985), 'On the variability of Hebridean English syntax: The verbal group', in M. Görlach (ed.), *Focus on Scotland: Varieties of English around the World,* pp. 125–43, Amsterdam: Benjamins.

SCCC (1976), *Scottish Literature in the Secondary School,* Edinburgh: Scottish Central Committee on the Curriculum.
SCCC/SFEU (1997), *English and Communication: Subject Guide,* Edinburgh: Scottish Consultative Council on the Curriculum/Scottish Further Education Unit.
Shuken, C. (1984), 'Highland and Island English', in P. Trudgill (ed.), pp. 152–66.
Sinclair, J. (1782), *Observations on the Scottish Dialect,* London.
Smith, J. J. (1994), 'Norse in Scotland', *Scottish Language,* 13, 18–33.
SOED (1991) *English Language 5–14,* Edinburgh: Scottish Office Education Department.
Stuart-Smith, J. (1999), 'Glasgow Accent and Voice Quality' in P. Foulkes and G. Docherty (eds), *Urban Voices: Variation and Change in British Accents,* pp. 201–22, London: Edward Arnold.
Trudgill, P. (ed.) (1984), *Language in the British Isles,* Cambridge: Cambridge University Press.
Tulloch, G. (1997), 'Lexis', in C. Jones (ed.), pp. 378–432.
Verma, M. (1995), 'Ethnic minority languages in Scotland: A sociolinguistic appraisal', *Scottish Language,* 14/15, 118–33.
Wells, J. (1982), *Accents of English,* 3 vols, Cambridge: Cambridge University Press.
Wilson, J. (1915), *Lowland Scotch, as Spoken in the Lower Strathearn District of Perthshire,* London: Oxford University Press.
—. (1923), *The Dialect of Robert Burns, as Spoken in Central Ayrshire,* Oxford: Oxford University Press.
—. (1926), *The Dialects of Central Scotland,* Oxford: Oxford University Press.
Young, D. (1947), *'Plastic Scots' and the Scottish Literary Tradition,* Glasgow: William Maclellan.

North West England

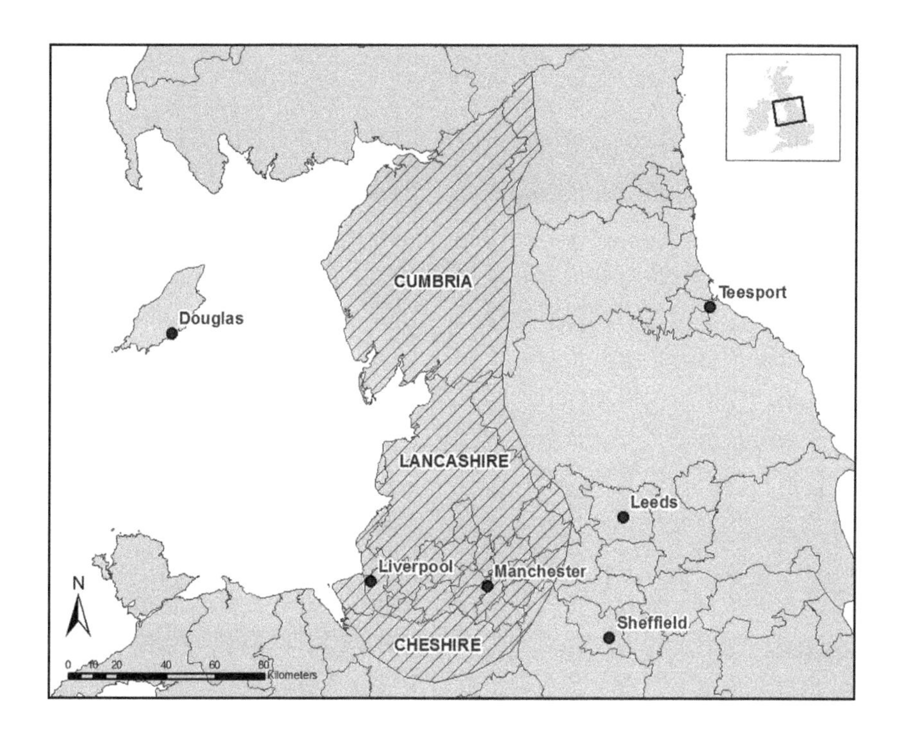

Chapter 8

North West English

Phillip Tipton

Geographical Position, Demographic Data and Historical Background as a 'Region'

Introduction

The area known today as the north west of England is made up of the traditional counties of Cheshire, Lancashire,[1] Westmorland and Cumberland.[2] It contains the large industrial cities of Liverpool and Manchester, along with smaller urban centres with city status such as Chester, Preston, Lancaster and Carlisle. In addition to the aforementioned cities, the North West is replete with both industrial and more rural towns. The industrial centre of the region is the hinterland in south Lancashire and north Cheshire between Liverpool and Manchester, through which runs the M62 motorway, which itself links the North West ultimately with the port city of Kingston-upon-Hull in East Yorkshire on the east coast, via Leeds, the largest city in the county of Yorkshire. Moreover, the region is bisected by the M6 motorway which originates in Warwickshire to the south and ultimately leads to the border between England and Scotland. Rural areas are to be found across the region. Travelling from south to north, these rural areas are especially to be found in mid- and south Cheshire, north Lancashire and throughout the inland areas of the administrative county of Cumbria.

The North West also benefits from a number of areas of natural beauty, not least the Lake District National Park in Cumbria, the Trough of Bowland in Lancashire and Delamere Forest in Cheshire.

The main centres of population are the metropolitan areas surrounding, and between, the cities of Manchester and Liverpool. The Greater Manchester conurbation has a population of 2,500,000, including 430,000 within the boundaries of the city of Manchester. The Merseyside conurbation, formed from the five unitary authorities of Liverpool, Knowsley, Sefton, Wirral and St Helens, has a population of 1,400,000 of whom approximately 450,000 live within the boundaries of the city of Liverpool itself. Due to their more rural nature, the administrative counties of Cheshire, Lancashire and Cumbria are more sparsely populated, though Lancashire has a population similar in size to that of Merseyside; it is, however, spread over a much larger geographical area.

The North West is governed centrally from London under the auspices of the Government Offices for the North West. In addition, certain responsibilities are delegated to local authorities. Two types of local government obtain in the North West. Some parts of the North West are administered by *unitary authorities* which provide all services for local residents, including education, social services, highway maintenance and waste management. The rest of the North West Region is administered by means of a *two-tier system* whereby each area is covered by a *district council* and a *county council*, the latter administering an area covered by a number of *district councils*. Certain services in an area administered by two-tier local government are the preserve of the county council, while some are reserved for provision on a much more local level by the district council.

The current local government arrangements are a legacy of the Redcliffe-Maud report published in the latter end of the 1960s. The report was the culmination of the Royal Commission on Local Government 1966–9 which looked into possible reforms for the structure of local government. Following the victory of the Conservative Party in the general election of 1970, the report's contents were revised radically when published as legislation, and the resulting Local Government Act 1972 was a much less wide-ranging set of proposals than those contained in the original report.

The Act created two types of county, metropolitan and non-metropolitan. Cumbria, created out of Cumberland, Westmorland, Lancashire north of the sands and Sedburgh Rural District in the North Riding of Yorkshire, is a two-tier non-metropolitan county. Lancashire is also a two-tier county, formed from the northern half of the traditional county, along with a small area around Barnoldswick and Earby, formerly within the West Riding of Yorkshire. To complete the triumvirate of two-tier non-metropolitan counties, we have Cheshire, whose land mass was somewhat depleted by the 1972 Act. The legislation removed most of the Wirral peninsula to Merseyside, and the so-called 'Cheshire pan-handle' area east of Manchester and a large swathe of land south of the Manchester Ship Canal, including Stockport, Hyde, Romiley and Cheadle, were combined with a large area of south east Lancashire to form Greater Manchester. Conversely, Cheshire gained a small area of south Lancashire north of the Manchester Ship Canal, such that Widnes and the whole of the borough of Warrington became part of the two-tier non-metropolitan county.[3] The most populous areas of south Lancashire and north Cheshire became the constituent elements of the metropolitan counties of Merseyside and Greater Manchester.

The local government changes wrought upon the North West were certainly not without their critics. As has been seen, the historic counties of Cumberland and Westmorland were wiped off the map completely; moreover, Cheshire and Lancashire were hardly left unscathed. Lancashire suffered a drastic cut in its population and the loss of its urban industrial heartlands in addition to its territory north of Morecambe Bay. Cheshire was significantly refashioned with the loss of the vast majority of the Wirral Peninsula and the pan-handle area in the Pennine Hills. Any account of the English spoken in the North West of England must be set against the backdrop of these administrative changes. The interplay of identity, regional affiliation and language is very much at the forefront of modern sociolinguistic research, and this chapter seeks to focus on some of the distinguishing features of the English spoken in the North West. First, it will address whether the North West can be regarded as a homogeneous geographical region and, if not, how it might be most appropriate to describe the relationship between the different communities within the larger region. Second, the notion of linguistic homogeneity within the North West will be examined: just how justified are we in postulating a North West variety within the United Kingdom? Third, some case studies of key linguistic variables will be presented with an analysis of how they might be integrated within a treatment of any North West English.

Sociocultural and linguistic background and linguistic description of the components of the grammar and English usage within the region

Where is the North West? Is there such a thing as North West English?

Honeybone (2007) looks at the distinctive variety of English known as Scouse which is spoken in and around the city of Liverpool. Any cursory examination of this variety will lead one quickly to the conclusion that it is in many ways different from the variety or varieties which surround it. The key aim of this chapter it to examine whether Scouse stands on its own in the North West in its distinctiveness from its neighbouring varieties, or, rather, if it is only one of many North West varieties that can be clearly differentiated from each other. First of all, however, it is necessary to examine whether there exists such a thing as a 'North West identity'.

Is a Mancunian, a resident of the city of Manchester, a 'north westerner' before he is Mancunian? Perhaps, more pertinently, is a life-long resident of the town of Bolton a north westerner before he is a Boltonian (or, in the local argot, a Trotter)? This latter example is rendered more pertinent by the existence in the North West of very local identities and affiliations. That a city-dweller should take on an identity closely associated with the home city is unsurprising; that there should also be an interplay of multiple and co-occurring identities and affiliations within a relatively small geographical area is perhaps more interesting and worthy of closer examination.

The role of identity has taken on an increasingly important role in sociolinguistic research over recent years (e.g. Eckert 2001, Moore 2003). An important aspect of this development in the field has been the ethnographic methodology it has employed. In broad terms, ethnographic methodology can be described as 'bottom-up', as opposed to 'top-down', in that it seeks to build theories and models, and draw conclusions, based on the data found in the field. This is in contrast to traditional sociolinguistic work which, in many cases, employed predetermined social class groups as a means of dividing up its sample groups and then drew causal relationships between such categories and the linguistic phenomena observed within the speech community (see Cameron 1997 for a critique of this approach). Ethnographic approaches do not rule out the use of such categories in linguistic research, but rather require that they, along with any other putative form of population categorization, be *salient* within the relevant speech community, and that any such salience or relevance is qualitatively established within the said community. This chapter, along with the other contributions covering what might be described as the 'linguistic north', shows that there exist certain linguistic features which are common to most, if not all, varieties spoken in the north of England. A key question is the extent to which the existence and use of these linguistic features play a role in representing and sustaining a generalized northern or, for the purposes of this chapter, a North West identity.

One of the leading scholars in the field of the relationship between language and regional identity is Carmen Llamas, whose work has examined this relationship in the town of Middlesbrough. Middlesbrough, as Llamas notes (2000: 127), is most commonly thought of as being situated in the North East of England. Before a local government reorganization in 1968, however, Middlesbrough was situated within the county of Yorkshire, an area of England which has a strong regional identity of its own. In the intervening period between 1968 and 1996, Middlesbrough went through two further administrative changes before the advent of the current situation, a Middlesbrough unitary authority. The most commonly known form of North East English is Tyneside English, and Llamas (*ibid*: 138) identifies a linguistic feature whose incidence is said to be typical of Tyneside English. This feature is the glottalization of the voiceless stops {p, t, k} in intervocalic position. She hypothesizes that as the incidence of this feature is higher in Tyneside English than in Middlesbrough English, her finding that this feature is increasingly used by younger speakers in Middlesbrough suggests Middlesbrough English is converging towards its more northerly counterpart. Importantly, she points out that this trend correlates 'neatly with the shifting identity of Middlesbrough and the pulling of the urban centre out of North Yorkshire and into the North East' (p. 127). This is an important example of how a linguistic variable can be manipulated by the speech community in order to reflect the prevailing and dominant identity taken on by that speech community. That the convergence towards Tyneside English norms should be most evident among the younger members of the population is unsurprising; many of them will have no recollection of the time when Middlesbrough was administered by Yorkshire. The increase in the use of Tyneside norms in the younger speakers seems to reflect the dynamic nature of a speech community in flux. Just as we are born without the history of our language to refer back to, the younger speakers in Middlesbrough have been born into a community whose affiliations and identity are in the process of change. The linguistic evidence suggests that they are anchoring themselves to an identity which is 'North East', yet which is principally derived from the dominant variant found within the geographical North East.

As already mentioned above, the North West region has two principal urban centres around which have grown large and adjacent conurbations. Liverpool and Manchester are situated barely 60 km apart, yet retain distinct, and often opposing, identities. This is reflected to a large extent in the distinctive varieties of English spoken in and around each city. Liverpool English is dealt with elsewhere in this volume, but it is sufficient here to mention that it very much stands alone in the North West in its distinctiveness as a variety of English. To what extent, however, is Manchester seen as the 'capital' of the region both in popular perception by outsiders and, more importantly, by those residing within the region itself? In this connection, it is perhaps important to consider the economic and cultural impact of the urban centres of the North West.

The relationship between the cities of Liverpool and Manchester is often stated in terms of opposition. This 'rivalry' is played out both in the popular imagination and on the football field. Liverpool FC and Manchester United are two of the United Kingdom's, and indeed the world's, biggest football (soccer) clubs. In 1996 Manchester was hit by a terrorist bomb, the largest device ever used on the British mainland, which was planted by the Provisional Irish Republican Army (IRA). Much of the city's central shopping area was destroyed though, mercifully, no life was lost in the incident. The 1996 bomb acted as the catalyst for the regeneration of Manchester city centre which, from the rubble of the blast, has risen like a modern phoenix from the ashes. Construction sites and cutting-edge buildings abound in today's Manchester. It is often said that Liverpool, at least over recent years, has languished in Manchester's shadow: it is certainly true that Liverpool has appeared to lack the self-confidence of its near-neighbour. Perceptions, however, are changing. Liverpool was recently chosen by the UK Government to be the country's designate for the 2008 European Capital of Culture. Plans are well underway to provide a year-long celebration of the cultural life of the city.

A glance at present-day media penetration in the North West reveals a similarly diverse picture emerging. No single newspaper claims coverage of the whole putative region. Rather there exist a number of morning and evening titles which cover large sections of the region and some, such as the (Liverpool) Daily Post, which extend their coverage far beyond the boundaries of the North West, into Wales in the case of the aforementioned title. The Manchester Evening News restricts its coverage to events occurring within the former Greater Manchester metropolitan county and selected areas just beyond the boundary, such as Warrington, Wilmslow and Macclesfield in Cheshire. Interestingly, such news is often titled 'North West News' in what is perhaps an unintended attempt at claiming the boundaries of the region.

In his 1954 study of the economic geography of south Lancashire, Green (1954: 4) seeks to delimit the boundaries of the North West by reference to the influence of Manchester and Liverpool. To quote him in full:

> This area will be taken to include those areas falling within the fields of influence of Manchester and Liverpool. It is bounded to the north by the Lake District watershed, to the east by the Pennines, to the west by the Irish Sea and parts of St George's Channel, and to the south by the Severn-Weaver watershed, the vale of Llangollen.

Green's description of the boundaries of the North West region differs somewhat from the area covered by the Government Office of the North West (henceforth GONW). In particular, he excludes the area to the north of the Lake District up to the Scottish Border which is currently under the remit of GONW. Moreover, he appears to include areas of north east Wales within a putative North West Region. Although written before the introduction of independent television (ITV) in 1955, Wright's North West region has very significant similarities with the area covered by Granada Television, the former ITV franchisee for the North West region. Based in Manchester, Granada Television was one of the first companies to be granted an ITV licence in 1955 and continues broadcasting to this day, albeit as part of the merged ITV plc. The area to the north of the Lake District is covered by Border Television (again, now part of ITV plc), based in Carlisle. This company acts as a cross-border franchisee covering areas either side of the England-Scotland border including north and west Cumbria, the extreme north of Northumberland and the Dumfriesshire, Galloway and Borders regions of Scotland. Moreover, the south of Wright's North West region is situated within Wales, and this again is a cross-over area for independent television franchisees. This area of north east Wales is ostensibly covered by the ITV Wales franchise (formerly HTV Wales), but many viewers choose to watch programmes originating from North West England, as it is felt by many to be more relevant to them than the output of a broadcaster situated many miles away in Cardiff.

Although this discussion is limited to the area covered by GONW, it is nevertheless important to remember that these boundaries are somewhat fuzzy. Cultural influences and home-to-work travel patterns clearly permeate administrative boundaries; the city of Chester is a paradigm example of such phenomena. Chester lies on the Welsh-English border, and though the city centre is in England, some of its dormitory suburbs such as Saltney and Broughton lie wholly or partially in Wales. In a vivid illustration of Chester's status as a border city, the pitch at Chester City Football Club's ground is in Wales, while the club offices and part of one of the ground's stands are to be found in England. Recent attempts by the British government to devolve a certain amount of power to the regions in the north of England were derailed after a lack of consent by the people of the north east of England in a referendum held on the matter. This region has historically been perhaps the most active in adopting a distinctive regional identity and it was with some surprise to those in regional affairs that the idea of a devolved regional assembly was rejected by such a large margin. Opponents of the assembly, however, referred to generalized notions of a 'lack of accountability' and, in this connection, it is worthy to note that, although the proposal to establish a north west regional assembly was not taken to a referendum, preliminary concerns often centred around such accountability concerns. In particular, there was a great deal of concern, which was most vocal in Cumbria, that the physical location of any such assembly would hinder its accountability to those in the northern-most reaches of the region. The most-often mentioned site for the assembly was Warrington, situated in the south of the north west region and many miles from areas around the border city of Carlisle.

It becomes difficult, therefore, at least in the view of the current author, to use the term 'North West English' as anything more than a convenient geographic label to describe the physical location of the area currently under consideration. It is very improbable that any resident of the geographic north west would describe the variety that they themselves spoke as 'North West English'. There do exist, however, a number of components of the grammar which are shared by the varieties found in the linguistic north, and it is to these that we now turn.

Linguistic Features

It is clear, then, that the North West poses problems for those who might wish to ascribe it with a static or unified identity. This is perhaps a surprising state of affairs considering the fact that the North West is a primarily monolingual region. English is the dominant language and there are no centres of population where another language can be seen to be the majority mode of communication. This is not to say, however, that there are no polyglots to be found within the region. The region has been a principal player in a number of historical population movements which have brought people from across the United Kingdom and the world to settle in the North West. Research has shown that a significant minority of the population of the city of Liverpool spoke Welsh as a first language during the nineteenth century. Moreover, the middle part of the twentieth century saw a large influx of immigrant workers from the former British colonies of the Caribbean and South Asia. The immigrant population of Caribbean heritage settled mainly in other parts of the United Kingdom, though there are small populations of this heritage in the larger cities of the region such as Manchester and Liverpool. The greatest lasting impact of this population movement is the large number of people of South Asian origin now resident in the northern half of Greater Manchester and in the towns of East Lancashire. Towns with a significant population of South Asian origin are Bolton, Burnley, Nelson, Accrington, Oldham and Blackburn. That this situation should have arisen was due to the predominant industry of these areas: textiles. Little or no work has been undertaken to investigate the linguistic impact of these population movements; this is especially true in the case of East Lancashire. Recent work (Kerswill et al.) carried out in the East End of London – the traditional 'Cockney heartland' – is pointing to the complex consequences of inter-ethnic dialect contact, the results of which are not easily analysable in terms of the effect of the incoming dialect on the 'native' variety.

An alternative model which could be more applicable in this connection is the famed so-called 'North South divide'. This phenomenon has long played a part in British popular culture. Administratively, the United Kingdom is a relatively centralized country such that London, in the south east, exerts a disproportionate hold in cultural and political terms over the rest of the country. Moreover, the densely populated nature of the British mainland has resulted in a demographic shift towards a vast commuter belt of suburbs and smaller towns radiating out of London along transportation corridors of motorways and railway lines. This geographical divide, then, is a salient one for many on either side of it. Popular stereotypes have been promulgated over the years by satirists and comedians; the north as a parochial place of men in flat caps who enjoy racing dogs, and the south as an area replete with people who love money and are indifferent to the needs of vulnerable people encountered in the streets.[4] As Jewell (1994: 28) notes, it is 'established that there is a north west/south east divide which is literally as old as the hills', this being a reference to geographical features such as the Pennine Hills which serve vividly to mark out territory in the northern portion of England.

This divide has often come to be represented linguistically by sociolinguists and dialectologists in their maps of the geographical distribution of linguistic features. Trudgill (2000) has referred to what he terms 'traditional', 'modern' and 'possible future' dialect areas. These dialect area maps do not map linguistic features of dialects *per se*, but rather seek to delimit areas which can be seen to share a number of features in common.

Map 1 shows the delimitation of Trudgill's 'modern' dialect areas. The north west, as currently described in this chapter, is covered by four of Trudgill's dialect areas: the Northwest Midlands, Merseyside, Central Lancashire and the Central North. The Merseyside dialect area is almost co-terminous with the former administrative county of the same name, though it is proposed to include a significant part of Cheshire, principally around the county city of Chester. Such areas are necessarily broad-brush, and it would not be fair to say that the whole of this area should be treated as synonymous with Liverpool English, a variety which will be dealt with elsewhere in this volume. Rather, the boundaries could be said to be convenient fictions which mask some of the more subtle local differences between varieties.

Map 2, on the other hand, illustrates what Trudgill believes to be the natural progression of the modern dialect areas into possible future versions of the same. Thus, four dialect areas are reduced to three and are named in such a way as to more closely resemble the places around which the dialect areas are centred.

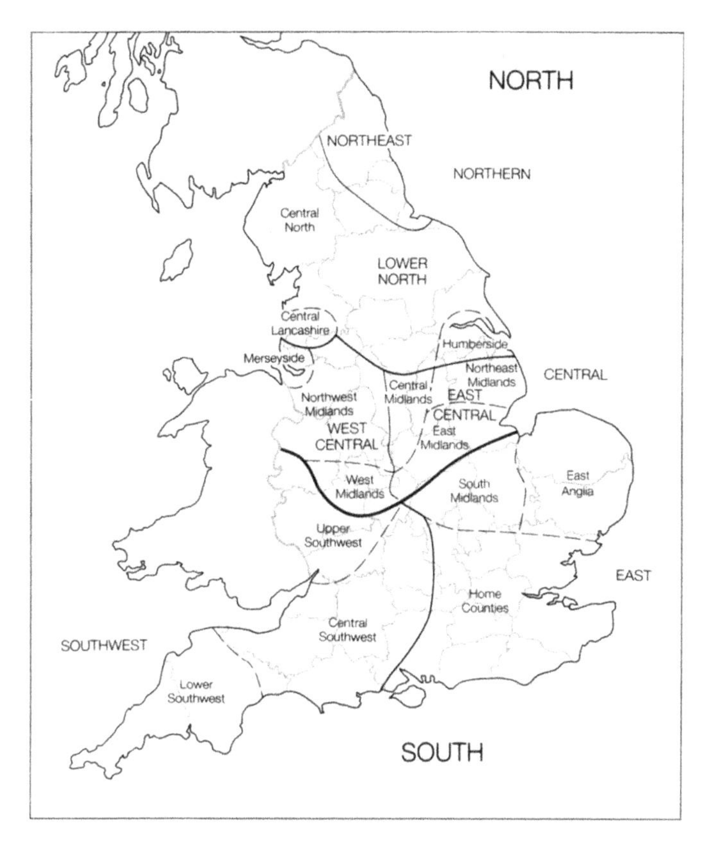

MAP 1

Thus 'Merseyside' becomes 'Liverpool' and increases in terms of its geographical reach, covering areas which were once part of the Central Lancashire and Northwest Midlands dialect regions. Much of the area covered by the former Northwest Midlands region is now, for the purposes of the north west region, covered by the new 'Manchester' dialect area which also supersedes a significant part of the former Central Lancashire area. The Central North, however, remains the same, but is renamed North Lancashire and Lake District. This very large geographical dialect area perhaps reflects the paucity of research on the varieties spoken in this area, and this part of the north west region would undoubtedly prove fruitful in coming to a better understanding of the linguistic north as a whole.

The possible future dialect areas of Trudgill are necessarily speculative, and further work will need to be done in the following years to assess their descriptive adequacy.

The lines drawn on these maps of dialect areas are known as *isoglosses*, and a particularly robust isogloss is often drawn between The Wash in the (relative) north east and the Severn Channel in the south west, thus producing two areas

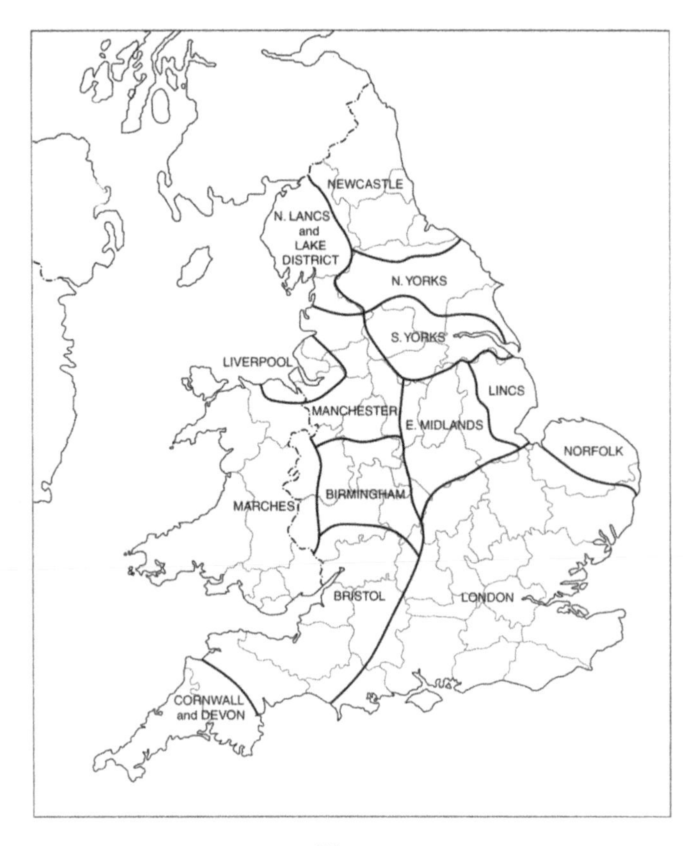

Map 2

which might broadly be characterized as the north west and the south east. The variable linguistic feature most often illustrated by this line is the BATH lexical set (see Wells 1982). Consider the following:

1. /bath/ → [bæθ]
2. /bath/ →[baːθ]

The first of the above examples is said to be typical of varieties to the north west of the Wash-Severn Channel isogloss while the latter example is associated with varieties to the south east of the line. This variable is perhaps one of the most well known within British English, and will be discussed with reference to the North West below. The difference between the two variants is represented by both vowel length and vowel quality. The 'northern' variant in (1) is shorter and more centralized than the 'southern' variant illustrated in (2).

A number of accounts of North West English accents and dialects have found this variable to be a consistent marker of the speech of the individuals studied in these locations. In his study of the grammar of the dialect of the Bolton area,

Shorrocks (1998) does not make use of Wells's lexical sets; rather he seeks to build up a picture of the phoneme inventory of a Bolton speaker. The evidence he has gathered from his fieldwork seems to point very strongly to the absence of variant (2) in the grammar of Bolton speakers, at least in the environments envisaged by Wells's BATH lexical set. Newbrook (1999), in his study of the western half of the Wirral Peninsula, undertook an examination of attitudes to linguistic norms (Received Pronunciation variants) as presented to informants who were asked to report on their self-usage of the 'norm' and the extent to which they perceived this variant as 'correct'. His hypothesis was that, whatever the usage of the informant, they would perceive the RP variant as more 'correct' than the localized variant. Although this proved to be borne out with respect to the majority of variables presented, the BATH lexical set proved to be one of a handful of exceptions to this general pattern of responses. In the majority of cases, the localized 'northern' variant was considered to be the 'correct' usage, a usage event of the 'norm'. Newbrook attempts to explain this in terms of social salience; the entrenchment of this local form is to such an extent that *supra*-regional, or prestige, norms are considered less 'correct' than the local usage forms. This conclusion relies upon at least two assumptions. First, that 'RP' howsoever defined has some currency within the speech community he is seeking to study. Second, that RP has attached to it a sufficient amount of overt or covert prestige. Perhaps the greatest criticism that can be made of Newbrook's work on West Wirral can be illustrated by his statement (1999: 101) that, with regard to the reporting of local norms as more 'correct' than the RP form, '[...] this was done, as it seemed, in full knowledge of which forms are found in RP, rather than out of any ignorance or confusion about the dialectological facts'. Newbrook labels such instances 'conscious rejections'. What, however, are the informants 'rejecting'? It seems, at least to the current author, that such a finding is only surprising if one has predetermined that the RP *should*, for whatever reason, lie at one extreme of an acceptability hierarchy. Wales (2006) comments that the constant referencing of northern Englishes against a principally southern RP standard has missed important insights into the input northern varieties have had into the standard and, importantly in this connection, the ways in which localized varieties can carry indexical meaning for the speech communities in which they operate. Importantly, this indexical meaning can quite often be free of reference to a generalized 'top-down' notion of a 'standard' variety. The vitality of so-called non-standard varieties is closely correlated to their ability to attract both overt and covert prestige in the consciousness of the speech communities in which they operate, and as Wales points out, prestige is not necessarily evaluated by speakers with reference to one single prestige variety which might, in fact, have its genesis outside of the region in which a particular non-standard variety is spoken.

To return momentarily to Wells's lexical sets, these provide a convenient framework in which to analyse phonological and phonetic variation, despite certain disadvantages when it comes to offering a fully descriptive account. They presume that the phoneme as a unit has psychological reality, though this is far from accepted by all scholars (Coleman 2002). The sets do, however, offer a straightforward descriptive account of much phonological variation and will provide the basis for the continuing account of the phonology of North West English. They operate by means of keywords, often orthographically represented by capital letters, which represent words proposed to contain the given vowel. Thus the FACE lexical set represents the vowel in words such as 'take' and 'trace'.

Another feature thought to be typical of varieties found within the linguistic north is, using Wells's lexical sets, the lack of a FOOT~STRUT split. Thus 'could' (stressed form) and 'cud' are realized with an identical vowel – [ʊ] as opposed to the latter vowel's realization as [ʌ] in most varieties of the linguistic south. As Wells (1982: 352) points out, there has been observed an intermediate phenomenon between the phonemic opposition given above, a realization termed 'Near-RP' by Wells. This intermediate vowel is [ə] and might be observed in a speaker trying to 'posh-up' (Wells 1982: 353) their accent but not quite reaching a hypothesized 'target' of [ʌ].

Until the advent of modern variationist studies in the sociolinguistic paradigm, much of our knowledge about different varieties of English came from traditional dialectology, the focus of which as discipline was somewhat different from modern variationist sociolinguistics, albeit that the two are similar in certain limited respects.

The Survey of English Dialects, a veritable opus of dialectology, was completed over a number of years at the beginning of the 1950s. It mainly surveyed non-mobile older rural males (NORMs), a practice somewhat out of current usage in modern sociolinguistics, in an attempt to record the 'true' local dialect of the places in which the fieldwork was undertaken. As such, it must be looked at with some caution when it comes to an examination of modern usage. It is, however, an invaluable resource for linguists who wish to track phonological and grammatical changes from the early twentieth century to the present day.

The organization of the results is somewhat different from Wells's convenient lexical sets but it remains possible to extract relevant tokens from the SED through resort to its own set of target words which were sought by the fieldworkers undertaking the project. Due to its completion before most of the governmental and administrative reorganizations, which started to take place in the United Kingdom in the early 1960s, the results are organized on a county-by-county basis. Interestingly, only Lancashire, Cumberland and Westmorland in the present-day north west region are included in the 'Six Northern Counties' subdivision of the survey. Cheshire, our remaining north west traditional county, is placed in the category of 'West Midlands'.

Going back to the lexical sets already discussed above, that is, BATH, TRAP, STRUT, FOOT and FACE, it can be seen that the situation described by, variously, Wells, Newbrook and Shorrocks for parts of the north west is a continuation of the situation in the SED. The FACE set, however, provides a possible illustration of change in progress. In most areas of today's north west, with the possible exception of Cheshire, the 'traditional' pronunciation of words in this has been monophthongal, that is, the first post-consonantal vowel is made up of one clear vocalic sound. It would seem, however, at least anecdotally, that the urban varieties of Liverpool and Manchester in today's north west are largely diphthongal for the FACE lexical set and this seems to be affecting the hinterland varieties through processes of dialect contact. The resistance of monophthongal FACE up to now may have its roots in its potential status as a supra-regional norm, that is, the extent to which it is seen as a marker of 'northern' speech as opposed to its 'southern' counterparts. The extent of this change is yet to be worked out fully, if indeed it is a change as opposed to stable variation, but may provide insights into the complex relationship between the different northern varieties.

Grammatical Variation: A Case Study of NEG/AUX Contraction

Much less is known about the grammatical features of North West English. Such a lack of data might be put down to the tradition in which much research on syntax and grammar has been carried out. Historically, much less emphasis has been placed upon the variation in such phenomena in favour of a unified account of speakers' linguistic 'competence' in which much is thought to be invariant. Recent work has sought to rectify this imbalance in the scholarly literature with an increasing importance placed upon linguistic variation as a vital consideration for linguistic theory.

It is probably true, however, that grammatical features are under much less conscious control on the part of the speakers than their phonological equivalents, but that should not lead us to ignore the variation which does indeed exist at this level of the grammar.

NEG/AUX contraction is a phenomenon which has only been studied in any detail in one small part of the north west, the town of Maryport in the modern county of Cumbria (Tagliamonte and Smith 2002). Consider the following examples:

(1) 'There isn't a lot to do'
(2) 'There's not a lot to do'

The first of the above examples illustrates the contraction of 'not' whereas the second example shows how the auxiliary BE can be contracted instead to produce a result with precisely the same meaning import. This latter consideration is vital in a study of grammatical variation in the sense that variation can only be said to exist if there are, essentially, two ways of saying exactly the same thing. Very little empirical research has been done on this phenomenon and, as the authors point out (2002: 253); most previous studies of this variable marker have not been quantitative in nature such that they relied on vague intuitions of linguists as to the descriptive reality.

Forty-three speakers were recorded in Maryport, and contractions of the auxiliaries BE, HAVE and WILL were considered. It had generally been presumed by linguists that northern locales would exhibit higher rates of AUX contraction than their southern counterparts, but Maryport proved to buck this putative trend. Only 14 per cent of tokens were AUX-contracted, though such patterns seemed to be largely observable according to the particular auxiliary involved. Thus, most of the tokens which made up the 14 per cent figure in Maryport were from the auxiliary BE.

It is clear that much more work is required on grammatical variation, not only in the north west, but also in mainstream variationist work which has been dominated by phonological variation for most of its history as a discipline.

Conclusion

It has been seen in the above sections that English provides the region with a means of expressing its difference from the standard. Studies have consistently shown the maintenance of regional forms over those which are presumed to demonstrate prestige. The United Kingdom is often said to be a monolingual country, yet the resurgence of the Welsh language, along with both long-settled and newly arrived immigrant communities, illustrates how linguistic diversity has long been present, including in the North West. The main immigrant communities in the North West came from the Indian subcontinent, bringing with them the linguistic diversity that entails. Recent political events in the United Kingdom have led to an increasing focus in rectifying what has been seen as a collective failure in 'integrating' the aforementioned communities. At the heart of this integration agenda has been placed a knowledge of the English language. Government agencies have long provided written and oral communication facilities in languages other than English, with the languages offered tailored on a regional basis according to the language background of the local non-indigenous population. An example of this phenomenon is to be found on the website of Bolton Metropolitan Borough Council which offers a limited amount of information in Urdu and Gujurati, in addition to the main information service in English.

It is clear, however, that, at least in the short to medium term, English has no obvious successor as the mode of communication in the North West of England and will continue to provide its speakers with the resources to mark out their membership of their community, whether familial, local, regional or national. The social and regional diversity of English as demonstrated by this glance at the situation in the North West of England illustrates the vitality of the language in all its forms. It might be thought that increasing mobility of individuals within society would naturally lead to a reduction in the extent to which varieties differ from each other. What can be seen, however, is the vitality of non-standard varieties against what is, and has always been, a socially imposed standard variety of Received Pronunciation. It has been demonstrated above that there do exist some features which are common to different varieties found within the north west, though its status as an easily identifiable unitary phenomenon is less clear when one considers the geographic, cultural and linguistic diversity within this region. North West English, to the extent that it is a homogeneous variety, is not likely to remain static, however, and its vitality as a variety is bound up with its constant renewal and renegotiation by both old and new members of the community, the latter provided by birth or migration. An important opposition in both dialectology and in the popular imagination has been between northern and southern, both in the linguistic and the sociocultural spheres. With increased movement of people between jobs and homes, it might be thought that such an opposition may be breaking down; such a position, however, does not acknowledge the ability of bodies of people, in addition to individuals, to create and recreate multi-modal identities. An important sub-strand of work within variationist linguistics has been the study of new dialect formation, a phenomenon arising out of situations with high levels of contact between speakers of previously distinct dialects. Such new resources, howsoever conceptualized, can be moulded by speakers, thus resulting in the aforementioned multi-modality, not least in the linguistic sphere.

Notes

[1] The composition of Lancashire and Cheshire was significantly altered by Local Government reorganization in 1974. Two new administrative Metropolitan Counties were created, Merseyside and Greater Manchester, out of the two traditional counties. The south Lancashire towns of Warrington and Widnes were transferred to Cheshire, whereas most of the Wirral Peninsula was included within the new Merseyside Metropolitan County and removed from Cheshire. The 1974 changes also saw Lancashire greatly reduce in size, losing the large cities of Liverpool and Manchester to Merseyside and Greater Manchester respectively, along with most of the south Lancashire industrial heartlands. Lancashire thus became a predominantly rural and light industrial county.

[2] Local Government reorganization in 1974 also abolished the counties of Westmoreland and Cumberland in favour of a new administrative county called 'Cumbria'. Cumbria also includes an area north of Morecambe Bay which was traditionally included within Lancashire. This area, centred on Barrow-in-Furness, is sometimes called 'Lancashire north of the sands'.

[3] In 1996, the structure concerning the local government of Warrington and Widnes was changed once again. Warrington and Halton (a borough covering Widnes and Runcorn) were removed from the remit of Cheshire County Council and became unitary authorities in their own right.

[4] Many other stereotypes of northerners and southerners persist, and the ones given above are just two examples of many.

Bibliography

Cameron, D. (1997), Demythologizing sociolinguistics, in N. Coupland and A. Jaworski (eds), Sociolinguistics: A Reader and Coursebook, Basingstoke: Palgrave Macmillan.

Coleman, J. S. (2002), Phonetic representations and the mental lexicon. In J. Durand and B. Laks, eds. *Phonetics, Phonology, and Cognition*. Oxford University Press, 96–130.

Eckert, P. (2001), *Style and Social meaning*. In Eckert, P. and J. Rickford (eds.), Style and Sociolinguistic variation. New York: Cambridge University Press, 119–26.

Green, P. (1954), An analysis of the urban spheres of influence of Manchester and Liverpool, with special reference to Central South Lancashire, Unpublished MA Thesis: University of Leeds.

—. (2006), An analysis of the urban spheres of influence of Manchester and Liverpool, with special reference to Central South Lancashire, Unpublished MA, Dissertation, University of Leeds.

Honeybone, P. (2007), 'New-dialect formation in nineteenth century Liverpool: a brief history of Scouse', In A. Grant and Grey, C. (eds), *The Mersey Sound: Liverpool's Language, People and Places*, pp. 106–40, Liverpool: Open House Press.

Jewell, H. M. (1994), *The North South Divide: The Origins of Northern Consciousness in England*, Manchester: Manchester University Press.

Kerswill, P. and A. Williams. (2000), Creating a new town Koine: children and language change in Milton Keynes, *Language in Society*, 29, 65–115.

Kerswill, P. and J. Cheshire (2008–11), Multicultural London English: the emergence, acquisition and diffusion of a new variety. Economic and Social Research Council.

Llamas, C. (2000), Middlesbrough English: convergent and divergent trends in a 'part of Britain with no identity', Leeds Working Papers in Linguistics 2000.

Moore, Emma (2003), Learning Style and Identity: A sociolinguistic analysis of a Bolton High School. Unpublished PhD Thesis at University of Manchester, Department of Linguistics.

Newbrook, M. (1999), West Wirral: self-reports, norms and usage, in P. Foulkes and G. Docherty (eds), *Urban Voices: Accent Studies in the British Isles*, London: Arnold.

Orton, H. and B. Eugen Dieth (1969), Survey of English Dialects. Leeds: Arnold for the University of Leeds.

Shorrocks, G. (1998), *A Grammar of the Dialect of the Bolton Area, Part 1*, Frankfurt am Main: Peter Lang.

Tagliamonte, S and J. Smith (2002), Either it isn't or it's not: NEG/AUX contraction in British dialects, *English World-Wide*, 23(2), 251–81.

Trudgill, P. (2000), *The Dialects of England*, Oxford: Blackwell.

Wales, K. (2006), *Northern English: A Social and Cultural History*, Cambridge: Cambridge University Press.

Wells, J. C. (1982), *Accents of English*, 3 vols, Cambridge: Cambridge University Press.

Wales

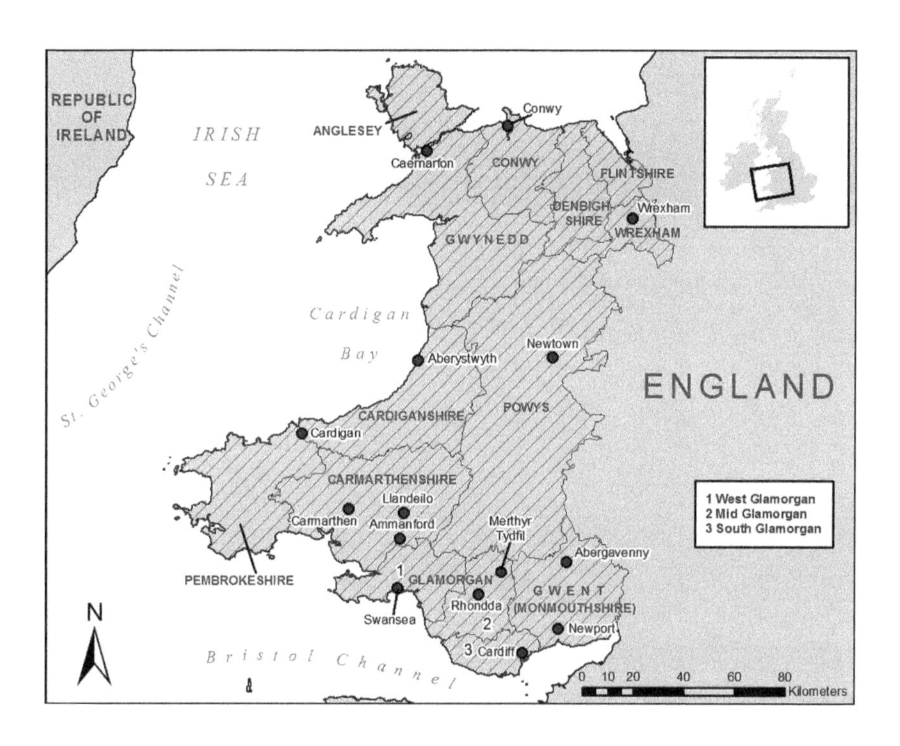
REPUBLIC OF IRELAND
IRISH SEA
ANGLESEY
Conwy
Caernarfon
CONWY
FLINTSHIRE
DENBIGH-SHIRE
Wrexham
WREXHAM
GWYNEDD
St. George's Channel
Cardigan Bay
Newtown
Aberystwyth
ENGLAND
CARDIGANSHIRE
POWYS
Cardigan
CARMARTHENSHIRE
Llandeilo
Carmarthen
Ammanford
Merthyr Tydfil
Abergavenny
PEMBROKESHIRE
GLAMORGAN
Rhondda
GWENT (MONMOUTHSHIRE)
Swansea
Newport
Cardiff
Bristol Channel
N
0 10 20 40 60 80 Kilometers
1 West Glamorgan
2 Mid Glamorgan
3 South Glamorgan

Chapter 9

English in Wales

Heli Paulasto

Introduction: Background Information

The majority language of Wales, one of the four constituent countries of the United Kingdom, is English. It is spoken by practically the entire population of c. 2,805,700 people.[1] The indigenous language of the area is Welsh, or *Cymraeg*, which according to the 2001 census is spoken by 20.5 per cent of the inhabitants, that is, some 575,640 people (Aitchison and Carter 2004: 49). A more recent survey conducted by the Welsh Language Board in 2004 and published in 2006 indicates that over the past few years, the figures had risen to 21.7 per cent (611,000) of all those aged three and above. For most Welsh speakers, it is their first language, but increasing numbers of people have learnt Welsh at school or in adult life.

The position of English as the dominant language was established through legislation in the sixteenth century, and it has been strengthened over time by various means: administrative, educational, economic and practical, but Welsh did not lose its majority status until the first decade of the twentieth century (Jones, 1998). In many parts of rural north and west Wales, language shift has not taken place to the same extent as in the south and east of the country, and Welsh continues to be spoken by the majority of the inhabitants. The recent and relatively rapid nature of Anglicization and the high degree of bilingualism in some regions have resulted in contact influence from Welsh into the local varieties of spoken English. Welsh English, used here as a cover term for the regional varieties, is characterized primarily by its distinctive phonology, but it also contains morpho-syntactic features arising from Welsh. Lexical borrowings or retentions are infrequent in general use, but localized dialect words of Welsh origin are more common (Thomas 1994; Parry 1999). In addition to Welsh, varieties of Welsh English have been influenced by West Midlands and south-west English dialects, urban varieties such as that of Liverpool, and mainstream modern dialects of English.

Conurbations, most significantly the Cardiff-Newport area, have developed distinct and distinctive regional accents of their own. Coupland et al. (1994: 485) point out that the Welsh dialect map is diverse enough that caution must be exercised when using labels such as Welsh English or southern Welsh English.

It might be advisable to opt for the more nondescript 'English in Wales' when analysing English language use in Wales from perspectives wider than that of the regional varieties. The term Welsh English itself is defined somewhat differently by scholars (see, e.g. Visser 1955; Penhallurick 1993; Awbery 1997). Penhallurick (1993: 33), for example, draws attention to the patterns of variation within Wales which extend from the cultural and socio-economic to the linguistic. He connects English language use with the political 'three-Wales model' proposed by Balsom (1985) and Osmond (1988), where the country is divided into *Y Fro Gymraeg*, the Welsh-speaking heartland; *Welsh Wales*, the southern industrial valleys; and *British Wales*, the longstanding English border and the coastal regions. Although patterns of this kind are of obvious relevance in determining the status of Welsh English versus English, there are multiple factors at play. It can be asked, for instance, whether a strong position of Welsh in the community is the only, or indeed the most influential, factor in maintaining distinctively Welsh patterns of speech in the regional dialects of English (see below, Paulasto 2006: 270f.).

Because of the range of regional and social variation, it is unclear to what extent the Welsh would define themselves as Welsh English speakers. Although the Welsh accent (or, e.g. the South Wales or North Wales accent) is a familiar and nationally recognized concept in the country (cf. Giles 1990; Garrett et al. 2003), interviews conducted by Penhallurick (for the sequel to the Survey of Anglo-Welsh Dialects; see Paulasto 2006) and Paulasto (ibid.) indicate that the Welsh are less comfortable with labelling English in Wales as a distinct national variety. Nor is there a 'Standard Welsh English', because, as pointed out by Coupland (1990b: 243), 'there is no single Welsh sociological base to sustain a regional standard, and groups and individuals will identify with and through competing models of speech'. The competing models range from Standard English English and RP to highly Welsh-influenced English. Although no variety of Welsh English can therefore be set apart as the regional prestige model of speech, Coupland et al. (1994) observe that certain varieties are regarded more favourably than others.

The History of Anglicization in Wales

Most of Wales has become Anglicized relatively recently compared to Ireland and, in particular, Scotland. Besides affecting the current position of the two languages of Wales, this has had an impact on the way in which the Welsh varieties of English have developed and continue to develop. The following account sketches the historical background for the present-day language situation from the point of view of Welsh as well as English. Before the *adventus Saxonum* in the fifth century, Brythonic, the predecessor of Welsh, Cornish and Breton, was spoken throughout England and Wales. The Anglicization of Wales is the end result of a language shift process which began with the increasingly influential role of the Anglo-Saxon tribes in the British Isles.

By the seventh century, the kingdom of Wessex extended to the river Severn, cutting off the connection between Wales and Cornwall (Jackson 1994: 203–6). The isolation led the Celtic languages of these areas to develop in their own directions. Although Brythonic continued to be spoken in most parts of England (Davies 1993: 68), Williams (1935: 242) finds that the east Radnorshire plain in Mid-Wales may have been largely English as early as the eighth century. By the high Middle Ages, the English language had spread across the border and along the southern coastline, replacing Welsh in what is today considered the longstanding English region of Wales: southern Pembrokeshire, the Gower peninsula, south Glamorganshire and Monmouthshire, and the border area. This development was largely due to the successful campaigning of the new rulers of England: Davies (1993: 109–14) writes that from the early twelfth century onwards, Wales was divided between *Marchia Wallie*, the territories of the Anglo-Norman Marcher lords in the south and east, and *Pura Wallia*, the Welsh kingdoms in the north and west. English and Flemish peasants emigrated to Pembrokeshire and the Gower at the command of Henry I, which strengthened the position of the king as well as that of the English language. Being English-speaking pockets surrounded by Welsh villages, these regions maintained distinct dialectal similarities with the southwestern varieties of English far into the twentieth century (for details, see Parry 1990; Penhallurick 1994).

While the longstanding English regions constituted the first stage in the Anglicization of Wales, the second stage entailed the advance of English, not in terms of geography, but of prestige and social functions. The last indigenous Prince of Wales, Llywelyn ap Gruffudd (Llywelyn II), was defeated in 1282, but although the Welsh nobles were brought under English rule, the peasantry remained overwhelmingly Welsh-speaking well into the nineteenth century. The Welsh gentry, on the other hand, felt the need to acquire English, which had become the language of law and administration after the decline of French and Latin. The position of English as the only official language of the nation was consolidated by the Laws in Wales Act included in the Acts of Union (1536 and 1543). The intention of the Act was to suppress Welsh, which was considered to stand in the way of the unity of the kingdom. Welsh speakers could no longer hold official positions in the land, which alienated the Welsh from their own administrative and legal institutions and prevented them from participating in the affairs of state.

The linguistic as well as social division between the Welsh peasantry and gentry eventually led to diglossia, bilingualism being rare beyond the Marcher lands and towns. Thomas (1994: 96) mentions that legal and commercial transactions between the peasantry and the gentry were often conducted using bilingual interpreters. The diglossia was heightened by prestige factors: while the status of Welsh was low, English represented prosperity and sophistication, which drove the gentry to abandon Welsh altogether. The position of Welsh was nevertheless improved by the translation of the Bible in 1588, giving the language a high, religious domain of use in addition to the domestic one. Several scholars (e.g. Williams 1990: 21) deem the translation to have been extremely important for the survival of the language, but Thomas (1994: 97) observes that it was also another good means of controlling the Welsh, who were now more likely to accept their disadvantaged position in other fields of life.

In spite of the Anglicization of the gentry and the chancery towns, the advance of English into the Welsh-speaking regions was extremely slow until the nineteenth century. There was little migration within Wales, and the average peasant had no pressing need to acquire English. On the borders between the two language regions, however, bilingualism was gradually increasing at all levels of society. It is also probable that the varieties of English spoken in these parts were affected by the Welsh language to some extent. Written evidence of early Welsh English is scarce, although Shakespeare is known to have used Welsh features of speech (see below) in the lines of some of his Welsh characters, most notably Fluellen in *Henry V* and Sir Hugh Evans in *The Merry Wives of Windsor* (Thomas 1994: 107). A more direct reference to the early impact of Welsh can be found in MacCann and Connolly (1933: 56, cited in Pryce, 1990: 50). They tell of a seventeenth-century gentleman from Abergavenny who wished that his son might acquire good English 'without any corruption from his mother tongue', as was common in the country. The monoglot English speakers on the Welsh side of the border, on the other hand, were in closer contact with the English than with the Welsh speakers, which is why the eastern and southern varieties of English absorbed characteristics of the West Midlands and south-west English dialects.

English began to spread into Wales considerably faster with the population movements and revolutionary changes in social structure which took place during the Industrial era, from c. 1770 onwards. The development was initially slow, but Pryce (1978: 229–30) states that by the end of the nineteenth century, 'Old Wales', rural and Welsh-speaking, had given way to 'new Wales', urban and predominantly English-speaking, and that the population and administration became centred in the south-east instead of the regional chancery towns. The effects of the thriving coal industry ultimately served the cause of promoting the English language, but until 1911, the number of Welsh speakers grew as well, as migration from the rural north and west into the south-eastern coalfields and iron works strengthened the position of Welsh and Welsh language culture in these parts of the country. Unlike in Ireland, thousands of people were able to find employment in their homeland. Williams (1985: 178) states that although emigration into England and America was also common, it did not erode the Welsh language to the extent it did in the case of Irish.

By 1881, English-speaking immigrants into the coalfield outnumbered the Welsh-speaking ones, and their numbers kept growing (see Jones 1998: 155). The English influx began to wear on the Welsh language, particularly as the status of Welsh had not improved: English remained the language that gave access to social advancement. There seemed to be no reason to hang on to Welsh, and the language shift in the most densely populated region of the country reached full momentum, advancing generation by generation from monoglot Welsh to bilingual to monoglot English (Williams 1935: 258). The communities in the industrial south-east were largely bilingual and the speakers of English and Welsh were in daily contact with each other. Linguistic transfer is common under these kinds of circumstances.

Although Thomas (1994: 99) observes that there is no evidence of a pidgin-type language having developed in the region, transfer did take place. This becomes clear in a response given by Rev John Griffith from Merthyr Tydfil to Ellis (1882), who investigated the linguistic border areas:

> It is difficult to answer your questions, as they do not apply to a district like this. [. . .] Most, or a very large proportion, speak both languages. You will find it very difficult to trace a boundary in towns. The English is peculiarly 'Welsh English', neither like Hereford nor Gloucester, in fact English in a Welsh idiom. (Ellis 1882: 205)

Ellis does not find a similar variety of English spoken in other localities on the linguistic border. He concludes that English has either been learnt at school, in which case it is close to the standard, or it resembles the dialects of the neighbouring West Midlands counties (op. cit.: 202).

In the late nineteenth century, the educational system was perhaps the most significant means of spreading English in the rural north and west of Wales. These regions were unaffected by immigration, which was directed to the industrial areas, but they did suffer from emigration, which weakened their social structure. Compared to the south and east of the country, the rural heartlands remained predominantly Welsh-speaking far longer. With the Education Act of 1870, however, primary level education through the medium of English became free and compulsory for the entire population. The introduction of the Act was partly the result of the Reports of the Commissioners of Inquiry, 1847, which examined the state of education in Wales. Based on their investigations, the commissioners concluded that the reason for the vast class differences and poverty among the Welsh was the Welsh language, which isolated them from 'polite society' and the benefits of progress (Aitchison and Carter 2000a: 34). Nationwide education in the English language was the solution to the problem. The conjoined effects of the Education Act and immigration caused the language shift to speed up between 1871 and 1921. A further blow for Welsh came with the mid-war depression, causing mass unemployment and forcing people to leave Wales for work. Socialist ideology, advocating the use of English, replaced the Liberalist and Nonconformist traditions which had supported the use of Welsh, (especially in the south-east (Jones 1980: 68–9; see also Thomas 1987: 437)). The number and percentage of Welsh speakers continued to decline until the census of 1981.

The final stage in the Anglicization process concerned rural, Welsh-speaking Wales. The language shift was clearly slower in the north and west: in the whole of Wales, barely a half of the population spoke Welsh by the census of 1901, but in the rural counties of Anglesey, Caernarfon, Cardigan, Merioneth and Carmarthen, Welsh was still spoken by 90–4 per cent of the inhabitants. What is more, the share of monoglot Welsh speakers was as high as 52–4 per cent in the first four counties (Aitchison and Carter 2000a: 34). During the 1900s, however, the whole of Wales came under the influence of the English language through newspapers, the radio and the cinema. The mobility of the population increased with the proliferation of cars, motorcycles and public transport systems; new roads and railways were built and English-speaking tourists began to find their way even to the remotest Welsh villages. The decline of Welsh was particularly rapid in the decades after World War II.

Although English became widely available in the society and acquiring it became a practical necessity in all of Wales, most Welsh speakers still had no pressing need to completely abandon the language. The shift from Welsh to English was therefore never completed in the Welsh heartlands; instead, the Anglicization process led to bilingualism. The position of Welsh was improved over the course of the twentieth century by legislative action, the reintroduction of Welsh-medium education and the foundation of Welsh language radio and TV-stations. The Welsh Language Act of 1993 finally gave Welsh equal rights with English at the institutional level, and today, support for the language is strong. Since the 1980s, there has been moderate increase in the numbers and percentage of Welsh speakers, particularly in the anglicized regions, where Welsh language teaching at schools and at adult level has begun to take effect. Aitchison and Carter (2004: 50) observe, however, that the English language slowly continues to gain ground in the traditional Welsh communities.

The Sociocultural and Linguistic Background of Welsh English

In many respects, English in Wales fits the descriptions of supra-regional mainstream English used in any part of the British Isles. There is no written Welsh English, and in formal spoken contexts, the grammar of the language does not generally differ from mainstream usage. Because of its history as the language of the colonizers, English is still not unanimously viewed as a 'language of Wales' (e.g. Penhallurick 1993). The significance of English for modern Welsh society is not questioned, unlike in the times of Saunders Lewis (the writer and inter-war President of Plaid Cymru, the National Party of Wales) or the most open and radical Welsh language activism in the 1960s and 1970s. Yet, the strong position of Welsh as the 'national language' of the country has diminished the possibility of Welsh English becoming regarded in national terms. The situation is quite different from Ireland and Scotland, where the indigenous Celtic languages have become more marginalized and therefore left space for a nationally recognized variety of English. In these countries, English also has a longer history than in Wales, where the concept of an Anglo-Welsh identity is barely more than a century old: dating the birth of Anglo-Welsh literature to *My People* by Caradoc Evans, published in 1915, is one indication of this (see Thomas 1999: 46).

Coupland and Thomas (1990: 2) recognize the controversies involved in the language situation in Wales and find that they have their consequences on the study of Welsh English. In their view,

> the language question in Wales is sufficiently highly charged that some might infer that even to pay analytic attention to English in Wales, or 'Welsh English' ... represents an ideological position, perhaps even a form of capitulation, or collusion with forces threatening the Welsh language.

With this statement in mind, Penhallurick (1993: 32) argues forcefully for the significance of a local, national variety of English, concluding that 'English in Wales belongs to the Welsh and is therefore Welsh English: nationalism cannot succeed, and perhaps the Welsh language cannot prosper, without embracing the fact of Welsh English'. Such national acknowledgement is not on the horizon, although the prospects have improved in some ways since the early 1990s.

Several studies show that in spite of its low profile, Welsh English (henceforth WE) retains a measure of social and national significance to its speakers. A large number of these are reviewed in Giles (1990), and the general findings indicate some straightforward patterns. In matched-guise experiments dealing with dialect convergence and divergence, Anglo-Welsh listeners evaluated WE speakers diverging from the RP interviewer as less intelligent but more kind-hearted and trustworthy than speakers who converged (e.g. Bourhis, Giles, and Lambert 1975; Bourhis 1977; summary in Giles, op. cit.: 260–2). Therefore maintaining or emphasizing one's Welshness in inter-group situations is in Giles's (1990: 261) words 'a valued tactic asserting cultural identity'. Integrative learners of Welsh also esteemed the Welsh accent as a symbol of national identity, until such time at least that it might be replaced by competence in the Welsh language (Bourhis, Giles, and Tajfel 1973; Giles et al. 1987; summary in Giles 1990: 263), which supports the notion that WE, as well as Welsh, possesses social and cultural significance. A later study by Coupland et al. (1994), focusing on the dialect evaluations of Welsh school teachers, showed that although the RP-type accent of English was deemed highly prestigious, it received low evaluations on the scales of pleasantness and dynamism. The WE varieties of Carmarthen and

Merthyr Tydfil, on the other hand, fared well in these respects, and also Carmarthen and Newtown received mid-level scores for prestige. The Welsh speakers' reactions to WE have been found more inconsistent than those of the Anglo-Welsh.

Cardiff, as a large conurbation, forms a dialectal and sociolinguistic area of its own. In the studies by Coupland, Garrett and Williams (1994, 1999) it receives low marks for perceived Welshness. The English-speaking born-and-bred Cardiffians do not relate with north Wales. They are more likely to consider themselves British than strongly Welsh, but English they do not confess to be. Coupland (1988: 98) indicates that Cardiffians do not in fact hold their local accent in very high regard at all; a trait shared by the speakers of other urban British speech forms.

The historical developments leading to the birth of a Welsh variety of English have been traced above. As indicated by Ellis (1882), there is evidence of Welsh structural transfer in Merthyr Tydfil English in the late nineteenth century. The extent and type of influence depend on various factors, however: the mode of transmission, whether through formal education or informal acquisition (Paulasto 2009), the individual speakers' grasp of English and opportunities to use it, and the role of English as a community language. The impact of Welsh on phonological and grammatical features in WE is noted by several more recent scholars (e.g. Parry 1977, 1979, 1999; Thomas 1984, 1985, 1994; Penhallurick 1991, 1996, 2004a, 2004b, 2007). There are also other contributing factors. The traditional dialects of the longstanding English regions mentioned earlier are distinguished by linguistic features arising from the English English (EngE) superstratum (e.g. periphrastic *do*, the use of second person singular forms, and certain anomalous forms of the verbs *be* and *do*). Of late, however, these dialects have lost a great deal of their distinctiveness and amalgamated into the varieties spoken in the neighbouring Welsh or English regions. In the south and north-east, on the other hand, spoken English is affected by the dialects of the large conurbations: Cardiff-Newport in the south and Liverpool in the north. Along with the increased contacts with other, more mainstream varieties of English, the regional Welsh varieties have on the whole become levelled quite significantly over the past century.

Regional variation among WE dialects was much more noticeable in the past. Paulasto (2006) presents an investigation of the diachronic changes as well as of the use of Welsh-influenced syntactic features in corpora representing early twentieth-century English spoken in the rural north and south-west and in the Rhondda valley of the south-east. The non-mobile, older, rural and mainly L1 Welsh informants recorded for the Survey of Anglo-Welsh Dialects (see Parry 1999) use substratum syntax in distinctive ways that correspond syntactically and functionally to similar constructions in Welsh. The frequencies of use are, however, much lower than those of the Rhondda informants, who are non-Welsh-speaking, and who have acquired English informally. In the Rhondda, on the other hand, the usages of these constructions are reminiscent of those found in EngE dialects. The results reflect the availability of English and its role in the community next to Welsh. The village of Llandybie in the south-east of Carmarthenshire is a locality where the traits of the first two corpora are combined: Llandybie remains Welsh-speaking, while being situated close to the highly anglicized and urbanized south-east. The variety of English spoken by the elderly generation is comparatively rich in Welsh-influenced patterns of syntax both in terms of forms and frequencies. The findings illustrate the complexities involved in the language shift process and the regional variation that can be observed in its outcomes.

The continued diversity of spoken varieties of English in Wales is also observed by Thomas (1984: 178–9), who states that distinguishing regional dialects or their sub-varieties on structural grounds is extremely difficult. He divides WE into two broad regional forms: northern and southern. The former is used in the bilingual communities of north and west Wales, receiving structural transfer from Welsh. The latter is typical of the southern regions where the language shift has been completed and where the influence of Welsh is therefore progressively wearing off, particularly in domains other than phonology. Garrett, Coupland and Williams (1999: 324) identify six to eight dialect regions based on the criteria of 'perceived linguistic features, affective qualities, prestige, urban/rural character, and . . . perceived Welshness'. In their view, there is a WE heartland which comprises, besides the north and south-west, also the south-eastern Valleys, whose English receives high scores for Welshness. Although the schoolteachers taking part in the study evaluated the rural, south-western dialect most positively, the teenaged informants considered the urban varieties spoken around Cardiff and near Liverpool in north-east Wales the most socially attractive (op. cit.: 330). The finding indicates that these regions are the present-day centres of linguistic innovation in Wales.

The Grammar of Welsh English

This section will present a summary of grammatical features which are common in spoken WE and/or frequently reported in various descriptions of the dialect. These are, in other words, some of the main features which differentiate WE from Standard English (StE) and other rural British dialects. As mentioned above, the traditional varieties of WE spoken in the longstanding English regions share characteristics with West Midlands or south-west English dialects, but in many cases, their relevance for present-day WE can be questioned (see, e.g. Penhallurick 1994; Parry 1990).

The focus of this section is on morphology and syntax, but also the phonology of WE is distinctive in a number of ways. Parry (1999: 11–12) gives a broad summary of the traditional rural WE phonemic inventory based on the Survey of Anglo-Welsh Dialects data. Penhallurick (2004a: 100) translates Parry's inventory into IPA symbols as follows:

Short vowels: / ɪ ɛ a ʌ ɔ ʊ/
Long vowels: /iː eː ɛː œː aː ɔː oː uː/
Diphthongs: /ɪu ai au ɔi oə iə/
Unstressed vowels: /i ə ɪ/
Consonants: /p b t d k g f v θ ð ɬ s z ʃ ʒ x h ʧ ʤ m n ŋ l w j r/

In the vowel system, the most noticeable differences from RP concern the long vowels [eː] and [oː] appearing in words such as *face, great* and *goat, pole,* and the rounded, half-open front vowel [œː] in *nurse.* The use of the former monophthongs follows the orthography of the word, particularly in the rural South WE dialects, so that words such as *clay, drain* and *weigh* or *cold, shoulder* and *snow* are likely to be pronounced with the diphthongs /ei/ and /ou/. In northern WE, on the other hand, the monophthongs are possible in words of all of the above types, whereas in the most anglicized regions, the diphthongs are the preferred choice (see Penhallurick 1993, 2004a). The long [œː] is associated with southern WE, and the Valleys' dialects, in particular. It also appears with an initial /j/ instead of the diphthong /iə/ in words such as *ear* and *here.*

The consonant system includes the additional phonemes /ɬ/ and /x/, but these only occur in Welsh loanwords and place names. The tremulant /r/ is typically rolled rather than retroflex, and /l/ tends to be consistently similar in the traditional dialects regardless of its position in the word: clear in south and mid-Wales and dark in the north. The longstanding English peripheries, again, follow the pattern of RP. Further regional characteristics include the de-voicing of sibilants in north Wales, resulting in words such as *chin* and *gin* or *seal* and *zeal* to be pronounced as homophones.

Most of the above features are substratal in origin: the Welsh phonetic system includes the long vowels [eː] and [oː], a rolled [r] and a regional distribution of clear and dark /l/ similar to that of WE. Another substratum element is the intonation, which is particularly striking in the Valleys dialects and in south-west Wales. The pitch range tends to be wider than in mainstream spoken English, with a higher degree of movement. The Welsh stress, too, functions differently from English, resulting in a distinctive rhythm which is carried over into WE. Middle consonants, for example, become lengthened after a stressed vowel in words such as *cooking, ladder, busy, any,* etc. See Parry (1999), Penhallurick (2004a) and Walters (2003) for further details on WE phonology.

As for lexicon, there are few Welsh words, proper names excepted, which have become integrated into the monolingual English-speakers' vocabulary (Thomas 1994: 142–3). *Eisteddfod,* the name of the Welsh cultural festival, is an example of a cultural loan without an English language equivalent, and certain other terms, for example, *cawl* 'mixed vegetable soup' or *twp* 'stupid, silly', are used also by the monoglot English. First-language Welsh speakers are perhaps more likely to drop in Welsh words, including *bach*, a common term of endearment meaning 'dear', 'little one' or *tŷ bach*, 'little house', a euphemism for 'outhouse, toilet'. Welsh words may also be found in regionally restricted use (e.g. *cariad* 'darling', *bopa* 'auntie' or *teishen lap* 'fruit cake' in Glamorganshire English; Lewis 1990: 110–11). Translation loans are another language contact element, particularly in older speakers' English: using the verb *rise* instead of *raise* (cf. Welsh *codi* 'to rise, to raise'; Thomas 1984: 194), or *turning the tea* instead of *stirring the tea* (cf. Welsh *troi* 'to turn, to stir, to revolve'; Morris Jones 1990: 202) may be influenced by the respective Welsh words containing both meanings (see Parry 1999 for traditional rural lexicon and Filppula et al. 2008 for a survey of Welsh lexical usage in WE).

The grammar of spoken WE is for the most part very similar to any mainstream modern dialect: it has many of the vernacular elements which are commonly found in other parts of the English-speaking world as well (cf. Trudgill 1999: 1–9; see also eWAVE, Kortmann and Lunkenheimer 2011), and in most respects, it fits effortlessly into the spoken British English continuum. This is perhaps the main reason why its speakers often do not distinguish WE as a dialect of its own. WE does, however, possess certain morpho-syntactic structures which are characteristic of Wales, and many of these structures have been forged by the language contact situation. In the case of bilingual speakers, these structures are sometimes the result of direct language transfer from Welsh to English, or they can be substratum features, relics of the language shift process, which remain a part of the speech of monolingual English speakers as well as bilinguals. Sometimes the structure of Welsh merely reinforces the use of an already existing standard or vernacular English structure, in which case the dialectal character of these features is a matter of frequency and/or function. The effects of language-historical processes and other dialects must not be overlooked, either.

Welsh-influenced varieties of WE have experienced a considerable degree of levelling over the twentieth century, as shown in Paulasto (2006). Apart from the result obtained on focus fronting and non-standard uses of the progressive form, examined in the above-mentioned study, there is little quantitative information on the present use of Welsh-influenced syntactic features in WE. Visitors to Wales can, nevertheless, witness that most of the constructions below remain in common use in many parts of the country. The examples are from the Survey of Anglo-Welsh Dialects (SAWD, in brief; either Parry 1999, or the corpus used in Paulasto 2006), as well as from corpora collected by the present writer in Llandybie and in north Wales. All of the features below can be found in the Welsh-speaking areas of south and north Wales, although some of them are more localized and less common than others.

The definite article can precede the names of common ailments and languages, and generally appear in contexts deviating from StE. The use of the indefinite article, absent in the Welsh language, can also be irregular in the English of the elderly bilingual speakers.

(1) She could come back to *the heat* again (SAWD: Gn [Gwynedd] 9: 2);
(2) ... put them peas in for the cows and for the cattle ... Very few put *the beans* for the animals [*beans* mentioned for the first time] (SAWD: Gn 7: 3);
(3) Yeah some say that it's go- *the Welsh* is going to die, to be wiped, you know- be- the language would be gone, you know, [*>Mm.] like<* the- in Scotland now it's *the Gaelic,* you know, [Yeah.] well they don't speak a lot of Gaelic now in Scotland you see (Llandybie: AM)
(4) I got *sister,* she's having a birthday that day (SAWD: Gn 8: 1)

In spite of the Welsh parallels, article use in WE does not always distinguish it from other spoken varieties of English: expressions such as *(got) the toothache* and *(got) the headache* are also widespread in the Survey of English Dialects (SED), and the dropping of the indefinite article is likewise recorded in the traditional dialects all over England (Parry 1999: 107–8). However, certain usages, such as definite articles with the names of languages, are specifically characteristic of WE and likely to arise from Welsh (see, e.g. Thorne 1993: 98), which strengthens the case for substratum influence in the irregularities found in article use more generally.

The use of periphrastic verb structures in non-standard contexts is typical of WE, although the forms these constructions take are not as elaborate as in Irish English. What mainly distinguishes WE verb structures from EngE is the less restricted aspectual use. The progressive '*be* + present participle' structure can be applied to habitual or stative contexts, or it can be attached to modal verb structures to convey a habitual meaning. The English progressive form resembles the Welsh periphrastic structure consisting of *bod* 'be', imperfective marker *yn* and a verbal noun, which corresponds in meaning both to the English progressive and habitual aspects:

(5) *Mae*'r dyn 'na *'n darllen* y Daily Telegraph.
be.PRES.3SG-the man that-IM read.VN the D.T.[2]
'That man is reading/reads the D.T.' (King 1993: 167)

The aspectual ambiguity in the Welsh imperfective periphrasis leads to the following types of habitual usages in WE:

(6) [How, if you want to know how heavy a thing is, *> you must ...]
Yes, yes, <* we are- we *are takin'* it to the barn to weigh them. (SAWD: Dy[fed] 4: 1)
(7) in the- in the summer months, when the weather was good, say from May forward until exams came, well, two or three of us *were riding* up to Llandeilo, every day. (Llandybie: ML)
(8) But she*'s* not *speaking* any English at all, she's all Welsh at the moment, she's only two. (Llwyngwril: BJ)

Stative verbs may also appear in the progressive form in contexts where they would be irregular in StE. This feature is shared by many other spoken varieties of English, but the WE usage is most likely prompted by the Welsh tendency to employ the periphrastic form with stative as well as dynamic verbs.

(9) Right, yeah, Saintess Tybie *was living* somewhere around the sixth century. (Llandybie: DD)
(10) [An' what did they look like?]
They *were looking* like er, gates, you know . . . (SAWD: Dy 4: 1)

Paulasto (2006) indicates that at present, the above verb forms remain used by speakers of all ages, but they are clearly more common in the speech of elderly rather than young informants and possibly in the process of being levelled out.

There is another habitual construction in the dialects of the historically Anglicized regions of south Wales: periphrastic *do*. Its distributional pattern indicates that it is probably of south-west English origin (see Parry 1999: 110):

(11) She *do wear* the trousers (said of a domineering wife) (SAWD: SG [South Glamorgan] 1, Gw[ent] 1/4/6/8)
(12) a machine *does do* it (SAWD: P[owys] 7, Dy 4)
(13) that *did serve* (SAWD: WG [West Glamorgan] 3)

Unlike habitual and stative uses of the progressive form, periphrastic *do* does not appear in the regions that are currently bilingual. In the south-eastern industrial Valleys, the two constructions are used side by side, although to a far lesser extent than in the past.

The Welsh imperfective structure resembles the English progressive form, but the verbal noun corresponds in meaning both to the English present participle and the infinitive. This is reflected in some WE structures. Parry (1999: 120) notes that in certain areas of Wales the verb *stop* can be used instead of *prevent*, and the present participle is replaced by the infinitive form.

(14) stop them to go backwards (SAWD: P 4, Dy 8/10/16)
(15) to stop the ashes to come out (SAWD: SG 4)

The reverse situation, the infinitive being replaced by the present participle, can be explained on the same grounds:

(16) you've got to put this sharp side . . . to cut the mouth . . . to make it *bleeding* (referring to the process of breaking a horse by using a special bit) (SAWD: Cl[wyd] 7)

The structure *for to* + infinitive is used in the same way as in Irish English, corresponding to the phrase *in order to*. It is mainly found in the Anglicized areas of Wales, which suggests that it is of English dialect origin, as this structure is also widely recorded in the SED.

The word order of the indirect question is sometimes inverted in WE, that is, the word order of the direct question is retained (e.g. Thomas 1985: 217). Indirect *wh*-questions involve a simple word order inversion, and in the case of indirect *yes/no*-questions, the connecting *if/whether* is left out.

(17) an' I am not sure now what *would that* be exactly . . . (SAWD: Cl 2: 1)
(18) And he asked him *would he* be interested in coming up as a family. (Llandybie: MT)

Thomas concludes that the inversion stems from the corresponding Welsh form, where the order of the verb and whatever follows right after it is identical in direct and indirect questions. Omitting the conjunction *if/whether* is also of Welsh origin: the corresponding Welsh conjunctions *os/a* are generally elided (Thorne 1993: 535). This feature remains productive in the bilingual regions.

The use of the grammatical focusing devices, fronting and clefting, differ somewhat from mainstream English usage. Focus fronting, or predicate fronting, is a common device of speech found all over Wales. The same structure is also used in other spoken, informal varieties of English, but it is noticeably frequent and varied in use in WE (Williams 2000: 212, Paulasto 2006). Paulasto demonstrates that the WE usage is defined by the frequent fronting of objects and adverbials, which are relatively rare in this position in EngE, and the relatively common use of the construction in the contrastive discourse function. According to Pitkänen (1998), focus fronting is more typical of WE than clefting. What points to Welsh influence most strongly with respect to cleft sentences is the occasional existential instance, as in example (22).

(19) An' *hens we had* an' eggs and . . . Erm, at Christmas my mother would fatten up cockerels and *turkey she bred* . . . (NWC: GN)
(20) [Do you have to travel far?]
Mm, *about seven miles I go.* (NWC: AP)
(21) [What do you say you do when you strip the feathers off a dead chicken?]
Feather them.
[Yes, would you ever say you pluck them?]
Pluck them, yes, *pluck them we do*, yes. (SAWD: Cl 1: 2)
(22) At one time, *it was* only these four houses that was here. (Llandybie: LZ)

Paulasto (2006) observes that focus fronting is not likely to be levelled out of the dialect in the near future; it is one of the few syntactic dialect features which have obtained positive salience in the WE-speaking community. It therefore has the potential to signify national and communal solidarity alongside the Welsh accent.

Another distinctive feature in WE is its prepositional usage. The Welsh language lacks a verb equivalent of the English verb *have*, and possession is indicated by an existential form of the verb *bod* 'be' followed by the object, *gyda* 'with', and the possessor, resulting in constructions such as *mae car gyda John*, 'John has a car'. A construction similar to that of Welsh can also be found in WE, receiving the form 'there's a car with us' (Parry 1999: 117–18). In addition to *have*, the structure '*with* + pronoun' sometimes replaces the possessive pronoun in WE, or indicates a more general 'possessive' relationship. The data in Parry indicate that this construction is particularly common in the south-west of Wales. Number (23) is an example of the first type, whereas (24) represents a variation of the theme.

(23) There's no horns *with the sheep* around this way. (SAWD: D 3)
(24) Well the boys are grown up *with her* now, you see? (Llandybie: LZ) 'her boys have grown up'
(25) [It was when she got older, she had problems with her]
*> Yes, yes, yes.
[hip as well I think but it <* was operated on.]
Oh but it was painful *with her*. (Llandybie: MP)

Example (25) is probably a modified translation of the Welsh phrase *oedd poen gyda hi*, meaning 'she had pain' (lit. 'was pain with her') (see King 1993: 236). In most cases, however, it appears that the non-standard use of *with* has expanded in WE beyond its original use in Welsh. Other prepositions used differently from StE include *on*, *for*, *of* and *out of*.

(26) There's no Welsh name *on these*. (Gn 9: 1) cf. Welsh *yr enw ar* 'the name on'
(27) They do, *on times*. (Dy 8); cf. Welsh *ar brydiau*
(28) to go *for bed* (Dy 14); We know *for places* that haven't got any (Dy 17). (Parry 1999: 118)
(29) Well, the- the queen, th- hey gotta make a ring for her, well every queen has been ma- a ring has been made *out of Wales*. (Cl 2: 1) cf. Welsh *o Gymru*, 'from, out of Wales'

In addition, certain phrases in WE originate from Welsh. These include the distinctive use of *there is/are* in expletives instead of the standard *how*, as in 'There's twp you are!' (Llandybie: BE). This correlates with the Welsh structure *dyna twp wyt ti*, literally 'there silly are you'. Another very common substratum feature is the use of the non-specific tags *is it* or *isn't it* (*innit* in colloquial usage) instead of practically every other tag question.

(30) Well he must have passed his BA to be a pharmacist, you know, *isn't it?* (Llandybie: ED)

(31) Is it ragwort, *is it*?
[Ragw . . . *> Er . . .]
The yellow <*, yellow . . .
[Yes, yes, could be.]
Bit of a nuisance, that, *is it*, you know. (SAWD: Gn 8: 2)

(32) Why are you stayin' so far away? Travellin' . . .
[Because I, er, spend my days at the university mostly.]
Down in Swansea?
[Mm.]
Is it?
[Yeah, yeah.] (Llandybie: BP)

In (32), the speaker uses the tag form as a truncated question, not to ask for confirmation of the locality but of the whole of the previous statement: 'Do you now?' Williams (2003: 206 f.) explores the development of these tags in WE from their original, focalizing function towards increasing invariability.

Further details about the above and other phonological and syntactic features of WE can be found in several sources. General descriptions are given by Parry (1999), Penhallurick (2004a, b) and Thomas (1984, 1985, 1994). Descriptions which focus on certain regional varieties are Parry (1977, 1979) and Penhallurick (1991, 1994). Coupland (1990a) contains papers on various southern accents and dialects of WE.

The Position of English/Welsh English in Wales: Present and Future Trends

The public uses of English in Wales are largely comparable to any other part of the British Isles: as the majority language, it is more common than Welsh in domains such as media, commerce, education and administration. Over the course of the twentieth century, Welsh has regained an institutional status equal to that of English, and it is used today side by side with English in every public domain. Examples of such everyday language contexts are Welsh-medium education from pre-school all the way through the university level (although not in every subject in every university), the Welsh TV channel S4C, and having the choice of Welsh language service in offices of law and administration. Welsh has the support of the authorities and most Welsh speakers are actively making use of their rights. Whereas previously it was commonly the case that enterprising English incomers had a strong representation in professional and managerial level jobs throughout the country, there is today a great need for bilingual staff in the field of public services, and the division of labour has begun to favour Welsh speakers.

Aitchison and Carter (2000a: 123–7) compare the three main ethnolinguistic communities, bilingual Welsh, Anglo-Welsh and incomers born outside of Wales, on the basis of the 1991 census figures. They observe that on the whole, bilinguals today hold a greater percentage of higher class positions than monoglot English speakers, who are more likely to obtain a skilled manual, part-skilled or unskilled job. However, it is still the non-Welsh incomers who take the majority of the highest positions. The Anglo-Welsh are at the greatest disadvantage: they cannot compete with the bilinguals for jobs where Welsh skills are required, but they also face strong competition from the incomers. The authors point out that the situation varies according to the region: job opportunities are best for the bilinguals in the Anglicized south-east, around the Cardiff area, whereas in the rural counties most of the higher class positions go to the English-speaking incomers. The Anglo-Welsh, again, draw the short straw both in the cities and in the countryside. Blackaby and Drinkwater (1996: 168) have come to similar conclusions, stating that 'for whatever reason, Welsh-speakers appear to do better in the Welsh labour market than their non-Welsh-speaking counterparts'. They also find that 'the occupational advantage of Welsh-speakers was most noticeable in areas where only a small minority of the population were able to speak Welsh', such as in the south-east of Wales.

The above studies do not account for the role of the regional Welsh varieties of English in the socio-economic situations they describe. The issue of dialect remains covert. Nor does WE have a clearly defined public or institutional profile any more than there can be said to be a 'standard' variety of WE. As pointed out above, Welsh English as a syntactically distinctive variety is restricted to informal spoken language use. It has little role in written language apart from a few Anglo-Welsh poets and novelists (such as Mike Jenkins, a Merthyr Tydfil spokesman for the Welsh Valley teenager) and humorous and popular dialect descriptions (most significantly, John Edwards's *Talk Tidy* books, 1985 and 1986).

Thomas (1994: 145–6) concludes that as a grammatically distinctive dialect, WE is likely to be a transitional phenomenon associated mainly with the bilingual regions. Paulasto (2006) demonstrates that this view is to a great extent justified: a comparison of speakers of different generations reveals that the uses of syntactic dialect features are apparently levelled over time in terms of form, function and frequency. There are, however, other factors at play as well, such as the location of the research area, whether in the strongly Welsh-speaking heartland or a more Anglicized bilingual region. In the latter kind of locality, where (Welsh) English functions as an important community language next to Welsh, the social and communal significance of the local English dialect is increased. As a result, speakers of the youngest generation, informants aged 16 to 30, maintain the use of syntactic dialect features such as focus fronting (see above). Based on these results, WE is unlikely to lose all of its dialectal distinctiveness in the near future.

At the level of phonology, the Welsh accent is alive and well. It has made its way from informal contexts to the spoken media over the past few decades: BBC Wales, for example, employs newsreaders and other presenters with mild regional accents, and Huw Edwards's Welsh accent on the BBC News is famous and apparently very well liked throughout the United Kingdom. The increased prominence of the Welsh accent in the spoken media follows quite naturally from similar trends in other parts of the British Isles. It also shows that the accent is received more positively today than it was a few decades ago. A number of matched-guise studies (see above) conducted in the 1970s showed that Welsh-accented speakers were evaluated poorly on the scales of intelligence, ambition and activeness both by Welsh as well as English listeners. At present, however, a newsreader with a Welsh accent is considered as intelligent and informed as an RP speaker, with the added benefits of trustworthiness and inter-group loyalty increasing his or her appeal within Wales.

In the field of politics, the Welsh accent can also be considered an asset rather than a disadvantage. Coupland (1990b) describes the accents of 13 Welsh Members of Parliament, some of whom have no WE features of speech, while others demonstrate clear WE usage. Coupland observes that the use of the regional accent may symbolize the politicians' involvement in specifically Welsh political life or create images of working class solidarity associated with the industrial south-east of the country. The use of RP, on the other hand, is in accordance with centralist and class ideologies. Coupland does not wish to draw definite correlations between accent use and political allegiance, but he points out that 'Welsh English has the potential to symbolise non-alignment' with the values traditionally represented by RP (op. cit.: 253). On the other hand, the semiotic value of a variety of speech is constantly redefined by the speakers themselves, and hence, the use of a Welsh accent in formal contexts can also be seen as 'a denial of non-standardness, an incipient standardising and institutionalising process' (ibid.).

The above changes in attitudes mainly apply to mild regional accents, but also the overall acceptability of the local, regional dialects has demonstrably increased among the Welsh: in January 2005, BBC News reported on a survey conducted for the BBC's Voices project, saying that although the Welsh accent is not among the most popular in Britain, the Welsh are on average prouder of their national accents than the British in general. It is well known that views such as these are some of the strongest factors supporting dialect maintenance. Although WE continues to evolve, levelling in some respects and being influenced by contacts with other varieties of English, it is likely to retain its distinctiveness at least at the phonological level. Certain syntactic and lexical idiosyncrasies will probably remain in the dialect as well. What the above survey also seems to indicate is that the local varieties of English have been able to carve out a 'national' space for themselves next to the Welsh language.

Notes

[1] Census of 2001 (Aitchison and Carter 2004: 33); the figure refers to the population resident and aged three and over at the time of the enumeration.
[2] PRES = present tense, SG = singular, IM = imperfective marker, VN = verbal noun.

Acknowledgement

This chapter was written with the support of the Research Council for Culture and Society, Academy of Finland (project no. 210702). Many thanks to the Centre for Research into the English Literature and Language of Wales for cooperation and assistance in granting me access to the Archive of Welsh English at Swansea University.

Bibliography

Aitchison, J. and Carter, H. (2000a), *Language, Economy and Society: The Changing Fortunes of the Welsh Language in the Twentieth Century*, Cardiff: University of Wales Press.

—. (2000b), 'The Welsh language 1921–91: a geolinguistic perspective', in G. Jenkins and M. A. Williams (eds), *Let's Do Our Best for the Ancient Tongue: The Welsh Language in the Twentieth Century*, pp. 29–108, Cardiff: University of Wales Press.

—. (2004), *Spreading the Word: The Welsh Language 2001*, Talybont: Y Lolfa.

Awbery, G. (1997), 'The English language in Wales', in H. L. C. Tristram (ed.), *The Celtic Englishes*, pp. 86–99, Heidelberg: Winter.

Balsom, D. (1985), 'The Three-Wales Model', in J. Osmond (ed.), *The National Question Again – Welsh Political Identity in the 1980s*, Llandysul, [Summarised in Osmond (1988), pp. 128–30].

Blackaby, D. and Drinkwater, S. (1996), 'Welsh-speakers and the labour market', *Contemporary Wales*, 9, 158–70.

Bourhis, R. Y. (1977), Language and social evaluation in Wales, Unpublished Ph.D. thesis, University of Bristol.

Bourhis, R. Y., Giles, H. and Lambert, W. E. (1975), 'Social consequences of accommodating one's style of speech: A cross-national investigation', *International Journal of the Sociology of Language*, 6, 55–72.

Bourhis, R. Y., Giles, H. and Tajfel, H. (1973), 'Language as a determinant of Welsh identity', *European Journal of Social Psychology*, 3, 447–60.

Coupland, N. (1988), *Dialect in Use: Sociolinguistic Variation in Cardiff English*, Cardiff: UWP.

—. (ed., in association with A. R. Thomas) (1990a), *English in Wales: Diversity, Conflict and Change*, Clevedon: Multilingual Matters.

—. (1990b), '"Standard Welsh English": a variable semiotic', in N. Coupland (1990a) (ed.), pp. 232–57.

Coupland, N. and Thomas, A. R. (1990), 'Social and linguistic perspectives on English in Wales', introduction to N. Coupland (1990a) (ed.), *English in Wales: Diversity, Conflict and Change*. Clevedon: Multilingual Matters, pp. 1–18.

Coupland, N., Williams, A. and Garrett, P. (1994), 'The social meanings of Welsh English: teachers' stereotyped judgements', *Journal of Multicultural and Multilingual Development*, 15(6), 471–89.

Davies, J. (1993), *A History of Wales*, London: Penguin.

Edwards, J. (1985), *Talk Tidy: The Art of Speaking Wenglish*, Cowbridge.

—. (1986), *More Talk Tidy*, Cowbridge.

Ellis, A. J. (1882), 'On the delimitation of the English and Welsh languages', *Y Cymmrodor*, 4, 173–208.

Filppula, M., Klemola, J. and Paulasto, H. (2008), *English and Celtic in Contact*, London/New York: Routledge.

Garrett, P., Coupland, N. and Williams, A. (1999), 'Evaluating dialect in discourse: teachers' and teenagers' responses to young English speakers in Wales', *Language in Society*, 28, 321–54.

—. (2003), *Investigating Language Attitudes: Social Meanings of Dialect, Ethnicity and Performance*, Cardiff: University of Wales Press.

Giles, H. (1990), 'Social meanings of Welsh English', in N. Coupland (1990a) (ed.), pp. 258–82.

Giles, H., Mulac, A., Bradac, J. J., and Johnson, P. (1987), 'Speech accommodation theory: The next decade and beyond', in M. McLaughlin (ed.), *Communication Yearbook 10*, Newbury Park, CA: Sage.

Jackson, K. (1994), *Language and History in Early Britain*, Reprint, Dublin: Four Courts Press.

Jones, D. (1998), Statistical evidence relating to the Welsh Language 1801–1911/ Tystiolaeth Ystadegol yn ymwneud â'r Iaith Gymraeg 1801–1911, Cardiff: University of Wales Press.

Jones, I. G. (1980), 'Language and community in nineteenth century Wales', in D. Smith (ed.), *A People and a Proletariat: Essays on the History of Wales 1780–1980*, pp. 47–71, London: Pluto Press in association with Llafur, the Society for the Study of Welsh Labour History.

Jones, R. O. (1993), 'The sociolinguistics of Welsh', in M. J. Ball and J. Fife (eds), *The Celtic Languages*, pp. 536–605, London: Routledge.

King, G. (1993), *Modern Welsh: A Comprehensive Grammar*, London: Routledge.

Kortmann, B. and Lunkenheimer, K. (eds) (2011), The electronic World Atlas of Varieties of English [eWAVE], Leipzig: Max Planck Institute for Evolutionary Anthropology, http://www.ewave-atlas.org/, accessed on 2012-08-01.

Lewis, J. W. (1990), 'Syntax and lexis in Glamorgan English', in N. Coupland (1990a) (ed.), pp. 109–20.

MacCann, J. and Connolly, H. (1933), *Memorials of Father Augustine Baker and Other Documents Relating to the English Benedictines*, Catholic Record Society Publications, vol. 33.

Morris Jones, B. (1990), 'Welsh influence on children's English', in N. Coupland (1990a) (ed.), pp. 195–231.

Osmond, J. (1988), *The Divided Kingdom*, London.

Parry, D. (1977), *The Survey of Anglo-Welsh Dialects, Vol. 1: The South-East,* Swansea: David Parry, University College.
—. (1979), *The Survey of Anglo-Welsh Dialects, Vol. 2: The South-West,* Swansea: David Parry, University College.
—. (1990), 'The conservative English dialects of South Pembrokeshire', in N. Coupland (1990a) (ed.), pp. 151–61.
—. (1999), *A Grammar and Glossary of Conservative Anglo-Welsh Dialects of Rural Wales,* NATCECT. Occasional Publications, No. 8, Sheffield: University of Sheffield.
Paulasto, H. (2006), *Welsh English Syntax: Contact and Variation,* Publications in the Humanities, No. 43. Joensuu: Joensuu University Press.
—. (2009), 'Regional effects of the mode of transmission in Welsh English', in E. Penttilä and H. Paulasto (eds), *Language Contacts Meet English Dialects: Studies in Honour of Markku Filppula.* Newcastle-upon-Tyne: Cambridge Scholars Publishing, pp. 211–29.
Penhallurick, R. (1991), *The Anglo-Welsh Dialects of North Wales.* University of Bamberg Studies in English Linguistics, Vol. 27. Frankfurt am Main: Peter Lang.
—. (1993), 'Welsh English: a national language?' *Dialectologia et Geolinguistica,* 1, 28–46.
—. (1994), *Gowerland and Its Language,* University of Bamberg Studies in English Linguistics, Frankfurt am Mein: Peter Lang.
—. (1996). 'The grammar of northern Welsh English: progressive verb phrases', in J. Klemola, M. Kytö, and M. Rissanen (eds), *Speech Past and Present, Studies in English Dialectology in Memory of Ossi Ihalainen,* University of Bamberg Studies in English Linguistics, Vol. 38. Frankfurt am Main: Peter Lang, pp. 308–42.
—. (2004a), 'Welsh English: phonology', in B. Kortmann, K. Burridge, R. Mesthrie, E. Schneider, and C. Upton (eds), *A Handbook of Varieties of English, Vol. 1: Phonology,* pp. 98–111, Berlin & New York: Mouton de Gruyter.
—. (2004b), 'Welsh English: morphology and syntax', in B. Kortmann, K. Burridge, R. Mesthrie, E. Schneider, and C. Upton (eds), *A Handbook of Varieties of English, Vol. 2: Morphology and Syntax,* pp. 102–13, Berlin and New York: Mouton de Gruyter.
—. (2007), 'English in Wales', in D. Britain (ed.), *Language in the British Isles,* pp. 152–70, Cambridge: Cambridge University Press.
Pitkänen, H. (1998), 'Only Welsh We Speak': Focusing in the English Dialect of Llandybie, South Wales, Unpublished *Pro gradu* MA thesis, University of Joensuu.
Pryce, W. T. R. (1978), 'Wales as a culture region: patterns of change 1750–1971', *Transactions in the Honourable Society of Cymmrodorion,* pp. 229–61.
—. (1990), 'Language shift in Gwent, c. 1770–1981', in N. Coupland (ed.), pp. 48–83.
Thomas, A. R. (1984), 'Welsh English', in P. Trudgill (ed.), *Languages in the British Isles,* pp. 178–94, Cambridge: Cambridge University Press.
—. (1985), 'Welsh English: a grammatical conspectus', in W. Viereck (ed.), *Focus on: England and Wales,* Amsterdam/Philadelphia: Benjamins.
—. (1994), 'English in Wales', in R. Burchfield (ed.), *The Cambridge History of the English Language, Vol. V: English in Britain and Overseas: Origins and Development,* pp. 94–147, Cambridge: CUP.
Thomas, B. (1987), 'A cauldron of rebirth: population and the Welsh language in the nineteenth century', *The Welsh History Review,* 17, 418–37.

Thomas, M. W. (1999), *Corresponding Cultures: The Two Literatures of Wales,* Cardiff: University of Wales Press.

Thorne, D. A. (1993), *A Comprehensive Welsh Grammar,* Oxford: Blackwell Publishers.

Trudgill, P. (1999), *The Dialects of England,* 2nd edn, Oxford: Blackwell.

Visser, G. J. (1955), 'Celtic influence in English', *Neophilologus,* 39, 267–93.

Walters, R. (2003), 'A study of the prosody of a South East Wales "Valleys Accent"', in H. L. C. Tristram (ed.), *Celtic Englishes III,* Heidelberg: Winter, pp. 224–39.

Williams, C. H. (1990), 'The anglicisation of Wales', in N. Coupland (1990a) (ed.), pp. 19–47.

Williams, D. T. (1935), 'Linguistic divides in South Wales; a historico-geographical study', *Archaeologia Cambrensis,* 90, 239–66.

Williams, G. A. (1985), *When Was Wales? A History of the Welsh,* London: Penguin.

Williams, M. (2000), 'The pragmatics of predicate fronting in Welsh English', in H. L. C. Tristram (ed.), *The Celtic Englishes II,* Heidelberg: Winter, pp. 210–30.

—. (2003), 'Information packaging in Rhondda speech: a second look at the research of Ceri George', in H. L. C. Tristram (ed.), *Celtic Englishes III,* Heidelberg: Winter, 201–24. '2004 Welsh Language Use Survey: the report', 2006, Cardiff: The Welsh Language Board. Date: 04 May 2006. Available from: http://www.bwrdd-yr-iaith.org.uk/cynnwys.php?pID = 109&nID = 2122&langID = 2

Ireland

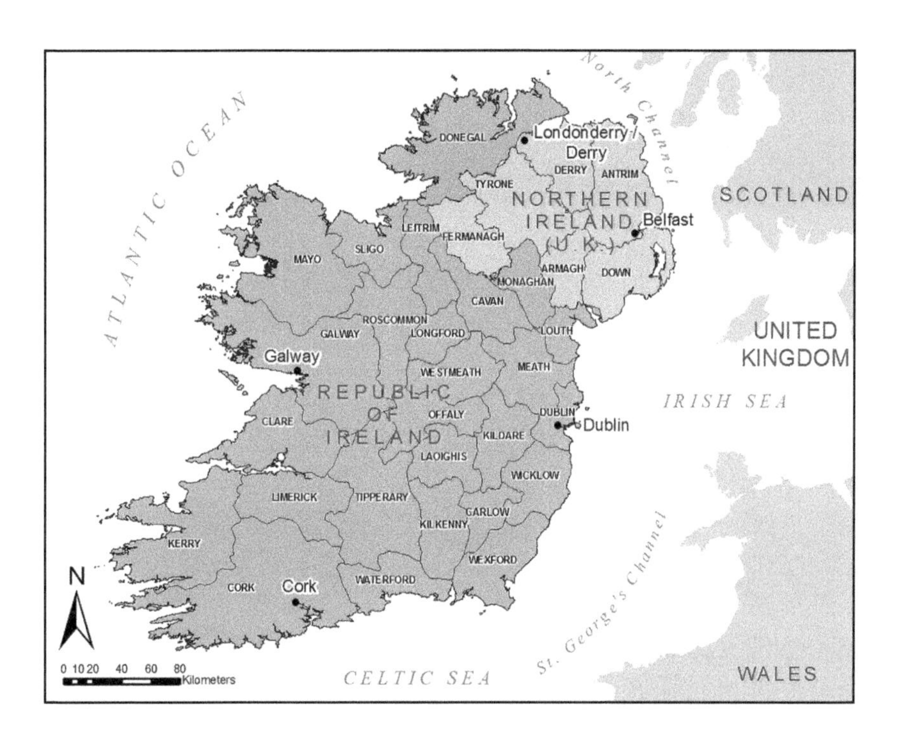

ATLANTIC OCEAN
North Channel
DONEGAL
Londonderry / Derry
DERRY
ANTRIM
TYRONE
NORTHERN IRELAND (U.K.)
Belfast
SCOTLAND
LEITRIM
FERMANAGH
SLIGO
MAYO
ARMAGH
DOWN
MONAGHAN
CAVAN
ROSCOMMON
GALWAY
LONGFORD
LOUTH
UNITED KINGDOM
Galway
WESTMEATH
MEATH
REPUBLIC OF IRELAND
IRISH SEA
CLARE
OFFALY
DUBLIN
Dublin
KILDARE
LAOIGHIS
WICKLOW
LIMERICK
TIPPERARY
CARLOW
KILKENNY
KERRY
WEXFORD
N
CORK
Cork
WATERFORD
St. George's Channel
0 10 20 40 60 80
Kilometers
CELTIC SEA
WALES

Chapter 10

English in Ireland

John Wilson and Sharon Millar

Geographical and Historical Background

Ireland is the third largest island in Europe, lying to the west of mainland Britain, between the Atlantic Ocean and the Irish Sea. Ireland has a long history dating back over 8000 years, but it is only from the Iron Age onwards that Ireland appears in the historical record, after the Celts arrived in a series of waves from 600 to 150 BC. They gradually took control of the island and established several kingdoms. The demise of the druid tradition is closely associated with the arrival of St Patrick (the exact date of this is not clear), Palladius and other Christian missionaries. Irish Christian scholars showed particular linguistic and artistic skills in developing and maintaining their theology. It is they who are often credited with maintaining Latin learning during the middle ages (although something similar is claimed for Early Christian scholars in England). In the ninth century Viking raiders started appearing in Ireland. For around 200 years they would continue to raid and plunder, later deciding to settle and establish towns across the island, including such places as Dublin, Cork and Limerick. The twelfth century saw the arrival of the Anglo-Normans with King Henry the Second, and so began many centuries of Anglo-Irish struggle. Although the Normans built many castles across the land for their protection, over time many assimilated within the Gaelic culture. By the time of Elizabeth I, English armies set about conquering the island, driven mainly by the strategic necessity of securing Ireland, the backdoor to England, from foreign invasion. During the Reformation most of the Irish, including descendants of the Anglo-Norman settlers, remained Catholic while England embraced Protestantism. Over a period of some 80 years under the rule of the Tudors, the island was gradually conquered. Of the four Irish provinces (Ulster, Leinster, Connacht and Munster), Ulster was the last to be brought under the control of the Crown, and these events are often symbolically represented by the Flight of the Earls (the Ulster Lords) in 1607. Following this, plantations of lowland Scots were established in Ulster from 1609, creating a firm Protestant footing in the north. Cromwell's attempt to resolve the Irish problem through dispossession of the Irish and the Old English was to leave a lasting legacy of bitterness, which in some parts of Ireland still survives today.

During what has become known as the Glorious Revolution (1688), the Protestants in the north were to prove decisive in the struggle for the British Crown between King James II, who wished to return England to Catholicism, and William of Orange who fought for the maintenance of a Protestant state. The defeat of King James was followed by punitive measures against the Catholic Irish, although some of these also impacted on the covenanting Scots in Ulster.

After the failure of the United Irish rebellion in 1798, Ireland became part of the United Kingdom of Great Britain and Ireland (1801), with religious tolerance granted in 1829 (Catholic emancipation). Between the years of 1846 and 1848, the potato crop failed in Ireland, leading to the great famine. Particularly stern interpretations of laissez-faire economic policy by English administrators led to the death, starvation and eventually migration of millions of Irish men and women. From 1858 onwards, various movements emerged, agitating for independence for Ireland. Under Charles Stewart Parnell, the Home Rule movement was able to force several home rule Bills from the British.

World War I, however, delayed the enactment of Home Rule, and in 1916 the Irish again rebelled in the unsuccessful Easter Rising. The execution of the leaders of the rising increased sympathy for independence and generated significant support for the Sinn Féin ('we ourselves') movement. Under Éamon de Valera, elected Sinn Féin deputies formed the first Irish parliament or Dáil Eireann. British efforts to eliminate Sinn Féin led to the Anglo Irish War of 1919–21. The war ended with the Anglo-Irish treaty of 1921, which created a partition of Ireland into the Irish Free State and Northern Ireland.

This separation was never fully accepted in Ireland and led to Civil war (1922–3) and later in Northern Ireland itself to what were to become known as 'the troubles'. After over 30 years of brutal terrorist conflict, the signing of the Good Friday agreement in 1998 provided a way forward for peace through a devolved, power-sharing assembly. This Northern Ireland Assembly was suspended from operations in 2002, but was restored to power in May 2007.

The island of Ireland remains politically divided between the independent Republic of Ireland, with a population of over 4 million, and Northern Ireland, part of the United Kingdom, with a population of 1.7 million. Ireland as a whole is divided into 32 counties, with 26 in the Republic (such as County Kerry, County Wicklow) and 6 in Northern Ireland (such as County Tyrone, County Armagh). There is also a division into four provinces: the provinces of Leinster, Munster and Connacht are in the Republic of Ireland while the province of Ulster straddles the political border to include Northern Ireland and three northern counties of the Republic of Ireland. Some use the term 'Ulster' to denote exclusively the political unit of Northern Ireland.

The main languages are English and Irish (although see the discussion below in relation to Ulster-Scots). According to the 2006 census, 1.66 million people in the Republic of Ireland claim to be Irish speaking, although 60 per cent of these state that they never speak the language or use it less frequently than once a week. (Central Statistics Office Ireland, 2007a). The officially recognized Irish-speaking areas, known as 'Gaeltachts', are located mainly along the western and south-western fringe of the country. Figures from the 2006 census reveal that Irish speakers represent about 71 per cent of the population of the Gaeltachts, an almost 2 per cent decline in numbers since the 2002 census. The most recent census in Northern Ireland from 2001 indicates that 1.45 million people claim to have no knowledge of Irish, 75,000 claim to be able to speak, read and write Irish, 7,183 to speak and read Irish, 24,536 to only speak Irish and 36,479 to only understand Irish (Northern Ireland Statistics and Research Agency 2007a). There is no officially recognized 'Gaeltacht' in Northern Ireland, but there is a government body ('Comhaírle na Gaelscolaiochta') which aims to develop Irish-medium education in Northern Ireland. It should also be noted that, given increased immigration, the modern linguistic landscape of Ireland is not populated only by Irish and English. Gallagher (2006), for instance, estimates that there are about 200 languages currently used in Ireland.

As linguistic and political borders do not necessarily overlap in Ireland, there is considerable potential for confusion in relation to terminology. In this chapter we will refer to English in Ireland as Irish English, with its two major geographical subdivisions, southern Irish English and northern Irish English. There are other alternative classifications available, which include Hiberno-English, Anglo Irish, Southern Irish English and Ulster English (see Filppula 1999; Henry 1977; Hickey, 2007a). A case can be made for the delimitation of each of these; but without dismissing these distinctions as irrelevant, we view these as forming a subset of the total set of Irish English. We agree with Hickey (2007a; see also McArthur 2002) that since we have American English, Australian English, Indian English etc, it makes sense to bring Irish English in line with these. If we look at American English, one can drill down to southern American English, or Appalachian English, to make a specific point about a region or grouping, or a specific historical or linguistic development. This should also be available in the case of Irish English, where one is free to nuance a specific issue or type of category or categories.

Adopting this approach highlights one specific issue however, that of what is known as Ulster-Scots in the north of Ireland, specifically within the province of Ulster. In previous reviews of English in Ireland, and indeed recent ones (Hickey, 2007a), Ulster-Scots is included as one of the varieties of English found in the north of Ireland, although Hickey (ibid.) also accepts that such an interpretation is now debated in terms of arguments which claim Ulster-Scots as a language in its own right. It would not be possible to rehearse the debates operating in this area in this short paper. But from Montgomery's (1997) argument that Ulster-Scots is a variety of Scots, and that Scots is not a variety of English, it seems reasonable to suggest that Ulster-Scots would not be a variety of English either. This is logical, but it presupposes that Scots is a distinct language in its own right. This too is an issue that has been controversial. Scots arose as a variant of Northumbrian English and Old Norse. In this sense it could be said to be derived from a similar root to English. This has led some to suggest that Ulster-Scots is a dialect of Scots which is a dialect of English, creating a commutative circle which would also have to suggest that Ulster-Scots is a dialect of English. This debate is a live one at this time. However, formally, it is worth noting that both Scots and Ulster-Scots have been recognized within the European Union as minority languages of Europe, and an Ulster-Scots Agency was established as part of the Good Friday agreement. It is extremely difficult to gauge the number of Ulster-Scots speakers, estimates can vary from 30,000 to 100,000. The 2011 census in Northern Ireland has included a question on Ulster-Scots with a view to ascertaining numbers of speakers.

Interest in Ulster-Scots has been growing in recent years, and the debate as to its linguistic status will continue in the light of not only reassessments of more traditional and older materials, but also new and emerging evidence. In this context then we will have little to say on Ulster-Scots directly, other than to note comments on its position within work developed under Irish English.

Linguistic Background and Contacts

In this section, we begin first by considering the complex linguistic and multilingual environment that English entered into when it arrived in Ireland with the Anglo-Normans in the twelfth century. Although many scholars begin historical accounts of English in Ireland with the arrival of the Anglo-Normans, we believe that this suggests a homogeneous view of the linguistic context of Ireland at that time which would not sit well with what is known (see Kallen 1997; Tymoczko 2003). Next we provide an overview of the historical impact of English within Ireland, highlighting a number of areas for consideration and debate.

There are few countries or peoples that have ideologized or romanticized their world as much as the Irish. It is with the Lebor Gabála Érenn that much of the mythic reflection of the sacred nature of Ireland and the Irish begins. This is translated as the 'Book of Invasions' and is seen as a 'history' of Ireland since the creation. It dates originally from around the seventh century, and although it was meant to tell the history of Ireland before AD 432, the suggested date for the arrival of St Patrick, it was extended and modified and its narratology is so modelled on classic myth formats that, as Scowcroft (1987, 1988) suggests, it is best viewed as 'invention', a 'mythopoetic faculty closer to the composition of saga than to modern historigraphy' (1988: 12, cited in Tymoczko 2003: 25).

What was not myth, however, was the fact that Old Irish texts showed a significant uniformity across an extended period of time. This homogeneity is often seen as evidence for an independent continuity in the development of the Irish language, freed from other external linguistic influences, something not easily enjoyed by many of the other languages of Europe. The written form and the spoken form of any language are not the same thing of course, and this difference is even more heightened when one is talking of more ancient times. Nevertheless, while the continuity provided by the written modality could be interpreted as support for the isolationist position of the Irish language, Tymoczko (2003) is probably correct in suggesting that this reflects perhaps more logically an institutionalization of a particular standard-at least within the written form of the time.

It is of course the case that Ireland, unlike most of Europe, and beyond, was never conquered by the Romans. It is also true that as an island located at the far reaches of the West of Europe, it might have been less likely to encounter other tribes or nations. So there are arguments in favour of the isolation of Ireland and the Irish at this time. But the reality, as Tymoczko (2003) notes, is that the rivers and the seas and oceans were the arteries of travel and communication for hundreds if not thousands of years. There are now several strands of evidence that Ireland was not only visited by various groups, for both invasion and commerce, but that the Irish themselves frequently travelled beyond their own shores, interacting with a variety of groups and encountering a variety of languages. As well as the more obvious links with the Scots, the Welsh and the English, recent genetic evidence links the Irish of the West of Ireland with Northern Spain. It is now speculated that this was not necessarily a one way relationship, and the Spanish may well have visited Ireland for trading purposes. Indeed, Michel Picard (2003) notes that the ports and coasts of Ireland were well known to Roman merchants and that Latin was probably used for general communication and bartering. Picard (2003: 45) further notes that in AD98 Tacitus mentions that Agricola hosted a King of Ireland ('probably re tuaithe' rendered in Latin as 'regulus gentis'). McManus (1991: 40–1, cited in Kallen 1997: 7) also argues that the Ogam script, seen as the first form of Irish writing, was developed from Latin orthography.

While the Romans may not have invaded Ireland, there was a significant social and linguistic impact on the country during the Viking raids in the ninth century. Parts of the country became Viking settlements and political marriages were used to maintain or extend Irish and Viking dynasties. Indeed, Tymoczko (2003: 38) goes as far as to suggest of the Irish-Scandinavian interface that '... bilingualism became a fact of life in certain sections of society at least, and such bilingualism persisted to the end of the twelfth century or later.'

Moreover, the Irish themselves were not passive in terms of raiding and they are known to have attacked up and down the Welsh and English coasts, taking slaves, as was normal at the time, back to Ireland (consider the case of St Patrick). Equally, the Irish could also find themselves captured as slaves and taken to other lands.

Following the establishment of Christianity in Ireland, which brought a wide distribution of Latin, a particular scholastic form of monastic life suited to the isolation of the island was established. But the Irish monks did not settle down to the permanency of monastic life, and 'wanderings' specific to the missionary activity central to Ireland meant that Irish missionaries began to travel throughout Europe and the world. These travels became renowned in both history and legend and are reflected in Irish literature, for example, The Voyage of St Brendan. We can see then that the Irish would have had a number of opportunities for linguistic mixing before the arrival of the Anglo-Normans in 1169, and with them the arrival of English.

Bliss (1979) suggests that the Anglo-Normans introduced spoken vernacular forms of Norman French and English, and that both were spoken alongside Irish. Over the next hundred years or so, Norman French was to decline with the Normans becoming very much Gaelicised. While English faired better than French, it too came under significant pressure in the fourteenth and fifteenth centuries. In reaction to this, the famous Statutes of Kilkenny (1366) were passed, bringing with them penalties for those of Anglo-Norman stock who were found to use Irish. By 1600 English, or as is termed in this period 'Old English,' only survived in parts of Wexford, producing the distinctive dialects known as Forth and Bargy, both of which, according to Bliss (1977), survived into the nineteenth century.

The impact of the early relationship between English and Irish is difficult to chart for a number of obvious, historical reasons. Reading general claims about the language from written texts is bound to represent a very limited glimpse of general language use, given that at such early periods the majority of speakers would have been illiterate. The suggestion that the initial development of English in Ireland represented a general diglossic situation makes sense, with French and Latin adopting the (H) High language position and English the (L) low position. This would seem to be supported by the fact that the statutes of Kilkenny were written in Norman French, and they contain the well-known exhortation that 'every Englishman use the English language and be named by an English name' (Cowley 2000:14).

Accordingly, use of the English language here must refer to everyday talk, as opposed to the (H) written form. But perhaps something more subtle beyond the purely linguistic was also being endorsed. While the statutes are often viewed as a particular form of linguistic control, Kallen (1997) suggests that they had a clear social agenda as well. The issue was not merely one of speaking Irish, but of becoming Irish. English was the linguistic vehicle which set the English apart as the English. The fact was that many of the Anglo-Normans had adopted an Irish way of life and were becoming assimilated in Gaelic culture, and language. As Berry notes (1907, cited in Kallen 1997a: 10):

> Englishmen also as degenerate in modern times, attire themselves in Irish garments and having their heads shaven grow and extend the hairs from the back of the head and call them Culan conforming themselves to the Irish as well in garb as in countenance, whereby it frequently happens that some Englishmen reported as Irishmen are slain.

Such comments reflect the pressure English was coming under at this time. Indeed Hogan (1927/1970: 36, cited in Filppula 1999: 4) suggests of the sixteenth century that '... there is probably no exaggeration in the accounts of the decay of the English in the country districts including the pale'.

From the seventeenth century a 'new English' was to emerge, forged out of the interaction of Irish and English, but this time on the basis of large plantations particularly in the north of Ireland, where lowland Scots was introduced into the linguistic equation. However, these plantations alone were not the core herald of the 'new English', rather it was to be the impact of the Cromwellian settlements throughout the island that proved crucial. These fundamentally changed the linguistic scene in Ireland by bringing greater numbers of English (and Scots) speakers into the country from diverse areas of England and Scotland. What has been debated is whether these plantations mark a starting point for the spread of English in Ireland or are a development in a linguistic diffusion process. The controversy is essentially based on temporal continuity versus discontinuity of usage between two periods in the history of the language, the medieval and the early modern (Hickey 2005). The continuity argument proposes that Irish English was alive and well in a diglossic relationship with Irish at the time of the plantations (see above and Kallen 1994, 1997a) while the discontinuity proposal maintains it was extinct, having died out during the fifteenth and sixteenth centuries (Bliss 1977), meaning that English was reintroduced into Ireland. The historical record tends to suggest the former, where the Anglo-Irish, the minority community, still used English. Hickey (2001) also finds evidence of features from the medieval period in eastern varieties of modern Irish English.

The influx of English speakers in the seventeenth century was destined to have significant consequences for the spread of English as it created a different spatiality, in the sense of physical, social and perceived space (Britain 2002). Irish speakers were increasingly marginalized to the south and west, towns were the focal points of English usage and English was used more widely across the social spectrum, no longer being confined to a landowning class. This is not to suggest that Irish was somehow driven out by these events. Indeed, Hindley (1990) argues that many of the Cromwellian settlers were monoglot Irish by the 1700s and that it was probably not until 1750 that Irish began to become less prevalent. In the mainly Scots settlement in Ulster, there is some modern evidence from the depositions following the 1641 Rebellion that many of the Irish in Ulster were, on some levels, bilingual (see Walker 2011), a situation not found in the rest of the country until the eighteenth century, when English began to hold sway and was adopted as a second language (Hindley 1990).

What Kallen (1997: 16) refers to as the 'new bilingualism' continued to develop in the eighteenth and nineteenth centuries as the language shift from Irish to English progressed, especially among the young, the more well-off sectors of society and urban dwellers. This ongoing shift to English was boosted by certain events of the nineteenth century which badly affected the fortunes of the Irish language, in particular the beginnings of mass education in the 1830s, which promoted English, and the major demographic effects brought about by the Famine of the latter half of the 1840s, where primarily Irish-speaking areas of the country were depopulated by deaths and migrations. With the formation of the Irish Free State in 1921, Irish was declared the national language and it rather than English remains the first official language of the state. Nonetheless, despite the 'ineradicable national significance' of Irish (Kallen 1997: 18), the dominant form of communication for the vast majority of people in Ireland is now English.

The emergence of Irish English is a story of one of the first and one of the oldest examples of the colonial impact of English on the world stage. Unfortunately, as noted above, much of the data required to review the early impacts of the Anglo-Norman invasions or other contacts becomes difficult, and perhaps in some cases, impossible to assess. It is somewhat ironic however, as Kallen (1997a) notes, that although Irish English was one of the first examples of its type, it was relatively neglected in terms of early analysis. This is in part because scholars viewed the concept of Irish English as only fully evolved in any relevant linguistic sense in the nineteenth century (see Hume 1858, cf. Kallen,1994).

Interestingly, Bauer (2002: 25) considers varieties of Irish and Scottish English not as 'colonial varieties but as colonising ones' given large-scale emigration from Ireland and Scotland to North America and Australasia. It has been suggested that features of Irish English are to be found in other varieties of English, including that of Australia, New Zealand, Newfoundland and Appalachia (Bauer 2002; Clarke 2002; Gordon and Trudgill 2002; Montgomery 2002).

One other area where Irish English has had a significant global impact is in the field of literature in English. For a small nation, Irish literary credentials are significantly impressive. The Irish language itself has a strong ancient tradition; it is claimed that Irish literature may be the third oldest literary tradition in the world. However, it is through Irish writing in English that the island may be said to have the greatest global impact. English, as a literary language in Ireland, provided a form of expression that enabled writers to negotiate the political, social, cultural and linguistic dimensions of their personal and national identities. It has provided a creative platform for the exploration of the ambiguities and paradoxes of Irish life. The utilization of style, form and technique in English granted Irish writers access to broader intellectual and commercial literary marketplaces and provided a means to influence readerships inside and outside of Ireland. Their work often sought to educate theit audiences on the political, social, cultural and aesthetic relationships between Britain and Ireland, which involved questioning the validity of British hegemony and affirming the author's rights to personal, national and artistic autonomy. For example, in the late seventeenth and eighteenth centuries a number of Irish-born dramatists achieved success in England with plays that made use of the stage-Irishman and his speech to highlight the excesses of English society; among these were the plays of George Farquhar and Thomas Sheridan.

The eighteenth century brought other great writers in English, for example Jonathan Swift and Oliver Goldsmith. Swift also carried on the tradition of using the English literary form as a mode of critique, publishing critical pamphlets under specific pseudonyms. The nineteenth and twentieth centuries saw a revival in the attention given to ancient stories and myths of older Irish traditions, particularly associated with the work of W. B. Yeats. The theatre also benefited from the Irish literary tradition in English, with the likes of George Bernard Shaw and Oscar Wilde. The linguistic tensions between Irish and English, both political and literaty, also found a place in the works of the theatre, notable examples being Sean O'Casey and J. M. Synge. Some of the greatest impact on world literature in English was provided by James Joyce, who broke with many literary and linguistic traditions to create what has sometimes been called a 'stream of consciousness' literature. Although Joyce sets much of his work in Ireland, and he clearly has an ear for the local linguistic voice, both he and his contemporary Samuel Beckett were painting on a much larger canvas than any set of specific languages or dialects. They were challenging the very underlying nature of the human linguistic capacity to understand ourselves and the world(s) we inhabit. The literary traditions established in Irish literature's use of the English language carry on in the works of such modern writers and poets as Patrick Kavanagh, Seamus Heaney and Flann O'Brian.

Linguistic Characteristics of Irish English

Generally the island of Ireland is divided up, primarily on the basis of phonology, into two major linguistic areas: northern and southern (Barry 1981; Harris 1984; Henry 1958). As already noted, these overlap with the north-south political division to some extent, but the geographical reach of the northern linguistic variety extends beyond political boundaries to include counties of the Republic of Ireland, namely Donegal, Monaghan and northern parts of Cavan and Louth (Kallen, 1997a, Hickey, 2007a). For this reason, it needs to be borne in mind that the terms southern Irish English and northern Irish English are being used here in a geolinguistic and not political sense. Kallen (2000) notes the general lack of effect of the political border on dialectal boundaries, at least with regard to the distribution of phonological variables from older survey materials, but speculates on possible current and future effects of the border on dialect divergence. He also points to a less well-acknowledged geolinguistic boundary, that of east (the provinces of Ulster and Leinster) versus west (the provinces of Munster and Connacht), which cuts across the north-south axis.

Within northern Irish English, three major dialects are recognized, again on the basis of phonology (Harris 1984; McCafferty 2007): Mid Ulster English, the most widely spoken variety, found in Belfast, the city of (London)Derry and the counties of Armagh, Tyrone and Fermanagh; Ulster-Scots, spoken in northern and eastern parts of Down, north-east (London)Derry, north-east Donegal and almost all of Antrim; South Ulster English, a transitional dialect spoken in south Armagh, south Fermanagh, south Donegal, south Monaghan and north Cavan. Given our current knowledge, it is not possible to delineate regional dialects within northern Irish English in terms of grammatical features, if such dialects actually exist. Indeed, the north-south axis itself may not be especially meaningful in relation to grammar (Harris 1993).

Less regional variation has traditionally been recognized within southern Irish English; indeed its relative uniformity has been a matter of comment (Adams 1977; Bliss 1977; Filppula 1999). Here, however, the emphasis has been more on grammar than phonology. Distinctions have usually been made on the basis of an urban-rural dichotomy rather than geographical boundaries as such, given the historical significance noted above of towns in the linguistic diffusion of English. An east – (south)west axis is, however, also apparent; for instance, Filppula (1999) in a corpus study of four southern Irish English varieties found that the syntactic features investigated occurred in all varieties, but the frequency of distribution differed between rural, especially south-western, dialects and urban, notably eastern, dialects. For this reason, Filppula prefers to conceptualize the geolinguistic situation in southern Irish English in terms of dialect continua rather than discrete dialects, despite qualitative differences between varieties in the east and south-west. Similarly, Hickey (2007a) views the major regional division in southern Irish English to be between the east coast and the south and west, defining qualitative differences between these two major areas in terms of phonology and syntax. That the east –(south)west axis should be so significant can be explained historically in terms of English settlement patterns; the south and west were the areas where the Irish language survived longest, and hence language contact was maintained longest. Another contributing factor to the relative uniformity of southern Irish English has been large-scale population movements from country to city, especially to Dublin, leading to dialect mixture where rural forms have influenced urban forms and vice versa (Filppula 1999). Processes of dialect levelling are also apparent, meaning that more marked variants are disappearing.

Features of Irish English

What follows is a brief overview of some of the main features of vernacular Irish English. It should be remembered that these features may vary in their occurrence according to region, style and social characteristics of the speaker. There is no discussion of the origins of these features, be these substratal influence from Irish, influence from Scots and English dialects, creolization or universalist principles of language learning. Some of the many discussions can be found in Corrigan (1993), Filppula (1999), Harris (1991a), Hickey (2007b) and Tristram (2003).

Phonology

Irish English is rhotic, although the realization of post-vocalic /r/ varies regionally; northern varieties, for instance, have a retroflex quality to vowels preceding /r/. A feature once considered characteristic of Irish English, namely use of clear /l/ in all phonetic contexts, seems to be changing with dark /l/ being observed in urban varieties such as Belfast, Dublin and (London)Derry (Hickey, 2007a; McCafferty, 2007). H-dropping is not a feature of Irish English, but the consonant is dropped in /hj/ clusters (e.g. huge, human) in the urban varieties of Dublin and Cork. Yod dropping in the cluster /nj/ (e.g. news) occurs in a number of dialects, including those of Cork and Dublin cities (Ó hÚrdail, 1997a). The distinction between /w/ and /hw/ (as in witch vs. which) characterizes many varieties of Irish English, but the distinction is increasingly being lost in urban dialects (e.g. Dublin, Cork, Belfast). A major difference between northern and southern Irish English is the dental stop realization of the dental fricatives /θ/ and /ð/ in southern varieties. A distinguishing feature of the Cork city accent is the use of alveolar rather than dental stop realizations in this context (e.g. three merges with tree), but, as noted by Ó hÚrdail (1997b), alveolar realizations to a greater or lesser degree occur in many varieties on southern Irish English, including those of Dublin city and county, Limerick city and county, Galway city. The evidence suggests an ongoing change towards alveolarity. Southern Irish English has also lenition of alveolar stops in positions of high sonority, for example, city, foot (Hickey 2005).

Vowel quality and quantity are subject to considerable regional and social variation. It is generally believed that a characteristic of southern Irish English (with the exception of Dublin) is monophthongization, but Collins (1997) found evidence of diphthongal realizations among the Claddagh community in Co. Galway, suggesting that processes of diphthongization are occurring outside the capital city. A distinctive feature of northern Irish English is a fronted realization of /u/ ([ʉ]) as opposed to the more backed allophones in southern varieties. A further contrast between these two major geolinguistic varieties is the nature of vowel length. Southern Irish English has phonemic vowel length whereas northern Irish English (with the exception of the south Ulster English dialect which follows southern Irish English in this respect) is variably affected by vowel length patterns from Scots, where vowel duration is determined by phonetic environment. For instance, the vowel /i/ is long before /r v z ð/, hiatus and morphemic or word boundary, but short elsewhere, for example, 'agreed' [əgɹi:d] but 'greed' [gɹid] (Harris 1984).

There have been very few studies of Irish English intonation. The variety that has received the most attention is that of Belfast English, which is characterized by a high incidence of rising intonation patterns in not only questions but also statements (Jarmen and Cruttenden 1976; Rahilly 1997). Lowry (2002) found an effect for style and gender in the use of rising nuclear accents among Belfast teenagers, where falling patterns were preferred in more formal styles, especially by girls. Grabe (2004), as part of a project on intonational variation in English, notes distributional differences in use of nuclear accents across seven dialects (London, Cambridge, Bradford, Leeds, Newcastle, Belfast, Dublin) and four utterance types. The Belfast speakers have the highest frequency of rising nuclear accents in declaratives, wh-questions, yes/no questions and declarative questions. In contrast, the Dublin speakers have the lowest frequency of rising nuclear accents in yes/no and declarative questions and incidence of rising nuclei in declaratives is low (6 per cent compared to Newcastle 16.7 per cent and Belfast 83.3 per cent). This preference for falling nuclear accents in statements was also observed in studies of Co. Cork and Co. Galway intonation from the 1940's (see Rahilly 1997).

Morphology

Many features of vernacular Irish English morphology are widely shared with other varieties of English (e.g. regularization of irregular verbs in past tense or past participle forms (e.g. I done, I seen, I have went), use of 'them' as a demonstrative (them chairs), multiple negation (I didn't see nothing). One distinctive feature is that of a 2nd person plural pronoun (yous/yiz or, in rural areas, ye), which contrasts with the singular form 'you'. In informal Dublin English, the –er suffix is used productively with both proper and common nouns to coin new words, for example, Mickser (from Mick), Chineser (Chinese take-away), sittiner (sitting room); some of these forms (such as chipper (fish and chip shop) have spread beyond Dublin (Kallen 1997b).

Syntax

The perfective system

There are a number of ways of expressing perfect aspect in Irish English and these will be exemplified from Harris (1993: 180–1). The 'resultative' perfect (events that have already happened but have current relevance) can be expressed in two ways depending on the transitivity of the verb:

a. I've the book read
b. I'm not too long left

Filppula (1999) observes from his corpus of four regional varieties (Dublin, Co. Wicklow, Co. Clare and Co. Kerry) that type a (what he terms the medial object perfect) occurs infrequently, but is more frequent in the (south)west than the east. Type b perfects (what he terms the BE perfect) occur slightly more frequently, but the divide is not so much east versus west as urban versus rural with rural varieties favouring syntactic contexts, such as adjectival and adverbial complements, that the construction does not occur with in Dublin speech, for example, 'the younger generations are gone idle over it' (Filppula, 1999:120).

The hot-news perfect (an event that has just occurred before speaking) employs a construction with be after + infinitive (or noun phase):

c. I'm after giving it to her
d. I'm only after my dinner

This construction had a notably low incidence in Filppula's corpus, but tended to occur more in Dublin than the other areas.

The extended-now perfect (situation started in past and extending into the present) uses present tense forms:

e. I know his family all my life
f. We're living here seventeen years

In Filppula's corpus, this type of perfect was more frequent in (south)western dialects, which also favoured constructions with a temporal preposition 'with' as in 'he is working with a couple o' weeks' (he has been working for a couple of weeks) (Filppula, 1997: 240).

The indefinite since-time perfect (events occurring at an unspecified time leading up to present) is expressed through the simple past:

g. I never saw a gun in my life nor never saw one fired

This construction showed no regional variation in Filppula's corpus, occurring in all varieties.

Habitual aspect

Habitual aspect in vernacular Irish English can be expressed by means of two forms: periphrastic do (be) (as in examples (h) and (i) from Filppula 1999: 130) or habitual be/be's (as in examples (j) and (k) from Filppula 1999: 135–6).

h. They does be lonesome by night, the priest does surely
i. Two lorries of them now in the year we do burn
j. When they be sowing the crops …
k. A lot of them be interested in football matches

Filppula (1999) notes that periphrastic do + be is very rare in his corpus, the more frequent construction being do + verb (as in example i). In contrast, Hickey (2007a) considers a preference for do + be in habitual aspect constructions to be a feature of (south)western varieties and cliticization of 'do' on 'be' to be a feature of eastern varieties. The habitual be/be's construction is generally seen as more typical of northern Irish English.

The Progressive

The progressive form occurs more frequently in Irish English than Standard British English, especially with stative verbs, including those of inert cognition and perception (such as think, understand, want, hear) and verbs of having and being (such as have, be, own) as in examples (l-n), taken from Ronan (2001: 45–7):

l. ... they'd be wanting to get in on the act
m. Aer Lingus is having a special offer in flights to Paris
n. Is anybody seeing the next speaker?

Ronan (2001: 48) also notes the use of the progressive with the imperative (as in 'don't be telling me that') and suggests that it may serve an intensifying function.

Subordination

Irish English uses a number of subordinators in characteristic ways. For example, 'till' is used in the sense of 'in order that' and 'from' and 'whenever' are used as temporal subordinators, the latter being equivalent to 'when' in northern Irish English. The examples below are from Harris (1993: 165):

o. Come here till I tell ye
p. I know him from he was a wee fella
q. My husband died whenever I was living in New Lodge Road

In addition, the form 'and' is used as a subordinating conjunction to introduce non-finite clauses and express temporal and concessive relations, which would usually be expressed by 'while' or 'although' in many other varieties of English.

r. Twas in harvest time and the weather bad (Filppula 1999: 196)
s. Ye'd wonder at that child being so stupid and the mother so clever (Harris, 1993: 166)

Clefting

Compared to other varieties of English, Irish English permits a greater degree of clefting and a greater freedom as to what type of constituent may be fronted. For instance, verb phrases, adverbials and quantifiers may be clefted as in examples (t-v), respectively (Filppula 1999: 250, 252, 253):

t. It's looking for more land a lot of them are
u. It's a handshears I used to shear with
v. It's plenty o' them would fall too

Filppula's corpus indicates regional variation in the use of clefting, the construction favoured most in Counties Clare and Kerry, least in Dublin with Co. Wicklow lying between.

Generally, clefting is used as a focusing device whereby the fronted element is to be understood as new or contrastive information. However, as noted by Harris (1993), the 'it-cleft' can be used to emphasize the entire sentence and not just the fronted constituent. A related focusing device is that of topicalization where an element is fronted in the sentence as in examples w and x below (taken from Ó hÚrdail, 1997a:190).

w. All round the country they brought me
x. Too much tea I'm drinking

Filppula (1999) found fewer instances of topicalization in his corpus compared to clefting.

Lexicon

Irish English has a substantial characteristic lexicon, with words deriving from Irish and from regional and archaic English (and Scots) usage as well as having many words with uncertain etymology (Dolan 2004; Macafee 1996). Words from Irish include geographical features, such as cnoc/knock ('hill/mountain'), sliabh/slieve (mountain/upland), loch/lough ('lake'), flora and fauna, such as sally ('willow'), cultural and culinary artefacts, such as Taoiseach ('Prime Minister'), Dáil ('Parliament'), feis ('usually competitive festival of dance, music, poetry'), colcannon ('potato dish with cabbage') as well as varied vocabulary, such as gonc/gunk ('unpleasant surprise'), slob ('mud', 'uncouth or untidy person'), gob ('mouth'), shebeen ('illegal drinking den'). Words reflecting dialectal (English and Scots) and/or archaic usage include crabbit/crabbed ('ill-tempered'), gab ('idle chatter'), boke ('to vomit'), gawp ('to stare/gape'), scuttered ('drunk'), dander ('leisurely stroll'), 'wee' ('small'). Moreover, certain semantic processes which have taken place in Ireland have led to distinctive meanings of English words: semantic extensions of agricultural terms have resulted in 'yoke' ('implement for harnessing draught animals together') and 'hames' ('collar on a horse') being understood as 'thing/device' and 'right mess', respectively; certain words have retained earlier meanings, such as 'bold' in the sense of 'naughty'; antonymic pairs in a complementary relation have merged so that 'rent/let', 'teach/learn', 'bring/take' are often used interchangeably (Hickey 2005). There are also many colloquial, idiomatic expressions, such as 'your man' to refer to a specific person ('give your man a pint'), 'deadly' and 'desperate' as both positive and negative intensifiers ('the crack was deadly', 'he's a desperate case'), 'altogether' meaning 'wholly/completely' ('he's a desperate man altogether').

Irish English permits the use of the positive 'anymore' construction, both in the sense of 'nowadays' (as in example y) and 'from now on' (as in example z); both examples are from Kallen (1997b: 153).

y. Wool is so expensive anymore
z. Maybe that's where they're going to be kept now anymore

As noted by Kallen (1997b), the lexicon exhibits regional variation both in terms of forms and pragmatic use, although it is not always easy to delimit forms regionally. An important division is that between the English of Ulster and the rest of Ireland (Macafee, 1996). Urban centres such as Dublin and Cork have localized vocabulary items, such as 'bazzer' (meaning 'haircut' in Cork) and 'goo' (meaning 'look' in Dublin).

Of course, it cannot be simply assumed that such vocabulary is necessarily known and/or used in modern-day Ireland. Sociolinguistic factors, such as age, social class, region and style, are likely to be relevant. Zwickl (2001) in a study of knowledge and use of dialect vocabulary in northern Irish English found that men claimed greater use of dialect vocabulary than women, and knowledge as well as use of such vocabulary increased with age. The highest knowledge, as opposed to use, of dialect words was claimed by the intermediate socio-economic group.

English Usage within the Region

In this section, we focus on the issue of norms and standards in Irish English. From a historical perspective, Irish English was generally perceived both within and outside Ireland as an inferior variety to 'proper' English, that is, the standard English of south-east England, and ridding oneself of 'provincialisms' was a common pastime of Irish and Scottish elites (gentry and bourgeoisie) in the eighteenth and nineteenth centuries. Essentially what the worried elites were engaging in, consciously and unconsciously, were processes of supralocalization or what Hickey (2005; 2007a; 2007b) prefers to label 'supraregionalisation', that is, processes of levelling where more marked local features are replaced by more standardized ones, in the Irish case often from an external source, namely Britain. The question as to whether a standard Irish English variety has emerged, however, remains open. Traditionally, normative thinking in Ireland assumes the view that standard English is something outside of, and different from, Irish English; hence Irish English, even in the linguistic literature, is often conceptualized by default as not standard English (Kallen and Kirk 2001). For many the core problem is a lack of codified prestige norms (Filppula 1999), and discussions in relation to standard norms in Ireland have, thus, often focused on the possible sources of prestige that are available in the context of wider questions about identities (national, social, ethnic etc); for instance, have English norms an influence on the development of prestige norms in Irish English generally, and have Scottish and southern Irish norms an influence on development of prestige norms in northern Irish English? Harris (1991b), for instance, suggested that, in Northern Ireland, political affiliation (i.e. unionist vs. nationalist) may affect the nature of prestige norms with nationalists looking to southern Irish English norms. However, such linguistic factors may shift as political circumstances shift (see, e.g. Gunn 1994).

Kallen and Kirk (2001) take a different approach to standardization in Ireland, arguing that standard Irish English is best seen as a dynamic variety (with its own variation) to be identified empirically in a wide range of contexts and modalities. They hypothesize that there is one standard for the entire island (but note their notion of standard excludes phonology) and that features of vernacular Irish English may well form part of any such standard. Based on the southern Irish English component and British sub-corpora of the International Corpus of English (a corpus designed to investigate standards across Englishes), they conclude that Irish Standard English does exist, finding a range of primarily quantitative differences between Irish and British spoken usage for features such as do-support with main verb 'have' (e.g. have you the time? versus do you have the time?), use of shall and will and use of the perfect with 'have'. For instance, Irish usage prefers no do-support with main verb 'have' (73.4 per cent) whereas British usage disfavours it (21.4 per cent). Another factor which differentiates Irish Standard English from many other standard varieties of English is that using the 'have' auxiliary to mark perfect is relatively infrequent; for example, 29.1 per cent in Irish English and 77.1 per cent in British English. In contrast, Irish English favours main verb 'have' considerably more than British English (70.9 per cent and 22.9 per cent, respectively). Note, however, that Kallan and Kirk (2001) in relation to the perfective system found that constructions such as those exemplified in a, b, e and f (above) were relatively rare and the 'after' construction did not occur at all. The Irish English 'perfects' may not necessarily form part of standard Irish English, given their sensitivity to style and social variables (see Kallen 1991).

Given our current knowledge, it is difficult to come to any firm conclusions about the nature of prestige norms in Irish English, both overt and covert, and their relation to spatial and social factors. The role played by ethnicity in Northern Ireland appears to be complex and not reducible to simple binary distinctions, such as Catholic English and Protestant English (Millar 1987; Todd 1984). Ethnicity was not significant in a sociolinguistic study of Belfast carried out in the 1970s (Milroy 1980) but was found to play a role in a more recent study of processes of linguistic variation and change in the city of (London)Derry, often interacting with social class (McCafferty 2001). Generally, however, there is a lack of empirical evidence in relation to the extent and nature of ethnic variation in Northern Ireland. The influence of urban varieties, such as Belfast English and Dublin English, on suburban and rural hinterlands is attested (Pitts 1985; Hickey 2005) and, given increasing urbanization, may be expected to continue. For instance, Hickey (2007a) refers to the new variant of Irish English which is spreading outside Dublin and includes features such as velarization of syllable-final /l/, intervocalic T-flapping and fronting and shortening of /a:/ before /r/ (e.g. [pæɹ̥t]). Not to be overlooked, however, are the effects of in-migration on Dublin English itself. Hickey (2005) suggests that there is currently a vowel shift in progress where low back vowels are being raised (e.g. [kɒt̞]- > [kɔt̞] 'cot') and diphthongs with low or back starting points are being retracted (e.g. [taɪm]- > [tɑɪm] 'time'). These changes are in turn currently spreading throughout the Republic of Ireland.

Current Trends

Current demographic trends in the Republic of Ireland indicate that the process of urbanization continues; the eastern area of Leinster has the heaviest concentration of population (1 in 2 people live in this region), and includes Dublin, with its commuter towns in especially Kildare, Meath and Wicklow, as well as the urban corridor developing between Dublin and Belfast, given recent improvements in transport infrastructure. The major future urban growth, however, is projected for smaller settlements, which are not necessarily close to the urban centres they are destined to serve (Hourihan 2006). There are likely to be linguistic implications of such developments in terms of not only dialect levelling but also koineization, where new varieties may emerge as former small, more rural villages and towns increasingly grow into urban conglomerates (cf. Kerswill and Williams 2005).

Another ongoing trend is that of immigration, where increasing numbers of non-English speaking peoples are settling in Ireland, especially in the Republic of Ireland, although the rate of increase has declined during the period 2006–11. This is likely to change the linguistic ecology of the island, but whether it will affect the nature of English spoken, such as the development of ethnovarieties, is an open question. Recent figures suggest that foreign-born residents in the Republic of Ireland now represent slightly over 10 per cent of the resident population. The figures for 2006 include 24,425 from European countries outside the European Union, 35,326 from Africa, and 46,952 from Asia (Central Statistics Office Ireland, 2007b). It is also estimated that there may be as many as 150,000 non-national Irish living in Dublin. There have been similar developments in Northern Ireland where the 2001 census suggested substantial increases in ethnic minorities, particularly those from Eastern Europe. Projections for Northern Ireland for 2005–6 suggested a migration figure of over 40,000 (Northern Ireland Statistics and Research Agency, 2007b). The island of Ireland, as a whole, is becoming a heterogeneous society with, as noted above, up to 200 languages being spoken, and as many 40 or more different nationalities. But what is the impact, if any, of this on the English language in Ireland? This is not easy to assess at present. Indeed, two factors suggest that the linguistic impact will be minimal for some significant time to come. First, the governments of the island both North and South have generally concentrated their efforts on issues of linguistic equality and access to the branches of government, as opposed to any core language planning. Two reports from the early part of this century (Holder, 2003; Leong, 2002) noted the lack of both community interpreters, and a serious and well organized policy of provision in the teaching of English as a second or other language.

Secondly, many migrant workers, such as the Polish or Lithuanians, do not necessarily intend to make Ireland their home. Consequently, they live within their own tight knit groups, some not learning other than basic functional English. Local stores are now seen to stock Polish or other foreign foods, and there are even some rudimentary newspapers in Polish. For those other groups who intend to make Ireland their long term home, such as new generation Chinese, Asians, Africans, Arabs and Portuguese, to mention only some possible examples, their numbers are in the main too small to impact on the forms of English that surround them. The main linguistic problem for these migrants is getting access to appropriate English language education, and in some cases any education; for instance, in 2007 an African community set up their own school in reaction to their inability to access mainstream education within the largely Catholic Church controlled system in the Republic of Ireland.

All in all, however, it is too early to predict whether immigrant varieties of Irish English will eventually develop; if they do, they are most likely to emerge in Dublin where the majority of non-national Irish reside.

Bibliography

Adams, G. B. (1977), 'The dialects of Ulster', in D. Ó Muirithe (ed.), *The English Language in Ireland,* pp. 56–70, Dublin: The Mercier Press.

Barry, M. V. (1981), 'The southern boundaries of northern Irish English speech', in M. V. Barry (ed.), *Aspects of English Dialects in Ireland,* pp. 52–95, Belfast: Institute of Irish Studies, Queen's University Belfast.

Bauer, L. (2002), *An Introduction to International Varieties of English,* Edinburgh: Edinburgh University Press.

Berry, H. F. (ed.) (1907), *Statues and Ordinances, and Acts of the Parliament of Ireland, King John to Henry V,* Dublin: Stationary Office.

Bliss, A. J. (1977), 'The emergence of modern English dialects in Ireland', in D. Ó Muirithe (ed.), *The English Language in Ireland,* Dublin: The Mercier Press, pp. 7–20

—. (1979), *Spoken English in Ireland 1600–1740,* Dublin: The Dolmen Press.

Britain, D. (2002), 'Space and spatial diffusion', in J. Chambers, P. Trudgill, and N. Schilling-Estes (eds), *The Handbook of Variation and Change,* pp. 603–37, Oxford: Blackwell.

Central Statistics Office Ireland. (2007a), 2006 Census Population – Volume 9 – Irish Language. Retrieved October 10, 2007 from http://www.cso.ie/census/census2006results/volume_9/volume_9_press_release.pdf.

—. (2007b), 2006 Census Population – Volume 4 – Usual Residences, Birthplaces, Migrations and Nationalities. Retrieved October 10, 2007 from http://beyond2020.cso.ie/Census/TableViewer/tableView.aspx? ReportId=5032.

Clarke, S. (2002), 'The legacy of British and Irish English in Newfoundland', in R. Hickey (ed.), *Legacy of Colonial Englishes: Studies in Transported Dialects,* pp. 242–61, Cambridge: Cambridge University Press.

Collins, A. (1997), 'Diphthongization of (o) in Claddagh Hiberno- English: a network study' in J. Kallen (ed.) *Focus on Ireland.* Amsterdam: John Benjamins 153–70.

Corrigan, K. (1993), 'Hiberno-English syntax: nature versus nurture in a creole context', *Newcastle and Durham Working Papers in Linguistics,* 1, 95–131.

Cowley, T. (2000), *The Politics of Language in Ireland,* London: Routledge.

Dolan, T. (2004), *A Dictionary of Hiberno-English: The Irish Use of English,* 2nd edn, Dublin: Gill and Macmillan.

Filppula, M. (1999), *The Grammar of Irish English: Language in Hibernian Style,* London: Routledge.

Gallagher, A. (2006), 'Speaking in tongues', *The Irish Times,* accessed October 2006, available from http://www.ireland.com/timeseye/whoweare/p3bottom.htm.

Gordon, E. and Trudgill, P. (2002), 'English input to New Zealand', in R. Hickey (ed.), *Legacy of Colonial Englishes: Studies in Transported Dialects,* pp. 440–55, Cambridge: Cambridge University Press.

Grabe, E. (2004), 'Intonational variation in urban dialects of English spoken in the British Isles', in P. Gilles and J. Peters (eds), *Regional Variation in Intonation,* pp. 9–31, Linguistische Arbeiten. Tuebingen: Niemeyer.

Gunn, B. (1994), '"No surrender": existentialist sociolinguistics and politics in Northern Ireland', *Belfast Working Papers in Language and Linguistics,* 12, 98–133.

Harris, J. (1984), 'English in the north of Ireland', in P. Trudgill (ed.), *Language in the British Isles,* pp. 115–35, Cambridge: Cambridge University Press.

—. (1991a), 'Conservatism versus substratal transfer in Irish English', in P. Trudgill and J. Chambers (eds), *Dialects of English: Studies in Grammatical Variation,* pp. 191–212, London: Longman.

—. (1991b), 'Ireland', in J. Cheshire (ed.), *English Around the World: Sociolinguistic Perspectives,* pp. 37–50, Cambridge: Cambridge University Press.

—. (1993), 'The grammar of Irish English', in J. Milroy and L. Milroy (eds), *Real English, The Grammar of English Dialects in the British Isles,* pp. 139–86, London: Longman.

Henry, P. L. (1958), 'A linguistic survey of Ireland: preliminary report', *Lochlann*, 1, 49–208.

—. (1977), 'Anglo-Irish and its Irish background', D. Ó Muirithe (ed.), *The English Language in Ireland*, pp. 20–37, Dublin: The Mercier Press.

Hickey, R. (2001), 'The south-east of Ireland. A neglected region of dialect study, in J. Kirk and D. Ó Baoill (eds), *Language Links. The Languages of Scotland and Ireland*, pp. 1–22, Belfast: Cló Ollscoil na Banríona.

—. (2005), 'Irish English in the context of previous research', in A. Barron and K. Schneider (eds), *The Pragmatics of Irish English*, pp. 17–44, Berlin: Mouton de Gruyter.

—. (2007a), 'Southern Irish English', in D. Britain (ed.), *Language in the British Isles*, 2nd edn, Cambridge: Cambridge University Press.

—. (2007b), *Irish English. History and Present-Day Forms*, Cambridge: Cambridge University Press.

Hindley, R. (1990), *The Death of the Irish Language*, London: Routledge.

Hogan, J. J. (1927/1970), *The English Language in Ireland*, College Park, MD: McGrath Publishing Company.

Holder, D. (2003), *In Other Words? Mapping Minority Languages in NI.* Belfast: Office of the First Minister and Deputy First Minister NI Assembly.

Hourihane, J. (2006), 'How Ireland is changing', *The Irish Times*, accessed October 2006, available from http://www.ireland.com/timeseye/whoweare/index.htm.

Hume, A. (1858), 'The Irish Dialect of the English Language', *The Ulster Journal of Archaeology*, 6, 47–56.

Jarmen, E. and Cruttenden, A. (1976), 'Belfast intonation and the myth of the fall', *Journal of the International Phonetic Association*, 6, 4–12.

Kallen, J. (1991), 'Sociolinguistic variation and methodology: after as a Dublin variable', in J. Cheshire (ed.), *English Around the World: Sociolinguistic Perspectives*, pp. 61–74, Cambridge: Cambridge University Press.

—. (1994), 'English in Ireland', in R. W. Burchfield (ed.), *The Cambridge History of the English Language V. English in Britain and Overseas: Origins and Development*, pp. 148–96, Cambridge: Cambridge University Press.

—. (1997a), 'Irish English: contexts and contacts', in J. Kallen (ed.), *Focus on Ireland*, pp. 1–34, Amsterdam: John Benjamins.

—. (1997b), 'Irish English and World English: lexical perspectives' in E. Schneider (ed.) *Englishes Around the World Volume 1.* Amsterdam: John Benjamins, 139–1 59.

—. (2000), 'Two languages, two borders, one island some linguistic and political borders in Ireland', *International Journal of the Sociology of Language*, 145, 29–63.

Kallen, J. and Kirk, J. (2001), 'Aspects of the verb phrase in standard Irish English: a corpus-based approach', in J. Kirk and D. Ó Baoill (eds), *Language Links. The Languages of Scotland and Ireland*, pp. 59–79, Belfast: Cló Ollscoil na Banríona.

Kerswill, P. and Williams, A. (2005), 'New towns and koineisation: linguistic and social correlates', *Linguistics*, 43(5), 1023–48.

Leong, Fee Ching. (2002), *ESOL:Interpreting the Way Forward*, Belfast: Department of Education and Learning.

Lowry, O. (2002), 'The stylistic variation of nuclear patterns in Belfast English', *Journal of the International Phonetic Association*, 32, 33–42.

Macafee, C. (1996), *A Concise Ulster Dictionary*, Oxford: Oxford University Press.

McArthur, T. (2002), *Oxford Guide to World English*, Oxford: Oxford University Press.

McCafferty, K. (2001), *Ethnicity and Language Change: English in (London) Derry, Northern Ireland*, Amsterdam: John Benjamins.

—. (2007), 'Northern Irish English', in D. Britain (ed.), *Language in the British Isles*, 2nd edn, Cambridge: Cambridge University Press.

McManus, D. (1991), *A Guide to Ogam (Maynooth Monographs 4)*, Maynooth: An Sagart.

Milroy, L. (1980), Language and Social Networks. Oxford: Blackwell.

Millar, S. (1987), 'The question of ethno-linguistic differences in Northern Ireland', *English World-Wide*, 8(2), 201–13.

Montgomery, M. (1997), 'The rediscovery of the Ulster-Scots language', in E. W. Schneider (ed.), *Englishes Around the World*, Vol 1, pp. 211–27, Amsterdam: John Benjamins.

—. (2002), 'Solving Kurath's puzzle: establishing the antecedent of the American midland dialect region', in R. Hickey (ed.), *Legacy of Colonial Englishes: Studies in Transported Dialects*, pp. 310–25, Cambridge: Cambridge University Press.

Northern Ireland Statistics and Research Agency. (2007a), Browse NI census. Retrieved October 10, 2007 from http://www.nicensus2001.gov.uk/nica/browser/profile.jsp?profile=Cultural&mainArea=Newry+and+Mourne&mainLevel=CouncilArea.rthern.

—. (2007b), Long-term International Migration Estimates (2005–6). Retrieved October 10 from http://www.nisra.gov.uk/archieve/demography/population/migration/NI_Migration_Report.pdf.

Ó hÚrdail, R. (1997a), 'Hiberno-English: historical background and synchronic features and variation', in H. Tristram (ed.) *The Celtic Englishes*. Heidelberg: Universitätsverlag C. Winter, 180–201.

—. (1997b), 'Confusion of dentality and alveolarity in dialects of Hiberno-English', in J. Kallen (ed.) *Focus on Ireland*. Amsterdam: John Benjamins 133–52.

Picard, J. M. (2003), 'The French language in medieval Ireland', in M. Cronin, M. and C. Ó Cuilleanain (eds), *The Languages of Ireland*, pp. 25–44, Dublin: Four Courts Press.

Pitts, A. (1985), 'Urban influence on phonological variation in a Northern Irish speech community', *English World-Wide*, 6(1), 59–86.

Rahilly, J. (1997), 'Aspects of prosody in Hiberno-English: the case of Belfast', in J. Kallen (ed.), *Focus on Ireland*, pp. 109–32, Amsterdam: John Benjamins.

Ronan, P. (2001), 'Observations on the progressive in Hiberno-English', in J. Kirk and D. Ó Baoill (eds), *Language Links. The Languages of Scotland and Ireland*, pp. 43–58, Belfast: Cló Ollscoil na Banríona.

Scowcroft, M. R. (1987), 'Leabhar gabhala-part II: the growth of the text', *Eriu*, 38, 81–142.

—. (1988), 'Leabhar gabhala-part II: the growth of the tradition', *Eriu*, 39, 1–66.

Todd, L. (1984), 'By their tongue divided: towards an analysis of speech communities in Northern Ireland', *English World-Wide*, 5(2), 159–80.

Tristram, H. (ed.) (2003), *The Celtic Englishes III.* Heidelberg: Winter Universitäts Verlag.

Tymoczko, M. (2003), 'Language interface in early Irish culture', in M. Cronin and C Ó Cuilleanain (eds), *The Languages of Ireland,* pp. 25–44, Dublin: Four Courts Press.

Walker, H. (2011), *A Social Constructionist Analysis of Ulster-Scots Identity in the 17th and 21st Centuries,* Ph.D. thesis, University of Ulster.

Zwickl, S. (2001), 'Dialect knowledge and use across the Northern Irish/Irish border: linguistic and extralinguistic factors', in J. Kirk and D. Ó Baoill (eds), *Language Links. The Languages of Scotland an Ireland,* pp. 149–69, Belfast: Cló Ollscoil na Banríona.

Isle of Man

Chapter 11

The Isle of Man

Andrew Hamer

Geographical Position

The Isle of Man is orientated south-west to north-east, with a maximum length of 48 kilometres (30 miles) and a breadth of 21 kilometres (13 miles). The Island is centrally placed within the British Isles, lying between the coasts of Northern Ireland and Cumbria. The hills of the English Lake District, and the Mourne Mountains in Northern Ireland, are clearly visible from different points of the Island, as are the hills of Galloway in Southern Scotland, and peaks of the Snowdon range in North Wales. Douglas, the Island's capital, faces east, and is 130 kilometres (80 miles) from Liverpool, the nearest port. But despite the geographical position of the Island, Manx natives justifiably feel their identity to be separate from those of the peoples of the surrounding countries. The Isle of Man is self-governing except for matters of foreign affairs and defence, for which it pays an annual fee to the British Government. It is not part of the United Kingdom, but is a Crown Dependency, the monarch having the title of Lord of Man.

Historical Background

The Island's strategic position in the Irish Sea has given it a historical importance far greater than its size might suggest, as successive waves of immigrants have been attracted to it. When settlers arrived from Ireland, probably in the fourth century, the Isle of Man was already inhabited, but it was the Goidelic Celtic language of the newcomers that became the language of the whole Island. This language, here referred to as Manx Gaelic, remained the first language of the majority of the population until the late eighteenth century. A large number of Norse place-names are the principal linguistic legacy of Scandinavian settlers, who arrived in the Island from the ninth century and ruled there till 1266. There followed a period of about seventy years, during which the Scots and English contended for control of the Island, before power passed to the English Crown (Hindley 1984: 15). The earliest significant date for the story of the English language on the Isle of Man is 1405, when Henry IV gifted the Island to Sir John Stanley and his descendants (Kinvig 1975: 88, 96). The

Stanleys, who were to rule the Island for over three hundred years, were a Lancashire family, and it was their variety of upper-class Lancashire speech that was to provide the first model of English for Manx Gaelic speakers.

Sociocultural and Linguistic Background

The Manx population adopted English as their first language over a period of centuries: the earliest record of Manx natives with first-language competence in English dates from the early seventeenth century, but the process of language shift was ended only when the last of the first-language Manx Gaelic speakers, Ned Maddrell, died in 1974 at the age of 97. The shift to English can be followed through a series of social networks, beginning with those at the upper end of the social scale. William Blundell, who stayed on the Island during the 1640s, is clear in his own mind that this first group learnt their English direct from their social equals among the Island's English administrators, and that therefore their English was that of the Lancashire gentry:

> For their gentry are truly gentle, courteous, affable, and more willingly will discourse with you in the English than in their own language, whom I observed even of all of them, not only to speak true English, but to pronounce so naturally as that I could not observe any different tone in their pronunciation of our English ... but in most imitating ... the Lancashire gentry, as having had so long converse with the house of Darby themselves, and all their officers and retinue, being all Lancashire men (Harrison 1876: 53).

Thus to Blundell, himself a Lancashire man from Crosby, no separate Manx dialect was detectable among the Manx upper classes. His remarks about 'their own language' imply, however, that this group was at this period bilingual – that is, that they had native-speaker competence in both languages, and kept the two codes separate, according greater prestige to English. It would appear that knowledge of English was largely restricted to the upper classes during the early part of the seventeenth century, to judge from comments made by John Speed (1611): 'the wealthier sort ... do imitate the people of Lancashire ... the commoner sort of people, both in their language and manners come nighest unto the Irish' (Stowell and Ó Breasláin 1996: 6). By the end of the century, however, knowledge of English had started to spread down the social scale (the following comments from Camden's *Britannia* are taken from the revised edition of 1695):

> Not only the gentry, but likewise such of the peasants as live in the towns or frequent the town-markets, do both understand and speak the English language (Harrison 1871: 18).

It is noteworthy from these remarks that the towns functioned as vectors of linguistic change. It may also be inferred from Camden's comments that those of the peasant classes who 'both understood and spoke' English at this date were not bilinguals, but probably used English as a second language, for business or trading purposes: those who lived in the towns were, according to Camden, 'for the most part mariners or fishermen' (Harrison 1871: 19), who would presumably have frequent opportunities to meet with English speakers. As second-language speakers of English, these urban peasants, like the upper-class bilinguals before them, can be assumed to have kept English and Manx Gaelic apart as separate codes.

The eighteenth century saw the development among the lower classes of an indigenous Manx variety of English – that is, a variety generated within the Manx speech-community, and not learnt from contact with foreigners. The absence of any contemporary sources prevents closer dating of this development, but by 1822 it was familiar enough to attract a gentle parody in the form of a letter in 'dialect' to the editor of *The Manx Advertiser*. The author of the letter signs himself 'A Northside Farmer', and it may therefore be inferred that the variety parodied in the letter was spoken among the rural population.

Another parody, in the form of a letter to the editor of *Mona's Herald*, 20th June 1834, was written ostensibly by a man whose friends were all fishermen. It is beyond the scope of this chapter to give a detailed examination of the language of these letters, but attention will be drawn later to certain linguistic features, as these letters are among the witnesses to what may be described as the earliest Manx English, a vernacular and (in modern terms) a working-class variety. This variety, showing considerable influence from Manx Gaelic, was to provide the basis for the literary dialect celebrated in the works of a number of authors, the first and most important of whom was T. E. Brown (1830–97), whose first volume of verse, *Betsy Lee, and other Poems*, was published in 1881. Its appearance as a literary dialect gave this variety an iconic status as the representative dialect of the Isle of Man.

English Usage within the Region

Since the fifteenth century, and the early days of Stanley rule, English has been the language of administration and law in the Isle of Man, and by the end of the seventeenth, as seen above, it had become the language of trade and commerce also. Manx Gaelic remained for another century and a half the language of church worship in the rural areas, although Bishop Barrow's education system, which was set up in 1669, began the long process of its replacement by English (Bird 1991: 12). The Celticist, Henry Jenner, attended a Manx Gaelic church service in 1875, at which the congregation were almost all 'above fifty years of age'; he reported that conversations in the churchyard before and after the service were 'almost always' in English (Jenner 1875–76: 192). It is clear from Jenner's account that the use of English had extended to all domains of spoken language, formal and informal, by this date. English had always been the dominant written language, and since the nineteenth century has been used for all literary purposes, including poetry and fiction, both in Standard English and in Manx English (Corkill 2000; Faragher 2000).

Demographic Data

Two periods of recession during the twentieth century revealed that the long-term economic viability of the Island was under threat from emigration. Census figures show that the first recession, in the 1920s, saw the population decrease from 60,284 in 1921 to 49,308 in 1931; by 1951 the population figure had recovered to 55,253, but a second recession reduced the population to 48,135 in 1961 (the 1861 figure, given here for comparison, was 52,469). Since 1961 there has been a dramatic increase in the population to 76,315 (2001 census), a rise that is entirely due to immigration, mainly the result of the rapid development of the finance sector, which now employs 17.5 per cent of the workforce and is the principal source of employment. The 2001 census shows that 51 per cent of the resident population were immigrants, with 38.2 per cent coming from England, and 8.1 per cent from Scotland and the island of Ireland. It is evident that England is by far the largest source of immigrants; some of the linguistic consequences of this immigration will be discussed below under 'Current trends'.

Linguistic Description of Manx English

Since at least the seventeenth century, when upper-class Lancashire speech provided the model for speakers of Manx Gaelic to adopt, standardized varieties of English have been in continuous use by the higher social classes among Manx natives. Early attempts to render the speech of the rural lower classes, such as in the letters to newspaper editors that were referred to above, show considerable admixture of Manx Gaelic accent and dialect features. Examples include *boy veen* ('dear boy', with a Gaelic loan-word and Gaelic word-order); *bethars* ('betters', with – presumably – a dental, rather than alveolar /t/). The material must be treated with caution, but conclusions to be drawn from it agree in general with comments made half a century later by Jenner: 'those who speak Manx [Gaelic] best frequently translate Manx idioms literally into English. Indeed, I expect there is often a very confused idea of language among the 'diglott' portion of the community (Jenner 1875–76: 195).

Grammar and Morphology

The development of Manx English during the nineteenth century was one of the changes towards Standard English. Manx English syntax is now relatively standard, but non-standard grammatical features recorded in the *Survey of*

English Dialects include some breach of number concord in *we/you was;* non-standard *them,* as *in them days, them ones up by the …*; the use of *for to* as a complementizer (which also occurs in the 1822 Manx English 'dialect' letter to the editor of *The Manx Advertiser* referred to above, and which is also found in representations of working-class Lancashire speech in the nineteenth century). Manx Gaelic lies behind non-standard *at,* as in *there's a big house at him* ('he has a big house'), a calque of *ta thie mooar echey*; non-standard (-ing) forms probably reflect earlier confusion among Manx speakers of the English continuous and habitual verbal aspects: *they were getting a sap of straw* ('they usually got a wisp of straw', Barry 1984: 176).

Noun and verb morphology is generally standard, although the plural form *childer* ('children'), found in the same 1822 letter, is also among the data recorded in the *Survey of English Dialects.* This form was apparently obsolescent in Standard English by the eighteenth century, and its source in Manx English was probably Lancashire vernacular (it is frequent in nineteenth-century Lancashire dialect literature). Forms of the copula are standard (the 1822 letter has *I is,* though this may be pseudo-dialect, as *I am* occurs in the same letter), while standard past tense and past participle verb forms include *break, broke, broken; take, took, taken.* Non-standard forms recorded by the *Survey of English Dialects* as minority variants, and present in nineteenth-century representations of the variety, include: present tense *I has; I does;* past tense *he give it me;* past participle *where has he went?* The non-standard simple past verb-form *beginned* occurs once in the *Survey of English Dialects* data.

Idiom and Lexis

Manx English developed as a rural variety, and much of its distinctive lexis is concerned with country life and the natural world. Examples, not borrowed from Manx Gaelic, include: *batter* to churn (butter); *bumbees* (bumble bees); *bink* (bench); *hedge* (a turf-covered boundary wall of a field); *on* (when making butter, and the butter formed, it was said to be 'on'); *throng* (thrust, push, also used of trees putting out new branches). Examples from Manx Gaelic include *curragh* – marshy ground; *broo* – low-lying land; *hibbin* – ivy; *brashlag* – 'charlock, wild mustard'; *gowag* – dog-fish; *thie* – house; *tholtan* – ruined house; *chiollagh* – 'hearth' (see below for pronunciation); *jouish* – pair of shears.

Phonology

Consonants

The consonant system is as that of RP, with the addition of the voiceless velar fricative /x/, found in loanwords from Manx Gaelic: *chiollagh* [tʃɒləx] – hearth; *loghtyn* [lɒxtən] – the native species of sheep.

1. Manx Gaelic has influenced the realization of /t/, /θ/ and /ð/.
   /t/ is frequently realized as a dental stop [t̪]. Examples in initial, medial, and final position include: *tea, tried, stream, daughter, bit of, shut, not.*
   Medially after /s/ there is a tendency towards realization as a dental fricative [θ] (examples: *master, Easter*).
   /θ/ is also realized by many speakers as a dental stop [t̪], examples including: *thaw, third, thousand, throw, Thursday.* The result is that for these speakers, *tree* and *three* are homophones.
   /ð/ may be realized by the same dental stop [t̪], initially in *this, that, these.* Medially, in *either, further* (also recorded with [d]), *mother,* [θ] is an alternative to [ð]

2. This realization of /ð/ as [θ] medially is part of a wider process, also influenced by Manx Gaelic, which devoices consonants in medial and final positions. In medial position /z/ is frequently realized as [s] in *busy, cousin, Tuesday, is it, dizzy* (also recorded as [z̥]). In final position, /v/ is frequently realized as [f] – *Christmas Eve, five* (also recorded as [v̥]); /z/ is frequently realized as [s] – *haze, lose, these* (with stopping of initial /ð/, as described above, recorded as [t̪iːs]); /d/ is frequently devoiced to [d̥], as in *neighbourhood, hundred, stupid.*
   The realization of final /z/ as [s] is common in noun plurals, as: *stars, years, boys, girls, cousins, eggs.*

3. /r/
   Non-prevocalic. Goodwin's phonetic transcriptions in Moore, Morrison and Goodwin (1924) are ambiguous as to whether Manx English was a rhotic or non-rhotic variety at that time. The data from the *Survey of English Dialects* point to a change from rhoticity to non-rhoticity at the end of the nineteenth century. Examples with the /r/ pronounced include: *first, years, turn, they're not, turf;* examples without /r/ include: *thirty, Thursday, morning, farmer, work, stars, on purpose.* Manx English is now non-rhotic.
   Prevocalic. Before stressed vowels, /r/ is usually either an alveolar trill [r] or tap [ɾ], whether word-initial or following a stop consonant, as in *road, ruts; trench, stream; break, bridge; grow, ground.*

4. /t/ is realized as a glottal stop only when /n/ is closely proximate, although in this environment it is regular. Examples of [ʔ] following /n/ include: *twenty, apprentice, winter,* while examples before /n/ (with or without intervening schwa) are: *getting* [gɛʔn], *cutting* [kʊʔən], *lightning* [leiʔnən], *frighten* [freiʔən], *straighten* [stræiʔn].

5. Many speakers lenite /t/ to [ʁ] medially between vowels, or in word-final position when before a vowel: *marrer* (matter); *arrer* (at her), *gorra* (got to).

6. Initial /w/ from earlier /hw/, as in *whey, whisker, wheel, white,* is often realized as /kw/.

7. The final consonant clusters /nd, ld, lt, st, lv/ are regularly simplified. Thus, from the *Survey of English Dialects*: *husban', len', poun'; chil', gol'; faul'; breakfas', firs', las'; twel'*. Spellings in dialect literature regularly reflect this loss of final consonant, which must have been a noticeable feature.

Vowels

Manx English has the following vowel system:
[iː ɪ e æː a ɒ ɔː uː ʊ ə ɜː]

1. Manx English speech has a different rhythm from varieties within England, caused by the frequent lengthening of /e, a, ɒ/ to [ɛː or ɛˑᵊ, æː, ɔː].
   The three vowels are not equally affected: /e/ and /a/ are frequently lengthened before voiceless and voiced stops (*gap, wrap; wet; sexton, back; dead, glad; eggs, bag*); voiceless and voiced fricatives (*nephew, after; west, last; seven, haven't*); nasals (*remember, dams; fence, anvil*); approximants (*twelve, pals; buried*). /ɒ/ is lengthened only before voiceless fricatives: *off, soft; boss, cross, gossiping.*
2. In other environments, /ɒ/ is fronted to [a], commonly in *not,* and frequently elsewhere, as in *lot, body, off, bothersome, from, once, holiday.*
3. Manx English shares the following with accents of Northern England:
   (a) [ʊ] where RP has /ʌ/, as in *butter, uncle;*
   (b) [a] (when not lengthened) where RP has /ɑː/, as in *laugh, ask, aunt;*
   (c) [uː] where RP has /ʊ/, particularly before /k/, and in certain other words: *book, look, cook, took; soot; good, could, would.*
4. There is a tendency to lower /ɪ/ to [e] before nasal consonants, as in *pinch, hinge; spring.*
5. Many speakers have no long low back vowel. Where RP has /ɑː/ these speakers have a fronted vowel [æː]. Examples include *aren't, half, arm, father.*
6. Manx English shares with many Irish varieties of English the pronunciation with [eː or e̞ɪ] of certain words which have /iː/ in England. Examples include *tea, pleased, steal, stream, clean.* This pronunciation is also attested for working-class speech in nineteenth-century Lancashire.
7. The back-rising diphthong in *house* (RP /ɑʊ/) typically has a fronted first element: [hæʊs].

Media Use of English

There have been English-language newspapers on the Island since 1792, and magazines since 1821 (Kelly 2000: 337). Although the first newspapers were aimed primarily at an immigrant readership, they clearly attracted a Manx readership fairly quickly, to judge by the evidence of the 'dialect' letters to editors that were mentioned above. Radio, at first provided by the BBC, was broadcast to the Island from 1922; the Island's own service, Manx Radio, has operated with Manx government subsidy since 1968 (Kelly 2000: 342), and as part of its programming has provided a forum for Manx English and Manx Gaelic. The earlier monopoly of programmes from England led to fears that the Island's vernacular speech would be threatened (Kelly 2000: 341), but the regular appearance now in Manx Radio programmes and local newspaper articles of Manx English idioms and lexical items can only help towards their survival.

Current Trends

Lexis

Moore, Morrison and Goodwin (1924) 'indicated the use of over 750 Manx Gaelic words in nineteenth-century Manx English literature', to which number Gill (1934) added 'a further 250' (Barry 1984: 175). Barry himself was only able to record 126 Manx Gaelic words during his 1958 fieldwork for the *Survey of English Dialects.* Manx English developed in the rural areas, and the loss of Manx Gaelic words is to a considerable extent explained by the fact that many of these words related to farming and fishing (e.g. 56 items out of the 126 Gaelic loans that Barry recorded), and some of these were becoming obsolete as technologies and occupational patterns changed. Many of these words are preserved in Manx English literature, from where Moore *et al.* and Gill took them, in fact. The modern popularity of dialect plays, and recitations and readings of Manx English literature, and the learning of dialect poems in Primary school, are all evidence of a widespread interest in Manx culture, and mean that at least a passive knowledge of these words is retained by those with such an interest. The figures of the 2001 census show that there has been a recent revival of interest in Manx Gaelic, too, with 2.2 per cent of the resident population now able to speak, read or write Manx Gaelic, up from less than 1% of the population in 1991. This development may well help the survival of non-obsolete Manx Gaelic loans in English.

Phonology

In 1984, during the period of rapid population growth that was referred to above, Barry suggested that:

> it seems likely that north-west Midland, (especially Liverpool) phonology and RP phonology will vie with one another for dominance in the pronunciation of English in Man during the next fifty years, so long as Liverpool remains the main port of access (Barry 1984: 177).

This prediction seems over-pessimistic, although it is true that many of the above distinctive sounds of Manx English are disappearing. In addition, the vowel lengthening which has been such a notable feature of Manx English, and which produced the variant [æː] in *last, after* (see above), is now heard mainly in the speech of the elderly. As a result, the rhythm of most Manx English speech is now not a distinctive feature of that variety. Manx English sounds which seem likely to remain distinctive include in particular those vowels which it shares with Northern English accents (see 3 above, under 'Phonology: Vowels').

/ɑː/ and /ʌ
Manx school pupils generally adopt the Northern variants [a] and [ʊ] in words like *last, aunt; butter,* despite the fact that many of them come from immigrant families with RP-like vowels in these words. It seems certain, therefore, that these Northern forms will continue to characterize Manx English for the foreseeable future.

/ʊ/
The Manx English variant [uː], found in words like *took, look, book,* as well as in *good, could, would,* remains a common feature in the speech of young adults, as well as older speakers, and may well survive, although some young speakers now use a more centralized pronunciation [üː].

/ɑʊ/
The Manx English pronunciation of this diphthong with a fronted first element, [æʊ], is still widespread.

Liverpool influence

Among the distinctive characteristics of Liverpool English is a tendency to aspirate heavily the voiceless stops /p, t, k/, or to replace them with affricates or fricatives (Knowles 1973: 324-325; Hughes, Trudgill and Watt 2005: 98). Aalin Clague, who did fieldwork in the west of the Island, reports that Manx schoolchildren as young as nine years are aware of this as a 'Scouse' feature when they hear it in the speech of their peers, but remarks that 'incomplete stops are uncommon' in the data she examined (Clague 2003: 84-85). Rachel Pressley researched the speech of Douglas and Onchan, in the east of the Island. Of her thirty-two informants, only four children and one adult affricated /t/, 'and each individual had a score of 6 per cent [of all tokens] or less ... Affricated /k/, on the other hand, was seen to have covert prestige for the working class, the males and the young, particularly the boys ... and its use is apparently on the increase' (Pressley 2002: 259). It would appear that Liverpool speech will continue as an influence on Manx English, though to nothing like the extent that Barry predicted.

Bibliography

Adams, G. B. (1967), 'Northern England as a source of Ulster dialects', *Ulster Folklife*, 13, 69–74.

Barry, M. V. (1984), 'Manx English', in P. Trudgill (ed.), *Language in the British Isles*, pp. 167–77, Cambridge: Cambridge University Press.

Belchem, J. (ed.) (2000), *A New History of the Isle of Man, Vol. V: The Modern Period 1830–1999*, Liverpool: Liverpool University Press.

Bird, H. (1991), *An Island that led – The History of Manx Education*, Vol. 1 (privately published, with financial assistance from the Manx Heritage Foundation).

Broderick, G. (1997), 'Manx English: an overview', in H. L. C. Tristram (ed.), *The Celtic Englishes*, pp. 123–34, Heidelberg: Universitätsverlag C. Winter.

—. (1999), *Language Death in the Isle of Man: An Investigation into the Decline and Extinction of Manx Gaelic as a Community Language in the Isle of Man*, Linguistische Arbeiten 395, Tübingen: Max Niemeyer Verlag.

Cain, P. (1939), 'Changes in speech and custom in Rushen', *Proceedings of the Isle of Man Natural History and Antiquarian Society* 4(1932–42), pp. 341–4.

Clague, K. A. (2003), 'Accent development in children and adolescents in the West of the Isle of Man', Unpublished M.Phil. thesis, University of Liverpool.

Corkill, U. (2000), 'Nineteenth-century literature in English relating to the Isle of Man', in J. Belchem (ed.), pp. 323–31.

De Lyon, H. B. (1981), 'A sociolinguistic study of aspects of the Liverpool accent', Unpublished. M.Phil. thesis, University of Liverpool.

Draskau, J. K. (1996), 'Gaelic influences in Anglo-Manx', in M. N. Craith (ed.), *Watching One's Tongue: Aspects of Romance and Celtic Languages*, Liverpool: Liverpool University Press, pp. 225–52.

—. (2000a), 'Linguistic codes in Manx vernacular English texts', *Proceedings of the Isle of Man Natural History and Antiquarian Society*, Vol. 11, no. 1, pp. 67–78.

—. (2000b), 'The use of Englishes', in J. Belchem (ed.), pp. 316–22.

Faragher, M. (2000), 'Literature in English since 1900', in J. Belchem (ed.), pp. 331–7.

Foulkes, P. and G. Docherty (1999), 'Urban voices – overview', in P. Foulkes, and G. Docherty (eds), *Urban Voices: Accent Studies in the British Isles*, pp. 1–24, London: Arnold.

Gill, W. W. (1934), *Manx Dialect: Words and Phrases*, London and Bristol: Arrowsmith.

—. (1941), 'Manx dialect words and phrases (Parts 1 to 3)', *Notes and Queries*, Vol. 181, pp. 185–6, 200–1, 215–17.

Harrison, W. (ed.) (1871), *The Old Historians of the Isle of Man*, Douglas: The Manx Society, Vol. 18.

—. (1876), *A History of the Isle of Man. Written by W. Blundell. 1648–56*, Vol. 1, Douglas: The Manx Society, Vol. 25.

Hindley, R. (1984), 'The decline of the Manx language: a study in linguistic geography', *Bradford Occasional Papers: Essays in Language, Literature and Area Studies*, pp. 15–39, University of Bradford.

Hughes, A., P. J. Trudgill and D. Watt (2005), *English Accents and Dialects: An Introduction to Social and Regional Varieties of English in the British Isles*, 4th edn, London: Hodder Arnold.

Isle of Man Government (2002), *Isle of Man Census Report 2001*, 2 vols., Douglas: Isle of Man Government Treasury.

Jenner, H. (1875–6), 'The Manx language: its grammar, literature and present state', *Transactions of the Philological Society*, pp. 172–97.

Kelly, R. T. (2000), 'The media', in J. Belchem (ed.), pp. 337–43.

Kinvig, R. H. (1975), *The Isle of Man: A Social, Cultural and Political History*, Liverpool: Liverpool University Press.

Knowles, G. O. (1973), 'Scouse: The urban dialect of Liverpool', Unpublished Ph.D. thesis, University of Leeds.

—. (1978), 'The nature of phonological variables in Scouse', in P. Trudgill (ed.), *Sociolinguistic Patterns in British English*, pp. 80–90, London: Edward Arnold.

Lockwood, W. B. (1966), 'Linguistic taboo in Manx and Anglo-Manx', *Journal of the Manx Museum*, 7, 29–32.

Maddrell, B. (2001), 'Contextualising a vocabulary of the Anglo-Manx dialect: developing Manx identities', Unpublished Ph.D. thesis, University of Liverpool.

Moore, A. W., with S. Morrison and E. Goodwin (1924, repr. 1991), *A Vocabulary of the Anglo-Manx Dialect*, Oxford University Press for Yn Cheshaght Ghailckagh.

Newbrook, M. (1986), *Sociolinguistic Reflexes of Dialect Interference in West Wirral*, Bern and Frankfurt am Main: Verlag Peter Lang.

Orton, H. *et al.* (1962–71), *Survey of English Dialects: Introduction*, 4 vols, Vol. 1 (in 3 parts): *The Six Northern Counties and Man*, Leeds: E. J. Arnold.

Pressley, R. J. (2002), 'Phonetic variation in the Douglas and Onchan area of the Isle of Man', Unpublished Ph.D. thesis, University of Liverpool.

Preuss, M. (1999), 'Remaining lexical and syntactic borrowings from Manx Gaelic in present day Manx English: a study of a declining phenomenon from a formal-linguistic viewpoint', Unpublished M.Phil. thesis, University of Liverpool.

Radcliffe, W. (1926), 'Pitfalls of Anglo-Manx', *Proceedings of the Isle of Man Natural History and Antiquarian Society* 3(1925–32), pp. 89–98.

Rhŷs, J. (1894), *The Outlines of the Phonology of Manx Gaelic*, Oxford University Press, for the Manx Society.

Rydland, K. (1972), 'Structural phonology and the survey of English dialects: a critical evaluation of the material', *Zeitschrift für Dialektologie und Linguistik*, Vol. 39, pp. 309–26.

Sangster, C. M. (2001), 'Lenition of alveolar stops in Liverpool English', *Journal of Sociolinguistics*, 5, 401–12.

Stowell, B. and D. Ó Breasláin (1996), *A Short History of the Manx Language*, Belfast: An Clochán.

Wells, J. C. (1982), *Accents of English*, 3 vols, Cambridge: Cambridge University Press.

Whittaker, I. B. (1954), 'The dialect of Dalby and Glen Maye', Unpublished B.A. dissertation, University of Leeds.

Winterbottom, D. (2000), 'Economic history, 1830–1996', in J. Belchem (ed.), pp. 207–78.

Wright, P. (1968), 'Fishing language around England and Wales', *Journal of the Lancashire Dialect Society*, 17, 2–14.

Orkney and Shetland Isles

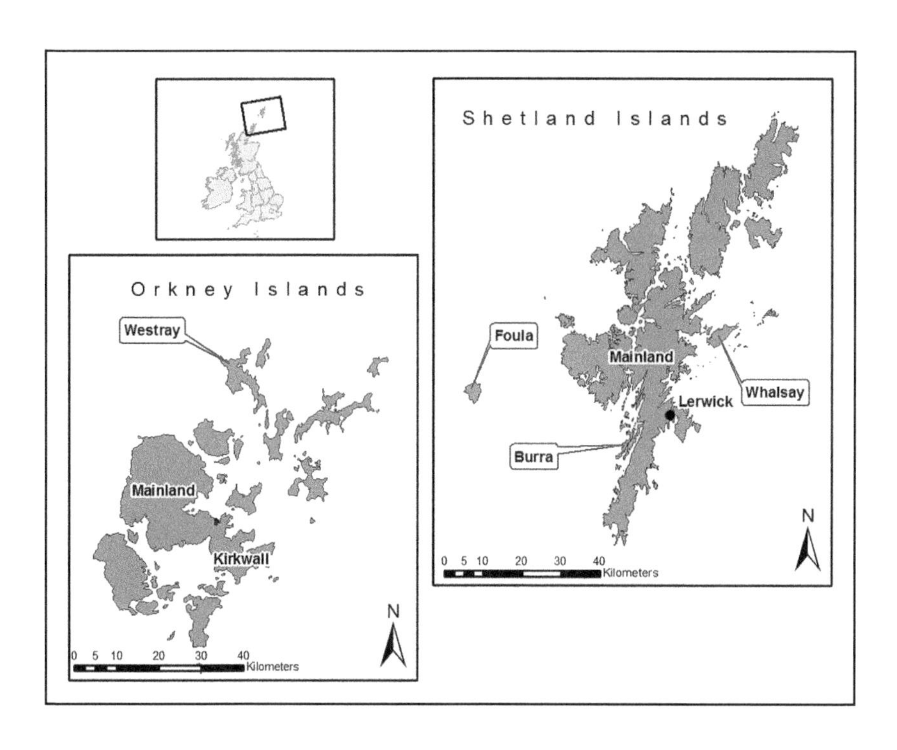

Chapter 12

English in Orkney and Shetland Isles

Klaske van Leyden

Introduction

Orkney and Shetland, collectively referred to as the Northern Isles, are the northernmost portions of the British Isles. Orkney lies just north off the coast of northern Scotland and consists of a group of over 70 islands, seventeen of which are inhabited. The Shetland Isles are located about 80 kilometres north-east of Orkney. There are over 100 islands in the Shetland archipelago, 15 of which are presently inhabited. Fair Isle, which is well known from the weather forecast, is situated equidistant between Orkney and Shetland, but belongs administratively to the latter.

The Orkney Isles are inhabited by 19,245 people (2001 Census). The administrative centre is the town of Kirkwall, with a population of about 7,500. Agriculture, tourism and, since the 1970s, North Sea oil provide the main sources of income. Shetland has a population of 21,988 (2001 Census), some 7,500 of whom live in the capital, Lerwick. Fisheries and North Sea oil and gas are key components of Shetland's economy, although in both Orkney and Shetland the importance of the oil industry has declined since the late 1990s.

There is a striking difference between the landscapes of the two island groups. Shetland has a landscape very similar to that of the Scottish Highlands, with peat-covered hills and little arable land, while Orkney is flat, green and fertile. Westerly salt-laden winds and gales account for the general scarcity of trees in both Orkney and Shetland. Thanks to the Gulf Stream, the climate in the Northern Isles is relatively mild for its latitude.

Historical Background

The first inhabitants of Orkney and Shetland appear to have arrived during the Stone Age. Archaeological evidence indicates that at the time of the first Viking raids, Pictish culture had become firmly rooted in both archipelagos.

Viking colonizers arrived in Orkney and Shetland in the first half of the ninth century. Linguistic evidence as well as literary sources, such as the *Orkneyinga Saga* (the Icelandic account of the Orkney Earldom; Pálsson and

Edwards 1978) suggest that the new settlers originated from western Norway. The Scandinavian language spoken by the immigrants and their descendants became known as Norn from *Norrœna* '(West) Norse language', and it completely obliterated whatever languages were spoken by the Pictish inhabitants of the Isles.

For several centuries, powerful Norwegian *jarls* 'earls' ruled both island groups from their base in Orkney. At its peak in the eleventh century, the Orkney Earldom extended from the Isle of Man in the south up to Shetland in the north, and included the Hebrides, Caithness and Sutherland. However, Viking power began to wane at the end of the twelfth century and the earldom was split in 1195, when Shetland was forfeited to the Norwegian king after a power struggle. A few years later, the last Norse earl died leaving no heir, and the earldom of Orkney passed to a Scottish family, although, officially, it remained Scandinavian territory. Meanwhile, Shetland maintained close relations with Norway. In 1468, Orkney and, in 1469, Shetland were pledged to Scotland by the impoverished King Christian I of Denmark and Norway as security for his daughter's dowry on her marriage to the future James III of Scotland. The dowry itself was never paid, and this is how the islands became a Scottish province. Through Scottish government and settlement in the Northern Isles, the Norn language was finally abandoned in favour of Lowland Scots in the course of the eighteenth century.

Linguistic Background

There are scarcely any written records dating from the Scandinavian period in the Northern Isles; only some fifty runic inscriptions have been found in Orkney and seven in Shetland. The language of this small corpus appears to be west Scandinavian in character, although it is unclear whether the runes were carved by native islanders or visiting Norwegians (Barnes 1996). Furthermore, there are about a dozen extant Scandinavian-language documents in the Roman alphabet originating from Orkney and Shetland, spanning the years 1329–c.1425 for Orkney and 1299–1586 for Shetland. Yet, the provenance of most of these documents is uncertain, and they could well have been written by Norwegians, possibly even in Norway itself (Smith 1996; Barnes 1998).

Literary references to the linguistic situation in the Northern Isles begin at the end of the sixteenth century; the relevant sources are provided in Marwick (1929). What we can gather from these brief remarks, penned by ministers and visitors to the Isles, is that in the sixteenth century Norn seems to have been the language of the native population, although Lowland Scots was also well understood. Around the beginning of the eighteenth century, it appears that Norn as a first language was starting to lose ground rapidly. By the end of the century, Norn was referred to largely as a language of the past, even though some fragments of rhymes were still living on in the folk memory. (For a detailed discussion of the death of Norn see Barnes (1996) and references therein.)

The most remarkable feature in the documentary sources, as Smith (1996) points out, is that the writers never refer to any communication difficulties. This is in striking contrast to the language problems faced by clergy working in Gaelic Scotland, and would suggest that by the late sixteenth century bilingualism was general in the islands.

Norn was never a literary language. Little is known about the development of Norn in the centuries preceding its death since all we have are a few snatches of speech and verse and most Norn fragments were collected only *after* the language had gone out of everyday use. Our knowledge of Norn at the time when it was possibly still understood, even though the language was by then in its final stages, is based almost entirely on material collected by the Reverend George Low on Foula (Shetland) in 1774, and published in 1879 in *A Tour through the Islands of Orkney and Schetland* (Low 1879). In Low (1879:104–14) we find the Lord's Prayer, a list of 34 everyday words and, most importantly, a 35-stanza ballad known as the *Hildina Ballad*. The word list and the Shetland Lord's Prayer, together with the Orkney Lord's Prayer printed in Wallace (1700), are discussed in Rendboe (1987, 1989–90); for a detailed analysis of the ballad, which contains just over 500 different words, see Hægstad (1900). The first verse of the Hildina ballad (from the corrected version provided by Hægstad (1900: 14)) is:

(1) Da vara Iarlin o Orkneyar
for frinda sĭn spýrde ro,
whirdì an skildè meun
or vannaro eidnar fuo –
Or glas buryon burtaga.

(Translation: It was the earl of Orkney, asked advice from his kinsman: whether he should take the maiden, get her out of her difficulties, out of the glass palace.)

The phonology, morphology and syntax of Low's Foula corpus are clearly west Scandinavian and seem to reveal that, by the eighteenth century, Shetland Norn was most closely related to Faroese and south-west Norwegian dialects (Barnes 1998).

More recent relics of Norn, mainly songs, rhymes and riddles, can be found in Jakobsen's (1928–32), and Marwick's (1929) etymological dictionaries. Jakobsen, a Faroese scholar, carried out his fieldwork trips to search out traces of Norn mainly in the 1890s, and Marwick was an Orcadian inspired by Jakobsen. The picture that emerges from the surviving vocabulary collected by these scholars is that, in its final stages, Norn had been reduced to a language of the hearth. In one sense, however, Norn has lived on until the present time (albeit imperfectly understood). The vast majority of place-names in the Northern Isles are of Norse origin (to give just three examples: *Kirkwall* < *Kirkjuvágr* 'kirk on the bay', *Lerwick* < *Leirvík* 'mud bay' and *Foula* < *Fugley* 'bird island').

The Linguistic Situation Today

The dialects now spoken in Orkney and Shetland are conservative varieties of Lowland Scots, with a substantial Scandinavian substratum. It is notable that the vowel systems of these dialects are still quite similar to that of Older Scots, and they are comparable to those of other peripheral Scots areas, such as Galloway in south-west Scotland. Scots was apparently taken to the Northern Isles by immigrants from Central Scotland in the sixteenth century at about the same time as the language replaced Gaelic in Galloway (Catford 1957a). Furthermore, many Older Scots words that have disappeared from most mainland dialects are still in everyday use in Orkney and Shetland, at least in the speech of the older generation. The occurrence of many archaic Scots words and pronunciation features, and the fact that natives generally compare their speech to Scottish Standard English, or even Standard English, rather than to other varieties of Lowland Scots, may lead speakers of the dialects to believe that the salient linguistic characteristics found in Orkney and Shetland are unique to the Isles and, therefore, must all originate from Norn.

It should also be noted that in Lowland Scots, we find many Scandinavian influences – both lexical and phonological – coming principally from the Anglo-Danish dialects of northern England. In the case of the Northern Isles, Norn and Older Scots – two closely linked languages – were spoken side by side for several centuries until relatively recently, and many speakers were also bilingual. Therefore, it is often very difficult to distinguish direct Norn borrowings from indirect Scandinavian loans. In Lowland Scots, Scandinavian influences are responsible for such phenomena as the absence of palatalization in words as *kirk* 'church', *kist* 'chest' and *brig* 'bridge'; the retention of [ʌu] in *nowt* 'cattle' and *grow*; and lexical loans such as *big* 'build', *harns* 'brains' and *lug* 'ear' (McClure 1994). These features are also found in the dialects of the Northern Isles.

Within both Orkney and Shetland there is considerable regional diversity. Most of the islands constituting the archipelagos are quite small, and, for many centuries, there was little contact between them. Children went to school locally, and people generally married within their own parish. New trends, linguistic or otherwise, entered through the administrative centres, Kirkwall and Lerwick, and from there, spread slowly to the outlying areas. The dialect of the island of Whalsay differs considerably from all other Shetland varieties, and even native Shetlanders sometimes experience difficulty understanding this conservative variety. Nevertheless, in spite of the regional variation, it can safely be said that Orcadians speak Orkney dialect, and Shetlanders speak Shetland.

As for social varieties, there is no Scottish Standard English speaking middle class, and virtually all native speakers from manual workers to university graduates employ the local dialect in their everyday speech. In fact, using a standardized form of English with locals, called *chanting* in Orkney and *knapping* in Shetland, is much frowned upon. Orcadians and Shetlanders take pride in the Norse heritage that sets them apart from mainland Scotland, and speaking the dialect is regarded as a way to emphasize this difference. Even so, natives of the Northern Isles are generally bidialectal, having command of both the traditional variety and of a form of modified Scottish Standard English. Note that, in the case of the Orcadians, the standard variety is spoken with a deviant intonation (see below).

Since the late 1970s, however, the linguistic situation in the Northern Isles has started to change. Many people have moved from the outer isles into the towns of Kirkwall and Lerwick. Furthermore, there has been a wave of immigration from mainland Scotland and England into the Northern Isles, while at the same time young people born in the Isles increasingly remain in Mainland Scotland after graduating from university. Until the 1960s, the percentage of people born outside Orkney or Shetland remained stable at around 10 per cent. These incomers, or at least their offspring, generally acquired the local dialect. Yet, from the 2001 Census it can be deduced that an estimated 25 to 30 per cent of the people now living in the Northern Isles are incomers, about half of them from England. This situation has led to an unprecedented levelling of the local varieties, and it appears that among school children and teenagers a type of Standard English – rather than the local dialect, or even Scots – is rapidly becoming the norm.

Linguistic Features of Orkney and Shetland Dialects

There exists no comprehensive account of twentieth-century Orkney and Shetland dialects. Most references in the literature to aspects of these varieties are based on sources such as the Linguistic Survey of Scotland (LLS, published in Mather and Speitel 1975, 1977, 1986). However, this survey was carried out largely in the 1950s, using predominantly elderly, rural informants; speakers from the towns of Kirkwall and Lerwick were not included. Johnston (1997), incorporating data from the LSS as well as from other sources, provides the most complete study to date of Insular Scots, as the two dialects are collectively known. In addition, it is noteworthy that nearly all relevant research dealing with the dialects of the Northern Isles focuses on Shetland, while Orkney is either discussed briskly or ignored altogether.

A detailed linguistic description of present-day Orkney and Shetland dialects falls outside the scope of the present chapter. What follows is a brief survey of some of the general characteristics of the local vernaculars, some of which might be attributed to Norn; the list does not aim to be exhaustive. Only features peculiar to Orkney and Shetland are mentioned here, a general description of Scots/Scottish Standard English is provided in Chapter 7, of this volume. Note that certain of the features listed below also occur in Caithness speech – a reflection of the fact that Norn was formerly also spoken in the coastal areas of Caithness.

Phonology and Phonetics

Orkney and Shetland dialects both preserve conservative Scots vowel inventories, even though lexical incidence is often radically different from mainland Scots dialects, and even varies considerably within the islands themselves. For example, in words like *find* [ɪ], *take* [a], *meat* [e] 'food' and *good* [ø] the Older Scots vowels have been retained, while in other cases vowels might, just as in certain mainland Scots varieties, be raised, diphthongized or fronted, as in *table* [i], *red* [i], fish [ɛi] and *part* [ɛ]. The front rounded /ø/ also occurs in Norn loans as *buil* (Sh) 'resting place for animals, nest', *böd* (Sh) 'a small house in which fishing tackle is kept', as well as in place-names, for example, *Ouse* (a small bay in Shapinsay, Orkney).

Although the vowels are certainly of considerable interest, the main evidence of Norn substratal influences is probably to be discovered in the consonants of the islands.

The use of [d] and [t] for /ð/ and /θ /, for example, *den* 'then', *tree* 'three' and *eart* 'earth', is generally thought to be due to the loss of these fricatives in Norn (Barnes 1998). This so-called TH stopping (Wells 1982) is still a general feature of Shetland speech, but has largely been reversed in Orkney, and the feature is now heard only in the speech of elderly, rural speakers. However, TH stopping seems to be creeping into the Standard English spoken by Shetland-born teenagers with English or mainland Scots parents (Cluness 2000; Scobbie 2006).

In both Orkney and Shetland dialects, initial /p t k/ have little or no aspiration, while initial /b d g/ are fully voiced. In Orkney, realization of non-initial /t/ as a glottal stop [ˀ] (/t/-glottalling), as in *better* [bɛˀər] and *but* [bʌˀ], has recently become widespread, while in Shetland this is predominantly a feature of Lerwick speech.

The voiced affricate /ʤ/ is typically devoiced to [ʧ], hence, *jar* and *just* become [ʧar] and [ʧʌst]; the occurrence of this devoicing decreases in more formal speech. Elderly speakers generally realize [ʧ] as [ʃ], so, *chair* is pronounced as *share*, while *chip* and *ship* become homophones [ʃɪp]. In addition, these speakers may have [ʧ] for /k/, giving [ʧɛtl] for *kettle*.

It is worth noting that with respect to consonant realization there seem to be dissimilarities between the two island groups, with Shetland pronunciation retaining a number of features that might be attributable to a Scandinavian substratum, while Orkney dialect seems to have lost many of these. In conservative Shetland speech, for example, initial /k/ and /g/ are palatalized, as in *kemp* [kjɛmp] 'to fight' and *gaan* [gja:n] 'going'. Furthermore, the initial consonant cluster /kn/ in *knee* and *knob* is retained, although pronounced with epenthetic schwa [kᵊni:]; this usage is now recessive. In most varieties of Shetland speech, we also find palatalization of post-vocalic alveolar consonants. As is typically the case with palatal consonants, this has the effect of raising the preceding vowel, and producing a palatal offglide, giving a diphthongal impression as can be heard in a local 'catch phrase' frequently employed to illustrate dialect features *ten men in the bed* [tɛⁱn mɛⁱn ɪn də bɛⁱd] and also in *later on* [ɔⁱn]. The feature is particularly noticeable in the pronunciation of speakers from Burra (south-west Shetland) and is somewhat stigmatized. According to Catford (1957b), palatalization of this type is not reported in mainland Scotland, but is, on the other hand, found in certain Norwegian dialects.

Furthermore, in Shetland, older speakers often do not distinguish between initial 'wh' and 'qu', with *white* and *quite* both pronounced as *white* in the south, but as *quite* in some western and central areas, a pattern which seems to reflect a split of Old Norse initial [hw] and [xw] in Shetland Norn (Barnes 1984). On Whalsay, and also in Lerwick and north Mainland, we find a crossover pattern resulting in realizations of *quite* for *white* and vice versa, and with *Whalsay* pronounced as [kwɑlsa:].

A further difference between the two varieties is heard in the typical realizations of /l/, with Shetland speakers producing word-initial /l/ with strikingly darker realizations than those found in Orkney speech. In intervocalic and final position, Shetland /l/ tends to vary, with some speakers having dark-ɫ in all contexts, while Orkney /l/ is generally clear in these positions. Note that clear-l is also a feature of Highland English and Gaelic, while dark-ɫ is commonly found in Lowland Scots varieties. In both Orkney and Shetland, /l/ is often dropped in certain words with open back vowels, for example, in *ba'* 'ball' [ba:], *fa'* 'fall' [fa:] and *wa'* 'wall' [wa:]. Historical loss of /l/, by a process known as l-vocalization, is a feature common to all Scottish dialects.

Finally, in Orkney speech, especially on Mainland (the largest of the Orkney Isles), word-final <–rse> is generally realized as [ɹʃ] as in, for example, *worse* [wʌɹʃ], *horse* [hɔɹʃ] and *nurse* [nʌɹʃ]; this feature seems to be unaffected by age or stylistic variation (Norquay 2003). This pronunciation is not found in Shetland; it does, however, occur in some varieties of Caithness speech.

Prosody

In Shetland dialect, the Norn substratum seems to be reflected in the syllable structure, with closed monosyllables generally containing either a phonetically short vowel followed by a phonetically long consonant or a long vowel followed by a short consonant; cf. Norwegian *tak* [ta:k] 'roof, ceiling' versus *takk* [tak:] 'thanks'. This feature of Shetland speech was first reported by Catford (1957b) and investigated experimentally by van Leyden (2002); in Orkney dialect, this particular relic of Norn has apparently been lost, most likely because of the strong influence of mainland Scots dialects (van Leyden 2002).

The most striking difference between Orkney and Shetland speech is the dissimilarity in intonation. Orkney dialect is characterized by very distinctive, 'lilting' patterns while Shetland speech has a somewhat level intonation. This difference seems to be accounted for by the location of the pitch peak relative to the stressed syllable with which it is associated. Shetland has a pitch-rise early in the stressed syllable, a pattern that is typical of the intonation of the vast majority of mother-tongue English speakers (including those of eastern Scotland) and many other languages. The rise in Orkney occurs much later, with the result that in disyllabic words with initial stress the pitch peak fails to coincide with the stressed syllable, but is delayed until the post-stress syllable (van Leyden 2004). Such a pattern is also found in certain Scandinavian varieties, as well as in Celtic languages, such as Welsh, Irish and possibly also Scots Gaelic. At this stage, however, it is unclear whether peak delay originated in the Celtic languages spoken in northern Scotland or whether the feature should be attributed to the Scandinavian substratum of Orkney dialect.

Syntax and Morphology

A friend, or someone younger, is addressed with familiar T-form, friendly *du* (Sh) or *thoo* (O); the respectful V-form *you* is used to parents, older people or strangers. The T/V pronoun system is still in common use in Shetland, whereas in Orkney it seems to be dying out, and is now only found among elderly people in Westray. Note that *du*, like the corresponding English form *thou*, is second person singular. The T/V pronoun system is of course by no means unique to the Northern Isles; until recently it was also found in mainland Scotland, as well as in Northern England and the South-West of England.

Gender-marked pronouns are used for weather and time, for example, *He lowsed wi da rain* (Sh) 'It began to rain heavily'; cf. *Han regner* in north-west Norwegian dialects (Standard Norwegian as well as Danish have *Det regner* 'it rains'). In Orkney, this usage seems to be on the way out.

The auxiliary *be* rather than *have* is used to form the perfect tense as in *I'm seen him* and *I'm bought biscuits.* The origin of this construction of *be* with transitive verbs is unclear. Owing to the lack of written evidence, we do not know whether this feature also occurred in Norn. Yet, since the construction is also found in Central Scotland (Trudgill and Hannah 1982), it might have been introduced to Orkney and Shetland by immigrants from this area (Melchers 1992; Pavlenko 1997). The Older Scots distinction of present participle *–an* and verbal noun *–in* is maintained in both Orkney and Shetland, for example, *I'm doan me cleanin,* a feature which is also found in other peripheral Lowland Scots dialects, such as Caithness and Dumfriesshire. As in Scots, some of the verbs that have remained strong in Standard English have become weak, like *catch – catched, tell – tel(l)t* and *sell – sel(l)t.* Certain archaic irregular past tense forms, such as *wrought* 'worked' and *clim – clam – clum* 'climb', are used as well.

Lexis

The vast majority of the words attributed to Norn as documented in Jakobsen's (1928–32) and Marwick's (1929) etymological dictionaries were directly bound to the traditional way of life in the Isles. As a result of the far-reaching modernization that has since taken place in the farming and fishing industries, many of these words are now rapidly disappearing from the language. Despite the large-scale loss of Norn elements from these semantic fields, however, there are still quite a number of Norn-derived words in daily use in the Isles, especially in Shetland.

Some Norn loan words still found today are: *arvi* (Sh) or *arvo* (O) 'chickweed' (ON *arfi*); *flukra* (Sh) 'snow falling in large flakes' (cf. Faer. *flykra*, snowflake); *grimlins* (O) 'twilight, first or last gleams of daylight' (deriv. of Norw. dial. *grimla* 'to glimmer, twinkle'); *guddick* 'riddle' (ON *gáta* with suffix *(i)ck*); *haaf* 'The deep or open sea as opposed to coastal waters, deep-sea fishing, especially for cod, ling, etc.' (ON *haf*, Norw. *hav*); *moorit* 'reddish yellow-brown', especially of wool (ON *mórauðr*); *piltock* 'young coalfish' (diminutive of ON *pilt* 'young boy'); *puggie, bogy* (O) 'belly, the intestines' (ON *búkr*); *skoit* (Sh) 'to cast an inquiring look' (ON *skoða*); *sk(y)imp* (Sh) 'to mock' (cf. Icel. *skimp*); *smero* (O) *smora* (Sh) 'clover' (cf. Norw. dial. *smæra*; Icel. *smári*); *uim* (O) 'mad, furious', said of animals (ON *ólmr*); and *voar* 'the spring of the year' (ON *vár*, Norw. *vår*).

Almost all birds commonly found in Orkney and Shetland are still known by their Norn names, for example, *bunxie* 'great skua' (deriv. of ON *bunki* 'heap', cf. Norw. *bunke* 'heap, corpulent woman'); *shalder* 'oystercatcher' (ON *tjaldr*, Faer. *tjaldur*); and *tystie* 'black guillemot' (ON *þeisti*).

The word *peerie* (Sh) or *peedie* (O; *peedie* is a recent development of *peerie* 'little' or 'small' often employed as a kind of positive shibboleth to emphasize Orkney or Shetland loyalty. This item is of uncertain origin (Grant and Murison 1931–76), but is usually connected with Norwegian *piren* (Norw. dial. 'niggardly, sickly, feeble, thin').

Recent Developments and Outlook

In recent years, the Shetland dialect in particular has undergone a revival of interest. In 2004, a Shetland dialect conference was held to discuss the state of the local tongue and ways to promote its future. The dialect's prestige is also helped with the growth of a strong dialect literature of which Haldane Burgess, Vagaland (T. A. Robertson), Rhoda Bulter and Christine de Luca are the most well-known exponents. There is no similar development in Orkney, where local authors generally write in English, rather than the local vernacular.

The second stanza of *Röd an Bled* by Rhoda Bulter (1986: 8) provides an example of Shetland dialect literature:

(2) Jöst a laar a wind is blaain,
Gently straikin mödoo flooers,
While peerie birds no geen ta baak yit,
Mak da maist a daylight ooers
A snippik cries oot ower da Hamars,
An da kyunnin ventirs furt ta dine;
Dir twartree things no muckle altered
Fae first I stöd here lang sin syne.

(Glossary: *jöst* 'just'; *laar a wind* 'gentle breeze'; *blaain* 'blowing'; *mödoo* 'meadow'; *flooers* 'flowers'; *peerie* 'small'; *geen* 'gone'; *baak* 'perch'; *ooers* 'hours'; *snippik* 'snipe'; *kyunnin* 'rabbit'; *ventirs* 'ventures'; *furt* 'outside'; *muckle* 'much'; *stöd* 'stood'; *lang sin syne* 'long ago'.)

In both Orkney and Shetland, the use of dialect in schools is actively encouraged – this is in strong contrast to the situation prevailing until the 1970s. Popular dialect dictionaries are readily available (Flaws and Lamb (2001) for Orkney and Graham (1999) for Shetland) and the dialect can also be heard on the local radio.

In conclusion, one can say that the future of the dialects is at best uncertain. Despite the encouraging level of support (especially as far as Shetland is concerned), the influence of the media, and the recent influx of incomers, mean that increasingly the day-to-day use of the dialect is confined to the over-30s. Whether it can survive among the younger generation is questionable in the extreme.

Bibliography

Barnes, M. P. (1984), 'Orkney and Shetland Norn', in P. Trudgill (ed.), *Language in the British Isles*, Cambridge: Cambridge University Press, pp. 352–66.

—. (1996), 'The origin, development and decline of Orkney and Shetland Norn', in H. F. Nielsen and L. Schøsler (eds), *The Origins and Development of Emigrant Languages* (RASK supplement 6, NOWELE supplement 17), pp. 169–99, Odense: Odense University Press.

—. (1998), *The Norn Language of Orkney and Shetland*, Lerwick: The Shetland Times.

Bulter, R. (1986), *Snyivveries. Shetland Poems*, Lerwick: The Shetland Times.

Catford, J. C. (1957a), 'Vowel systems of Scots dialects', *Transactions of the PhilologicalSociety*, pp. 107–17.

—. (1957b), 'Shetland dialect', *Shetland Folkbook*, Vol. 3, pp. 71–6.

Cluness, M. A. (2000), 'An investigation into the parental influence on dialect acquisition', Unpublished Honours Project, Queen Margaret University College, Edinburgh.

Flaws, M. and G. Lamb (2001), *The Orkney Dictionary*, 2nd edn, Kirkwall: The Orkney Language and Culture Group.

General Register Office for Scotland (2001), *Census 2001 Scotland*, retrieved 2006 from http://scrol.gov.uk/scrol/common/home.jsp.

Graham, J. J. (1999), *The Shetland Dictionary*, Lerwick: The Shetland Times.

Grant, W. and D. D. Murison (eds) (1931–76), *The Scottish National Dictionary*, Aberdeen: Aberdeen University Press.

Hægstad, M. (1900), *Hildinakvadet* (Vidensbabsselskabets Skrifter. II. Historisk-filosofiske Klasse. 1900. No. 2), Christiana.

Jakobsen, J. (1928–32), *An Etymological Dictionary of the Norn Language in Shetland*, 2 vols, London/Copenhagen: David Nutt/Vilhelm Prior. (Reprinted 1985, Lerwick: Shetland Folk Society.)

Johnston, P. (1997), 'Regional variation', in C. Jones (ed.), *The Edinburgh History of the Scots Language*, pp. 433–513, Edinburgh: Edinburgh University Press.

von Leyden, K. (2002), 'The relationship between vowel and consonant duration in Orkney and Shetland dialects', *Phonetica*, 59, 1–19.

—. (2004), *Prosodic Characteristics of Orkney and Shetland Dialects. An Experimental Approach*, Doctoral Dissertation, Leiden University (LOT Dissertation Series 92, Utrecht: LOT).

Low, G. (1879), *A Tour through the Islands of Orkney and Schetland*, Kirkwall: William Peace.

Marwick, H. (1929), *The Orkney Norn*, London: Oxford University Press.

Mather, J. Y. and H. H. Speitel (1975, 1977, 1986), *The Linguistic Atlas of Scotland*, Vols I–III, London: Croom Helm.

McClure, J. D. (1994), 'English in Scotland', in R. Burchfield (ed.), *The Cambridge History of the English Language*, Vol. V, pp. 23–103, Cambridge: Cambridge University Press.

Melchers, G. (1992), '"Du's no heard da last o'dis"– on the use of *be* as a perfective auxiliary in Shetland dialect', in M. Riisanen (ed.), *History of Englishes: New Methods and Interpretations in Historical Linguistics*, pp. 602–10, Berlin: Mouton de Gruyter.

Norquay, T. (2003), 'Is the consonant system of Orcadian changing? An apparent-time group study', Unpublished Honours Project, Queen Margaret University College, Edinburgh.

Pálsson, H. and P. Edwards (1978), Orkney. *Orkneyinga Saga: The History of the Earls of London*, Hogarth Press.

Pavlenko, A. (1997), 'The origin of the be-perfect with transitives in the Shetland dialect', *Scottish Language*, 16, 88–96.

Rendboe, L. (1987), *Det Gamle Shetlandse Sprog* (*NOWELE* Supplement Vol. 3), Odense Universitetsforlag.

—. (1989–90), The Lord's prayer in Orkney and Shetland Norn 1–2, *NOWELE* 14, 77–112; 15; 49–111.

Scobbie, J. M. (2006, forthcoming), Flexibility in the face of incompatible English VOT systems, in L. Goldstein, D. Whalen, and C. T. Best (eds), *Laboratory Phonology VIII*, Berlin: Mouton de Gruyter.

Smith, B. (1996), The development of the spoken and written Shetland dialect: a historians view, in D. J. Waugh (ed.), *Shetland's Northern Links: Language and History*, pp. 30–43, Edinburgh: Scottish Society for Northern Studies.

Trudgill, P. and J. Hannah (1982), *International English*, London: Edward Arnold.

Wallace, J. (1700), *An Account of the Islands of Orkney*, London: Jacob Tonson.

Wells, J. C. (1982), *Accents of English*, Vols I–III, Cambridge: Cambridge University Press.

Channel Islands

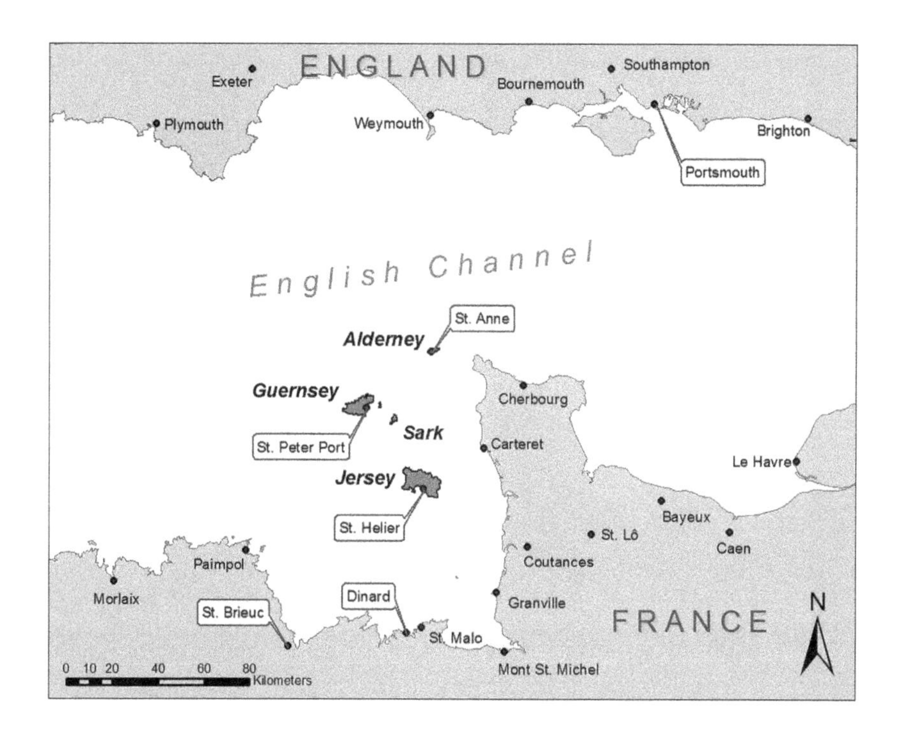

Chapter 13

English in the Channel Islands

Heinrich Ramisch

Geographical Setting

The Channel Islands (Jersey, Guernsey, Alderney and Sark) lie off the northwestern coast of France, west of the Cotentin peninsula. A brief look at the map (see p. 311, this volume) shows that from a geographical point of view, they are much closer to France than to England. Alderney is just 9 miles away from Cap de la Hague in France, while Jersey is only about 15 miles from the French coast but 90 miles south of England. As the original language in these islands is a form of Norman French, they have traditionally been regarded in dialectology as a French-speaking area.[1] Yet the exclusive interest of traditional dialectology in Channel Islands French is no adequate reflection of the current linguistic situation. Today, English clearly is the dominant language in the Channel Islands. The number of speakers of Norman French is relatively small and constantly decreasing. Over the last 200 years, English has gained more and more influence and has gradually replaced the local Norman French dialects. Indeed, there are clear indications that they will become extinct within the foreseeable future.[2]

Political Setting

From a political point of view, the islands have been connected with England for a long time.[3] Originally, the islands were part of the Duchy of Normandy, but after the Battle of Hastings in 1066, Duke William II of Normandy (William the Conqueror) also became King of England, and the Duchy of Normandy was united with England under one ruler. Thus, 1066 is the date that first associates the Channel Islands with England and the English Crown, and this association has existed ever since.[4]

The exceptional political situation of the Channel Islands really arose after the year 1204, when King John (Lackland) lost all his territories on the Continent to King Philippe Auguste of France, but the Channel Islands were *not* conquered by the French. As a result, they became the only part of the former Duchy of Normandy to remain in the possession of the English king, who continued to reign in the islands in his function as Duke of Normandy.

After the separation of the Channel Islands from the Norman mainland, their political links with England at first had no far-reaching consequences (cf. Guillot 1975: 31–2; Le Patourel 1937: 35). The native inhabitants, their culture and their language were Norman, keeping them in close contact with their neighbours on the Norman mainland. At a time when distances played a far greater role than today, trade with the outside world mainly took place with Normandy. On the whole, it seems that English influence in the Channel Islands during the Middle Ages was rather limited. However, the situation began to change towards the late eighteenth and early nineteenth centuries, when larger military units from England were brought to the islands to defend them against the French. It was above all the tradespeople and the inhabitants of the capital towns St. Helier (in Jersey) and St. Peter Port (in Guernsey) who first came into contact with English through the medium of soldiers stationed in the area. Furthermore, English merchants had also settled in these towns, which had developed into international trade centres.

But during the first half of the nineteenth century the Channel Islands were still largely French-speaking. There is an interesting comment from the 1830s by an Englishman called Henry Inglis. Writing in a guidebook, he comments:

> . . . there are certain points of interest attached to the Channel Islands, peculiarly their own . . . their native civilized inhabitants, their vicinity to the coast of France, and the general use of the French language. (Inglis 1844: 2)

Talking about Jersey, he makes clear what he means by 'French language':

> The universal language is still a barbarous dialect. (Inglis 1844: 72)

But Inglis also reports on the beginnings of a process of anglicization:

> Children are now universally taught English; and amongst the young, there is an evident preference of English. The constant intercourse of the tradespeople with the English residents; and the considerable sprinkling of English residents in Jersey society, have also their effect. (Inglis 1844: 73)

English Usage in the Islands

English influence really started to grow after the Napoleonic wars (1815), when a larger number of English immigrants came to live in the Channel Islands. And immigration from Britain continued throughout the nineteenth century. The census figures of 1891 (Census 1891: 4) reveal, for instance, that 5,844 people (or 15.49 per cent) of the inhabitants of Guernsey were immigrants from England, Wales, Scotland or Ireland. At the same time, immigration from France had been rather low, comprising only 2.92 per cent of the total population. Other factors that contributed to an increased influence of English are to be seen in the growing trade relations with England, the emergence of tourism, and improvements in communication and traffic links. For example, the introduction of steamboats played an important role. From 1824 onwards a regular service between England and the islands was established, which offered new opportunities for commerce and made it much more convenient for British tourists to visit the islands (cf. Tupper 1876: 403). Towards the end of the nineteenth century a historian comments:

> During the present century the English language has both in Guernsey and Jersey, made vast strides, so that it is difficult now to find a native even in the country parishes who cannot converse fairly well in that tongue. (Nicolle 1893: 387)

The influence of English continued to rise during the twentieth century. The mass media, such as radio and television, brought English into practically every home. Tourism greatly increased and became a major industry. Moreover, immigration from Britain has remained remarkably high. The 2001 census figures show that 33.5 per cent of the resident population of Jersey (total: 87,186) were born in the United Kingdom and 2.3 per cent in the Republic of Ireland. In Guernsey 27.4 per cent of the population (total: 59,807) originally came from the United Kingdom and 0.7 per cent from Ireland.

The decline of the Norman French dialects has rapidly progressed over the last 100 years and it seems certain that they will not survive as a living language. In Alderney, Norman French has already disappeared. The results of the 2001 census, see Table 13.1 below, show that only 3.3 per cent (2,874 people) of the population in Jersey still claim to be active speakers of Jersey French (cf. Table 13.1). About two-thirds of these speakers are in fact aged 60 and above. In Guernsey 1,327 people (2.2 per cent of the total population) stated that they 'speak Guernsey French fluently'. But most of them (934 or 70.4 per cent) are 65 or older. As for Sark (total population: 550) local estimates assume that 50 people still speak Sark French.

All present speakers of Norman French are bilingual, that is, they are also speakers of English. They are local people who live mainly in the rural areas,

Table 13.1 Languages spoken in Jersey (Census of Jersey 2001: 23)

	Main language	Secondary language	Total number of speakers	Percentage of population
English	82,349	3,443	85,792	98.4
Jersey French	113	2,761	2,874	3.3
Portuguese	4,002	3,303	7,305	8.4
French	338	14,776	15,114	17.3
Other languages	384	4,496	4,880	5.6

where they typically work as farmers, growers, fishermen or simple craftsmen. Moreover, the use of the Norman French dialect is limited to family members, friends and neighbours whom the speaker knows are able to understand the language. It is particularly in the case of older couples where both husband and wife are dialect speakers that Norman French is still the daily language at home.

Linguistic Features of Channel Island English

The second part of this chapter takes a closer look at the linguistic variation of English in the Channel Islands.[5] First, due to the language contact between English and the local Norman French dialects, there are features in English which can be attributed to an influence from Norman French. Following Clyne (1975), these features may be called *transference phenomena*. On the morphosyntactic level, for instance, one can notice that the objective forms of the personal pronouns (*me, you,* etc.) occur at the end of a sentence for emphatic purposes.

- *I went to prison for the Germans, me – for a month.*
- *There was a few [crystal sets]. My brother-in-law had one. But we didn't have any, us.*

Syntactic structures like these are obviously based on a parallel structure in Norman French where the personal pronouns [mɛ], [tɛ], etc. are also used for emphatic purposes in sentence-final position.

Another transference is the use of the definite article in certain contexts, for example, in connection with names of languages:

- *Well, my father knew the good French and the English and the patois.*

In this case, the entire phrase '*the good French*' is indeed a literal translation from [lə bwõ frãse] ('le bon français'). Similarly, the expression *But yes* used as an emphatic form of consent (cf. 'Yes, of course' in St.E.) obviously is a direct translation of [me wi] ('mais oui'). It is particularly noteworthy that transference phenomena may occur not only with speakers of Norman French but also with (younger) people who are monolingual speakers of English. Consequently, features of this type are not just transitional phenomena in the process of acquiring English. Some of the features have become an integral part of the local language variety and continue to exist even if the speakers themselves are no longer bilingual.

Secondly, Channel Island English includes general non-standard features that occur in numerous other varieties of British English.[6] For example, one encounters instances of multiple negation:

- *I can't say nothing about Alderney, I've only been there once.*

Or after a numeral, nouns of measurement such as *pound* or *year* are not marked for plurality:

- *You get 14 pound a month.*
- *two year ago.*

On the phonological level one can notice that the ending *-ing* may be realized with an alveolar nasal [ɪn], as in *fishing* or *living*. Other features are more recent and can be found especially in the speech of younger people in St. Helier (Jersey) and St. Peter Port (Guernsey), for example, T-glottalization (the glottalling of intervocalic and word-final [t]) or TH-fronting (the use of [f] and [v] instead of [θ] and [ð]). There is no evidence that transference from Norman French has ever played a role in any of these cases. One can assume that these general non-standard features have arrived in the islands as a result of the close connections with Britain and because of the many British immigrants.

Thirdly, Channel Island English may be characterized – at least theoretically – by independent developments with no influence from either Norman French or other varieties of English.

Table 13.2 below lists the typical vowel realizations in Channel Island English. One prominent feature is discussed here in more detail, namely the realization of RP /aɪ/.[7] In Channel Island English, the starting point of the diphthong /aɪ/ tends to be further back than in RP. Words such as *fight* or *buy* are pronounced [fɑɪt] and [bɑɪ]. Additionally, the first element of the glide may be rounded, resulting in [fɒɪt] and [bɒɪ]. The realization of /aɪ/ as [ɑɪ] or [ɒɪ] is certainly not restricted to the Channel Islands, but commonly found in many other accents of English. It is particularly typical of the Cockney accent (London) and of urban areas in the south of England in general (cf. Wells 1982: 149, 308). Certain varieties of Irish English equally have [ɑɪ] or [ɒɪ] in place of /aɪ/, which has led to the stereotype view in the United States that

Table 13.2 Vowel realizations in Channel Island English – summary

KIT	ɪ ~ ɪ̈	FLEECE	iː ~ ɪi	NEAR	ɪə ~ iə
DRESS	ɛ ~ ɛ̈	FACE	eɪ ~ e̞ɪ	SQUARE	ɛə
TRAP	æ	PALM	ɑː ~ ɑ̹ː	START	ɑː ~ ɑ̹ː
LOT	ɒ ~ ɒ̈	THOUGHT	ɔː ~ oː	NORTH	ɔː ~ oː
STRUT	ɔ ~ ʌ	GOAT	ɔʊ ~ əʊ	FORCE	ɔː ~ oː
FOOT	ʊ	GOAL	ɔʊ ~ əʊ	CURE	jʊə
BATH	ɑː ~ ɑ̟ː	GOOSE	uː ~ ʉː	happY	i ~ iː
CLOTH	ɒ ~ ɒ̈	PRICE	ɒɪ ~ ɑɪ ~ aɪ	lettER	œ ~ ə
NURSE	ɜː ~ əː	CHOICE	ɔɪ ~ oɪ	horsES	ɪ ~ ɪ̈
		MOUTH	aʊ	commA	ə

speakers of Irish English pronounce *nice time* as 'noice toime' (cf. Wells 1982: 425–6).

The question of whether the variable pronunciation of /aɪ/ in the Channel Islands may also be due to the influence of Norman French cannot be resolved conclusively. It cannot be a case of phone substitution, since the diphthong [aɪ] does exist in Channel Island French. But it is noteworthy that the diphthong [ɑɪ] is a typical and frequently occurring sound in the local French dialects. Verbs which end in *-er* in St.F. have the diphthong [ɑɪ] in the same position in Guernsey French, for example: [dunɑɪ] (St.F. *donner*). Similarly, the ending [ɑɪ] is used in the second person plural of the present tense [vu dunɑɪ] (St.F. *vous donnez*), in the imperative plural [dunɑɪ] (St.F. *donnez!*) and in the past participle forms of verbs [dunɑɪ] (St.F. *donné*).

Table 13.3 below presents the results for /aɪ/ among 40 informants in Guernsey, divided into 4 different groups: MO = older (60+), male informants and speakers of Guernsey French; FO = older (60+), female informants and speakers of Guernsey French; MY = younger (19–32), male informants and monolingual speakers of English; FY = younger (19–32), female informants and monolingual speakers of English. The feature occurred most frequently with group MO. In slightly more than a third of all cases /aɪ/ was realized as [ɑɪ] or [ɒɪ]. The feature was quite common with the younger men (group MY) as well. Their percentage value is still above that of group FO. The younger women (group FY) clearly came closest to the standard in their pronunciation of /aɪ/.

As for consonants, two features will be discussed here, namely non-prevocalic /r/ and H-dropping. Channel Island English is variably rhotic, but only to a lesser degree. Thus, non-prevocalic /r/ may be pronounced in preconsonantal (e.g. *farm*) or in absolute final positions (eg. *far*). The typical local realization is a retroflex approximant, for example, [fɑɻm], [fɑɻ]. The pronunciation of non-prevocalic /r/ in accents of British English is of a complex nature, involving both regional and social factors. In the traditional rural accents of England, three areas can generally be described as still preserving non-prevocalic /r/: Northumberland, Lancashire and a larger area in the south-west, ranging from Kent to Cornwall in the west and to Shropshire in the West Midlands (cf. Upton and Widdowson 1996: 30–1). In recent times, the rhotic areas have definitely become

Table 13.3 Realization of the diphthong /aɪ/ as [ɑɪ] or [ɒɪ] in Guernsey

Informant group	Percentages
MO	35.8
FO	21.0
MY	27.1
FY	12.2

smaller. Non-prevocalic /r/ is still present in parts of Lancashire such as Blackburn and Burnley, and in the southwest of England including Cornwall, Devon, Somerset, Dorset, Gloucester, Hereford and Wiltshire (cf. Trudgill 1999: 53–6).

The realization of non-prevocalic /r/ in the Channel Islands can certainly be attributed to an influence from other varieties of English. But on the other hand, an influence from Channel Island French seems equally possible. Speakers of the Norman French dialects are accustomed to pronouncing [r] (normally an apical type of *r*, pronounced with different degrees of vibration) both in preconsonantal (e.g. [parti], St.F. *parti*) and in absolute-final position (e.g. [vɛr] St.F. *vert*). Moreover, it is reasonable to assume that Norman French speakers of earlier periods who learnt English only at school tended to realize non-prevocalic /r/ under the influence of English orthography; in other words, their pronunciation of non-prevocalic /r/ would be based on a spelling pronunciation.

A clear indication that the realization of non-prevocalic /r/ is indeed influenced by Norman French becomes apparent in the ending *-er* in Guernsey English, which can be pronounced as [œr] (cf. Table 13.2). Thus, the pronunciation of words such as *better* or *youngster* is ['betœr] and ['jʌŋstœr]. There is evidently an influence from Norman French here, the same ending [œr] also being used in Guernesey French as in [lə pɔrtœr] (St.F. *le porteur*). Another argument for the English ending *-er* being identified with the ending [œr] in Guernsey French is based on the fact that the latter is also found in English loanwords used in Guernsey French. In this way, the English words *shutter* and *mourner* have become [lə ʃɔtœr] and [lə mɔrnœr] in Guernsey French (cf. Tomlinson 1981: 265, 325). The realization of non-prevocalic /r/ was not very widespread among the 40 informants in Guernsey. The feature was mostly found in group MO at a rate of 9.2 per cent. With the younger informants, it occurred only very occasionally, and solely in group MY. One can conclude, therefore, that the pronunciation of non-prevocalic /r/ is becoming increasingly rare in the Channel Islands.

H-dropping or the non-realization of /h/ in initial position in stressed syllables before vowels (e.g. in *happy* ['æpi] or *hedge* [edʒ]) is one of the best-known non-standard features in British English. It has achieved a high level of public awareness, is clearly stigmatized and commonly regarded as uneducated. For Wells (1982: 254) H-dropping is even 'the single most powerful pronunciation shibboleth in England'. Its presence in Channel Island English is hardly surprising. Moreover, there are individual items in which the initial position of /h/ is filled by a semivowel [j], for example, in *hear* [jɪə(ɹ)] or *head* [jɛd], parallels of which can also be found in English dialects (cf. SED VI.4.2 'hear', VI.1.1 'head'). It is an intriguing question to ask whether there can also be an influence from Channel Island French on H-dropping.

Nearly all varieties of French, including Standard French, do not realize initial /h/. But the Norman French dialects of the Channel Islands belong to the few varieties of French that have indeed preserved initial Germanic /h/, as in [haʃ] (St.F. *hache* 'axe') or [humar] (St.F. *homard* 'lobster'). Consequently, initial /h/ is a familiar sound for speakers of Norman French and should not lead to H-dropping in English. But, on the other hand, it has to be pointed out that the realization of initial /h/ in Channel Island French is by no means categorical but variable. Individual speakers may vary considerably in their use of initial /h/ and it appears likely that this variability as such has some effect on H-dropping in English.

Furthermore, Channel Island English is characterized by features on the suprasegemental level (stress, intonation) which sound 'foreign' and which are either caused by an influence from Norman French or can at least be explained originally in terms of non-natives using English. Such features are more common with older people who are still regular speakers of Norman French. One may come across unusual stress patterns, for example, in *Guernseyman* ['gɜːnzi'mæn], *educated* [ˌedju'keɪtɪd] or *grandfather* [ˌgrænd'fɑːðə]. Alternatively, the difference between stressed and unstressed syllables may be less marked with the use of secondary stresses on normally unstressed syllables as in *potatoes* ['pɔˌteɪˌtəʊz], *tomatoes* ['tɔˌmaˌtəʊz], *English* ['ɪŋˌglɪʃ].

On the syntactic level, the particle *eh* is frequently employed as a tag in Channel Island English. *Eh* is usually realized as a diphthong [eɪ], but it can also be pronounced as a short [e]. From a functional point of view, *eh* induces the hearer to express his opinion on what is said by the speaker.

- *There was no television eh, we had no electric anyway eh – yes a gramophone eh.*
- *The Red Arrows – you've heard of them, eh?*

Eh has indeed become a stereotype. Channel Islanders refer to it when they are asked about typical features of their own variety of English. Although *eh* generally occurs in present-day English (cf. e.g. Quirk et al. 1985: 814), the question is why *eh* occurs with such a high frequency in the Channel Islands. A transference from Norman French immediately suggests itself, because *eh* is equally common in the local French dialects and is also used as a tag as in English.

Another interesting feature is the syntactic structure *there is* or *there was* + plural subject, which is frequently employed in Channel Island English (cf. Ramisch 1989: 92–103):

- *There's no cars in Sark at all, you got the horse carriage, you know.*
- *There was two kinds of milk.*

The construction *there is* + plural subject is common in many varieties of English and characterized by Quirk et al. (1985: 1405) as 'informal'. Therefore, it is only natural that it occurs in the Channel Islands as well. But there are indications which suggest that a transference from Norman French may have contributed to the frequent use of *there is* + plural subject. One finds examples in which *there is* occurs in combination with a time reference, something which constitutes a clear parallel to a construction with [ja] in Norman French *(il y a* in Standard French):

- *I don't smoke now. . . . There's four years I don't smoke.*
  (cf. Norman French: [ja katr ã kə ʒən fym pɑ]
  ('Il y a quatre ans que je ne fume pas.')

- . . . *after the Norman conquest, there's nearly a thousand years we are British – we are not English we are British.*
  (cf. Norman French: [ja kazi ɛ̃ mil ã kə nuze õgje]
  ('Il y a quasi un mille ans que nous sommes anglais.')

Syntactic structures like these are not found in Standard English and are obviously based on a transference. Moreover, it seems realistic to assume that the syntactic pattern with [ja] has generally exerted an influence on *there is* in English. It should be remembered that [ja] is a very common syntactic structure in Norman French, as is *il y a* in Standard French. Therefore, it appears likely that a frequent and familiar syntactic pattern such as [ja] is generally translated by *there is* in English. One should also note the formal parallels between [ja] and *there is.* [ja] is singular in form, and remains unchanged even if the following subject is plural. The same is true of *there is* in English. The syntactic structure *there was* + plural subject can likewise be explained by transference, the source of influence here being the past tense form [javɛ] (*il y avait*).

It follows that there are two good explanations for the frequent use of *there is/was* + plural subject. On the one hand, the feature may have been adopted from other varieties of British English; on the other hand, an influence from Norman French may have contributed to the high frequency of this feature.[8]

In summary, Channel Island English is a variety that is characterized by a unique blend of features originating from different sources. On the one hand, one encounters non-standard features of British English that have arrived in the Channel Islands as a result of the close connections with Britain and because of the many British immigrants. This influence has existed for a long time and continues to be effective today. Yet on the other hand, Channel Island English comprises features that have their origin in Channel Island French. It is of particular relevance that they occur not only with speakers of Norman French but also with (younger) people who are monolingual speakers of English.

But our discussion of various features has shown that in quite a number of cases the analysis is rather more complex because both a Norman French influence and an influence from other varieties of English seem plausible. If there is more than one explanation for a particular feature, then they should not necessarily be regarded as mutually exclusive; rather, it is reasonable to assume that there is a convergence of different sources of influence, reinforcing and complementing each other.

Notes

[1] The Channel Islands are included in J. Gilliéron and E. Edmont's *Atlas Linguistique de la France* (1902ff), and also in the regional dialect atlas for Normandy, *Atlas Linguistique et Ethnographique Normand* by P. Brasseur (1980ff). The European project *Atlas Linguarum Europae* (ALE) likewise regards the Channel Islands as a French-speaking area only (cf. Alinei 1997:XLVIII).

[2] A more detailed account of the sociolinguistic situation in the Channel Islands and their linguistic history can be found in Ramisch (1989: 5–62). Cf. also Jones (2001), Tomlinson (1981: 3–20) and Viereck (1988).

[3] For the history of the Channel Islands cf. in particular Lemprière (1974), Guillot (1975: 24–55) and Syvret and Stevens (1998).

[4] These historical facts form the background of a longstanding joke. When asking local people whether they think that the Channel Islands belong to England, they will tell you that just the opposite is true. They will point out that after all they were on the winning side in the Battle of Hastings, and it was them who conquered England.

[5] For a detailed description of features to be found in Guernsey and Jersey English cf. in particular Ramisch (1989: 91ff), Barbé (1995) and Ramisch (1994, 2004).

[6] Cf., e.g. Hughes et. al. (2005: 24–33, 59–68).

[7] An earlier version of the phonological section of this article was also published in B. Kortmann and C. Upton (eds.), *Varieties of English. The British Isles.* Berlin, 2004 (Mouton de Gruyter), pp. 204–16. (This is the hardcover edition, the paperback edition is 2008 and pp. 223–36).

[8] There is a parallel case in the Gaelic-speaking area of Scotland where, according to Shuken (1984:155), sentences starting with *there is/was* are typical (e.g. *There's that many English people here now, it's English you talk mostly*). Shuken states that this particular syntactic structure is a transference from Gaelic. But here again one has to acknowledge that an influence from other, especially Scottish, varieties is also possible.

Bibliography

Alinei, M. (1997), *Atlas Linguarum Europae. Perspectives Nouvelles en Géolinguistique*, Roma: Istituto Poligrafico.

Barbé, P. (1995), 'Guernsey English: A Syntax Exile?', *English World-Wide,* 16, 1–36.

Brasseur, P. (1980ff.), *Atlas Linguistique et Ethnographique Normand,* Paris: Editions du CNRS.

Census. (1891), 'Census 1891. Islands in the British Seas. Isle of Man, Jersey, Guernsey and Adjacent Islands', London: Her Majesty's Stationery Office.

Census of Guernsey. (2001), '2001 Guernsey Census. Report on the Census of Population and Households', Guernsey: States of Guernsey.

Census of Jersey. (2001), 'Report on the 2001 Census', Jersey: States of Jersey.

Clyne, M. (1975), *Forschungsbericht Sprachkontakt*, Kronberg (Taunus): Scriptor Verlag.

Gilliéron, J. and Edmont, E. (1902ff.), *Atlas Linguistique de la France*, Paris: Honoré Champion.

Guillot, C. (1975), *Les Iles Anglo-Normandes*, Paris: Presses Universitaires de France.

Hughes, A., Trudgill, P. and Watt, D. (2005), *English Accents and Dialects*, 4th edn, London: Hodder Arnold.

Inglis, H. (1844), *The Channel Islands*, 4th edn, London: Whittaker & Co.

Jones, M. C. (2001), *Jersey Norman French: A Linguistic Study of an Obsolescent Dialect*, Oxford: Blackwell.

Lemprière, R. (1974), *History of the Channel Islands*, London: Robert Hale (reprinted with revisions 1980).

Le Patourel, J. (1937), *The Medieval Administration of the Channel Islands 1199–1399*, London: OUP.

Nicolle, E. T. (ed.) (1893), *The Channel Islands*, 3rd edn, in: D. T. Ansted and R. G. Latham (eds), London: Allen & Co.

Orton, H., et al. (1962–71), *Survey of English Dialects. The Basic Material*, Leeds: E. J. Arnold [SED].

Quirk, R., Greenbaum, S., Leech, G. and Svartvik, J. (1985), *A Comprehensive Grammar of the English Language*, London: Longman.

Ramisch, H. (1989), *The Variation of English in Guernsey/Channel Islands*, Frankfurt/Main: Lang.

—. (1994), 'English in Jersey', in W. Viereck (ed.), *Proceedings of the International Congress of Dialectologists* (Bamberg, 29.7. – 4.8.1990, Vol. 3), pp. 452–62, Stuttgart: Steiner.

—. (2004), 'Channel Island English: phonology', in B. Kortmann, E. Schneider, K. Burridge, R. Mesthrie, and C. Upton (eds), *A Handbook of Varieties of English. Vol. 1: Phonology*, pp. 204–16, Berlin: Mouton de Gruyter.

Shuken, C. (1984), 'Highland and Island English', in P. Trudgill (ed.), *Language in the British Isles*, pp. 152–66, Cambridge: CUP.

Syvret, M. and Stevens, J. (1998), *Balleine's History of Jersey*, West Sussex: Phillimore and Co.

Tomlinson, H. (1981), 'Le Guernesiais – Etude Grammaticale et Lexicale du Parler Normand de l'Ile de Guernesey', Edinburgh (unpublished Ph.D. thesis).

Trudgill, P. (1999), *The Dialects of England*, 2nd edn, Oxford: Blackwell.

Tupper, F. B. (1876), *The History of Guernsey and its Bailiwick*, 2nd edn, London: Simpkin, Marshall & Co.

Upton, C. and Widdowson, J. (1996), *An Atlas of English Dialects*, Oxford: Oxford University Press.

Viereck, W. (1988), 'The Channel Islands: An Anglicist's No Man's Land', in J. Klegraf and D. Nehls (eds), *Essays on the English Language and Applied Linguistics on the Occasion of Gerhard Nickel's 60th Birthday*, pp. 468–78, Heidelberg: Groos.

Wells, J. (1982), *Accents of English*, 3 vols, Cambridge: CUP.

Index